Webster's New
Business Writers Guide

Webster's
New
Business
Writers Guide

Created in Cooperation
with the Editors of
MERRIAM-WEBSTER

Based on the Merriam-Webster Concise Handbook for Writers *and* Merriam-Webster's Guide to Business Correspondence
Copyright © 1988 by Merriam-Webster Inc.

This edition published in 1996 by
SMITHMARK Publishers,
a division of US Media Holdings, Inc.
16 East 32nd Street,
New York, NY 10016.

SMITHMARK books are available for bulk purchase for sales promotion and premium use. For details, write or call the manager of special sales, SMITHMARK Publishers,
16 East 32nd Street, New York, NY 10016 (212) 532-6600

Library of Congress Cataloging-in-Publication data

Webster's new business writers guide / created in cooperation with the editors of Merriam-Webster
p. cm.
ISBN 0-8317-7159-3
1. Business writing. 2. English language—Business English.
I. Merriam-Webster, Inc.
HF5718.3.W43 1996
808'.06665—dc20

95-46614
CIP

Printed in the United States of America

10 9 8 7 6 5 4 3 2 1

Contents

Preface

WEBSTER'S NEW BUSINESS WRITERS GUIDE is a practical guide to the conventions of the English language in its written form and to effective business-letter writing. It is designed to be an aid not only to executives, secretaries, and other businesspeople but also to anyone else who writes business-related correspondence.

The book discusses such day-to-day matters as punctuating sentences, capitalizing names and terms, using italics or underlining, spelling compound words and the plural and possessive forms of words, and deciding when to use abbreviations and numerals. The book also offers information and advice on composition and grammar, notes and bibliographies, and the treatment of quotations.

Comprehensive guidance on a variety of topics having to do with business correspondence is intended to help writers achieve concise, accurate, and effective communication. Sample letters designed to meet the needs of common business-related situations make up a large portion of the book. Each sample letter includes a facsimile of the finished letter, accompanied by a description of the elements that go into such a letter.

Webster's New Business Writers Guide was created in cooperation with the editors of Merriam-Webster Inc., a company that has been publishing dictionaries and reference books for over 150 years.

Chapter 1

Punctuation

CONTENTS

Punctuation marks are used in the English writing system to help clarify the structure and meaning of sentences. To some degree, they achieve this end by corresponding to certain elements of the spoken language, such as pitch, volume, pause, and stress. To an even greater degree, however, punctuation marks serve to clarify structure and meaning by virtue of the fact that they conventionally accompany certain grammatical elements in a sentence, no matter how those elements might be spoken. In many cases, the relationship between punctuation and grammatical structure is such that the choice of which mark of punctuation to use in a sentence is clear and unambiguous. In other cases, however, the structure of a sentence may be such that it allows for several patterns of punctuation. In cases like these, varying notions of correctness have grown up, and two writers might, with equal correctness and with equal clarity, punctuate the same sentence quite differently.

This chapter is designed to help writers and editors make decisions about which mark of punctuation to use. In situations where more than one pattern of punctuation may be used, each is explained; if there are reasons to prefer one over another, the reasons are presented, but there are many instances in which one styling is no more preferable or common than another. Therefore, even after having read this chapter, writers and editors will find that they still encounter questions requiring them to exercise their judgment and taste.

The descriptions in this chapter focus on the ways in which punctuation marks are used to convey grammatical structure. The chapter does not explain in any detailed way the use of some punctuation marks to style individual words and compounds. Specifically, this chapter does not discuss the use of quotation marks to style titles and other kinds of proper nouns, the use of apostrophes to form plurals and possessives, the use of hyphens to form compounds, or the use of periods to punctuate abbreviations. For a discussion of these topics, see Chapter 2, "Capitals, Italics, and Quotation Marks"; Chapter 3, "Plurals, Possessives, and Compounds"; and Chapter 4, "Abbreviations."

General Principles

In addition to the rules that have been developed for individual marks of punctuation, there are also conventions and principles that apply to marks of punctuation in general, and these are explained in the paragraphs that follow.

Open and Close Punctuation

Two terms frequently used to describe patterns of punctuation, especially in regard to commas, are *open* and *close*. An open punctuation pattern is one in which commas and other marks of punctuation are used sparingly, usually only to separate major syntactical units, such as main clauses, or to prevent misreading. A close punctuation pattern, on the other hand, makes liberal use of punctuation marks, often putting one wherever the grammatical structure of the sentence will allow it. Close punctuation is often considered old-fashioned, and open punctuation more modern; however, contemporary writing displays a wide range of practices in regard to commas, and some grammatical constructions are still punctuated in ways traditionally associated with close punctuation (see paragraphs 8 and 22 under Comma in this chapter).

Multiple Punctuation

The term *multiple punctuation* describes the use of two or more marks of punctuation following the same word in a sentence. A conventional rule says that multiple punctuation is to be avoided except in cases involving brackets, parentheses, quotation marks, and sometimes dashes. Unfortunately, it is not possible to formulate any simple general instructions that would allow writers and editors to apply this rule. This book addresses the question of multiple punctuation by including a section entitled "With Other Marks of Punctuation" at the end of the treatment of each mark of punctuation for which there is a specific convention regarding multiple punctuation.

Boldface and Italic Punctuation

In general, marks of punctuation are set in the same typeface (lightface or boldface, italic or roman) as the word that precedes them, but most writers and editors allow themselves a number of exceptions to this rule. Brackets and parentheses are nearly always set in the font of the surrounding text, usually lightface roman, regardless of the text they enclose. Quotation marks are usually handled in the same manner; however, if the text they enclose is entirely in a contrasting typeface, they are set in a typeface to match. Some writers and editors base decisions regarding the typeface of exclamation points and question marks on the context in which they are used. If the exclamation point or question mark is clearly associated with the word or words that precede it, it is set in a matching typeface. If, on the other hand, it punctuates the sentence as a whole, it is set in the same typeface as the rest of the sentence.

> **Summary:** Recently completed surveys tend to confirm the theory that . . .
>
> He lived up to his reputation as an *homme d'esprit*; only once did he fail to come up with a witty reply.
>
> You did *that!*
>
> We were talking with the author of the book *Who Did That?*
>
> Have you seen the latest issue of *Saturday Review*?

Spacing

The conventions regarding the amount of space that precedes or follows a mark of punctuation vary from mark to mark. In general, the usual spacing around each mark of punctuation should be clear from the example sentences included for each mark of punctuation. In cases where additional explanation is needed, it is included at the end of the discussion, often under the heading "Spacing."

Ampersand

An ampersand is typically written &, although it has other forms, as *&*, *&*, and &. The character represents the word *and*; its function is to replace the word when a shorter form is desirable. However, the ampersand is an acceptable substitute for *and* only in a few constructions.

1. The ampersand is used in the names of companies but not in the names of agencies that are part of the federal government.

   American Telephone & Telegraph Co.
   Gulf & Western Corporation
   Occupational Safety and Health Administration
   Securities and Exchange Commission

   NOTE: In styling corporate names, writers and editors often try to reproduce the form of the name preferred by the company (taken from an annual report or company letterhead). However, this information may not be available and, even if it is available, following the different preferences of different companies can lead to apparent inconsistencies in the text. Publications that include very many corporate names usually choose one styling, usually the one with the ampersand, and use it in all corporate names that include *and*.

2. Ampersands are frequently used in abbreviations. Style varies regarding the spacing around the ampersand. Publications that make heavy use of abbreviations, such as business or technical publications, most often omit the spaces. In general-interest publications, both the spaced and the unspaced stylings are common.

   The R&D budget looks adequate for the next fiscal year.
   Apply for a loan at your bank or S & L.

3. The ampersand is often used in cases where a condensed text is necessary, as in tabular material. While bibliographies, indexes, and most other listings use *and*, some systems of parenthetical documentation do use the ampersand. For more on parenthetical documentation, see Chapter 7, "Notes and Bibliographies."

   (Carter, Good & Robertson 1984)

4. When an ampersand is used between the last two elements in a series, the comma is omitted.

   the law firm of Shilliday, Fraser & French

Apostrophe

1. The apostrophe is used to indicate the possessive case of nouns and indefinite pronouns. For details regarding this use, see the section on Possessives, beginning on page 88, in Chapter 3, "Plurals, Possessives, and Compounds."

2. Apostrophes are sometimes used to form plurals of letters, numerals, abbreviations, symbols, and words referred to as words. For details regarding this use, see the section on Plurals, beginning on page 82, in Chapter 3, "Plurals, Possessives, and Compounds."

3. Apostrophes mark omissions in contractions made of two or more words that are pronounced as one word.

didn't	o'clock
you're	shouldn't've

4. The apostrophe is used to indicate that letters have been intentionally omitted from the spelling of a word in order to reproduce a perceived pronunciation or to give a highly informal flavor to a piece of writing.

    "Head back to N'Orleans," the man said.

    Get 'em while they're hot.

    dancin' till three

    NOTE: Sometimes words are so consistently spelled with an apostrophe that the spelling with the apostrophe becomes an accepted variant.

    fo'c'sle for *forecastle*
    bos'n for *boatswain*
    rock 'n' roll for *rock and roll*

5. Apostrophes mark the omission of numerals.

    class of '91
    politics in the '90s

    NOTE: Writers who use the apostrophe for styling the plurals of words expressed in numerals usually avoid the use of the apostrophe illustrated in the second example above. Either they omit the apostrophe that stands for the missing figures, or they spell the word out.

    90's *or* nineties *but not* '90's

6. Apostrophes are used to produce the inflected forms of verbs that are made of numerals or individually pronounced letters. Hyphens are sometimes used for this purpose also.

> 86'ed our proposal
> OK'ing the manuscript
> TKO'd his opponent

7. An apostrophe is often used to add an *-er* ending to an abbreviation, especially if some confusion might result from its absence. Hyphens are sometimes used for this purpose also. If no confusion is likely, the apostrophe is usually omitted.

> 4-H'er   CBer
> AA'er   DXer

8. The use of apostrophes to form abbreviations (as *ass'n* for *association* or *sec'y* for *secretary*) is avoided in most formal writing.

Brackets

Brackets work like parentheses to set off inserted material, but their functions are more specialized. Several of their principal uses occur with quoted material, as illustrated below. For other aspects of styling quotations, see Chapter 8, "The Treatment of Quotations."

With Editorial Insertions

1. Brackets enclose editorial comments, corrections, clarifications, or other material inserted into a text, especially into quoted matter.

> "Remember, this was the first time since it became law that the Twenty-first Amendment [outlining procedures for the replacement of a dead or incapacitated President or Vice President] had been invoked."
>
> "But there's one thing to be said for it [his apprenticeship with Samuels]: it started me thinking about architecture in a new way."
>
> He wrote, "I am just as cheerful as when you was [sic] here."

NOTE: While the text into which such editorial insertions are made is almost always quoted material, they are sometimes also used in nonquoted material, particularly in cases where an editor wishes to add material to an author's text without disturbing the author's original wording.

> Furthermore the Committee anticipates additional expenses in the coming fiscal year [October 1985–September 1986] and seeks revenues to meet these expenses.

2. Brackets set off insertions that supply missing letters.

> "If you can't persuade D[israeli], I'm sure no one can."

3. Brackets enclose insertions that take the place of words or phrases that were used in the original version of a quoted passage.

> The report, entitled "A Decade of Progress," begins with a short message from President Stevens in which she notes that "the loving portraits and revealing accounts of [this report] are not intended to constitute a complete history of the decade. . . . Rather [they] impart the flavor of the events, developments, and achievements of this vibrant period."

4. Brackets enclose insertions that slightly alter the form of a word used in an original text.

> The magazine reported that thousands of the country's children were "go[ing] to bed hungry every night."

5. Brackets are used to indicate that the capitalization or typeface of the original passage has been altered in some way.

> As we point out on pages 234–235, "The length of a quotation usually determines whether it is run into the text or set as a block quotation. . . . [L]ength can be assessed in terms of the number of words, the number of typewritten or typeset lines, or the number of sentences in the passage."

> They agreed with and were encouraged by her next point: "In the past, many secretaries have been placed in positions of responsibility *without being delegated enough authority to carry out the responsibility*. [Italics added.] The current pressures affecting managers have caused them to rethink the secretarial function and to delegate more responsibility and authority to their secretaries."

NOTE: The use of brackets to indicate altered capitalization is optional in many situations. For more on this use of brackets, see the section on Alterations, Omissions, and Interpolations, beginning on page 238, in Chapter 8, "The Treatment of Quotations."

As a Mechanical Device

6. Brackets function as parentheses within parentheses.

> The company was incinerating high concentrations of pollutants (such as polychlorinated biphenyls [PCBs]) in a power boiler.

7. Brackets set off phonetic symbols or transcriptions.

> [t] in British *duty*

8. Brackets are used in combination with parentheses to set off units in mathematical expressions. They are also used in chemical formulas.

> $x + 5[(x + y)(2x - y)]$
> $Ag[Pt(NO_2)_4]$

With Other Marks of Punctuation

9. No punctuation mark (other than a period after an abbreviation) precedes bracketed material within a sentence. If punctuation is required, the mark is placed after the closing bracket.

> The report stated, "If we fail to find additional sources of supply [of oil and gas], our long-term growth will be limited."

10. When brackets enclose a complete sentence, the required punctuation should be placed within the brackets.

> [A pawprint photographed last month in the Quabbin area has finally verified the cougar's continued existence in the Northeast.]

NOTE: Unlike parentheses, brackets are rarely used to enclose complete sentences within other sentences.

Spacing

11. No space is left between brackets and the material they enclose or between brackets and any mark of punctuation immediately following.

12. In typewritten material, two spaces precede an opening bracket and follow a closing bracket when the brackets enclose a complete sentence. In typeset material, only one space is used.

```
We welcome the return of the cougar.  [A paw
print photographed last month has verified its
existence locally.]  Its habitation in this area
is a good sign for the whole environment.
```

> We welcome the return of the cougar. [A paw print photographed last month has verified its existence locally.] Its habitation in this area is a good sign for the whole environment.

Colon

The colon is a mark of introduction. It indicates that what follows it—whether a clause, a phrase, or even a single word—is linked with some element that precedes it. Many uses of the colon are similar to those of the dash. Like the dash, the colon gives special emphasis to whatever follows it; lengthy material introduced by a colon is often further emphasized by indention. (For information on the question of capitalizing the first word following a colon, see the section on Beginnings, starting on page 53, in Chapter 2, "Capitals, Italics, and Quotation Marks.")

With Phrases and Clauses

1. A colon introduces a clause or phrase that explains, illustrates, amplifies, or restates what has gone before.

> The sentence was poorly constructed: it lacked both unity and coherence.
>
> Throughout its history, the organization has combined a tradition of excellence with a dedication to human service: educating the young, caring for the elderly, assisting in community-development programs.
>
> Disk cartridges provide high-density storage capacity: up to 16 megabytes of information on some cartridges.
>
> Time was running out: a decision had to be made.

2. A colon directs attention to an appositive.

> The question is this: where will we get the money?
>
> He had only one pleasure: eating.

3. A colon is used to introduce a series. The introductory statement often includes a phrase such as *the following* or *as follows*.

> The conference was attended by representatives of five nations: England, France, Belgium, Spain, and Portugal.
>
> Anyone planning to participate should be prepared to do the following: hike five miles with a backpack, sleep on the ground without a tent, and paddle a canoe through rough water.

NOTE: Opinion varies regarding whether a colon should interrupt the grammatical continuity of a clause (as by coming between a verb and its objects). Although most style manuals and composition handbooks advise against this practice and recommend that a full independent clause precede the colon, the interrupting colon is common. It is especially likely to be used before a lengthy and complex list, in which case the colon serves to set the list distinctly apart from the normal flow of running text. With shorter or less complex lists, the colon is usually not used.

> Our programs to increase profitability include: continued modernization of our manufacturing facilities; consolidation of distribution terminals; discontinuation of unprofitable retail outlets; and reorganization of our personnel structure, along with across-the-board staff reductions.
>
> Our programs to increase profitability include plant modernization, improved distribution and retailing procedures, and staff reductions.
>
> Our programs to increase profitability include the following: continued modernization of our manufacturing facilities; consolidation of distribution terminals; discontinuation of unprofitable retail outlets; and reorganization of our personnel structure, along with across-the-board staff reductions.

4. A colon is used like a dash to introduce a summary statement following a series.

> Physics, biology, sociology, anthropology: he discusses them all.

With Quotations

5. A colon introduces lengthy quoted material that is set off from the rest of a text by indentation but not by quotation marks. For more on the treatment of lengthy quoted material, see Chapter 8, "The Treatment of Quotations."

> He took the title for his biography of Thoreau from a passage in *Walden*:
>> I long ago lost a hound, a bay horse, and a turtle-dove, and am still on their trail. . . . I have met one or two who had heard the hound, and the tramp of the horse, and even seen the dove disappear behind a cloud, and they seemed as anxious to recover them as if they had lost them themselves.
>
> However, the title *A Hound, a Bay Horse, and a Turtle-Dove* probably puzzled some readers.

6. A colon may be used before a quotation in running text, especially when (1) the quotation is lengthy, (2) the quotation is a formal statement or is being given special emphasis, or (3) the quotation is an appositive.

> Said Murdoch: "The key to the success of this project is good planning. We need to know precisely all of the steps that we will need to go through, what kind of staff we will require to accomplish each step, what the entire project will cost, and when we can expect completion."
>
> The inscription reads: "Here lies one whose name was writ in water."
>
> In response, he had this to say: "No one knows better than I do that changes will have to be made soon."

As a Mechanical Device

7. In transcriptions of dialogue, a colon follows the speaker's name.

> Robert: You still haven't heard from her?
> Michael: No, and I'm beginning to worry.

8. A colon follows a brief heading or introductory term.

> NOTE: The library will be closed on the 17th while repairs are being made to the heating system.
>
> 1977: New developments in microchip technology lead to less-expensive manufacturing.

9. A colon separates elements in page references, bibliographical and biblical citations, and fixed formulas used to express ratios and time.

Journal of the American Medical Association 48:356
Springfield, Mass.: Merriam-Webster Inc.
John 4:10
8:30 a.m.
a ratio of 3:5

10. A colon separates titles and subtitles (as of books).

The Tragic Dynasty: A History of the Romanovs

11. A colon is used to join terms that are being contrasted or compared.

Seventeenth-century rhymes include *prayer : afar* and *brass : was : ass.*

12. A colon follows the salutation in formal correspondence.

Dear General Smith:
Dear Mr. Jiménez:
Dear Product Manager:
Ladies and Gentlemen:

13. A colon punctuates memorandum and government correspondence headings and subject lines in general business letters.

TO:
SUBJECT:
VIA:
REFERENCE:

14. A colon separates writer/dictator/typist initials in the identification lines of business letters.

WAL:jml
WAL:WEB:jml

15. A colon separates carbon-copy or blind carbon-copy abbreviations from the initials or names of copy recipients in business letters.

cc:RWP
    JES

bcc:MWK
     FCM

With Other Marks of Punctuation

16. A colon is placed outside quotation marks and parentheses.

There's only one thing wrong with "Harold's Indiscretion": it's not funny.

I quote from the first edition of *Springtime in Savannah* (published in 1952):

Spacing

17. In typewritten material, two spaces follow a colon used in running text, bibliographical references, publication titles, and letter or memorandum headings. In typeset material, only one space follows.

> The answer is simple: don't go.
> SUBJECT: Project X
> New York: Macmillan, 1980.
> *Typewriting: A Guide*

18. When a colon is being used between two correlated terms (see paragraph 11), it is centered with equal spacing on each side.

> The stature of the two sexes shows the same female : male proportions.

19. No space precedes or follows a colon when it is used between numerals.

> 9:30 a.m.
> a ratio of 2:4

20. No space precedes or follows a colon in a business-letter identification line or in a carbon-copy notation that indicates a recipient designated by initials.

> FCM:hg
> cc:FCM

21. Two spaces follow a colon in a carbon-copy notation that indicates a recipient designated by a full name.

> cc: Mr. Johnson

Comma

The comma is the most frequently used punctuation mark in the English writing system. Its most common uses are to separate items in a series and to set off syntactical elements within sentences. Within these two broad categories, there are a great many specific uses to which commas can be put. This section explains the most common aspects of the comma, listed under the following headings.

> Between Main Clauses
> With Compound Predicates
> With Subordinate Clauses and Phrases
> With Appositives
> With Introductory and Interrupting Elements

With Contrasting Expressions
With Items in a Series
With Compound Modifiers
In Quotations, Questions, and Indirect Discourse
With Omitted Words
With Addresses, Dates, and Numbers
With Names, Degrees, and Titles
In Correspondence
Other Uses
With Other Marks of Punctuation

Between Main Clauses

1. A comma separates main clauses joined by a coordinating conjunction (as *and, but, or, nor,* and *for*). For use of commas with clauses joined by correlative conjunctions, see paragraph 24 below.

   She knew very little about him, and he volunteered nothing.

   We will not respond to any more questions on that topic this afternoon, nor will we respond to similar questions at any time in the future.

   His face showed disappointment, for he knew that he had failed.

   NOTE: Some reference books still insist that *so* and *yet* are adverbs rather than conjunctions and that therefore they should be preceded by a semicolon when they join main clauses. However, our evidence indicates that the use of *so* and *yet* as conjunctions preceded by a comma is standard.

   The acoustics in this hall are good, so every note is clear.

   We have requested this information many times before, yet we have never gotten a satisfactory reply.

2. When one or both of the clauses are short or when they are closely related in meaning, the comma is often omitted.

   The sun was shining and the birds were singing.

   We didn't realize it at the time but the spot we had picked for our home was the same spot one of our ancestors had picked for his home.

   Six thousand years ago, the top of the volcano blew off in a series of powerful eruptions and the sides collapsed into the middle.

   Many people want to take their vacations in August so it may be difficult for some of them to find good accommodations.

   NOTE: In punctuating sentences such as the ones illustrated above, writers have to use their own judgment regarding whether clauses are short enough or closely related enough to warrant omitting the comma. There are no clear-cut rules to follow; however, factors such as the rhythm, parallelism, or logic of the sentence often influence how clearly or smoothly it will read with or without the comma.

3. Commas are sometimes used to separate main clauses that are not joined by conjunctions. This styling is especially likely to be used if the clauses are short and feature obvious parallelism.

> One day you are a successful corporate lawyer, the next day you are out of work.
>
> The city has suffered terribly in the interim. Bombs have destroyed most of the buildings, disease has ravaged the population.

NOTE: Using a comma to join clauses that are neither short nor obviously parallel is usually called *comma fault* or *comma splice* and most writers and editors avoid such a construction. In general, clauses not joined by conjunctions are separated by semicolons.

4. If a sentence is composed of three or more clauses, the clauses may be separated by either commas or semicolons. Clauses that are short and relatively free of commas can be separated by commas even if they are not joined by a conjunction. If the clauses are long or heavily punctuated, they are separated with semicolons, except for the last two clauses which may be separated by either a comma or a semicolon. Usually a comma will be used between the last two clauses only if those clauses are joined by a conjunction. For more examples of clauses separated with commas and semicolons, see paragraph 5 under Semicolon in this chapter.

> The pace of change seems to have quickened, the economy is uncertain, the technology seems sometimes liberating and sometimes hostile.
>
> Small fish fed among the marsh weed, ducks paddled along the surface, and a muskrat ate greens along the bank.
>
> The policy is a complex one to explain; defending it against its critics is not easy, nor is it clear the defense is always necessary.

With Compound Predicates

5. Commas are not usually used to separate the parts of a compound predicate.

> The firefighter tried to enter the burning building but was turned back by the thick smoke.

NOTE: Despite the fact that most style manuals and composition handbooks warn against separating the parts of compound predicates with commas, many authors and editors use commas in just this way. They are particularly likely to do so if the predicate is especially long and complicated, if they want to stress one part of the predicate, or if the absence of a comma could cause even a momentary misreading of the sentence.

The board helps to develop the financing, new product planning, and marketing strategies for new corporate divisions, and issues periodic reports on expenditures, revenues, and personnel appointments.

This is an unworkable plan, and has been from the start.

I try to explain to him what I want him to do, and get nowhere.

With Subordinate Clauses and Phrases

6. Adverbial clauses and phrases that precede a main clause are usually set off with commas.

> As cars age, they depreciate.
>
> Having made that decision, we turned our attention to other matters.
>
> To understand the situation, you must be familiar with the background.
>
> From the top of this rugged and isolated plateau, I could see the road stretching out for miles across the desert.
>
> In 1919, his family left Russia and moved to this country.
>
> In addition, staff members respond to queries, take new orders, and initiate billing.

7. If a sentence begins with an adverbial clause or phrase and can be easily read without a comma following it, writers will often omit the comma. In most cases where the comma is omitted, the phrase will be short—four words or less. But some writers will omit the comma even after a longer phrase if the sentence can be easily read or seems more forceful that way.

> In January the company will introduce a new line of entirely redesigned products.
>
> On the map the town appeared as a small dot in the midst of vast emptiness.
>
> If the project cannot be done profitably perhaps it should not be done at all.

8. Adverbial clauses and phrases that introduce a main clause other than the first main clause are usually set off with commas. However, if the adverbial clause or phrase follows a conjunction, style varies regarding how many commas are required to set it off. In most cases, two commas are used: one before the conjunction and one following the clause or phrase. Writers who prefer close punctuation usually use three commas: one before the conjunction and two more to enclose the clause or phrase. If the writer prefers open punctuation, the phrase may not be set off at all. In this case, only one comma that separates the main clauses is used. For more on open and close punctuation, see page 2.

His parents were against the match, and had the couple not eloped, their plans for marriage would have come to nothing.

They have redecorated the entire store, but, to the delight of their customers, the store retains much of its original flavor. [close]

We haven't left Springfield yet, but when we get to Boston we'll call you. [open]

9. A comma is not used after an introductory phrase if the phrase immediately precedes the main verb.

> In the road lay a dead rabbit.

10. Subordinate clauses and phrases that follow a main clause or that fall within a main clause are usually not set off by commas if they are restrictive. A clause or phrase is considered restrictive if its removal from the sentence would alter the meaning of the main clause. If the meaning of the main clause would not be altered by removing the subordinate clause or phrase, the clause or phrase is considered nonrestrictive and usually is set off by commas.

> We will be delighted if she decides to stay. [restrictive]
>
> Anyone who wants his or her copy of the book autographed by the author should get in line. [restrictive]
>
> Her new book, *Fortune's Passage,* was well received. [nonrestrictive]
>
> That was a good meal, although I didn't particularly like the broccoli in cream sauce. [nonrestrictive]

11. Commas are used to set off an adverbial clause or phrase that falls between the subject and the verb.

> The weather, fluctuating from very hot to downright chilly, necessitated a variety of clothing.

12. Commas enclose modifying phrases that do not immediately precede the word or phrase they modify.

> Hungry and tired, the soldiers marched back to camp.
>
> We could see the importance, both long-term and short-term, of her proposal.
>
> The two children, equally happy with their lunches, set off for school.

13. Absolute phrases are set off with commas, whether they fall at the beginning, middle, or end of the sentence.

> Our business being concluded, we adjourned for refreshments.
>
> We headed southward, the wind freshening behind us, to meet the rest of the fleet in the morning.
>
> I still remember my first car, its bumpers sagging, its tires worn, its body rusting.

With Appositives

14. Commas are used to set off a word, phrase, or clause that is in apposition to a noun and that is nonrestrictive.

> My husband, Larry, is in charge of ticket sales for the fair.
>
> The highboy, or tallboy, is a tall chest of drawers typically made between 1690 and 1780.
>
> George Washington, first president of the United States, has been the subject of countless biographies.
>
> We were most impressed by the third candidate, the one who brought a writing sample and asked so many questions.

NOTE: A nonrestrictive appositive sometimes precedes the word with which it is in apposition. It is set off by commas in this position also.

> A cherished landmark in the city, the Hotel Sandburg has managed once again to escape the wrecking ball.

15. Restrictive appositives are not set off by commas.

> My daughter Andrea had the lead in the school play.
>
> Alfred Hitchcock's thriller "Psycho" will be screened tonight.

With Introductory and Interrupting Elements

16. Commas set off transitional words and phrases (as *finally, meanwhile,* and *after all*).

> Indeed, close coordination between departments can minimize confusion during this period of expansion.
>
> We are eager to begin construction; however, the necessary materials have not yet arrived.
>
> The most recent report, on the other hand, makes clear why the management avoids such agreements.

NOTE: Adverbs that can serve as transitional words can often serve in other ways as well. When these adverbs are not used to make a transition, no comma is necessary.

> The materials had finally arrived.

17. Commas set off parenthetical elements, such as authorial asides and supplementary information, that are closely related to the rest of the sentence.

> All of us, to tell the truth, were completely amazed by his suggestion.
>
> The headmaster, now in his sixth year at the school, was responsible for the changes in the curriculum.

NOTE: When the parenthetical element is digressive or otherwise not closely related to the rest of the sentence, it is often set off by dashes or parentheses. For contrasting examples, see paragraph 3 under Dash and paragraphs 1 and 9 under Parentheses in this chapter.

18. Commas are used to set off words or phrases that introduce examples or explanations.

> He expects to visit three countries this summer, namely, France, Spain, and Germany.
>
> I would like to develop a good, workable plan, i.e., one that would outline our goals and set a timetable for their accomplishment.

NOTE: Words and phrases such as *i.e., e.g., namely, for example,* and *that is* are often preceded by a dash, open parenthesis, or semicolon, depending on the magnitude of the break in continuity represented by the examples or explanations that they introduce; however, regardless of the punctuation that precedes the word or phrase, a comma always follows it. For contrasting examples of dashes, parentheses, and semicolons with these words and phrases, see paragraph 6 under Dash, paragraph 2 under Parentheses, and paragraph 6 under Semicolon in this chapter.

19. Commas are used to set off words in direct address.

> We would like to discuss your account, Mrs. Reid.
>
> The answer, my friends, lies within us.

20. Commas set off mild interjections or exclamations such as *ah* or *oh.*

> Ah, summer—season of sunshine and goodwill.
>
> Oh, what a beautiful baby.

NOTE: The vocative *O* is not set off by commas.

> O Time! O Death!
>
> Have mercy, O Lord.

With Contrasting Expressions

21. A comma is used to set off contrasting expressions within a sentence.

> This project will take six months, not six weeks.
>
> He has merely changed his style, not his ethics.

22. Style varies regarding use of the comma to set off two or more contrasting phrases used to describe a single word that follows immediately. In open punctuation, a comma follows the first modifier but is not used between the final modifier and the word modified. In close punctuation, the contrasting phrase is treated as a nonrestrictive modifier and is, therefore, both preceded and followed by a comma. For more on open and close punctuation, see page 2.

The harsh, although eminently realistic critique is not going to make you popular. [open]

The harsh, although eminently realistic, critique is not going to make you popular. [close]

This street takes you away from, not toward the capitol building. [open]

This street takes you away from, not toward, the capitol building. [close]

23. Adjectives and adverbs that modify the same word or phrase and that are joined by *but* or some other coordinating conjunction are not separated by a comma.

> a bicycle with a light but sturdy frame
> a multicolored but subdued rag rug
> errors caused by working carelessly or too quickly

24. A comma does not usually separate elements that are contrasted through the use of a pair of correlative conjunctions (as *either . . . or, neither . . . nor,* and *not only . . . but also*).

> The cost is either $69.95 or $79.95.
>
> Neither my brother nor I noticed the mistake.
>
> He was given the post not only because of his diplomatic connections but also because of his great tact and charm.

NOTE: Correlative conjunctions are sometimes used to join main clauses. If the clauses are short, a comma is not added; however, if the clauses are long, a comma usually separates them.

> Either you do it my way or we don't do it at all.
>
> Not only did she have to see three salesmen and a visiting reporter during the course of the day, but she also had to prepare for the next day's meeting with the president.

25. Long parallel contrasting and comparing clauses are separated by commas; short parallel phrases are not.

> The more I heard about this new project, the greater was my desire to volunteer.
>
> "The sooner the better," I said.

With Items in a Series

26. Words, phrases, and clauses joined in a series are separated by commas. If main clauses are joined in a series, they may be separated by either semicolons or commas. For more on the use of commas and semicolons to separate main clauses, see paragraphs 1, 3, and 4 above and paragraph 5 under Semicolon in this chapter.

Men, women, and children crowded aboard the train.

Her job required her to pack quickly, to travel often, and to have no personal life.

He responded patiently while reporters shouted questions, flashbulbs popped, and the crowd pushed closer.

NOTE: Style varies regarding the use of the comma between the last two items in a series if those items are also joined by a conjunction. In some cases, as in the example below, omitting the final comma (often called the serial comma) can result in ambiguity. Some writers feel that in most sentences the use of the conjunction makes the comma superfluous, and they favor using the comma only when a misreading could result from omitting it. Others feel that it is easier to include the final comma routinely rather than try to consider each sentence separately to decide whether a misreading is possible without the comma. Most reference books, including this one, and most other book-length works of nonfiction use the serial comma. In all other categories of publishing, according to our evidence, usage is evenly or nearly evenly divided on the use or omission of this comma.

We are looking for a house with a big yard, a view of the harbor, and beach and docking privileges. [with serial comma]

We are looking for a house with a big yard, a view of the harbor and beach and docking privileges. [without serial comma]

27. A comma is not used to separate items in a series that are joined with conjunctions.

I don't understand what this policy covers or doesn't cover or only partially covers.

I have talked to the president and the vice president and three other executives.

28. When the elements in a series are long or complex or consist of clauses that themselves contain commas, the elements are usually separated by semicolons, not commas. For more on this use of the semicolon, see paragraphs 7 and 8 under Semicolon in this chapter.

With Compound Modifiers

29. A comma is used to separate two or more adjectives, adverbs, or phrases that modify the same word or phrase. For the use of commas with contrasting modifiers, see paragraphs 22 and 23 above.

She spoke in a calm, reflective manner.

We watched the skier move smoothly, gracefully through the turns.

His story was too fantastic, too undersupported by facts for us to take seriously.

30. A comma is not used between two adjectives when the first modifies the combination of the second adjective plus the word or phrase it modifies.

a little brown jug
a modern concrete-and-glass building

31. A comma is not used to separate an adverb from the adjective or adverb that it modifies.

a truly distinctive manner
running very quickly down the street

In Quotations, Questions, and Indirect Discourse

32. A comma separates a direct quotation from a phrase identifying its source or speaker. If the quotation is a question or an exclamation and the identifying phrase follows the quotation, the comma is replaced by a question mark or an exclamation point.

Mary said, "I am leaving."
"I am leaving," Mary said.
Mary asked, "Where are you going?"
"Where are you going?" Mary asked.
"I am leaving," Mary said, "even if you want me to stay."
"Don't do that!" Mary shouted.

NOTE: In some cases, a colon can replace a comma preceding a quotation. For more on this use of the colon, see paragraph 6 under Colon in this chapter.

33. A comma does not set off a quotation that is tightly incorporated into the sentence in which it appears.

Throughout the session his only responses were "No comment" and "I don't think so."

Just because he said he was "about to leave this minute" doesn't mean he actually left.

34. Style varies regarding the use of commas to set off shorter sentences that fall within longer sentences and that do not constitute actual dialogue. These shorter sentences may be mottoes or maxims, unspoken or imaginary dialogue, or sentences referred to as sentences; and they may or may not be enclosed in quotation marks. (For more on the use of quotation marks with sentences like these, see paragraph 6 under Quotation Marks, Double, in this chapter.) Typically the shorter sentence functions as a subject, object, or complement within the larger sentence and does not require a comma. Sometimes the structure of the larger sentence will be styled like actual quoted dialogue, and in such cases a comma is used to separate the shorter sentence from the text that introduces or identifies it. In some cases, where an author decides not to use quotation marks, a comma may be inserted simply to mark the beginning of the shorter sentence clearly.

> "The computer is down" was the response she dreaded.
>
> Another confusing idiom is "How do you do?"
>
> He spoke with a candor that seemed to insist, This actually happened to me and in just this way.
>
> The first rule is, When in doubt, spell it out.

When the shorter sentence functions as an appositive in the larger sentence, it is set off with a comma when nonrestrictive and not when restrictive. (For more on restrictive modifiers and appositives, see paragraphs 10, 14, and 15 above.)

> He was fond of the slogan "Every man a king, but no man wears a crown."
>
> We had the club's motto, "We make waves," printed on our T-shirts.

35. A comma introduces a direct question regardless of whether it is enclosed in quotation marks or if its first word is capitalized.

> I wondered, what is going on here?
>
> The question is, How do we get out of here?
>
> What bothered her was, who had eaten all of the cookies?

36. The comma is omitted before quotations that are very short exclamations or representations of sounds.

> He jumped up suddenly and cried "Yow!"
>
> When she was done, she let out a loud "Whew!"

37. A comma is not used to set off indirect discourse or indirect questions introduced by a conjunction (such as *that* or *what*).

> Mary said that she was leaving.
>
> I wondered what was going on there.
>
> The clerk told me that the book I had ordered had just come in.

With Omitted Words

38. A comma indicates the omission of a word or phrase, especially in parallel constructions where the omitted word or phrase appears earlier in the sentence.

> Common stocks are preferred by some investors; bonds, by others.

39. A comma often replaces the conjunction *that*.

> The road was so steep and winding, we thought for sure that we would go over the edge.
>
> The problem is, we don't know how to fix it.

With Addresses, Dates, and Numbers

40. A comma is used to set off the individual elements of an address except for zip codes. In current practice, no punctuation appears between a state name and the zip code that follows it. If prepositions are used between the elements of the address, commas are not needed.

> Mrs. Bryant may be reached at 52 Kiowa Circle, Mesa, Arizona.
>
> Mr. Briscoe was born in Liverpool, England.
>
> The collection will be displayed at the Wilmington, Delaware, Museum of Art.
>
> Write to the Bureau of the Census, Washington, DC 20233.
>
> The White House is located at 1600 Pennsylvania Avenue in Washington, D.C.

NOTE: Some writers omit the comma that follows the name of a state when no other element of an address follows it. This is most likely to happen when a city name and state name are being used in combination to modify a noun that follows; however, our evidence indicates that retaining this comma is still the more common practice.

> We visited their Enid, Oklahoma plant.
> *but more commonly*
> We visited their Enid, Oklahoma, plant.

41. Commas are used to set off the year from the day of the month. When only the month and the year are given, the comma is usually omitted.

> On October 26, 1947, the newly hired employees began work on the project.
>
> In December 1903, the Wright brothers finally succeeded in keeping an airplane aloft for a few seconds.

42. A comma groups numerals into units of three to separate thousands, millions, and so on; however, this comma is generally not used in page numbers, street numbers, or numbers within dates. For more on the styling of numbers, see Chapter 5, "The Treatment of Numbers."

> a population of 350,000
> 4509 South Pleasant Street
> the year 1986
> page 1419

With Names, Degrees, and Titles

43. A comma punctuates an inverted name.

> Sagan, Deborah J.

44. A comma is often used between a surname and *Junior, Senior,* or their abbreviations. For more on the use of *Jr.* and *Sr.,* see paragraph 45 in the section on Specific Styling Conventions, beginning on page 112, in Chapter 4, "Abbreviations."

> Morton A. Williams, Jr.
> Douglas Fairbanks, Senior

45. A comma is often used to set off the word *Incorporated* or the abbreviation *Inc.* from the rest of a corporate name; however, many companies elect to omit this comma from their names.

> Leedy Manufacturing Company, Incorporated
> Tektronics, Inc.
> Merz-Fortunata Inc.

46. A comma separates a surname from a following academic, honorary, military, or religious degree or title.

> Amelia P. Artandi, D.V.M.
> John L. Farber, Esq.
> Sister Mary Catherine, S.C.
> Robert Menard, M.A., Ph.D.
> Admiral Herman Washington, USN

In Correspondence

47. The comma follows the salutation in informal correspondence and follows the complimentary close in both informal and formal correspondence. In formal correspondence, a colon follows the salutation. For examples of this use of the colon, see paragraph 12 under Colon in this chapter.

> Dear Rachel,
> Affectionately,
> Very truly yours,

Other Uses

48. The comma is used to avoid ambiguity when the juxtaposition of two words or expressions could cause confusion.

> Whatever will be, will be.
> To John, Marshall was someone special.
> I repaired the lamp that my brother had broken, and replaced the bulb.

49. A comma often follows a direct object or a predicate nominative or predicate adjective when they precede the subject and

verb in the sentence. If the meaning of the sentence is clear
without this comma, it is often omitted.

> That we would soon have to raise prices, no one disputed.
> Critical about the current state of affairs, we might have been.
> A disaster it certainly was.

With Other Marks of Punctuation

50. Commas are used in conjunction with brackets, ellipsis points,
parentheses, and quotation marks. Commas are not used in
conjunction with colons, dashes, exclamation points, question
marks, or semicolons. If one of these latter marks falls at the
same point in a sentence at which a comma would fall, the
comma is dropped and the other mark is retained. For more
on the use of commas with other marks of punctuation, see
the heading With Other Marks of Punctuation in the sections
of this chapter covering those marks of punctuation.

Dash

In many of its uses, the dash functions like a comma, a colon, or
a pair of parentheses. Like commas and parentheses, dashes set
off parenthetic material such as examples, supplemental facts, or
appositional, explanatory, or descriptive phrases. Like colons,
dashes introduce clauses that explain or expand upon some element of the material that precedes them. The dash is sometimes
considered to be a less formal equivalent of the colon and parenthesis, and it does frequently take their place in advertising and
other informal contexts. However, dashes are prevalent in all
kinds of writing, including the most formal, and the choice of
which mark to use is usually a matter of personal preference.

The dash exists in a number of different lengths. The dash
in most general use is the em dash, which is approximately the
width of an uppercase M in typeset material. In typewritten material, it is represented by two hyphens. The en dash and the two-
and three-em dashes have more limited uses which are explained
in paragraphs 15–18 below.

Abrupt Change or Suspension

1. The dash marks an abrupt change in the flow of a writer's
thought or in the structure of a sentence.

> The mountain that we climbed is higher than—well, never mind
> how high it is.
> The students seemed happy enough with the new plan, but the
> alumni—there was the problem.

2. Dashes mark a suspension in the writer's flow of thought or in the sentence structure. Such suspensions are frequently caused by an authorial aside.

> He was—how shall we put it?—a controversial character to say the least.

> If I had kept my notes—and I really wish that I had—I would be able to give you the exact date of the sale.

Parenthetic and Amplifying Elements

3. Dashes are used in place of other punctuation (such as commas or parentheses) to emphasize parenthetic or amplifying material or to make such material stand out more clearly from the rest of the sentence.

> She is willing to discuss all problems—those she has solved and those for which there is no immediate solution.

> In 1976, they asked for—and received—substantial grants from the federal government.

> The privately owned consulting firm—formerly known as Aborjaily and Associates—is now offering many new services.

NOTE: When dashes are used to set off parenthetic elements, they often indicate that the material is more digressive than elements set off with commas but less digressive than elements set off by parentheses. For contrasting examples see paragraph 17 under Comma and paragraphs 1 and 9 under Parentheses in this chapter.

4. Dashes are used to set off or to introduce defining and enumerating phrases.

> The fund sought to acquire controlling positions—a minimum of 25% of outstanding voting securities—in other companies.

> The essay dealt with our problems with waste—cans, bottles, discarded tires, and other trash.

5. A dash is often used in place of a colon or semicolon to link clauses, especially when the clause that follows the dash explains, summarizes, or expands upon the clause that precedes it.

> The test results were surprisingly good—none of the tested models displayed serious problems.

> The deterioration of our bridges and roads has been apparent for many years—parts of the interstate highway system are 30 years old, after all, and most of our bridges are older than that.

6. A dash or a pair of dashes often sets off parenthetic or amplifying material introduced by such phrases as *for example, namely, that is, e.g.,* and *i.e.*

After some discussion the motion was tabled—that is, it was removed indefinitely from the board's consideration.

Sports develop two valuable traits—namely, self-control and the ability to make quick decisions.

Not all "prime" windows—i.e., the ones installed when a house is built—are equal in quality.

NOTE: Commas, parentheses, and semicolons are often used for the same purpose. For contrasting examples, see paragraph 18 under Comma, paragraph 2 under Parentheses, and paragraph 6 under Semicolon in this chapter.

7. A dash introduces a summary statement that follows a series of words or phrases.

Unemployment, inflation, stock prices, mortgage rates—all are part of the economy.

Once into bankruptcy, the company would have to pay cash for its supplies, defer maintenance, and lay off workers—moves that could threaten its long-term profitability.

As a Mechanical Device

8. A dash precedes the name of an author or source at the end of a quoted passage.

Winter tames man, woman and beast.

—William Shakespeare

"A comprehensive, authoritative, and beautifully written biography."—*National Review*

NOTE: This method of attribution is most often used when the quoted material is not part of the main text. Examples of such situations are quotations set as epigraphs and quotations set as extracts. The attribution may appear immediately after the quotation, or it may appear on the next line.

9. A dash is used to indicate interrupted speech or a speaker's confusion or hesitation.

"The next point I'd like to bring up—" the speaker started to say. "I'm sorry. I'll have to stop you there," the moderator broke in.

"Yes," he went on, "yes—that is—I guess I agree."

NOTE: There is some disagreement among style manuals regarding the use of a comma between a quotation ending with a dash and its attribution. Our evidence indicates that the comma is usually omitted in such circumstances. This follows the general practice regarding the use of commas with dashes described in paragraph 11 below.

10. Dashes are used variously as elements in page design. They may, for example, precede items in a vertical enumeration, set off elements in the dateline of a newspaper report, or separate words from their definitions in a glossary. The use of dashes in such circumstances is usually determined by the editor or designer of the publication.

> Required skills are:
> — Shorthand
> — Typing
> — Transcription

With Other Marks of Punctuation

11. If a dash appears at a point in a sentence where a comma could also appear, the dash is retained and the comma is dropped. For one situation in which this practice is not always followed, see paragraph 9 above.

> If we don't succeed—and the critics say we won't—then the whole project is in jeopardy.
> Our lawyer has read the transcript—all 1200 pages of it—and he has decided that an appeal would not be useful.
> Some of the other departments, however—particularly Accounting, Sales, and Credit Collection—have expanded their computer operations.

12. If the second of a pair of dashes appears at a point in a sentence where a period or semicolon would also appear, the period or semicolon is retained and the dash is dropped.

> His conduct has always been exemplary—near-perfect attendance, excellent productivity, a good attitude; nevertheless, his termination cannot be avoided.

13. Dashes are used with exclamation points and question marks. When a pair of dashes sets off parenthetic material calling for either of these marks of punctuation, the exclamation point or the question mark is placed inside the second dash. If the parenthetic material falls at the end of a sentence ending with an exclamation point or question mark, the closing dash is not required.

> His hobby was getting on people's nerves—especially mine!—and he was extremely good at it.
> When the committee meets next week—are you going to be there?—I will present all of the final figures.
> Is there any way to predict the future course of this case—one which we really cannot afford to lose?

14. Dashes and parentheses are used in combination to indicate parenthetic material appearing within parenthetic material. Our evidence indicates that dashes within parentheses and parentheses within dashes occur with about equal frequency.

We were looking for a narrator (or narrators—sometimes a script calls for more than one) who could handle a variety of assignments.

On our trip south we crossed a number of major rivers—the Hudson, the Delaware, and the Patapsco (which flows through Baltimore)—without paying a single toll.

NOTE: If the inner parenthetic element begins with a dash and its closing dash would fall in the same position as the closing parenthesis, the closing dash is omitted and the parenthesis is retained, as in the first example above. If the inner phrase begins with a parenthesis and its closing parenthesis would coincide with the closing dash, the closing parenthesis and the closing dash are both retained, as in the second example above.

En Dash

15. En dashes appear only in typeset material. The en dash is shorter than the em dash but slightly longer than the hyphen, and it is used in place of the hyphen in some situations. The most common use of the en dash is as an equivalent to "(up) to and including" when used between numbers, dates, or other notations that indicate range.

1984–85	Monday–Friday
$20–$40	35–40 years
levels D–G	ages 10–15
8:30 a.m.–4:30 p.m.	pages 128–34

NOTE: The use of the en dash to replace the hyphen in such cases, although urged by most style manuals, is by no means universal. Writers and editors who wish to have en dashes set in their copy need to indicate on their manuscripts which hyphens should be set as en dashes, and this need to mark en dashes can obviously be an inconvenience and an invitation to errors. However, many writers and editors prefer to use en dashes because of the visual clarity they provide between numbers and because of the distinction they make between en dashes used to mean "to" and hyphens used to connect elements in compound words.

16. Publishers make various uses of the en dash, and no one set of rules can be said to be standard. Some common uses of the en dash include using it as a replacement for the hyphen following a prefix that is added to an open compound, as a replacement for the word *to* between capitalized names, and to indicate linkages, such as boundaries, treaties, or oppositions.

pre–Civil War architecture
the New York–Connecticut area

    Chicago–Memphis train
    Washington–Moscow diplomacy
    the Dempsey–Tunney fight

Long Dashes

17. A two-em dash is used to indicate missing letters in a word
and, less frequently, to indicate a missing word.

    Mr. P—— of Baltimore
    That's b——t and you know it.

18. A three-em dash indicates that a word has been left out or
that an unknown word or figure is to be supplied. For the use
of this dash in bibliography listings, see Chapter 7, "Notes and
Bibliographies," page 227.

    The study was carried out in ———, a fast-growing Sunbelt city.
    We'll leave New York City on the ——— of August.

Spacing

19. Style varies as to spacing around the dash. Some publications
insert a space before and after the dash, others do not. Our
evidence indicates that the majority of publishers style the
dash without spaces.

Ellipsis Points

Ellipsis points is the name most often given to periods when they
are used, usually in groups of three, to signal an omission from
quoted material or to indicate a pause or trailing off of speech.
Other names for periods used in this way include *ellipses, points of
ellipsis,* and *suspension points.* Ellipsis points are often used in conjunction with other marks of punctuation, including periods used
to mark the ends of sentences. When ellipsis points are used in
this way with a terminal period, the omission is sometimes thought
of as being marked by four periods. This discussion of ellipsis
points is illustrated with examples of ellipsis points used with
quoted material enclosed in quotation marks. For examples of ellipsis points used to indicate omissions from quoted material set
as extracts, see Chapter 8, "The Treatment of Quotations," especially the section on Alterations, Omissions, and Interpolations,
beginning on page 238.

    NOTE: The examples given below present passages in which
    ellipsis points indicate omission of material. In most cases, the
    full text from which these omissions have been made is some
    portion of the headnote above.

1. Ellipsis points indicate the omission of one or more words within a quoted sentence.

> One book said, "Other names . . . include *ellipses, points of ellipsis,* and *suspension points.*"

2. Ellipsis points are usually not used to indicate the omission of words that precede the quoted portion. However, style varies on this point, and in some formal contexts, especially those in which the quotation is introduced by a colon, ellipsis points are used.

> The book maintained that "the omission is sometimes thought of as being marked by four periods."
>
> The book maintained: ". . . the omission is sometimes thought of as being marked by four periods."

3. Punctuation used in the original that falls on either side of the ellipsis points is often omitted; however, it may be retained, especially if such retention helps clarify the sentence.

> According to the book, "*Ellipsis points* is the name most often given to periods when they are used . . . to signal an omission from quoted material or to indicate a pause or trailing off of speech."
>
> According to the book, "When ellipsis points are used in this way . . . , the omission is sometimes thought of as being marked by four periods."
>
> According to the book, "*Ellipsis points* is the name most often given to periods when they are used, usually in groups of three, . . . to indicate a pause or trailing off of speech."

4. If an omission comprises an entire sentence within a passage, the last part of a sentence within a passage, or the first part of a sentence other than the first quoted sentence, the end punctuation preceding or following the omission is retained and is followed by three periods.

> That book says, "Other names for periods used in this way include *ellipses, points of ellipsis,* and *suspension points.* . . . When ellipsis points are used in this way with a terminal period, the omission is sometimes thought of as being marked by four periods."
>
> That book says, "*Ellipsis points* is the name given to periods when they are used, usually in groups of three, to signal an omission from quoted material. . . . Other names for periods used in this way include *ellipses, points of ellipsis,* and *suspension points.*"
>
> That book says, "Ellipsis points are often used in conjunction with other marks of punctuation, including periods used to mark ends of sentences. . . . The omission is sometimes thought of as being marked by four periods."

NOTE: The capitalization of the word *The* in the third example is acceptable. For more on the capitalization of words in quotations, see the section on Alterations, Omissions, and Interpolations, beginning on page 238, in Chapter 8, "The Treatment of Quotations."

5. If the last words of a quoted sentence are omitted and if the original sentence ends with a period, that period is retained and three ellipsis points follow. However, if the original sentence ends with punctuation other than a period, the end punctuation often follows the ellipsis points, especially if it helps clarify the quotation.

> Their book said, "Ellipsis points are often used in conjunction with other marks of punctuation. . . ."
>
> He always ends his harangues with some variation on the question, "What could you have been thinking when you . . . ?"

NOTE: Many writers and editors, especially those writing in more informal contexts, choose to ignore the styling considerations presented in paragraphs 4 and 5. They use instead an alternative system in which all omissions are indicated by three periods and all terminal periods that may precede or follow an omission are dropped.

6. Ellipsis points are used to indicate that a quoted sentence has been intentionally left unfinished. In situations such as this the terminal period is not included.

> In that section, the introductory paragraph begins, "*Ellipsis points is the name most often given* . . ."

7. A line of ellipsis points indicates that one or more lines of poetry have been omitted from a text. For more on this use of ellipsis points, see the section on Quoting Verse, beginning on page 242, in Chapter 8, "The Treatment of Quotations."

8. Ellipsis points are used to indicate faltering speech, especially if the faltering involves a long pause between words or a sentence that trails off or is left intentionally unfinished. In these kinds of sentences most writers treat the ellipsis points as terminal punctuation, thus removing the need for any other punctuation; however, style does vary on this point, and some writers routinely use other punctuation in conjunction with ellipsis points.

> The speaker seemed uncertain how to answer the question. "Well, that's true . . . but even so . . . I think we can do better."
>
> "Despite these uncertainties, we believe we can do it, but . . ."
>
> "I mean . . ." he said, "like . . . How?"

9. Ellipsis points are sometimes used as a stylistic device to catch and hold a reader's attention.

> They think that nothing can go wrong . . . but it does.

10. Each ellipsis point is set off from other ellipsis points, from adjacent punctuation (except for quotation marks, which are closed up to the ellipsis points), and from surrounding text by a space. If a terminal period is used with ellipsis points, it precedes them with no space before it and one space after it.

Exclamation Point

The exclamation point is used to mark a forceful comment. Writers and editors usually try to avoid using the exclamation point too frequently, because its heavy use can weaken its effect.

1. An exclamation point can punctuate a sentence, phrase, or interjection.

> This is the fourth time in a row he's missed his cue!
> No one that I talked to—not even the accounting department!—seemed to know how the figures were calculated.
> Oh! you startled me.
> Ah, those eyes!

2. The exclamation point replaces the question mark when an ironic or emphatic tone is more important than the actual question.

> Aren't you finished yet!
> Do you realize what you've done!
> Why me!

3. Occasionally the exclamation point is used with a question mark to indicate a very forceful question.

> How much did you say?!
> You did what!?

NOTE: The interrobang, printed ‽ , was created to punctuate the types of sentences described in paragraphs 2 and 3 above. However, the character is not available to most typesetters, and it is rarely used.

4. In mathematical expressions, the exclamation point indicates a factorial.

> $n! \cdot m \geq (n)(m!)$

5. The exclamation point is enclosed within brackets, dashes, parentheses, and quotation marks when it punctuates the material so enclosed rather than the sentence as a whole. It should be placed outside them when it punctuates the entire sentence.

> He expressed his feelings in a letter to his wife: "Such a long delay would be a catastrophie [sic]!"
>
> All of this proves—at long last!—that we were right from the start.
>
> Somehow the dog got the gate open (for the third time!) and ran into the street.
>
> He shouted, "Wait!" and sprinted toward the train.
>
> The correct word is "mousse," not "moose"!

6. Exclamatory phrases that occur within a sentence are set off by dashes or parentheses.

> And now our competition—get this!—wants to start sharing secrets.
>
> The board accepted most of the recommendations, but ours (alas!) was not even considered.

7. If an exclamation point falls at a place in a sentence where a comma or a terminal period could also go, the comma or period is dropped and the exclamation point is retained.

> "Absolutely not!" he snapped.
>
> She has written about sixty pages so far—and with no help!

NOTE: If the exclamation point is part of a title, as of a play, book, or movie, it may be followed by a comma. If the title falls at the end of a sentence, the terminal period is usually dropped.

> Marshall and Susan went to see the musical *Oklahoma!*, and they enjoyed it very much.
>
> They enjoyed seeing the musical *Oklahoma!*

8. In typewritten material, two spaces follow an exclamation point that ends a sentence. If the exclamation point is followed by a closing bracket, closing parenthesis, or closing quotation marks, the two spaces follow the second mark. In typeset material, only one space follows the exclamation point.

> The time is now! Decide what you are going to do.
> She said, "The time is now!" That meant we had to decide what to do.
> The time is now! Decide what you are going to do.
> She said, "The time is now!" That meant we had to decide what to do.

Hyphen

1. Hyphens are used to link elements in compound words. For more on the styling of compound words, see the section on Compounds, beginning on page 92, in Chapter 3, "Plurals, Possessives, and Compounds."

2. A hyphen marks an end-of-line division of a word when part of the word is to be carried down to the next line.

   > We went to three different showrooms (it wasn't a pleasant experience; prices in this area have gone up) and asked every question we could think of.

3. A hyphen divides letters or syllables to give the effect of stuttering, sobbing, or halting speech.

   S-s-sammy   ah-ah-ah   y-y-es

4. Hyphens indicate a word spelled out letter by letter.

   p-r-o-b-a-t-i-o-n

5. A hyphen indicates that a word element is a prefix, suffix, or medial element.

   anti-   -ship   -o-

6. A hyphen is used in typewritten material as an equivalent to the phrase "(up) to and including" when placed between numbers and dates. In typeset material this hyphen is very often replaced by an en dash. For more on the use of the en dash, see paragraphs 15 and 16 under Dash in this chapter.

7. Hyphens are sometimes used to produce inflected forms of verbs that are made of individually pronounced letters or to add an -er ending to an abbreviation; however, apostrophes are more commonly used for this purpose. For more on these uses of the apostrophe, see paragraphs 6 and 7 under Apostrophe in this chapter.

   D.H.-ing for the White Sox
   a loyal AA-er

Parentheses

Parentheses enclose supplementary elements that are inserted into a main statement but that are not intended to be part of the statement; in fact, parenthetic elements often interrupt the main structure of the sentence. For some of the cases described below, especially those listed under the heading "Parenthetic Elements," commas and dashes are frequently used instead of parentheses. (For contrasting examples, see paragraph 17 under Comma and paragraph 3 under Dash in this chapter.) In general, commas tend to be used when the inserted material is closely related, logically or grammatically, to the main clause; parentheses are more often used when the inserted material is incidental or digressive. Some newspapers and news magazines avoid the use of parentheses in straight news reporting and rely instead on the dash. In most cases, however, the choice of dashes or parentheses to enclose parenthetic material is a matter of personal preference.

Parenthetic Elements

1. Parentheses enclose phrases and clauses that provide examples, explanations, or supplementary facts. Supplementary numerical data may also be enclosed in parentheses.

   Nominations for the association's principal officers (president, vice president, treasurer, and secretary) were heard and approved at the last meeting.

   Although we liked the restaurant (their Italian food was the best), we seldom went there.

   Three old destroyers (all now out of commission) will be scrapped.

   Their first baseman was hitting well that season (.297, 84 RBIs), and their left fielder was doing well also (21 HRs, 78 RBIs).

2. Parentheses enclose phrases and clauses introduced by expressions such as *namely, that is, e.g.,* and *i.e.* Commas, dashes, and semicolons are also used to perform this function. (For contrasting examples, see paragraph 18 under Comma, paragraph 6 under Dash, and paragraph 6 under Semicolon in this chapter.)

   In writing to the manufacturer, be as specific as possible (i.e., list the missing or defective parts, describe the nature of the malfunction, and provide the name and address of the store where the unit was purchased).

3. Parentheses set off definitions, translations, or alternate names for words in the main part of a sentence.

   The company sold off all of its retail outlets and announced plans to sell off its houseware (small appliance) business as well.

   He has followed the fortunes of the modern renaissance (*al-Nahdad*) in the Arab-speaking world.

   The hotel was located just a few blocks from San Antonio's famous Paseo del Rio (river walk).

They were scheduled to play Beethoven's Trio in B-flat major, Opus 97 ("The Archduke").

4. Parentheses enclose abbreviations synonymous with spelled-out forms and occurring after those forms, or they may enclose the spelled-out form occurring after the abbreviation.

She referred to a ruling by the Federal Communications Commission (FCC).

They were involved with a study regarding the manufacture and disposal of PVC (polyvinyl chloride).

5. Parentheses are used in running text to set off bibliographical or historical data about books, articles, or other published or artistic works. (For full information regarding the use of parentheses with bibliographical references, see the section on Parenthetical References, beginning on page 211, in Chapter 7, "Notes and Bibliographies."

His work was influenced by several of Freud's essays, including "Some Character Types Met with in Psychoanalytic Work" (1916).

Ohio Impromptu (1981) was written for a special performance at Ohio State University.

Another book in this category is Alice Schick's *Serengeti Cats* (Lippincott, $10.53).

6. Parentheses often set off cross-references.

Telephone ordering service is also provided (refer to the list of stores at the end of this catalog).

Textbooks are available at the bookstore for all on-campus courses. (See page 12 for hours.)

The diagram (Fig. 3) illustrates the action of the pump.

7. Parentheses enclose Arabic numerals that confirm a spelled-out number in a text.

Delivery will be made in thirty (30) days.

8. Parentheses enclose the name of a city or state that is inserted into a proper name for identification.

the Norristown (Pa.) State Hospital
the *Tulsa* (Okla.) *Tribune*

9. Some writers use parentheses to set off personal asides.

It was largely as a result of this conference that the committee was formed (its subsequent growth in influence is another story).

10. Parentheses are used to set off quotations, either attributed or unattributed, that illustrate or support a statement made in the main text.

After he had had a few brushes with the police, his stepfather had him sent to jail as an incorrigible ("It will do him good").

As a Mechanical Device

11. Parentheses enclose unpunctuated numbers or letters in a series within running text.

> We must set forth (1) our long-term goals, (2) our immediate objectives, and (3) the means at our disposal.

NOTE: Some writers and editors use only a single parenthesis following the number; however, most style books advise that parentheses be used both before and after, and most publications do follow that style.

12. Parentheses indicate alternative terms.

> Please indicate the lecture(s) you would like to attend.

13. Parentheses are used in combination with numbers for several mechanical purposes, such as setting off area codes in telephone numbers, grouping elements in mathematical expressions, and indicating losses in accounting.

> (413) 256-7899
> $3(a+b) + 4(a+b)$

Operating Profits (in millions)	
Cosmetics	26.2
Food products	47.7
Food services	54.3
Transportation	(17.7)
Sporting goods	(11.2)
Total	99.3

With Other Marks of Punctuation

14. If a parenthetic expression is an independent sentence, its first word is capitalized and a period is placed *inside* the last parenthesis. On the other hand, a parenthetic expression that occurs within a sentence—even if it could stand alone as a separate sentence—does not end with a period. It may, however, end with an exclamation point, a question mark, a period after an abbreviation, or a set of quotation marks. A parenthetic expression within a sentence does not require capitalization unless it is a quoted sentence. (For more on the use of capitals with parenthetic expressions, see the section on Beginnings, starting on page 53, in Chapter 2, "Capitals, Italics, and Quotation Marks.")

> The discussion was held in the boardroom. (The results are still confidential.)

Although several trade organizations worked actively against the legislation (there were at least three paid lobbyists working on Capitol Hill at any one time), the bill passed easily.

After waiting in line for an hour (why do we do these things?), we finally left.

The conference was held in Vancouver (that's in B.C.).

He was totally confused ("What can we do?") and refused to see anyone.

15. If a parenthetic expression within a sentence is composed of two independent clauses, capitalization and periods are avoided. To separate the clauses within the parentheses, semicolons are usually used. If the parenthetic expression occurs outside of a sentence, normal patterns of capitalization and punctuation prevail.

> We visited several showrooms, looked at the prices (it wasn't a pleasant experience; prices in this area have not gone down), and asked all the questions we could think of.

> We visited several showrooms and looked at the prices. (It wasn't a pleasant experience. Prices in this area have not gone down.) If salespeople were available, we asked all of the questions we could think of.

16. No punctuation mark (other than a period after an abbreviation) is placed before parenthetic material within a sentence; if a break is required, the punctuation is placed after the final parenthesis.

> I'll get back to you tomorrow (Friday), when I have more details.

17. Parentheses sometimes appear within parentheses, although the usual practice is to replace the inner pair of parentheses with a pair of brackets. (For an example of brackets within parentheses, see paragraph 6 under Brackets in this chapter.)

> Checks must be drawn in U.S. dollars. (PLEASE NOTE: In accordance with U.S. Department of Treasury regulations, we cannot accept checks drawn on Canadian banks for amounts less than four U.S. dollars ($4.00). The same regulation applies to Canadian money orders.)

18. Dashes and parentheses are often used together to set off parenthetic material within a larger parenthetic element. For details and examples, see paragraph 14 under Dash in this chapter.

Spacing

19. In typewritten material, a parenthetic expression that is an independent sentence is followed by two spaces. In typeset material, the sentence is followed by one space. In typewritten or

typeset material, a parenthetic expression that falls within a sentence is followed by one space.

```
We visited several showrooms and looked at the
prices. (It wasn't a pleasant experience. Prices
in this area have gone up.) We asked all the
questions we could think of.
```

We visited several showrooms and looked at the prices. (It wasn't a pleasant experience. Prices in this area have gone up.) We asked all the questions we could think of.

NOTE: Paragraphs 14 and 15 above are followed by examples that illustrate the appearance in typeset material of parenthetic expressions that are independent sentences.

Period

This section describes uses of the period in running text. For rules regarding use of the period in bibliographies, see Chapter 7, "Notes and Bibliographies." For the use of three periods to indicate a pause or omission, see the section on Ellipsis Points in this chapter.

1. A period terminates a sentence or a sentence fragment that is neither interrogative nor exclamatory.

Do your best.
I did my best.
Total chaos. Nothing works.

2. A period punctuates some abbreviations. For more on the punctuation of abbreviations, see the section on Punctuation, beginning on page 109, in Chapter 4, "Abbreviations."

a.k.a.	U.S.	e.g.
fig.	Dr.	Co.
N.W.	No.	Ph.D.
Assn.	Inc.	ibid.
in.	Jr.	Corp.

3. A period is used with an individual's initials. If all of the person's initials are used instead of the name, however, the unspaced initials may be written without periods.

F. Scott Fitzgerald
F.D.R. *or* FDR
Susan B. Anthony
T. S. Eliot

4. A period follows Roman and Arabic numerals and also letters when they are used without parentheses in outlines and vertical enumerations.

> I. Objectives
>   A. Economy
>   1. Low initial cost
>   2. Low maintenance cost
>   B. Ease of operation
>
> Required skills are:
>   1. Shorthand
>   2. Typing
>   3. Transcription

5. A period is placed within quotation marks even when it does not punctuate the quoted material.

> The charismatic leader was known to his followers as "the guiding light."
>
> "I said I wanted to fire him," Henry went on, "but she said, 'I don't think you have the contractual privilege to do that.' "

6. When brackets or parentheses enclose a sentence that is independent of surrounding sentences, the period is placed inside the closing parenthesis or bracket. However, when brackets or parentheses enclose a sentence that is part of a surrounding sentence, the period for the enclosed sentence is omitted.

> On Friday the government ordered a 24-hour curfew and told all journalists and photographers to leave the area. (Authorities later confiscated the film of those who did not comply.)
>
> I took a good look at her (she was standing quite close to me at the time).

7. In typewritten material, two spaces follow a period that ends a sentence. If the period is followed by a closing bracket, closing parenthesis, or quotation marks, the two spaces follow the second mark. In typeset material, only one space follows this period.

> Here is the car.   Do you want to get in?
> He said, "Here is the car."   I asked if I should get in.
> Here is the car. Do you want to get in?

8. One space follows a period that comes after an initial in a name. If a name is composed entirely of initials, no space is required; however, the usual styling for such names is to omit the periods.

> Mr. H. C. Matthews
> F.D.R. *or* FDR

9. No space follows an internal period within a punctuated abbreviation.

f.o.b.	Ph.D.	p.m.
i.e.	A.D.	R.S.V.P.

Question Mark

1. The question mark terminates a direct question.

> What went wrong?
> "When do they arrive?" she asked.

NOTE: The intent of the writer, not the word order of the sentence, determines whether or not the sentence is a question. Polite requests that are worded as questions, for instance, usually take periods, because they are not really questions. Similarly, sentences whose word order is that of a statement but whose force is interrogatory are punctuated with question marks.

> Will you please sit down.
> He did that?

2. The question mark terminates an interrogative element that is part of a sentence. An indirect question is not followed by a question mark.

> The old arithmetic books were full of How-much-wallpaper-will-it-take-to-cover-a-room? questions.
> How did she do it? was the question on everybody's mind.
> She wondered, will it work?
> She wondered whether it would work.

3. The question mark punctuates each element of an interrogative series that is neither numbered nor lettered. When an interrogative series is numbered or lettered, only one question mark is used, and it is placed at the end of the series.

> Can you give us a reasonable forecast? back up your predictions? compare them with last year's earnings?
> Can you (1) give us a reasonable forecast, (2) back up your predictions, (3) compare them with last year's earnings?

4. The question mark indicates a writer's or editor's uncertainty about a fact.

> Geoffrey Chaucer, English poet (1340?–1400)

5. The question mark is placed inside a closing bracket, dash, parenthesis, or pair of quotation marks when it punctuates only the material enclosed by that mark and not the sentence as a whole. It is placed outside that mark when it punctuates the entire sentence.

> What did Andrew mean when he called the project "a fiasco from the start"?

> I had a vacation in 1975 (was it really that long ago?), but I haven't had time for one since.

> "She thought about it for a moment," Alice continued, "and finally she said, 'Can you guarantee this will work?' "

> He asked, "Do you realize the extent of the problem [the housing shortage]?"

6. In typewritten material, two spaces follow a question mark that ends a sentence. If the question mark is followed by a closing bracket, closing parenthesis, or quotation marks, the two spaces follow the second mark. In typeset material, only one space follows the question mark.

> `She wondered, will it work?    He said he thought`
> `it would.`

> `She asked,  "Will it work?"    He said he thought it`
> `would.`

> She wondered, will it work? He said he thought it would.

7. One space follows a question mark that falls within a sentence.

> Are you coming today? tomorrow? the day after?

Quotation Marks, Double

This section describes the use of quotation marks to enclose quoted matter in running text. It also describes the mechanical uses of quotation marks, such as to set off translations of words or to enclose single letters within sentences. For the use of quotation marks to enclose titles of poems, paintings, or other works, see the section on Proper Nouns, Pronouns, and Adjectives, beginning on page 56, in Chapter 2, "Capitals, Italics, and Quotation Marks." For a discussion of extended quotations set off from the rest of the text by indention, see Chapter 8, "The Treatment of Quotations."

Basic Uses

1. Quotation marks enclose direct quotations but not indirect quotations.

> She said, "I am leaving."

> "I am leaving," she said, "and I'm not coming back."

"I am leaving," she said. "This has gone on long enough."

She said that she was leaving.

2. Quotation marks enclose fragments of quoted matter when they are reproduced exactly as originally stated.

The agreement makes it clear that he "will be paid only upon receipt of an acceptable manuscript."

As late as 1754, documents refer to him as "yeoman" and "husbandman."

3. Quotation marks enclose words or phrases borrowed from others, words used in a special way, or words of marked informality when they are introduced into formal writing.

That kind of corporation is referred to as "closed" or "privately held."

Be sure to send a copy of your résumé, or as some folks would say, your "biodata summary."

They were afraid the patient had "stroked out"—had had a cerebrovascular accident.

4. Quotation marks are sometimes used to enclose words referred to as words. Italic type is also frequently used for this purpose. For more on this use of italics, see the section on Other Uses of Italics, beginning on page 78, in Chapter 2, "Capitals, Italics, and Quotation Marks."

He went through the manuscript and changed every "he" to "she."

5. Quotation marks enclose short exclamations or representations of sounds. Representations of sounds are also frequently set in italic type. For more on this use of italics, see the section on Other Uses of Italics, beginning on page 78, in Chapter 2, "Capitals, Italics, and Quotation Marks."

"Ssshh!" she hissed.

They never say anything crude like "shaddap."

6. Quotation marks enclose short sentences that fall within longer sentences, especially when the shorter sentence is meant to suggest spoken dialogue. Kinds of sentences that may be treated in this way include mottoes and maxims, unspoken or imaginary dialogue, or sentences referred to as sentences.

Throughout the camp, the spirit was "We can do."

She never could get used to his "That's the way it goes" attitude.

In effect, the voters were saying "You blew it, and you don't get another chance."

Their attitude could only be described as "Kill the messenger."

Another example of a palindrome is "Madam, I'm Adam."

NOTE: Style varies regarding the punctuation of sentences such as these. In general, the force of the quotation marks is to set the shorter sentence off more distinctly from the surrounding sentence and to give the shorter sentence more of the feel of spoken dialogue; omitting the quotation marks diminishes the effect. (For a description of the use of commas in sentences like these, see paragraphs 33 and 34 under Comma in this chapter.)

The first rule is, When in doubt, spell it out.

They weren't happy with the impression she left: "Don't expect favors, because I don't have to give them."

7. Quotation marks are not used to enclose paraphrases.

Build a better mouse trap, Emerson says, and the world will beat a path to your door.

8. Direct questions are usually not enclosed in quotation marks unless they represent quoted dialogue.

The question is, What went wrong?

As we listened to him, we couldn't help wondering, Where's the plan?

She asked, "What went wrong?"

NOTE: As in the sentences presented in paragraph 6 above, style varies regarding the use of quotation marks with direct questions; and in many cases, writers will include the quotation marks.

As we listened to him, we couldn't help wondering, "Where's the plan?"

9. Quotation marks are used to enclose translations of foreign or borrowed terms.

The term *sesquipedalian* comes from the Latin word *sesquipedalis*, meaning "a foot and a half long."

While in Texas, he encountered the armadillo ("little armored one") and developed quite an interest in it.

10. Quotation marks are sometimes used to enclose single letters within a sentence.

The letter "m" is wider than the letter "i."

We started to work on the dictionary, beginning with the letter "A."

Put an "x" in the right spot.

The metal rod was shaped into a "V."

NOTE: Style varies on this point. Sans serif type is most often used when the shape of the letter is being stressed. Letters referred to as letters are commonly set in italic type. (For more on this use of italics, see the section on Other Uses of Italics, beginning on page 78, in Chapter 2, "Capitals, Italics, and Quotation Marks.") Finally, letters often appear in the same typeface as the surrounding text if no confusion would result from the styling.

> a "V"-shaped blade
> He was happy to get a B in the course.
> How many e's are in her name?

With Other Marks of Punctuation

11. When quotation marks follow a word in a sentence that is also followed by a period or comma, the period or comma is placed within the quotation marks.

    > He said, "I am leaving."
    > Her camera was described as "waterproof," but "moisture-resistant" would have been a better description.

    NOTE: Some writers draw a distinction between periods and commas that belong logically to the quoted material and those that belong to the whole sentence. If the period or comma belongs to the quoted material, they place it inside the quotation marks; if the period belongs logically to the sentence that surrounds the quoted matter, they place it outside the quotation marks. This distinction was previously observed in a wide range of publications, including U.S. Congressional publications and Merriam-Webster® dictionaries. In current practice, the distinction is made in relatively few publications, although the distinction is routinely made for dashes, exclamation points, and question marks used with quotation marks, as described in paragraph 13 below.

    > The package was labeled "Handle with Care".
    > The act was referred to as the "Army-Navy Medical Services Corps Act of 1947".
    > Her camera was described as "waterproof", but "moisture-resistant" would have been a better description.
    > He said, "I am leaving."

12. When quotation marks follow a word in a sentence that is also followed by a colon or semicolon, the colon or semicolon is placed outside the quotation marks.

    > There was only one thing to do when he said, "I may not run": promise him a larger campaign contribution.
    > She spoke of her "little cottage in the country"; she might better have called it a mansion.

13. The dash, question mark, and exclamation point are placed inside quotation marks when they punctuate the quoted matter only. They are placed outside the quotation marks when they punctuate the whole sentence.

> He asked, "When did she leave?"
> What is the meaning of "the open door"?
> Save us from his "mercy"!
> "I can't see how—" he started to say.
> He thought he knew where he was going—he remembered her saying, "Take two lefts, then stay to the right"—but the streets didn't look familiar.

14. One space follows a quotation mark that is followed by the rest of a sentence.

> "I am leaving," she said.

15. In typewritten material, two spaces follow a quotation mark that ends a sentence. In typeset material one space follows.

> He said, "Here is the car. "   I asked if I should get in.
> He said, "Here is the car." I asked if I should get in.

Quotation Marks, Single

1. Single quotation marks enclose a quotation within a quotation in conventional English.

> The witness said, "I distinctly heard him say, 'Don't be late,' and then I heard the door close."
> The witness said, "I distinctly heard him say, 'Don't be late.' "

NOTE: When both single and double quotation marks occur at the end of a sentence, the period typically falls *within* both sets of marks.

2. Single quotation marks are sometimes used in place of double quotation marks especially in British usage.

> The witness said, 'I distinctly heard him say, "Don't be late," and then I heard the door close.'

3. On rare occasions, authors face the question of how to style a quotation within a quotation within a quotation. Standard styling practice would be to enclose the innermost quotation in double marks; however, this construction can be confusing, and in many cases rewriting the sentence can remove the need for it.

> The witness said, "I distinctly heard him say, 'Don't you say "Shut up" to me.' "
> The witness said that she distinctly heard him say, "Don't you say 'Shut up' to me."

4. In some specialized fields, such as theology, philosophy, and linguistics, special terminology or words referred to as words are enclosed within single quotation marks. When single quotation marks are used in this way, any other punctuation following the word enclosed is placed outside the quotation marks.

> She was interested in the development of the word 'humongous', especially during the 1960s.

Semicolon

The semicolon is used in ways that are similar to those in which periods and commas are used. Because of these similarities, the semicolon is often thought of as either a weak period or a strong comma. As a weak period, the semicolon marks the end of a complete clause and signals that the clause that follows it is closely related to the clause that precedes it. As a strong comma, the semicolon clarifies meaning usually by distinguishing major sentence divisions from the minor pauses that are represented by commas.

Between Clauses

1. A semicolon separates independent clauses that are joined together in one sentence without a coordinating conjunction.

> He hemmed and hawed for over an hour; he couldn't make up his mind.
> The river rose and overflowed its banks; roads became flooded and impassable; freshly plowed fields disappeared from sight.
> Cream the shortening and sugar; add the eggs and beat well.

2. Ordinarily a comma separates main clauses joined with a coordinating conjunction. However, if the sentence might be confusing with a comma in this position, a semicolon is used in its place. Potentially confusing sentences include those with other commas in them or with particularly long clauses.

> We fear that this situation may, in fact, occur; but we don't know when.
> In a society that seeks to promote social goals, government will play a powerful role; and taxation, once simply a means of raising money, becomes, in addition, a way of furthering those goals.

As recently as 1988 the company felt the operation could be a successful one that would generate significant profits in several different markets; but in 1991 the management changed its mind and began a program of shutting down plants and reducing its product line.

3. A semicolon joins two statements when the grammatical construction of the second clause is elliptical and depends on that of the first.

> The veal dishes were very good; the desserts, too.
>
> In many cases the conference sessions, which were designed to allow for full discussions of topics, were much too long and tedious; the breaks between them, much too short.

4. A semicolon joins two clauses when the second begins with a conjunctive adverb, as *accordingly, also, besides, consequently, furthermore, hence, however, indeed, likewise, moreover, namely, nevertheless, otherwise, still, then, therefore,* and *thus.* Phrases such as *by the same token, in that case, as a result, on the other hand,* and *all the same* can also act as conjunctive adverbs.

> Most people are covered by insurance of one kind or another; indeed, many people don't even see their medical bills.
>
> It won't be easy to sort out the facts of this confusing situation; however, a decision must be made.
>
> The case could take years to work its way through the court system; as a result, many plaintiffs will accept out-of-court settlements.

NOTE: Style varies regarding the treatment of clauses introduced by *so* and *yet.* Although many writers continue to treat *so* and *yet* as adverbs, it has become standard to treat these words as coordinating conjunctions that join clauses. In this treatment, a comma precedes *so* and *yet* and no punctuation follows them. (For examples, see paragraph 1 under Comma in this chapter.)

5. When three or more clauses are separated by semicolons, a coordinating conjunction may or may not precede the final clause. If a coordinating conjunction does precede the final clause, the final semicolon is often replaced with a comma. (For the use of commas to separate three or more clauses without conjunctions, see paragraph 4 under Comma in this chapter.)

> Their report was one-sided and partial; it did not reflect the facts; it distorted them.
>
> They don't understand; they grow bored; and they stop learning.
>
> The report recounted events leading up to the incident; it included observations of eyewitnesses, but it drew no conclusions.

NOTE: The choices of whether to use a conjunction and whether to use a semicolon or comma with the conjunction are matters of personal preference. In general, the force of the semicolon is to make the transition to the final clause more abrupt, which often serves to place more emphasis on that clause. The comma and conjunction ease the transition and make the sentence seem less choppy.

With Phrases and Clauses Introduced by *for example*, *i.e.*, etc.

6. A semicolon is sometimes used before expressions (as *for example, for instance, that is, namely, e.g.,* or *i.e.*) that introduce expansions or series. Commas, dashes, and parentheses are also used in sentences like these. For contrasting examples, see paragraph 18 under Comma, paragraph 6 under Dash, and paragraph 2 under Parentheses in this chapter.

> On one point only did everyone agree; namely, that too much money had been spent already.
>
> We were fairly successful on that project; that is, we made our deadlines and met our budget.
>
> Most of the contestants had traveled great distances to participate; for example, three had come from Australia, one from Japan, and two from China.

In a Series

7. A semicolon is used in place of a comma to separate phrases in a series when the phrases themselves contain commas. A comma may replace the semicolon before the last item in a series if the last item is introduced with a conjunction.

> She flung open the door; raced up the stairs, taking them two at a time; locked herself in the bathroom; and, holding her sides, started to laugh uncontrollably.
>
> The visitor to Barndale was offered three sources of overnight accommodation: The Rose and Anchor, which housed Barndale's oldest pub; The Crawford, an American-style luxury hotel; and Ellen's Bed and Breakfast on Peabody Lane.
>
> We studied mathematics in the morning; English, French, and Spanish right after lunch, and science in the late afternoon.

8. When the individual items in an enumeration or series are long or are sentences themselves, they are usually separated by semicolons.

> Among the committee's recommendations: more hospital beds in urban areas where there are waiting lists for elective surgery; smaller staff size in half-empty rural hospitals; review procedures for all major purchases.
>
> There is a difference between them: she is cross and irritable; he is merely moody.

As a Mechanical Device

9. A semicolon separates items in a list in cases where a comma alone would not clearly separate the items or references.

(Friedlander 1957; Ballas 1962)
(Genesis 3:1–19; 4:1–16)

With Other Marks of Punctuation

10. A semicolon is placed outside quotation marks and parentheses.

They referred to each other as "Mother" and "Father"; they were the archetypal happily married elderly couple.

She accepted the situation with every appearance of equanimity (but with some inward qualms); however, all of that changed the next day.

Virgule

The virgule is known by many names, including *diagonal, solidus, oblique, slant, slash,* and *slash mark.* Most commonly, the virgule is used to represent a word that is not written out or to separate or set off certain adjacent elements of text.

In Place of Missing Words

1. A virgule represents the word *per* or *to* when used with units of measure or when used to indicate the terms of a ratio.

40,000 tons/year   price/earnings ratio
14 gm/100 cc   a 50/50 split
9 ft./sec.   risk/reward tradeoff

2. A virgule separates alternatives. In this context, the virgule usually represents the words *or* or *and/or.*

alumni/ae
his/her
introductory/refresher courses
oral/written tests

3. A virgule replaces the word *and* in some compound terms.

molybdenum/vanadium steel
in the May/June issue
1973/74
in the Falls Church/McLean, Va., area
an innovative classroom/laboratory

4. A virgule is used, although less commonly, to replace a number of prepositions, such as *at, versus, with,* and *for.*

U.C./Berkeley	parent/child issues
table/mirror	Vice President/Editorial

With Abbreviations

5. A virgule punctuates some abbreviations.

c/o	w/	A/1C	d/b/a
A/R	A/V	V/STOL	S/Sgt

NOTE: In some cases the virgule may stand for a word that is not represented in the abbreviation (e.g., *in* in *W/O*, the abbreviation for *water in oil*).

To Separate Elements

6. The virgule is used in a number of mechanical ways to separate groups of numbers, such as elements in a date, numerators and denominators in fractions, and area codes in telephone numbers. For more on the use of virgules with numbers, see Chapter 5, "The Treatment of Numbers."

7. The virgule serves as a divider between lines of poetry that are run in with the text around them. This method of quoting poetry is usually limited to passages of no more than three or four lines. Longer passages are usually set off from the text as extract quotations, as shown in Chapter 8, "The Treatment of Quotations."

    When Samuel Taylor Coleridge wrote in "Christabel" that "'Tis a month before the month of May, /And the Spring comes slowly up this way," he could have been describing New England.

8. The virgule sets off certain elements—such as the parts of an address that are normally placed on separate lines—when they appear run in with the surrounding text.

    Mlle Christine Lagache/20, Passage des Écoliers/75051 Paris/France

9. The virgule sets off phonemes and phonemic transcriptions.

    /b/ as in *but*
    pronounced /ˌekə'nämik/ or /ˌēkə'nämik/

Spacing

10. In general, no space is used between the virgule and the words, letters, or figures separated by it. Some authors and editors prefer to place spaces around a virgule used to separate lines of poetry, but most omit the space. In the case of virgules used to set off phonemes and phonemic transcriptions, however, a space precedes the first virgule and follows the second virgule.

Chapter 2

Capitals, Italics, and Quotation Marks

CONTENTS

Words and phrases are capitalized, italicized, or enclosed in quotation marks in order to indicate that they have a special significance in a particular context. Some rules regarding capitals, italics, and quotation marks are backed by long tradition and are quite easy to apply ("The first word of a sentence or sentence fragment is capitalized"); others require arbitrary decisions or personal judgment ("Foreign words and phrases that have not been fully adopted into the English language are italicized"). Careful writers and editors usually make notes or keep a style sheet to record the decisions that they make so they can be consistent in their use of capitals, italics, and quotation marks.

This chapter is divided into four sections. The first section explains the use of capitalized words to begin sentences and phrases. The second section explains the use of capitals, italics, and quotation marks to indicate that a word or phrase is a proper noun, pronoun, or adjective. The third and fourth sections explain other uses of capital letters and italics. For other uses of quotation marks, see the section on Quotation Marks beginning on page 43, in Chapter 1, "Punctuation." For a discussion of the treatment of extended quotations, see Chapter 8, "The Treatment of Quotations."

Beginnings

---

1. The first word of a sentence or sentence fragment is capitalized.

The meeting was postponed.
No! I cannot do it.
Will you go?
Total chaos. Nothing works.

2. The first word of a sentence contained within parentheses is capitalized; however, a parenthetical sentence occurring inside another sentence is not capitalized unless it is a complete quoted sentence.

> The discussion was held in the boardroom. (The results are still confidential.)
>
> Although we liked the restaurant (their Italian food was the best), we could not afford to eat there often.
>
> After waiting in line for an hour (why do we do these things?), we finally left.
>
> He was totally demoralized ("There is just nothing we can do") and was contemplating resignation.

3. The first word of a direct quotation is capitalized; however, if the quotation is interrupted in midsentence, the second part does not begin with a capital.

> The President said, "We have rejected this report entirely."
>
> "We have rejected this report entirely," the President said, "and we will not comment on it further."

4. When a quotation, whether a sentence fragment or a complete sentence, is syntactically dependent on the sentence in which it occurs, the quotation does not begin with a capital.

> The President made it clear that "there is no room for compromise."

5. The first word of a sentence within a sentence is usually capitalized. Examples of sentences within sentences include mottoes and rules, unspoken or imaginary dialogue, sentences referred to as sentences, and direct questions. (For an explanation of the use of commas and quotation marks with sentences such as these, see paragraphs 34 and 35 in the section on Comma, beginning on page 12, and paragraph 6 in the section on Quotation Marks, Double, beginning on page 43, in Chapter 1, "Punctuation."

> You know the saying, "A stitch in time saves nine."
>
> The first rule is, When in doubt, spell it out.
>
> The clear message coming back from the audience was "We don't care."
>
> My question is, When can we go?
>
> She kept wondering, how did they get here so soon?

NOTE: In the cases of unspoken or imaginary dialogue and of direct questions, it is a matter of individual preference whether or not to capitalize the first word; however, the most common practice is to capitalize it.

6. The first word of a line of poetry is conventionally capitalized.

> The best lack all conviction, while the worst
> Are full of passionate intensity.
>   —W. B. Yeats

7. The first word following a colon may be either lowercased or capitalized if it introduces a complete sentence. While the former is the usual styling, the latter is also quite common, especially when the sentence introduced by the colon is fairly lengthy and distinctly separate from the preceding clause.

> The advantage of this particular system is clear: it's inexpensive.

> The situation is critical: This company cannot hope to recoup the fourth-quarter losses that were sustained in five operating divisions.

NOTE: For the sake of consistency, many authors and editors prefer to use one style or the other in all cases, regardless of sentence length. The capitalized style is more common in newspapers, but overall the lowercased styling is more frequently used.

8. If a colon introduces a series of sentences, the first word of each sentence is capitalized.

> Consider the following steps that we have taken: A subcommittee has been formed to evaluate our past performance and to report its findings to the full organization. New sources of revenue are being explored, and relevant organizations are being contacted. And several candidates have been interviewed for the new post of executive director.

9. The first words of run-in enumerations that form complete sentences are capitalized, as are the first words of phrasal lists and enumerations arranged vertically beneath running texts. Phrasal enumerations run in with the introductory text, however, are lowercased.

> Do the following tasks at the end of the day: 1. Clean your typewriter. 2. Clear your desktop of papers. 3. Cover office machines. 4. Straighten the contents of your desk drawers, cabinets, and bookcases.

> This is the agenda:
>   Call to order
>   Roll call
>   Minutes of the previous meeting
>   Treasurer's report

On the agenda will be (1) call to order, (2) roll call, (3) minutes of the previous meeting, (4) treasurer's report . . .

10. The introductory words *Whereas* and *Resolved* are capitalized in minutes and legislation, as is the word *That* or an alternative word or expression which immediately follows either.

Resolved, That . . .
Whereas, Substantial benefits . . .

11. The first word in an outline heading is capitalized.

    I. Editorial tasks
   II. Production responsibilities
       A. Cost estimates
       B. Bids

12. The first word of the salutation of a letter and the first word of a complimentary close are capitalized.

Dear Mary,   Ladies and Gentlemen:
Gentlemen: Sincerely yours,
Dear Sir or Madam: Very truly yours,

13. The first word and each subsequent major word following a SUBJECT or TO heading (as in a memorandum) are capitalized.

SUBJECT: Pension Plans
TO: All Department Heads and Editors

Proper Nouns, Pronouns, and Adjectives

This section describes the ways in which a broad range of proper nouns, pronouns, and adjectives are styled—with capitals, italics, quotation marks, or some combination of these devices. In almost all cases, proper nouns, pronouns, and adjectives are capitalized. The essential distinction in the use of capitals and lowercase letters lies in the particularizing or individualizing significance of capitals as against the generalizing significance of lowercase. A capital is used with a proper noun because it distinguishes some individual person, place, or thing from others of the same class. A capital is used with a proper adjective because it takes its descriptive meaning from a proper noun.

In many cases, proper nouns are italicized or enclosed in quotation marks in addition to being capitalized. No clear distinctions can be drawn between the kinds of words that are capitalized and italicized, capitalized and enclosed in quotation marks, or simply capitalized, as styling on these points is governed almost wholly by tradition.

The paragraphs in this section are grouped under the following alphabetically arranged headings:

Abbreviations	Legal Material
Abstractions and	Medical Terms
Personifications	Military Terms
Academic Degrees	Numerical Designations
Animals and Plants	Organizations
Awards, Honors, and Prizes	People
Derivatives of Proper Names	Pronouns
Geographical and	Religious Terms
Topographical References	Scientific Terms
Governmental, Judicial, and	Time Periods and Zones
Political Bodies	Titles
Historical Periods and Events	Trademarks
Hyphenated Compounds	Transportation

Abbreviations

1. Abbreviated forms of proper nouns and adjectives are capitalized, just as the spelled-out forms would be. For more on the capitalization of abbreviations, see the section on Capitalization, beginning on page 110, in Chapter 4, "Abbreviations."

    Dec. for *December*
    Col. for *Colonel*
    Wed. for *Wednesday*
    Brit. for *British*

Abstractions and Personifications

2. Abstract terms, such as names of concepts or qualities, are usually not capitalized unless the concept or quality is being presented as if it were a person. If the term is simply being used in conjunction with other words that allude to human characteristics or qualities, it is usually not capitalized. For more on the capitalization of abstract terms, see the section on Other Uses of Capitals in this chapter.

    a time when Peace walked among us
    as Autumn paints each leaf in fiery colors
    an economy gripped by inflation
    hoping that fate would lend a hand

3. Fictitious names used as personifications are capitalized.

    Uncle Sam   John Bull
    Ma Bell   Jack Frost
    Big Oil squirmed under the new regulations.

Academic Degrees

4. The names of academic degrees are capitalized when they follow a person's name. The names of specific academic degrees not following a person's name are capitalized or not capitalized according to individual preference. General terms referring to degrees, such as *doctorate, master's degree,* or *bachelor's* are not capitalized. Abbreviations for academic degrees are always capitalized.

> Martin Bonkowski, Doctor of Divinity
> earned her Doctor of Laws degree
>   *or* earned her doctor of laws degree
> working for a bachelor's degree
> Susan Wycliff, M.S.W.
> received her Ph.D.

Animals and Plants

5. The common names of animals and plants are not capitalized unless they contain a proper noun as a separate element, in which case the proper noun is capitalized, but any element of the name following the proper noun is lowercased. Elements of the name preceding the proper noun are usually but not always capitalized. In some cases, the common name of the plant or animal contains a word that was once a proper noun but is no longer thought of as such. In these cases, the word is usually not capitalized. When in doubt about the capitalization of a plant or animal name, consult a dictionary. (For an explanation of the capitalization of genus names in binomial nomenclature or of New Latin names for groups above genera in zoology and botany, see paragraphs 67 and 68 below.)

> cocker spaniel   Great Dane
> great white shark   wandering Jew
> Steller's jay   ponderosa pine
> Rhode Island red   Kentucky bluegrass
> black-eyed Susan   Japanese beetle
> lily of the valley   Brown Swiss
> Hampshire hog   holstein

NOTE: In references to specific breeds, as distinguished from the animals that belong to the breed, all elements of the name are capitalized.

> Gordon Setter   Holstein
> Rhode Island Red

Awards, Honors, and Prizes

6. Names of awards, honors, and prizes are capitalized. Descriptive words and phrases that are not actually part of the award's name are lowercased. (For an explanation of capitalizing the names of military decorations, see paragraph 44 below.)

Academy Award
Nobel Prize
Nobel Prize winner
Rhodes Scholarship
Emmy
Nobel Prize in medicine
Nobel Peace Prize
Rhodes scholar
New York Drama Critics' Circle Award

Brand Names—See **Trademarks** below.

Computer Terms—See **Scientific Terms** below.

Derivatives of Proper Names

7. Derivatives of proper names are capitalized when they are used in their primary sense. However, if the derived term has taken on a specialized meaning, it is usually not capitalized.

Roman architecture	pasteurized milk
an Americanism	manila envelope
Keynesian economics	french fries
Victorian customs	a quixotic undertaking
an Egyptologist	cesarean section

Geographical and Topographical References

8. Terms that identify divisions of the earth's surface and distinct areas, regions, places, or districts are capitalized, as are derivative nouns and adjectives.

Chicago, Illinois
the Middle Eastern situation
the Southwest
Tropic of Capricorn
the Western Hemisphere
the Sunbelt

9. Popular names of localities are capitalized.

the Big Apple	the Twin Cities
the Village	Hell's Kitchen
the Loop	the Valley

10. Compass points are capitalized when they refer to a geographical region or when they are part of a street name. They are lowercased when they refer to a simple direction.

back East
up North
out West

West Columbus Avenue
South Pleasant Street
down South
east of the Mississippi
traveling north on I-91

11. Nouns and adjectives that are derived from compass points
    and that designate or refer to a specific geographical region
    are usually capitalized.

    a Southern accent
    Northerners
    a Western crop
    part of the Eastern establishment

12. Words designating global, national, regional, or local political
    divisions are capitalized when they are essential elements of
    specific names. However, they are usually lowercased when
    they precede a proper name or when they are not part of a
    specific name.

    the British Empire
    Washington State
    Hampden County
    New York City
    Ward 1
    Ohio's Ninth Congressional District
    the fall of the empire
    the state of Washington
    the county of Hampden
    the city of New York
    fires in three wards
    carried her district

    NOTE: In legal documents, these words are often capitalized
    regardless of position.

    the State of Washington
    the County of Hampden
    the City of New York

13. Generic geographical terms (as *lake, mountain, river, valley*) are
    capitalized if they are part of a specific proper name.

    Crater Lake   Atlantic Ocean
    the Columbia River   Strait of Gibraltar
    Great Barrier Reef   Rocky Mountains
    Hudson Bay   Long Island
    Lake Como   Niagara Falls
    Ohio Valley   Bering Strait

14. Generic geographical terms preceding names are usually capi-
    talized.

Lakes Mead and Powell
Mounts Whitney and Shasta

NOTE: When *the* precedes the generic term, the generic term is lowercased.

the river Thames

15. Generic geographical terms that are not used as part of a proper name are not capitalized. These include plural generic geographical terms that follow two or more proper names and generic terms that are used descriptively or alone.

the Himalaya and Andes mountains
the Atlantic coast of Labrador
the Mississippi delta
the river valley
the Missouri and Platte rivers
the Arizona desert
the Caribbean islands
the valley

16. The names of streets, monuments, parks, landmarks, well-known buildings, and other public places are capitalized. However, generic terms that are part of these names (as *avenue, bridge,* or *tower*) are lowercased when they occur after multiple names or are used alone (but see paragraph 17 below).

Golden Gate Bridge
Eddystone Lighthouse
the San Diego Zoo
the Pyramids
the Capitol
the Dorset Hotel
the Dorset and Drake hotels
on the bridge

Coit Tower
the Statue of Liberty
Rock Creek Park
Fanueil Hall
the Mall
Peachtree Street
Fifth and Park avenues
walking through the park

17. Well-known informal or shortened forms of place-names are capitalized.

the Avenue for *Fifth Avenue*
the Street for *Wall Street*
the Exchange for the *New York Stock Exchange*

Governmental, Judicial, and Political Bodies

18. Full names of legislative, deliberative, executive, and administrative bodies are capitalized, as are easily recognizable short forms of these names. However, nonspecific noun and adjective references to them are usually lowercased.

United States Congress
the Congress
the Federal Bureau of Investigation

the Federal Reserve Board
the House
the Fed
a federal agency
congressional hearings

NOTE: Style varies regarding the capitalization of words such as *department, committee,* or *agency* when they are being used in place of the full name of a specific body. They are most often capitalized when the department or agency is referring to itself in print. In most other cases, these words are lowercased.

The Connecticut Department of Transportation is pleased to offer this new booklet on traffic safety. The Department hopes that it will be of use to all drivers.

We received a new booklet from the Connecticut Department of Transportation. This is the second pamphlet the department has issued this month.

19. The U.S. Supreme Court and the short forms *Supreme Court* and *Court* referring to it are capitalized.

the Supreme Court of the United States
the United States Supreme Court
the Supreme Court
the Court

20. Official and full names of higher courts and names of international courts are capitalized. Short forms of official higher court names are often capitalized in legal documents but lowercased in general writing.

The International Court of Arbitration
the United States Court of Appeals for the Second Circuit
the Virginia Supreme Court
the Court of Queen's Bench
a ruling by the court of appeals
the state supreme court

21. Names of city and county courts are usually lowercased.

the Lawton municipal court
the Owensville night court
small claims court
police court
the county court
juvenile court

22. The single designation *court,* when specifically applicable to a judge or a presiding officer, is capitalized.

It is the opinion of this Court that . . .
The Court found that . . .

23. The terms *federal* and *national* are capitalized only when they are essential elements of a name or title.

> Federal Trade Commission
> National Security Council
> federal court
> national security

24. The word *administration* is capitalized in some publications when it refers to the administration of a specific United States president; however, the word is more commonly lowercased in this situation. If the word does not refer to a specific presidential administration, it is not capitalized except when it is a part of an official name of a government agency.

> the Truman administration *or* the Truman Administration
> the administration *or* the Administration
> the Farmers Home Loan Administration
> The running of the White House varies considerably from one administration to another.

25. Names of political organizations and their adherents are capitalized, but the word *party* may or may not be capitalized, depending on the writer's or publication's preference.

> the Democratic National Committee
> Tories
> the Republican platform
> Nazis
> the Democratic party *or* the Democratic Party
> the Communist party *or* the Communist Party

26. Names of political groups other than parties are usually lowercased, as are their derivative forms.

> rightist
> right wing
> left winger
>
> *but usually*
> the Left
> the Right

27. Terms describing political and economic philosophies and their derivative forms are usually capitalized only if they are derived from proper names.

> authoritarianism
> isolationist
> democracy
> nationalism
> supply-side economics
>
> civil libertarian
> Marxist
> social Darwinism
> fascism *or* Fascism

Historical Periods and Events

28. The names of conferences, councils, expositions, and specific sporting, historical, and cultural events are capitalized.

the Yalta Conference
the Minnesota State Fair
the World Series
the Boston Tea Party
the Bonus March of 1932
the Golden Gate International Exposition
the Congress of Vienna
the Games of the XXIII Olympiad
the Series
the San Francisco Earthquake
the Philadelphia Folk Festival

29. The names of some historical and cultural periods and movements are capitalized. When in doubt about such a name, consult a dictionary or encyclopedia.

Augustan Age	Stone Age
Prohibition	space age
Renaissance	fin de siècle
the Enlightenment	cold war *or* Cold War
the Great Depression	

30. Numerical designations of historical time periods are capitalized only when they are part of a proper name; otherwise they are lowercased.

the Third Reich	seventeenth century
Roaring Twenties	eighties

31. Full names of treaties, laws, and acts are capitalized.

Treaty of Versailles
The Controlled Substances Act of 1970

32. The full names of wars are capitalized; however, words such as *war, revolution, battle,* and *campaign* are capitalized only when they are part of a proper name. Descriptive terms such as *assault, siege,* and *engagement* are usually lowercased even when used in conjunction with the name of the place where the action occurred.

the French and Indian War
the War of the Roses
the American Revolution
the Revolution of 1688
the Battle of the Bulge
the Peninsular Campaign
the Spanish American War
the War of the Spanish Succession
the Whiskey Rebellion
the Battle of the Coral Sea
the second battle of Manassas
the Meuse-Argonne offensive

the assault on Iwo Jima
the naval battle of Guadalcanal
the American and French revolutions
the siege of Yorktown
the winter campaign
was in action throughout most of the war

Hyphenated Compounds

33. Elements of hyphenated compounds are capitalized if they are proper nouns or adjectives.

Arab-Israeli negotiations
East-West trade agreements
Tay-Sachs disease
U.S.-U.S.S.R. détente
American-plan rates
an eighteenth-century poet

NOTE: If the second element in a two-word compound is not a proper noun or adjective, it is lowercased.

French-speaking peoples
an A-frame house
Thirty-second Street

34. Word elements (as prefixes and combining forms) may or may not be capitalized when joined to a proper noun or adjective. Common prefixes (as *pre-* or *anti-*) are usually not capitalized when so attached. Geographical and ethnic combining forms (as *Anglo-* or *Afro-*) are capitalized; *pan-* is usually capitalized when attached to a proper noun or adjective.

the pro-Soviet faction
un-American activities
post–Civil War politics
Sino-Soviet relations
Pan-Slavic nationalism
Afro-Americans
Greco-Roman architecture
the Pan-African Congress

Languages—See **People** below.

Legal Material—See also **Governmental, Judicial, and Political Bodies** above.

35. The names of both plaintiff and defendant in legal case titles are italicized. The *v.* for *versus* may be roman or italic. Cases that do not involve two opposing parties have titles such as *In re Watson* or *In the matter of John Watson;* these case titles are also italicized. When the person involved rather than the case itself is being discussed, the reference is not italicized.

Jones v. *Massachusetts*
In re Jones
Smith et al. v. *Jones*
She covered the Jones trial for the newspaper.

NOTE: In running text a case name involving two opposing parties may be shortened.

The judge based his ruling on a precedent set in the *Jones* decision.

Medical Terms

36. Proper names that are elements in terms designating diseases, symptoms, syndromes, and tests are capitalized. Common nouns are lowercased.

> Down's syndrome
> Duchenne-Erb paralysis
> German measles
> Parkinson's disease
> Rorschach test
> syndrome of Weber
> acquired immunodeficiency syndrome
> measles
> mumps
> herpes simplex

37. Taxonomic names of disease-causing organisms follow the rules established for binomial nomenclature discussed in paragraph 67 below. The names of diseases or pathological conditions derived from taxonomic names of organisms are lowercased and not italicized.

> a neurotoxin produced by *Clostridium botulinum*
> nearly died of botulism

38. Generic names of drugs are lowercased; trade names should be capitalized.

> a prescription for chlorpromazine
> had been taking Thorazine

Military Terms

39. The full titles of branches of the armed forces are capitalized, as are easily recognized short forms of full branch designations.

U.S. Air Force	the Coast Guard
the Navy	the Marines
U.S. Coast Guard	U.S. Navy
the Marine Corps	the Army
the Air Force	U.S. Marine Corps
U.S. Army	the Corps

40. The terms *air force, army, coast guard, marine(s)*, and *navy* are lowercased unless they form a part of an official name or refer back to a specific branch of the armed forces previously named. They are also lowercased when they are used collectively or in the plural.

> the combined air forces of the NATO nations
> the navies of the world
> the American army
>
> In some countries the duty of the coast guard may include ice-breaking in inland waterways.

41. The adjectives *naval* and *marine* are lowercased unless they are part of a proper name.

> naval battle   Naval Reserves
> marine barracks

42. The full titles of units and organizations of the armed forces are capitalized. Elements of full titles are lowercased when they stand alone.

> U.S. Army Corps of Engineers   the corps
> the Reserves   a reserve commission
> First Battalion   the battalion
> 4th Marine Regiment   the regiment
> Eighth Fleet   the fleet
> Cruiser Division   the division
> Fifth Army   the army

43. Military ranks are capitalized when they precede the names of their holders, and when they take the place of a person's name (as in direct address). Otherwise they are lowercased.

> Admiral Nimitz
> General Creighton W. Abrams
> I can't get this rifle any cleaner, Sergeant.
> The major arrived precisely on time.

44. The specific names of decorations, citations, and medals are capitalized.

> Medal of Honor   Distinguished Service Medal
> Navy Cross   Silver Star
> Purple Heart

Nicknames—See paragraphs 49, 51, and 52 below.

Numerical Designations

45. A noun introducing a reference number is usually capitalized.

> Order 704
> Flight 409

Form 2E
Policy 118-4-Y

46. Nouns used with numbers or letters to designate major reference headings (as in a literary work) are capitalized. However, nouns designating minor reference headings are typically lowercased.

Book II   page 101
Volume V   line 8
Division 4   note 10
Figure 1   paragraph 6.1
Table 3   question 21

Organizations

47. Names of firms, corporations, schools, and organizations and terms derived from those names to designate their members are capitalized. However, common nouns used descriptively or occurring after the names of two or more organizations are lowercased.

Merriam-Webster Inc.
University of Michigan
Smith College
Washington Huskies
played as a Pirate last year
Rotary International
Kiwanians
American and United airlines
Minnesota North Stars

NOTE: The word *the* at the beginning of such names is capitalized only when the full legal name is used.

48. Words such as *agency, department, division, group,* or *office* that designate corporate and organizational units are capitalized only when they are used with a specific name.

worked at the Criminal Division in the Department of Justice
a notice to all department heads

NOTE: Style varies regarding the capitalization of these words when they are used in place of the full name of a specific body. For more on this aspect of styling, see the note following paragraph 18 above.

49. Nicknames, epithets, or other alternate terms for organizations are capitalized.

referred to IBM as Big Blue
the Big Three automakers
trading stocks on the Big Board

People

50. The names and initials of persons are capitalized. If a name is hyphenated, both elements are capitalized. Particles forming the initial elements of surnames (as *de, della, der, du, la, ten, ter, van,* and *von*) may or may not be capitalized, depending on the styling of the individual name. However, if a name with a lowercase initial particle begins a sentence, the particle is capitalized.

> Thomas de Quincey
> Sir Arthur Thomas Quiller-Couch
> James Van Allen
> the paintings of de Kooning
> E. I. du Pont de Nemours
> Gerald ter Hoerst
> Heinrich Wilhelm Von Kleist
> De Kooning's paintings are . . .

51. The name of a person or thing can be added to or replaced entirely by a nickname or epithet, a characterizing word or phrase. Nicknames and epithets are capitalized.

> Calamity Jane   Dusty Rhodes
> Buffalo Bill   Bird Parker
> Louis the Fat   Night Train Lane
> Bubba Smith   Doctor J.
> Goose Gossage   Attila the Hun
> Big Mama Thornton   Dizzy Gillespie
> the Golden Bear   Rusty Staub
> Wilt the Stilt   Meadowlark Lemon
> Murph the Surf   Lefty Grove

52. Nicknames and epithets are frequently used in conjunction with both the first and last names of a person. If it is placed between the first and last name, it will often be enclosed in quotation marks or parentheses; however, if the nickname is expected to be very well known to readers, the quotation marks or parentheses are often omitted. If the nickname precedes the first name, it is sometimes enclosed in quotation marks, but more often it is not.

> Thomas P. "Tip" O'Neill
> Earl ("Fatha") Hines
> Mary Harris ("Mother") Jones
> Joanne "Big Mama" Carner
> Dennis (Oil Can) Boyd
> Anna Mary Robertson "Grandma" Moses
> Kissin' Jim Folsom
> Slammin' Sammy Snead
> Blind Lemon Jefferson
> Mother Maybelle Carter

53. Words of family relationship preceding or used in place of a person's name are capitalized. However, these words are lowercased if they are part of a noun phrase that is being used in place of a name.

> Cousin Mercy
> Grandfather Barnes
> I know when Mother's birthday is.
> I know when my mother's birthday is.

54. Words designating languages, nationalities, peoples, races, religious groups, and tribes are capitalized. Descriptive terms used to refer to groups of people are variously capitalized or lowercased. Designations based on color are usually lowercased.

> | | |
> |---|---|
> | Latin | Ibo |
> | Caucasians | Christians |
> | Canadians | Afro-American |
> | Muslims | Navajo |
>
> Bushman (for a nomadic hunter of southern Africa)
> bushman (for an inhabitant of the Australian bush)
> the red man in America
> black, brown, and white people

55. Corporate, professional, and governmental titles are capitalized when they immediately precede a person's name, unless the name is being used as an appositive.

> | | |
> |---|---|
> | President Roosevelt | Professor Greenbaum |
> | Doctor Malatesta | Senator Henry Jackson |
> | Queen Elizabeth | Pastor Linda Jones |
>
> They wanted to meet the new pastor, Linda Jones.
> Almost everyone has heard of Chrysler's president, Lee Iacocca.

56. When corporate or governmental titles are used as part of a descriptive phrase to identify a person rather than as a person's official title, the title is lowercased.

> Senator Ted Stevens of Alaska
> *but* Ted Stevens, senator from Alaska
> Lee Iacocca, president of Chrysler Corporation

NOTE: Style varies when governmental titles are used in descriptive phrases that precede a name.

> Alaska senator Ted Stevens *or* Alaska Senator Ted Stevens

57. Specific governmental titles may be capitalized when they are used in place of particular individuals' names. In minutes and official records of proceedings, corporate titles are capitalized when they are used in place of individuals' names.

The Secretary of State gave a news conference.

The Judge will respond to questions in her chambers.

The Treasurer then stated his misgivings about the project.

58. Some publications always capitalize the word *president* when it refers to the United States presidency. However, the more common practice is to capitalize the word *president* only when it refers to a specific individual.

> It is one of the duties of the President to submit a budget to Congress.
>
> It is one of the duties of the president to submit a budget to Congress.

59. Titles are capitalized when they are used in direct address.

> Tell me the truth, Doctor.
>
> Where are we headed, Captain?

Personifications—See **Abstractions and Personifications** above.

Prefixes—See **Hyphenated Compounds** above.

Pronouns

60. The pronoun *I* is capitalized. For pronouns referring to the Deity, see rule 62 below.

> He and I will attend the meeting.

Religious Terms

61. Words designating the Deity are capitalized.

> Allah   Yahweh
> Jehovah   Christ
> God Almighty   the Holy Spirit

62. Personal pronouns referring to the Deity are usually capitalized. Relative pronouns (as *who, whom,* and *whose*) usually are not.

> God in His mercy
> when God asks us to do His bidding
> believing that it was God who created the universe

NOTE: Some style manuals maintain that the pronoun does not need to be capitalized if it is closely preceded by its antecedent; however, in current practice, most writers capitalize the pronoun regardless of its position.

63. Traditional designations of apostles, prophets, and saints are capitalized.

> our Lady   the Lawgiver
> the Prophet

64. Names of religions, denominations, creeds and confessions, and religious orders are capitalized, as are adjectives derived from these names. The word *church* is capitalized only when it is used as part of the name of a specific body or edifice or, in some publications, when it refers to organized Christianity in general.

> Judaism
> the Church of Christ
> Apostles' Creed
> the Poor Clares
> Hunt Memorial Church
> Islamic
> the Thirty-nine Articles of the Church of England
> Catholicism
> the Southern Baptist Convention
> the Society of Jesus
> Franciscans
> a Buddhist monastery
> the Baptist church on the corner

65. Names of the Bible or its books, parts, versions, or editions of it and other sacred books are capitalized but not italicized. Adjectives derived from the names of sacred books are variously capitalized and lowercased. When in doubt, consult a dictionary.

> Authorized Version   Apocrypha
> Koran   Pentateuch
> Talmud   talmudic
> Gospel of Saint Mark   biblical
> Old Testament   Vedic
> Genesis   Koranic

66. The names of prayers and well-known passages of the Bible are capitalized.

> Ave Maria
> Ten Commandments
> the Lord's Prayer
> the Sermon on the Mount
> the Beatitudes
> the Our Father

Scientific Terms

67. Genus names in biological binomial nomenclature are capitalized; species names are lowercased, even when derived from a proper name. Both genus and species names are italicized.

> Both the wolf and the domestic dog are included in the genus *Canis*.
>
> The California condor (*Gymnogyps californianus*) is facing extinction.

Trailing arbutus (*Epigaea repens*) and rue anemone (*Anemonella thalictroides*) are among the earliest wildflowers to bloom in the spring.

NOTE: When used, the names of races, varieties, or subspecies are lowercased. Like genus and species names, they are italicized.

Hyla versicolor chrysoscelis
Otis asio naevius

68. The New Latin names of classes, families, and all groups above the genus level in zoology and botany are capitalized but not italicized. Their derivative adjectives and nouns in English are neither capitalized nor italicized.

Gastropoda	gastropod
Thallophyta	thallophyte

69. The names, both scientific and informal, of planets and their satellites, asteroids, stars, constellations, groups of stars, and other unique celestial objects are capitalized. However, the words *sun, earth,* and *moon* are usually lowercased unless they occur with other astronomical names. Generic terms that are the final element in the name of a celestial object are usually lowercased.

Ganymede	Venus
the Milky Way	Big Dipper
Pleiades	Great Bear
studying the Moon and Mars	Ursa Major
Sirius	Barnard's star

70. Names of meteorological phenomena are lowercased.

aurora australis	northern lights
aurora borealis	parhelic circle

71. Terms that identify geological eras, periods, epochs, and strata are capitalized. The generic terms that follow them are lowercased. The words *upper, middle,* and *lower* are capitalized when they are used to designate an epoch or series within a period; in most other cases, they are lowercased. The word *age* is capitalized in names such as *Age of Reptiles* or *Age of Fishes.*

Mesozoic era	Middle Ordovician
Oligocene epoch	Upper Cretaceous
Quaternary period	Lower Silurian

72. Proper names forming essential elements of scientific laws, theorems, and principles are capitalized. However, the common nouns *law, theorem, theory,* and the like are lowercased.

Boyle's law
the Pythagorean theorem
Planck's constant
Einstein's theory of relativity

NOTE: In terms referring to popular or fanciful theories or observations, descriptive words are usually capitalized as well.

Murphy's Law
the Peter Principle

73. The names of chemical elements and compounds are lowercased.

hydrogen fluoride
ferric ammonium citrate

74. The names of computer services and data bases are usually trademarks and should always be capitalized. The names of computer languages are irregularly styled either with an initial capital letter or with all letters capitalized. The names of some computer languages are commonly written either way. When in doubt, consult a dictionary.

CompuServe	COBOL *or* Cobol
Atek	PL/1
BASIC	APL
PENTA	FORTRAN *or* Fortran
TeleTransfer	Dow Jones News Retrieval
Pascal	Service

Time Periods and Zones

75. The names of days of the week, months of the year, and holidays and holy days are capitalized.

Easter	Yom Kippur
Passover	June
Tuesday	Thanksgiving
Independence Day	Ramadan
Memorial Day	

76. The names of time zones are capitalized when abbreviated but usually lowercased when written out except for words that are themselves proper names.

CST
central standard time
mountain time
Pacific standard time

77. Names of the seasons are lowercased if they simply declare the time of year; however, they are capitalized if they are personified.

My new book is scheduled to appear this spring.

the sweet breath of Spring

Titles—For titles of people, see **People** above.

78. Words in titles of books, long poems, magazines, newspapers, plays, movies, novellas that are separately published, and works of art such as paintings and sculpture are capitalized except for internal articles, conjunctions, prepositions, and the *to* of infinitives. The entire title is italicized. For the styling of the Bible and other sacred works, see paragraph 65 above.

> *The Lives of a Cell*
> *Saturday Review*
> Shakespeare's *Othello*
> Gainsborough's *Blue Boy*
> *Of Mice and Men*
> *Christian Science Monitor*
> *The Old Man and the Sea*
> the movie *Wait until Dark*

NOTE: Some publications also capitalize prepositions of five or more letters (as *about* or *toward*).

79. An initial article that is part of a title is often omitted if it would be awkward in context. However, when it is included it is capitalized and italicized. A common exception to this style regards books that are referred to by an abbreviation. In this case, the initial article is neither capitalized nor italicized.

> *The Oxford English Dictionary*
> the 13-volume *Oxford English Dictionary*
> the *OED*

80. Style varies widely regarding the capitalization and italicization of initial articles and city names in the titles of newspapers. One style rule that can be followed is to capitalize and italicize any word that is part of the official title of the paper as shown on its masthead. However, this information is not always available, and even if it is available it can lead to apparent inconsistencies in styling. Because of this, many publications choose one way of styling newspaper titles regardless of their official titles. The most common styling is to italicize the city name but not to capitalize or italicize the initial article.

> the *New York Times*
> the *Des Moines Register*
> the *Wall Street Journal*
> the *Washington Post*

81. Many publications, especially newspapers, do not use italics to style titles. They either simply capitalize the words of the title or capitalize the words and enclose them in quotation marks.

the Heard on the Street column in the Wall Street Journal
our review of "The Lives of a Cell" in last week's column

82. The first word following a colon in a title is capitalized.

John Crowe Ransom: An Annotated Bibliography

83. The titles of short poems, short stories, essays, lectures, dissertations, chapters of books, articles in periodicals, radio and television programs, and novellas that are published in a collection are capitalized and enclosed in quotation marks. The capitalization of articles, conjunctions, and prepositions is the same as it is for italicized titles, as explained in paragraph 78 above.

Robert Frost's "Dust of Snow"
Katherine Anne Porter's "That Tree"
John Barth's "The Literature of Exhaustion"
The talk, "Labor's Power: A View for the Eighties," will be given next week.
the third chapter of *Treasure Island*, entitled "The Black Spot"
Her article, "Computer Art on a Micro," was in last month's *Popular Computing*.
listening to "A Prairie Home Companion"
watching "The Tonight Show"
D. H. Lawrence's "The Woman Who Rode Away"

84. Common titles of sections of books (as a preface, introduction, or index) are capitalized but not enclosed in quotation marks when they refer to a section of the same book in which the reference is made. If they refer to another book, they are usually lowercased.

See the Appendix for further information.
In the introduction to her book, the author explains her goals.

85. Style varies regarding the capitalization of the word *chapter* when it is used with a cardinal number to identify a specific chapter in a book. In some publications the word is lowercased, but more commonly it is capitalized.

See Chapter 3 for more details.
is discussed further in Chapter Four
   but   in the third chapter

86. The titles of long musical compositions such as operas and symphonies are capitalized and italicized; the titles of short compositions are capitalized and enclosed in quotation marks. The titles of musical compositions identified by the nature of the musical form in which they were written are capitalized only.

Verdi's *Don Carlos*
Ravel's "Bolero"
"America the Beautiful"
Serenade No. 12 in C Minor

Trademarks

87. Registered trademarks, service marks, collective marks, and brand names are capitalized.

Band-Aid	Diet Pepsi
College Board	Kleenex
Kellogg's All-Bran	Realtor
Jacuzzi	Lay's potato chips
Grammy	Planned Parenthood

Transportation

88. The names of individual ships, submarines, airplanes, satellites, and space vehicles are capitalized and italicized. The designations *U.S.S.*, *S.S.*, *M.V.*, and *H.M.S.* are not italicized.

Apollo 11	*Enola Gay*
Mariner 5	*Explorer 10*
Spirit of Saint Louis	M.V. *West Star*

Other Uses of Capitals

1. Full capitalization of a word is sometimes used for emphasis or to indicate that a speaker is talking very loudly. Both of these uses of capitals are usually avoided or at least used very sparingly in formal prose. Italicization of words for emphasis is more common. For examples of this use of italics, see paragraph 8 of the section on Other Uses of Italics in this chapter.

Results are not the only criteria for judging performance. HOW we achieve results is important also.

All applications must be submitted IN WRITING before January 31.

The waiter rushed by yelling "HOT PLATE! HOT PLATE!"

2. A word is sometimes capitalized to indicate that it is being used as a philosophical concept or to indicate that it stands for an important concept in a discussion. Style manuals generally discourage this practice, but it is still in common use today even in formal writing.

Many people seek Truth, but few find it.

the three M's of advertising, Message, Media, and Management

3. Full capitals or a mixture of capitals and lowercase letters or sometimes even small capitals are used to reproduce the text of signs, labels, or inscriptions.

> a poster reading SPECIAL THRILLS COMING SOON
> a Do Not Disturb sign
> a barn with CHEW MAIL POUCH on the side
> a truck with WASH ME written in the dust

4. A letter used to indicate a shape is usually capitalized. If sans serif type is available, it is often used for such a letter, because it usually best approximates the shape that is being referred to.

> an A-frame house   V-shaped
> a J-bar

Other Uses of Italics

Italic type is used to indicate that there is something out of the ordinary about a word or phrase or about the way in which it is being used. For some of the uses listed below, quotation marks can be substituted. For more on this use of quotation marks, see the section on Quotation Marks, Double, in Chapter 1, "Punctuation," beginning on page 43. For each of the uses listed below, underlining is used in place of italicizing when the text is typewritten instead of typeset.

1. Foreign words and phrases that have not been fully adopted into the English language are italicized. The decision whether or not to italicize a word will vary according to the context of the writing and the audience for which the writing is intended. In general, however, any word that appears in the main A–Z vocabulary section of *Webster's Ninth New Collegiate Dictionary* does not need to be italicized.

> These accomplishments will serve as a monument, *aëre perennius*, to the group's skill and dedication.
> They looked upon this area as a *cordon sanitaire* around the city.
> "The cooking here is *wunderbar*," he said.
> After the concert, the crowd headed en masse for the parking lot.
> The committee meets on an ad hoc basis.

NOTE: A complete sentence (such as a motto) can also be italicized. However, passages that comprise more than one sentence, or even a single sentence if it is particularly long, are usually treated as quotations; i.e., they are set in roman type and enclosed in quotation marks.

2. Unfamiliar words or words that have a specialized meaning are set in italics, especially when they are accompanied by a short definition. Once these words have been introduced and defined, they do not need to be italicized in subsequent references.

> *Vitiligo* is a condition in which skin pigment cells stop making pigment.

> Another method is the *direct-to-consumer* transaction in which the publisher markets directly to the individual by mail or door-to-door.

3. Style varies somewhat regarding the italicization of Latin abbreviations. During the first half of this century, these abbreviations were most commonly set in italic type. Some authors and publishers still italicize them, either by tradition or on the grounds that they should be treated like foreign words. However, most authors and publishers now set these abbreviations in roman type. (For an explanation of the use of *ibid., op. cit.,* and other Latin bibliographical abbreviations, see Chapter 7, "Notes and Bibliographies.")

> et al.   cf.   e.g.   i.e.   viz.

4. Italic type is used to indicate words referred to as words, letters referred to as letters, or numerals referred to as numerals. However, if the word referred to as a word was actually spoken, it is often enclosed in quotation marks. If the letter is being used to refer to its sound and not its printed form, virgules or brackets can be used instead of italics. And if there is no chance of confusion, numerals referred to as numerals are often not italicized. (For an explanation of the ways in which to form the plurals of words, letters, and numerals referred to as such, see the section on Plurals, beginning on page 82, in Chapter 3, "Plurals, Possessives, and Compounds.")

> The panel could not decide whether *data* was a singular or plural noun.

> *Only* can be an adverb modifying a verb, as in the case of "I *only* tried to help."

> We heard his warning, but we weren't sure what "other repercussions" meant in that context.

> You should dot your *i*'s and cross your *t*'s.

> She couldn't pronounce her *s*'s.

> He was still having trouble with the /p/ sound.

> The first *2* and the last *1* are barely legible.

5. A letter used to indicate a shape is usually capitalized but not set in italics. For more on this use of capital letters, see the section on Other Uses of Capitals in this chapter.

6. Individual letters are sometimes set in italic type to provide additional typographical contrast. This use of italics is common when letters are used in run-in enumerations or when they are used to identify elements in an illustration.

> providing information about (*a*) typing, (*b*) transcribing, (*c*) formatting, and (*d*) graphics
> located at point *A* on the diagram

7. Italics are used to indicate a word created to suggest a sound.

> From the nest came a high-pitched *whee* from one of the young birds.
> We sat listening to the *chat-chat-chat* of the sonar.

8. Italics are used to emphasize or draw attention to a word or words in a sentence.

> Students must notify the dean's office *in writing* of all courses added or dropped from their original list.
> She had become *the* hero, the one everyone else looked up to.

NOTE: Italics serve to draw attention to words in large part because they are used so infrequently. Writers who overuse italics for giving emphasis may find that the italics lose their effectiveness.

Chapter 3

Plurals, Possessives, and Compounds

CONTENTS

This chapter describes the ways in which plurals, possessives, and compound words are most commonly formed. In doing so, it treats some of the simplest and some of the most problematic kinds of questions that are faced by writers and editors. For some of the questions raised in this chapter, various solutions have been developed over the years, but no single solution has come to be universally accepted. This chapter describes the range of solutions that are available; however, many of the questions raised in this chapter inevitably require arbitrary decisions and personal judgments. In cases like these, careful writers and editors usually make notes or keep a style sheet so that they can be consistent in the way that they form plurals, possessives, and compounds for certain specific words or categories of words.

Writers and editors are frequently told that consulting a good dictionary will solve many of the problems that are discussed in this chapter. To some extent this is true, and this chapter does recommend consulting a dictionary at a number of points. In this regard, the best dictionary to consult is an unabridged dictionary, such as *Webster's Third New International Dictionary*. In the absence of such a comprehensive reference book, writers and editors should consult a good desk dictionary, such as *Merriam-Webster's Collegiate Dictionary*. Any dictionary that is much smaller than the *Collegiate* will often be more frustrating in what it fails to show than helpful in what it shows.

In giving examples of plurals, possessives, and compounds, this chapter uses both *or* and *also* to separate variant forms of the same word. The word *or* is used when both forms of the word are used with approximately equal frequency in standard prose; the form that precedes the *or* is probably slightly more common than the form that follows it. The word *also* is used when one form of the word is much more common than the other; the more common precedes the less common.

Plurals

The plurals of most English words are formed by adding -*s* to the singular. If the noun ends in -*s*, -*x*, -*z*, -*ch*, or -*sh*, so that an extra syllable must be added in order to pronounce the plural, -*es* is added to the singular. If the noun ends in a -*y* preceded by a consonant, the -*y* is changed to -*i*- and -*es* is added. Most proper nouns ending in -*y* (as *Mary* or *Germany*), however, simply add -*s* to the singular.

Many English nouns do not follow the general pattern for forming plurals. Most good dictionaries give thorough coverage to irregular and variant plurals, so they are often the best place to start to answer questions about the plural form of a specific word. The paragraphs that follow describe the ways in which plurals are formed for a number of categories of words whose plural forms are most apt to raise questions.

The symbol → is used throughout this section of the chapter. In each case, the element that follows the arrow is the plural form of the element that precedes the arrow.

Abbreviations

1. The plurals of abbreviations are commonly formed by adding -*s* or an apostrophe plus -*s* to the abbreviation; however, there are some significant exceptions to this pattern. For more on the formation of plurals of abbreviations, see the section on Plurals, Possessives, and Compounds, beginning on page 110, in Chapter 4, "Abbreviations."

   COLA → COLA's   Ph.D. → Ph.D.'s
   f.o.b. → f.o.b.'s   bldg. → bldgs.
   CPU → CPUs   p. → pp.

Animals

2. The names of many fishes, birds, and mammals have both a plural formed with a suffix and one that is identical with the singular. Some have only the -*s* plural; others have only an uninflected plural.

   flounder → flounder *or* flounders
   quail → quail *or* quails
   mink → mink *or* minks
   buffalo → buffalo *or* buffalos

cow → cows	hen → hens
bison → bison	sheep → sheep
rat → rats	monkey → monkeys
shad → shad	moose → moose

3. Many of the animals that have both plural forms are ones that are hunted, fished, or trapped, and those who hunt, fish for, and trap them are most likely to use the uninflected form. The -s form is especially likely to be used to emphasize diversity of kinds.

> caught four trout
> *but*
> trouts of the Rocky Mountains
> a place where fish gather
> *but*
> the fishes of the Pacific Ocean

Compounds and Phrases

4. Most compounds composed of two nouns, whether styled as one word or two words or as hyphenated words, are pluralized by pluralizing the final element.

> matchbox → matchboxes
> judge advocate → judge advocates
> city-state → city-states
> face-lift → face-lifts
> spokeswoman → spokeswomen
> tree house → tree houses
> crow's-foot → crow's-feet
> battle-ax → battle-axes

5. The plural form of a compound consisting of an -*er* agent noun and an adverb is made by pluralizing the noun element.

> hanger-on → hangers-on
> looker-on → lookers-on
> onlooker → onlookers
> passerby → passersby

6. Nouns made up of words that are not nouns form their plurals on the terminal element.

> also-ran → also-rans
> put-down → put-downs
> changeover → changeovers
> ne'er-do-well → ne'er-do-wells
> set-to → set-tos
> blowup → blowups

7. Plurals of compounds that are phrases consisting of two nouns separated by a preposition are regularly formed by pluralizing the first noun.

aide-de-camp → aides-de-camp
auto-da-fe → autos-da-fe
man-of-war → men-of-war
attorney-at-law → attorneys-at-law
lady-in-waiting → ladies-in-waiting
power of attorney → powers of attorney
base on balls → bases on balls
mother-in-law → mothers-in-law
coup d'état → coups d'état

8. Compounds that are phrases consisting of two nouns separated by a preposition and a modifier form their plurals in various ways.

flash in the pan → flashes in the pan
jack-in-the-box → jack-in-the-boxes *or* jacks-in-the-box
jack-of-all-trades → jacks-of-all-trades
son of a gun → sons of guns
stick-in-the-mud → stick-in-the-muds

9. Compounds consisting of a noun followed by an adjective are regularly pluralized by adding a suffix to the noun.

cousin-german → cousins-german
heir apparent → heirs apparent
knight-errant → knights-errant

NOTE: If the adjective in such a compound tends to be construed as a noun, the compound may have more than one plural form.

attorney general → attorneys general *or* attorney generals
sergeant major → sergeants major *or* sergeant majors
poet laureate → poets laureate *or* poet laureates

Foreign Words and Phrases

10. Many nouns of foreign origin retain the foreign plural; most of them also have a regular English plural.

alumnus → alumni
beau → beaux *or* beaus
crisis → crises
emporium → emporiums *or* emporia
index → indexes *or* indices
larynx → larynges *or* larynxes
phenomenon → phenomena *or* phenomenons
schema → schemata *also* schemas
seraph → seraphim *or* seraphs
series → series
tempo → tempi *or* tempos

NOTE: A foreign plural may not be used for all senses of a word or may be more commonly used for some senses than for others.

antenna (on an insect) → antennae
antenna (on a radio) → antennas

11. Phrases of foreign origin may have a foreign plural, an English plural, or both.

beau monde → beau mondes *or* beaux mondes
carte blanche → cartes blanches
charlotte russe → charlottes russe
felo-de-se → felones-de-se *or* felos-de-se
hors d'oeuvre → hors d'oeuvres

-ful Words

12. A plural *-fuls* can be used for any noun ending in *-ful,* but some of these nouns also have an alternative, usually less common plural with -s- preceding the suffix.

eyeful → eyefuls
barnful → barnfuls
mouthful → mouthfuls
worldful → worldfuls
barrelful → barrelfuls *or* barrelsful
bucketful → bucketfuls *or* bucketsful
cupful → cupfuls *also* cupsful
tablespoonful → tablespoonfuls *also* tablespoonsful

Irregular Plurals

13. A small group of English nouns form their plurals by changing one or more of their vowels.

foot → feet
goose → geese
louse → lice
man → men

mouse → mice
woman → women
tooth → teeth

14. A few nouns have *-en* or *-ren* plurals.

ox → oxen
child → children
brother → brethren

15. Some nouns ending in *-f, -fe,* and *-ff* have plurals that end in *-ves.* Some of these also have regularly formed plurals.

elf → elves
knife → knives
life → lives
loaf → loaves
beef → beefs *or* beeves
staff → staffs *or* staves
wharf → wharves *also* wharfs
dwarf → dwarfs *or* dwarves

Italic Elements

16. Italicized words, phrases, abbreviations, and letters in roman context are variously pluralized with either an italic or roman *s*. Most stylebooks urge use of a roman *s*, and our evidence indicates that that is the form used most commonly. If the plural is formed with an apostrophe and an *-s*, the *-s* is almost always roman.

> fifteen *Newsweek*s on the shelf
> answered with a series of *uh-huh*s
> a row of *x*'s

Letters

17. The plurals of letters are usually formed by the addition of an apostrophe and an *-s*, although uppercase letters are sometimes pluralized by the addition of an *-s* alone.

> p's and q's
> V's of geese flying overhead
> dot your *i*'s
> straight As

Numbers

18. Numerals are pluralized by adding an *-s,* or, less commonly, an apostrophe and an *-s*.

> two par 5s   1960's
> 1970s   the mid-$20,000s
> in the 80s   DC-10's

19. Spelled-out numbers are usually pluralized without an apostrophe.

> in twos and threes
> scored two sixes

-o Words

20. Most words ending in an *-o* are pluralized by adding an *-s*; however, some words ending in an *-o* preceded by a consonant have *-s* plurals, some have *-es* plurals, and some have both. When you are in doubt about such a word, consult a dictionary.

> alto → altos
> echo → echoes
> motto → mottoes   *also*   mottos
> tornado → tornadoes   *or*   tornados

Proper Nouns

21. The plurals of proper nouns are usually formed with *-s* or *-es*.

> Bruce → Bruces

> Charles → Charleses
> John Harris → John Harrises
> Hastings → Hastingses
> Velasquez → Velasquezes

22. Proper nouns ending in *-y* usually retain the *-y* and add *-s.*

> Germany → Germanys
> Mary → Marys
> Mercury → Mercurys
>   *but*
> Ptolemy → Ptolemies
> Sicily → The Two Sicilies
> The Rockies

NOTE: Words that were originally proper nouns and that end in *-y* are usually pluralized by changing *-y* to *-i-* and adding *-es,* but a few retain the *-y.*

> bobby → bobbies
> Jerry → Jerries
> johnny → johnnies
> Tommy → Tommies
>
> Bloody Mary → Bloody Marys
> Typhoid Mary → Typhoid Marys

Quoted Elements

23. Style varies regarding the plural form of words in quotation marks. Some writers form the plural by adding an *-s* or an apostrophe plus *-s* within the quotation marks; others add an *-s* outside the quotation marks. Both arrangements look awkward, and writers generally try to avoid this construction.

> too many "probably's" in the statement
> didn't hear any "nays"
> One "you" among millions of "you"s
> a response characterized by its "yes, but"s

Symbols

24. Although symbols are not usually pluralized, when a symbol is being referred to as a character in itself without regard to meaning, the plural is formed by adding an *-s* or an apostrophe plus *-s.*

> used &'s instead of *and*'s
> his π's are hard to read
> printed three *s

Words used as Words

25. Words used as words without regard to meaning usually form their plurals by adding an apostrophe and an *-s.*

five *and*'s in one sentence
all those *wherefore*'s and *howsoever*'s

NOTE: When a word used as a word has become part of a fixed phrase, the plural is usually formed by adding a roman -*s* without the apostrophe.

oohs and aahs
dos and don'ts

Possessives

The possessive case of most nouns is formed by adding an apostrophe or an apostrophe plus -*s* to the end of the word. For most other uses of the apostrophe, such as to form contractions, see the section on Apostrophe, beginning on page 5, in Chapter 1, "Punctuation." For the use of the apostrophe to form plurals, see the section on Plurals in this chapter.

Common Nouns

1. The possessive case of singular and plural common nouns that do not end in an *s* or *z* sound is formed by adding an apostrophe plus -*s* to the end of the word.

   the boy's mother   children's books
   men's clothing   the potato's skin
   at her wit's end   the symposia's themes

2. The possessive case of singular nouns ending in an *s* or *z* sound is usually formed by adding an apostrophe plus -*s* to the end of the word. Style varies somewhat on this point, as some writers prefer to add an apostrophe plus -*s* to the word only when the added -*s* is pronounced; if it isn't pronounced, they add just an apostrophe. According to our evidence, both approaches are common in contemporary prose, although always adding an apostrophe plus -*s* is the much more widely accepted approach.

   the press's books
   the boss's desk
   the index's arrangement
   the horse's saddle
   the audience's reaction   *also*   the audience' reaction
   the waitress's duties   *also*   the waitress' duties
   the conference's outcome   *also*   the conference' outcome

NOTE: Even writers who follow the pattern of adding an apostrophe plus -*s* to all singular nouns will often make an exception for a multisyllabic word that ends in an *s* or *z* sound if it is followed by a word beginning with an *s* or *z* sound.

for convenience' sake
for conscience' sake
the illness' symptoms   *or*   the illness's symptoms
to the princess' surprise   *or*   to the princess's surprise

3. The possessive case of plural nouns ending in an *s* or *z* sound
is formed by adding only an apostrophe to the end of the
word. One exception to this rule is that the possessive case of
one-syllable irregular plurals is usually formed by adding an
apostrophe plus *-s*.

horses' stalls
consumers' confidence
geese's calls
mice's habits

Proper Names

4. The possessive forms of proper names are generally made in
the same way as they are for common nouns. The possessive
form of singular proper names not ending in an *s* or *z* sound
is made by adding an apostrophe plus *-s* to the name. The
possessive form of plural proper names is made by adding
just an apostrophe.

Mrs. Wilson's store   the Wattses' daughter
Utah's capital   the Cohens' house
Canada's rivers   Niagara Falls' location

5. As is the case for the possessive form of singular common
nouns (see paragraph 2 above), the possessive form of singular proper names ending in an *s* or *z* sound may be formed
either by adding an apostrophe plus *-s* or by adding just an
apostrophe to the name. For the sake of consistency, most
writers choose one pattern for forming the possessive of all
singular names ending in an *s* or *z* sound, regardless of the
pronunciation of individual names (for exceptions see paragraphs 6 and 7 below). According to our evidence, adding an
apostrophe plus *-s* to all such names is more common than
adding just the apostrophe.

Jones's car   *also*   Jones' car
Bliss's statue   *also*   Bliss' statue
Dickens's novels   *also*   Dickens' novels

6. The possessive form of classical and biblical names of two or
more syllables ending in *-s* or *-es* is usually made by adding
an apostrophe without an *-s*. If the name has only one syllable,
the possessive form is made by adding an apostrophe and
an *-s*.

Aristophanes' plays   Odysseus' journey

Judas' betrayal   Zeus's anger
Achilles' heel   Mars's help

7. The possessive forms of the names *Jesus* and *Moses* are always formed with just an apostrophe.

Jesus' time
Moses' law

8. The possessive forms of names ending in a silent *-s*, *-z*, or *-x* usually include the apostrophe and the *-s*.

Arkansas's capital
Delacroix's paintings
Camus's *The Stranger*
Josquin des Prez's work

9. For the sake of convenience and appearance, some writers will italicize the possessive ending when adding it to a name that is in italics; however, most frequently the possessive ending is in roman.

the U.S.S. *Constitution*'s cannons
Gone With the Wind's ending
the *Mona Lisa*'s somber hues
High Noon's plot

Pronouns

10. The possessive case of indefinite pronouns such as *anyone, everybody,* and *someone* is formed by adding an apostrophe and an *-s*.

everyone's   anybody's
everybody's   someone's
anyone's   somebody's

NOTE: Some indefinite pronouns usually require an *of* phrase rather than inflection to indicate possession.

the rights of each
the inclination of many
the satisfaction of all

11. Possessive pronouns include no apostrophes.

mine   his
its   theirs
yours   hers
ours

Phrases

12. The possessive form of a phrase is made by adding an apostrophe or an apostrophe plus *-s* to the last word in the phrase.

board of directors' meeting
his brother-in-law's sidecar

from the student of politics' point of view
a moment or so's thought

NOTE: Constructions such as these can become awkward, and it is often better to rephrase the sentence to eliminate the need for the possessive ending. For instance, the last two examples above could be rephrased as follows:

from the point of view of the student of politics
thinking for a moment or so

Words in Quotation Marks

13. Style varies regarding the possessive form of words in quotation marks. Some writers place the apostrophe and -s inside the quotation marks; others place them outside the quotation marks. Either arrangement will look awkward, and writers usually try to avoid this construction.

the "Today Show' "'s cohosts
the "Grande Dame's" escort
but more commonly
the cohosts of the "Today Show"
escort to the "Grande Dame"

Abbreviations

14. Possessives of abbreviations are formed in the same way as those of nouns that are spelled out. The singular possessive is formed by adding an apostrophe plus -s to the abbreviation; the plural possessive, by adding an apostrophe only.

the AMA's executive committee
Itek Corp.'s Applied Technology Division
the Burns Bros.' stores
the MPs' decisions

Numerals

15. The possessive form of nouns composed of or including numerals is made in the same way as for nouns composed wholly of words. The possessive of singular nouns is formed by adding an apostrophe plus -s; the possessive form of plural nouns, by adding an apostrophe only.

1985's most popular model
Louis XIV's court
the 1980s' most colorful figure

Individual and Joint Possession

16. Individual possession is indicated when an apostrophe plus -s is added to each noun in a sequence. Joint possession is most commonly indicated by adding an apostrophe or an apostrophe plus -s to the last noun in the sequence. In some cases,

joint possession is also indicated by adding a possessive ending
to each name.

Kepler's and Clark's respective clients
John's, Bill's, and Larry's boats
Kepler and Clark's law firm
Christine and James's vacation home
   or Christine's and James's vacation home

Compounds

A compound is a word or word group that consists of two or more
parts working together as a unit to express a specific concept.
Compounds can be formed by combining two or more words (as
in *eye shadow, graphic equalizer, farmhouse, cost-effective, blue-pencil,
around-the-clock,* or *son of a gun*), by combining word elements (as
prefixes or suffixes) with words (as in *ex-president, shoeless, presorted,
uninterruptedly,* or *meaningless*), or by combining two or more word
elements (as in *supermicro* or *photomicrograph*). Compounds are
written in one of three ways: solid (as *cottonmouth*), hyphenated (as
player-manager), or open (as *field day*).

Some of the explanations in this section make reference to
permanent and temporary compounds. Permanent compounds
are those that are so commonly used that they have become established as permanent parts of the language; many of them can be
found in dictionaries. Temporary compounds are those made up
to fit the writer's need at the particular moment. Temporary compounds, of course, cannot be found in dictionaries and therefore
present the writer with styling problems.

Presenting styling problems similar to those of temporary
compounds are self-evident compounds. These are compounds
(as *baseball game* or *economic policy*) that are readily understood
from the meanings of the words that make them up. Self-evident
compounds, like temporary compounds, are not to be found in
dictionaries.

In other words, writers faced with having to use compounds
such as *farm stand* (*farm-stand? farmstand?*), *wide body* (*wide-body?
widebody?*), or *picture framing* (*picture-framing? pictureframing?*) cannot rely wholly on dictionaries to guide them in their styling of
compounds. They need, in addition, to develop an approach for
dealing with compounds that are not in the dictionary. A few of
those approaches are explained below.

One approach is simply to leave open any compound that is
not in the dictionary. Many writers do this, but there are draw-
backs to this approach. A temporary compound may not be as
easily recognized as a compound by the reader when it is left

open. For instance if you need to use *wide body* as a term for a kind of jet airplane, a phrase like "the operation of wide bodies" may catch the reader unawares. And if you use the open style for a compound modifier, you may create momentary confusion (or even unintended amusement) with a phrase like "the operation of wide body jets."

Another possibility would be to hyphenate all compounds that aren't in the dictionary. Hyphenation would give your compound immediate recognition as a compound. But hyphenating all such compounds runs counter to some well-established American practice. Thus you would be calling too much attention to the compound and momentarily distracting the reader.

A third approach is to use analogy to pattern your temporary compound after some other similar compound. This approach is likely to be more complicated than simply picking an open or hyphenated form, and will not free you from the need to make your own decisions in most instances. But it does have the advantage of making your compound less distracting or confusing by making it look as much like other more familiar compounds as possible.

The rest of this section is aimed at helping you to use the analogical approach to styling compounds. You will find compounds listed according to the elements that make them up and the way that they function in a sentence.

This section deals first with compounds formed from whole English words, then compounds formed with word elements, and finally with a small collection of miscellaneous styling conventions relating to compounds. The symbol + in the following paragraphs can be interpreted as "followed immediately by."

Compound Nouns

Compound nouns are combinations of words that function in a sentence as nouns. They may consist of two or more nouns, a noun and a modifier, or two or more elements that are not nouns.

1. **noun + noun** Compounds composed of two nouns that are short, commonly used, and pronounced with falling stress— that is, with the most stress on the first noun and less or no stress on the second—are usually styled solid.

teapot	birdbath
catfish	handsaw
football	railroad
cottonmouth	handmaiden
sweatband	farmyard
handlebar	bandwagon

2. When a noun + noun compound is short and common but pronounced with equal stress on both nouns, the styling is more likely to be open.

bean sprouts	fire drill
fuel oil	head louse
fuel cell	pine tar
beach buggy	dart board
duffel bag	rose fever

3. Many short noun + noun compounds begin as temporary compounds styled open. As they become more familiar and better established, there is a tendency for them to become solid.

> data base   *is becoming*   database
> chain saw   *is becoming*   chainsaw
> lawn mower   *is becoming*   lawnmower

4. Noun + noun compounds that consist of longer nouns, are self-evident, or are temporary are usually styled open.

> wildlife sanctuary
> football game
> reunion committee
> television camera

5. When the nouns in a noun + noun compound describe a double title or double function, the compound is hyphenated.

city-state	secretary-treasurer
decree-law	player-manager
dinner-dance	author-critic

6. Compounds formed from a noun or adjective followed by *man, woman, person,* or *people* and denoting an occupation are regularly solid.

salesman	salesperson
congresswoman	spokesperson
saleswoman	salespeople
handyman	policewoman

7. Compounds that are units of measurement are hyphenated.

foot-pound	column-inch
kilowatt-hour	light-year
man-hour	board-foot

8. **adjective + noun**   Most temporary or self-evident adjective + noun compounds are styled open. Permanent compounds formed from relatively long adjectives or nouns are also open.

automatic weapons	minor seminary
religious freedom	modular arithmetic
pancreatic juice	graphic equalizer
modal auxiliary	white lightning
automatic pilot	

9. Adjective + noun compounds consisting of two short words may be styled solid when pronounced with falling stress. Just as often, however, short adjective + noun compounds are styled open; a few are hyphenated.

bigfoot	dry cleaner
blueprint	dry rot
drywall	dry run
highland	dry well
longboat	high gear
longhand	long haul
redline	red tape
shortcake	short run
shortcut	short story
shorthand	sick leave
sickbed	wet nurse
wetland	yellow jacket
yellowhammer	red-eye
big deal	red-hot

10. participle + noun Most participle + noun compounds are styled open, whether permanent, temporary, or self-evident.

frying pan	nagging backache
whipped cream	shredded wheat
furnished apartment	whipping boy

11. noun's + noun Compounds consisting of a possessive noun followed by another noun are usually styled hyphenated or open.

crow's-feet	cat's-eye
cat's cradle	fool's gold
stirred up a hornet's nest	cat's-paw
lion's share	

NOTE: Compounds of this type that have become solid have lost the apostrophe.

foolscap
menswear
sheepshead

12. noun + verb + -er; noun + verb + -ing Temporary compounds in which the first noun is the object of the verb to which the suffix has been added are most often styled open; however, many writers use a hyphen to make the relationships of the words immediately apparent. Permanent compounds like these are sometimes styled solid as well.

temporary		
	gene-splicing	career planning
	risk-taking	cost-cutting
	opinion maker	English-speakers

permanent	lifesaver	penny-pinching
	data processing	flyswatter
	lawn mower	fund-raising
	copyediting	bookkeeper
	bird-watcher	

13. object + verb   Noun compounds consisting of a verb preceded by a noun that is its object are variously styled.

clambake	face-lift
car wash	turkey shoot

14. verb + object   A few compounds are formed from a verb followed by a noun that is its object. These are mostly older words, and they are solid.

tosspot	carryall
cutthroat	pinchpenny
breakwater	pickpocket

15. noun + adjective   Compounds composed of a noun followed by an adjective are styled open or hyphenated.

battle royal	mayor-elect
governor-designate	secretary-general
sum total	letters patent
consul general	president-elect
heir apparent	

16. particle + noun   Compounds consisting of a particle (usually a preposition or adverb having prepositional, adverbial, or adjectival force in the compound) and a noun are usually styled solid, especially when they are short and pronounced with falling stress.

downpour	outpatient
output	aftershock
offshoot	crossbones
inpatient	input
throughput	overskirt
undershirt	upkeep

17. A few particle + noun compounds, especially when composed of longer elements or having equal stress on both elements, may be hyphenated or open.

off-season	off year
down payment	cross-fertilization

18. verb + particle; verb + adverb   These compounds may be hyphenated or solid. Compounds with two-letter particles (*by, to, in, up, on*) are most frequently hyphenated, since the hyphen aids quick comprehension. Compounds with three-letter particles (*off*, *out*) are hyphenated or solid with about equal frequency. Those with longer particles or adverbs are more often but not always solid.

call-up	get-together	rollback
sign-on	giveaway	breakthrough
wrap-up	layout	takeover
brush-off	lead-in	letup
dropout	trade-in	sick-out
lay-up	flyby	tryout
sit-in	show-off	set-to
write-in	strikeout	warm-up
shoot-out	run-on	pileup
follow-through	turn-on	write-off
gadabout	breakdown	turnoff

19. verb + -er + particle; verb + -ing + particle Except for *passerby*, these compounds are hyphenated.

hanger-on	falling-out
summing-up	goings-on
diner-out	runner-up
talking-to	looker-on

20. compounds of three or four elements Compounds of three or four elements are styled either hyphenated or open. Those consisting of noun + prepositional phrase are generally open, although some are hyphenated. Those formed from other combinations are usually hyphenated.

base on balls	by-your-leave
lily of the valley	pick-me-up
good-for-nothing	lady of the house
love-in-a-mist	son of a gun
know-it-all	lady-in-waiting
justice of the peace	Johnny-jump-up
lord of misrule	stick-to-itiveness
jack-of-all-trades	

21. letter + noun Compounds formed from a single letter (or sometimes a combination of them) followed by a noun are either open or hyphenated.

A-frame	H-bomb
C ration	I beam
ABO system	Rh factor
B-girl	T-shirt
D day	T square
J-bar lift	H and L hinge

Compounds That Function as Adjectives

Compound adjectives are combinations of words that work together to modify a noun—that is, they work as unit modifiers. As

unit modifiers they should be distinguished from other strings of
adjectives that may also precede a noun. For instance, in "a low,
level tract of land" or "that long, lonesome road" the two adjectives each modify the noun separately. We are talking about a
tract of land that is both low and level and about a road that is
both long and lonesome. These are coordinate modifiers.

In "a low monthly fee" or "a wrinkled red necktie" the first
adjective modifies the noun plus the second adjective. In other
words, we mean a monthly fee that is low and a red necktie that
is wrinkled. These are noncoordinate modifiers. But in "low-level
radiation" we do not mean radiation that is low and level or level
radiation that is low; we mean radiation that is at a low level. Both
words work as a unit to modify the noun.

Unit modifiers are usually hyphenated. The hyphens not only
make it easier for the reader to grasp the relationship of the
words but also avoid confusion. The hyphen in "a call for more-
specialized controls" removes any ambiguity as to which word *more*
modifies. A phrase like "graphic arts exhibition" may seem clear
to its author, but may have an unintended meaning for some
readers.

22. Before the Noun (attributive position)   Most two-word permanent or temporary compound adjectives are hyphenated
when placed before the noun.

> tree-lined streets
> an iron-clad guarantee
> class-conscious persons
> well-intended advice
> a profit-loss statement
> arrested on a trumped-up charge
> fast-acting medication
> a tough-minded negotiator
> Spanish-American relations
> the red-carpet treatment
> an input-output device
> a risk-free investment

23. Temporary compounds formed of an adverb (as *well, more,
less, still*) followed by a participle (or sometimes an adjective)
are usually hyphenated when placed before a noun.

> more-specialized controls
> a still-growing company
> these fast-moving times
> a just-completed survey
> a well-funded project
> a now-vulnerable politician

24. Temporary compounds formed from an adverb ending in -*ly*
followed by a participle may sometimes be hyphenated but are

more commonly open, because adverb + adjective + noun is
a normal word order.

> a widely-read feature
> internationally-known authors
> > *but more often*
> generally recognized categories
> publicly supported universities
> a beautifully illustrated book
> our rapidly changing plans

25. The combination of *very* + adjective is not a unit modifier.

> a very satisfied smile

26. Many temporary compound adjectives are formed by using a
compound noun—either permanent or temporary—to modify another noun. If the compound noun is an open compound, it is usually hyphenated so that the relationship of the
words is more immediately apparent to the reader.

> the farm-bloc vote
> a short-run printing press
> a tax-law case
> a picture-framing shop
> a secret-compartment ring
> ocean-floor hydrophones

27. Some open compound nouns are considered so readily recognizable that they are frequently placed before a noun without
a hyphen.

> a high school diploma *or* a high-school diploma
> a data processing course *or* a data-processing course
> a dry goods store *or* a dry-goods store

28. A proper name placed before a noun to modify it is not hyphenated.

> a Thames River marina
> a Korean War veteran
> a Huck Finn life
> a General Motors car

29. Compound adjectives of three or more words are hyphenated
when they precede the noun. Many temporary compounds
are formed by taking a phrase, hyphenating it, and placing it
before a noun.

> spur-of-the-moment decisions
> higher-than-anticipated costs
> her soon-to-be-released movie

30. Compound adjectives composed of foreign words are not hyphenated when placed before a noun unless they are always hyphenated.

> the per capita cost
> a cordon bleu restaurant
> an a priori argument
> a ci-devant professor

31. Chemical names used as modifiers before a noun are not hyphenated.

> a sodium hypochlorite bleach
> a citric acid solution

32. Following the Noun (as a complement or predicate adjective)   When the words that make up a compound adjective follow the noun they modify, they tend to fall in normal word order and are no longer unit modifiers. They are therefore no longer hyphenated.

> Controls have become more specialized.
> The company is still growing.
> a device for both input and output
> a statement of profit and loss
> arrested on charges that had been trumped up
> decisions made on the spur of the moment
> They were ill prepared for the journey.

33. Many permanent and temporary compounds keep their hyphens after the noun in a sentence if they continue to function as unit modifiers. Compounds consisting of adjective or noun + participle, adjective or noun + noun + -ed (which looks like a participle), or noun + adjective are most likely to remain hyphenated.

> Your ideas are high-minded but impractical.
> streets that are tree-lined
> You were just as nice-looking then.
> metals that are corrosion-resistant
> tends to be accident-prone

34. Permanent compound adjectives that are entered in dictionaries are usually styled in the way that they appear in the dictionary whether they precede or follow the noun they modify.

> The group was public-spirited.
> The problems are mind-boggling.
> is well-read in economics

35. Compound adjectives of three or more words are normally not hyphenated when they follow the noun they modify.

> These remarks are off the record.

36. Permanent compounds of three or more words may be entered as hyphenated adjectives in dictionaries. In such cases the hyphens are retained as long as the phrase is being used as a unit modifier.

> the plan is still pay-as-you-go
> *but* a plan in which you pay as you go

37. It is possible that a permanent hyphenated adjective from the dictionary may appear alongside a temporary compound in a position where it would normally be open (as "one who is both ill-humored and ill prepared"). Editors usually try to resolve these inconsistencies, either by hyphenating both compounds or leaving both compounds open.

38. When an adverb modifies another adverb that is the first element of a compound modifier, the compound may lose its hyphen. If the first adverb modifies the whole compound, however, the hyphen should be retained.

> a very well developed idea
> a delightfully well-written book
> a most ill-humored remark

39. Adjective compounds that are names of colors may be styled open or hyphenated. Color names in which each element can function as a noun (as *blue green* or *chrome yellow*) are almost always hyphenated when they precede a noun; they are sometimes open when they follow the noun. Color names in which the first element can only be an adjective are less consistently treated; they are often not hyphenated before a noun and are usually not hyphenated after.

> blue-gray paint
> paint that is blue-gray   *also*   paint that is blue gray
> bluish gray paint   *or*   bluish-gray paint
> paint that is bluish gray

40. Compound modifiers that include a number followed by a noun are hyphenated when they precede the noun they modify. When the modifier follows the noun, it is usually not hyphenated. For more on the styling of numbers, see Chapter 5, "The Treatment of Numbers."

> five-card stud   ten-foot pole
> an 18-inch rule   twelve-year-old girl
> an essay that is one page   a child who is ten years old

41. An adjective that is composed of a number followed by a noun in the possessive is not hyphenated.

> a two weeks' wait
> a four blocks' walk

Compounds That Function as Adverbs

42. Adverb compounds consisting of preposition + noun are almost always written solid; however, there are a few well-known exceptions.

downtown	upstairs
downwind	upfield
onstage	offhand
overseas	underhand
but	

in-house	off-line	on-line

43. Compound adverbs of more than two words are usually styled open, and they usually follow the words they modify.

every which way	hook, line, and sinker
little by little	off and on
high and dry	over and over

44. A few three-word adverbs are homographs of hyphenated adjectives and are therefore styled with hyphens. But many adverbs are styled open even if an adjective formed from the same phrase is hyphenated.

> back-to-back (adverb or adjective)
> face-to-face (adverb or adjective)
> *but*
> hand-to-hand combat
> off-the-cuff remarks
> fought hand to hand
> spoke off the cuff

Compound Verbs

45. Two-word verbs consisting of a verb followed by an adverb or a preposition are styled open.

get together	strike out
set to	run across
break through	put down
run around	print out
run wild	

46. A compound composed of a particle followed by a verb is styled solid.

upgrade	overcome
outflank	bypass

47. A verb derived from an open or hyphenated compound noun—permanent, temporary, or self-evident—is hyphenated.

blue-pencil	tap-dance
sweet-talk	poor-mouth
double-check	water-ski

48. A verb derived from a solid noun is styled solid.

bankroll	mainstream
roughhouse	steamroller

Compounds Formed with Word Elements

Many new and temporary compounds are formed by adding word elements to existing words or by combining word elements. There are three basic word elements: prefixes (as *anti-*, *re-*, *non-*, *super-*), suffixes (as *-er*, *-ly*, *-ness*, *-ism*), and what the dictionaries call combining forms (as *mini-*, *macro-*, *pseud-*, *ortho-*, *-ped*, *-graphy*, *-gamic*, *-plasty*). Prefixes and suffixes are usually attached to existing words; combining forms are usually combined to form new words.

49. prefix + word Except as specified below, compounds formed from a prefix and a word are usually styled solid.

precondition	suborder
interagency	overfond
refurnish	postwar
misshapen	unhelpful

50. If the prefix ends with a vowel and the word it is attached to begins with the same vowel, the compound is usually hyphenated.

anti-inflation	de-emphasize
co-owner	multi-institutional

NOTE: Many exceptions to this styling (such as *cooperate* and *reentry*) can be found by checking a dictionary.

51. If the base word to which a prefix is added is capitalized, the compound is hyphenated.

anti-American	pro-Soviet
post-Victorian	inter-Caribbean

NOTE: The prefix is usually not capitalized in such compounds. But if the prefix and the base word together form a new proper name, the compound may be solid with the prefix capitalized (as *Postimpressionist, Precambrian*). Such exceptions can be found in a dictionary.

52. Compounds made with *self-* and *ex-* meaning "former" are hyphenated.

    self-pity
    ex-wife

53. If a prefix is added to a hyphenated compound, it may be either followed by a hyphen or closed up solid to the next element. Permanent compounds of this kind should be checked in a dictionary.

    unair-conditioned
    ultra-up-to-date
    non-self-governing
    unself-conscious

54. If a prefix is added to an open compound, the prefix is followed by a hyphen in typewritten material. In typeset material, this hyphen is often represented by an en dash. (For more on this use of the en dash, see paragraph 16 in the section on Dash, beginning on page 25, in Chapter 1, "Punctuation.")

    ex–Boy Scout
    post–coup d'état

55. A compound that would be identical with another word if styled solid is usually hyphenated to prevent misreading.

    a multi-ply fabric
    re-collect the money
    un-ionized particles

56. Some writers and editors like to hyphenate a compound that might otherwise be solid if they think the reader might be momentarily puzzled (as by consecutive vowels, doubled consonants, or simply an odd combination of letters.)

    coed   *or*   co-ed
    coworker *or*   co-worker
    overreact *or*   over-react
    interrow *or*   inter-row

57. Temporary compounds formed from *vice-* are usually hyphenated; however, some permanent compounds (as *vice president* and *vice admiral*) are open.

58. When prefixes are attached to numerals, the compounds are hyphenated.

    pre-1982 expenses
    post-1975 vintages
    non-20th-century ideas

59. Compounds formed from combining forms like *Anglo-*, *Judeo-*, or *Sino-* are hyphenated when the second element is an independent word and solid when it is a combining form.

Judeo-Christian   Francophone
Italophile   Sino-Soviet
Austro-Hungarian   Anglophobe

60. Prefixes that are repeated in the same compound are separated by a hyphen.

sub-subheading

61. Some prefixes and initial combining forms have related independent adjectives or adverbs that may be used where the prefix might be expected. A temporary compound with *quasi(-)* or *pseudo(-)* therefore may be written open as modifier + noun or hyphenated as combining form + noun. A writer or editor must thus decide which style to follow.

quasi intellectual   *or*   quasi-intellectual
pseudo liberal   *or*   pseudo-liberal

NOTE: in some cases (as *super, super-*), the independent modifier may not mean quite the same as the prefix.

62. Compounds consisting of different prefixes with the same base word and joined by *and* or *or* are sometimes shortened by pruning the first compound back to the prefix. The missing base word is indicated by a hyphen on the prefix.

pre- and postoperative care
anti- or pro-Revolutionary sympathies

63. word + suffix Except as noted below, compounds formed by adding a suffix to a word are styled solid.

Darwinist   landscaper
fortyish   powerlessness

64. Permanent or temporary compounds formed with a suffix are hyphenated if the addition of the suffix would create a sequence of three like letters.

bell-like   a coffee-er coffee
will-less

65. Temporary compounds made with a suffix are often hyphenated if the base word is more than three syllables long, if the base word ends with the same letter the suffix begins with, or if the suffix creates a confusing sequence of letters.

tunnel-like   industry-wide
umbrella-like   jaw-wards
Mexican-ness   battle-worthy

66. Compounds made from a number + *odd* are hyphenated whether the number is spelled out or in numerals; a number + *-fold* is solid if the number is spelled out but hyphenated if it is in numerals.

20-odd	twenty-odd
12-fold	twelvefold

67. Most compounds formed from an open or hyphenated compound + a suffix do not separate the suffix by a hyphen. But such suffixes as *-like, -wide, -worthy,* and *-proof,* all of which are homographs of independent adjectives, are attached by a hyphen.

good-humoredness	do-it-yourselfer
dollar-a-yearism	a United Nations-like agency

    NOTE: Open compounds often become hyphenated when a suffix is added unless they are proper nouns.

    middle age   *but*   middle-ager
    tough guy   *but*   tough-guyese
    New Englandism
    Wall Streeter

68. **combining form + combining form**   Many new terms in technical fields are created by adding combining form to combining form or combining form to a word or a word part. Such compounds are generally intended to be permanent, even though many never get into the dictionary. They are regularly styled solid.

Miscellaneous Styling Conventions

69. Compounds that would otherwise be styled solid according to the principles described above are written open or hyphenated to avoid ambiguity, to make sure of rapid comprehension, or to make the pronunciation more obvious.

meat-ax *or* meat ax	umbrella-like
re-utter	tri-city
bi-level	un-iced

70. When typographical features such as capitals or italics make word relationships in a sentence clear, it is not necessary to hyphenate an open compound (as when it precedes a noun it modifies).

    a *Chicago Tribune* story
    I've been Super Bowled to death.
    a *noblesse oblige* attitude
    an "eyes only" memo

71. Publications (as technical journals) aimed at a specialized readership likely to recognize the elements of a compound and their relationship tend to use open and solid stylings more frequently than more general publications would.

electrooculogram
radiofrequency
rapid eye movement

72. Words that are formed by reduplication and so consist of two similar-sounding elements (as *hush-hush, razzle-dazzle,* or *hugger-mugger*) present styling questions like those of compounds. Words like these are hyphenated if each of the elements is made up of more than one syllable. If each element has only one syllable, the words are variously styled solid or hyphenated. The solid styling is slightly more common overall; however, for very short words (as *no-no, go-go,* and *so-so*), for words in which both elements may have primary stress (as *tiptop* and *sci-fi*), and for words coined in the twentieth century (as *ack-ack* and *hush-hush*), the hyphenated styling is more common.

goody-goody	boo-boo
palsy-walsy	tip-top
teeter-totter	crisscross
topsy-turvy	peewee
agar-agar	knickknack
ack-ack	singsong

Chapter 4

Abbreviations

CONTENTS

Abbreviations are used for a variety of reasons. They serve to save space, to avoid repetition of long words and phrases that may distract the reader, and to reduce keystrokes for typists and thereby increase their output. In addition, abbreviations are used simply to conform to conventional usage.

The frequency of abbreviations in typewritten or printed material is directly related to the nature of the material itself. For example, technical literature (as in the military and in the fields of aerospace, engineering, data processing, and medicine) features many abbreviations, but formal literary writing has relatively few. By the same token, the number of abbreviations in a piece of business writing depends on the nature of the business, as do the particular abbreviations employed. A person working in a university English department will often see *ibid.*, *ll.*, and *TESOL*, while the employee of an electronics firm will instead see *CAD*, *CPU*, and *mm* from day to day.

Unfortunately, the contemporary styling of abbreviations is to a large extent inconsistent and arbitrary. No set of rules can hope to cover all the possible variations, exceptions, and peculiarities actually encountered in print. The styling of abbreviations— whether capitalized or lowercased, closed up or spaced, punctuated or unpunctuated—depends most often on the writer's preference or the organization's policy. For example, some companies style the abbreviation for *cash on delivery* as *COD*, while others prefer *C.O.D.*, and still others, *c.o.d.*

All is not confusion, however, and general patterns can be discerned. Some abbreviations (as *a.k.a.*, *e.g.*, *etc.*, *i.e.*, *No.*, and *viz.*) are governed by a strong tradition of punctuation, while others (as *NATO*, *NASA*, *NOW*, *OPEC*, and *SALT*) that are pronounced as words tend to be all-capitalized and unpunctuated. Styling problems can be dealt with by consulting a good general dictionary such as *Webster's Ninth New Collegiate Dictionary*, especially for capitalization guidance, and by following the guidelines of one's own organization or the dictates of one's own preference. An abbreviations dictionary such as *Webster's Guide to Abbreviations* may also be consulted.

Punctuation

The paragraphs that follow describe a few broad principles that apply to abbreviations in general; however, there are many specific situations in which these principles will not apply. For instance, U.S. Postal Service abbreviations for names of states are always unpunctuated, as are the abbreviations used within most branches of the armed forces for the names of ranks. The section on Specific Styling Conventions in this chapter contains more information on particular kinds of abbreviations.

1. A period follows most abbreviations that are formed by omitting all but the first few letters of a word.

   > bull. for *bulletin*
   > bro. for *brother*
   > fig. for *figure*
   > Fr. for *French*

2. A period follows most abbreviations that are formed by omitting letters from the middle of a word.

   > secy. for *secretary*
   > mfg. for *manufacturing*
   > agcy. for *agency*
   > Mr. for *Mister*

3. Punctuation is usually omitted from abbreviations that are made up of initial letters of words that constitute a phrase or compound word. However, for some of these abbreviations, especially ones that are not capitalized, the punctuation is retained.

   > GNP for *gross national product*
   > EFT for *electronic funds transfer*
   > PC for *personal computer*
   > f.o.b. for *free on board*

4. Terms in which a suffix is added to a numeral, such as *1st, 2nd, 3d, 8vo,* and *12mo,* are not abbreviations and do not require a period.

5. Isolated letters of the alphabet used to designate a shape or position in a sequence are not punctuated.

T square	I beam
A 1	V sign

6. Some abbreviations are punctuated with one or more virgules in place of periods.

c/o for *care of*
d/b/a for *doing business as*
w/o for *without*
w/w for *wall to wall*

Capitalization

1. Abbreviations are capitalized if the words they represent are proper nouns or adjectives.

F for *Fahrenheit*
NFL for *National Football League*
Nov. for *November*
Brit. for *British*

2. Abbreviations are usually capitalized when formed from the initial letters of the words or word elements that make up what is being abbreviated. There are, however, some very common abbreviations formed in this way that are not capitalized.

TM for *trademark*
ETA for *estimated time of arrival*
CATV for *community antenna television*
EEG for *electroencephalogram*
FY for *fiscal year*
a.k.a. for *also known as*
d/b/a for *doing business as*

3. Most abbreviations that are pronounced as words, rather than as a series of letters, are capitalized. If they have been assimilated into the language as words in their own right, however, they are most often lowercased.

OPEC	quasar
NATO	laser
MIRV	sonar
NOW account	scuba

Plurals, Possessives, and Compounds

1. Punctuated abbreviations of single words are pluralized by adding -s before the period.

bldgs.	figs.
bros.	mts.

2. Punctuated abbreviations that stand for phrases or compounds are pluralized by adding *-'s* after the last period.

Ph.D.'s	J.P.'s
f.o.b.'s	M.B.A.'s

3. Unpunctuated abbreviations that stand for phrases or compound words are usually pluralized by adding *-s* to the end of the abbreviation.

COLAs	PCs
CPUs	DOSs

NOTE: Some writers pluralize such abbreviations by adding *-'s* to the abbreviation; however, this styling is far less common than the one described above.

4. The plural form of most lowercase single-letter abbreviations is made by repeating the letter. For the plural form of single-letter abbreviations that are abbreviations for units of measure, see paragraph 5 below.

cc. for *copies*
ll. for *lines*
pp. for *pages*
ff. for *and the following ones*
nn. for *notes*
vv. for *verses*

5. The plural form of abbreviations of units of measure is the same as the singular form.

30 sec.	20 min.
30 d.	50 m
24 ml	200 bbl.
24 h.	10 mi.

6. Possessives of abbreviations are formed in the same way as those of spelled-out nouns: the singular possessive is formed by the addition of *-'s*, the plural possessive simply by the addition of an apostrophe.

the CPU's memory
Brody Corp.'s earnings
most CPUs' memories
Bay Bros.' annual sale

7. Compounds that consist of an abbreviation added to another word are formed in the same way as compounds that consist of spelled-out nouns.

    a Kalamazoo, Mich.-based company
    an AMA-approved medical school

8. Compounds formed by adding a prefix or suffix to an abbreviation are usually styled with a hyphen.

    an IBM-like organization
    non-DNA molecules
    pre-HEW years

Specific Styling Conventions

The following paragraphs describe styling practices commonly followed for specific kinds of situations involving abbreviations. The paragraphs are arranged under the following alphabetical headings.

A and An
A.D. and B.C.
Agencies, Associations, and
  Organizations
Beginning a Sentence
Books of the Bible
Company Names
Compass Points
Contractions
Dates
Degrees
Division of Abbreviations
Footnotes
Full Forms

Geographical and
  Topographical Names
Latin Words and Phrases
Latitude and Longitude
Laws and Bylaws
Military Ranks and Units
Number
Personal Names
Saint
Scientific Terms
Time
Titles
Units of Measure
Versus

A and An

1. The choice of the article *a* or *an* before abbreviations depends on the *sound* with which the abbreviation begins. If an abbreviation begins with a consonant sound, *a* is normally used. If an abbreviation begins with a vowel sound, *an* is used.

    a B.A. degree   an FCC report
    a YMCA club   an SAT score
    a UN agency   an IRS agent

A.D. and B.C.

2. The abbreviations A.D. and B.C. are usually styled in typeset matter as punctuated, unspaced small capitals; in typed material they usually appear as punctuated, unspaced capitals.

    in printed material   41 B.C.   A.D. 185
    in typed material   41 B.C.   A.D. 185

3. The abbreviation A.D. usually precedes the date; the abbreviation B.C. usually follows the date. However, many writers and editors place A.D. after the date, thus making their placement of A.D. consistent with their placement of B.C. In references to whole centuries, the usual practice is to place A.D. after the century. The only alternative is not to use the abbreviation at all in such references.

> A.D. 185   *but also*   185 A.D.
> the fourth century A.D.

Agencies, Associations, and Organizations

4. The names of agencies, associations, and organizations are usually abbreviated after they have been spelled out on their first occurrence in a text. The abbreviations are usually all capitalized and unpunctuated.

EPA	NAACP	USO
SEC	NCAA	NOW

NOTE: In contexts where the abbreviation is expected to be instantly recognizable, it will generally be used without having its full form spelled out on its first occurrence.

Beginning a Sentence

5. Most writers and editors avoid beginning a sentence with an abbreviation that is ordinarily not capitalized. Abbreviations that are ordinarily capitalized, on the other hand, are commonly used to begin sentences.

> Page 22 contains . . .   *not*   P. 22 contains . . .
> Doctor Smith believes . . .   *or*   Dr. Smith believes . . .
> OSHA regulations require . . .
> PCB concentrations that were measured at . . .

Books of the Bible

6. Books of the Bible are generally spelled out in running text but abbreviated in references to chapter and verse.

> The minister based his sermon on Genesis.
> In the beginning God created the heavens and the earth.
> —Gen. 1:1

Capitalization—See section on Capitalization in this chapter.

Chemical Elements and Compounds—See **Scientific Terms** below.

Company Names

7. The styling of company names varies widely. Many published style manuals say that the name of a company should not be abbreviated unless the abbreviation is part of its official name; however, many publications routinely abbreviate words such as *Corporation, Company,* and *Incorporated* when they appear in company names. Words such as *Airlines, Associates, Fabricators, Manufacturing,* and *Railroad,* however, are spelled out.

> Ginn and Company   *or*   Ginn and Co.
> The Bailey Banks and Biddle Company
>   *or*   The Bailey Banks and Biddle Co.
> Gulf & Western Industries, Inc.
> Canon, U.S.A., Inc.

NOTE: An ampersand frequently replaces the word *and* in official company names. For more on this use of the ampersand, see paragraph 1 in the section on Ampersand, beginning on page 4, in Chapter 1, "Punctuation."

8. If a company is easily recognizable from its initials, its name is usually spelled out for the first mention and abbreviated in all subsequent references. Some companies have made their initials part of their official name, and in those cases the initials appear in all references.

> *first reference*   General Motors Corp. released figures
>   today . . .
> *subsequent reference*   A GM spokesperson said . . .
> MCM Electronics, an Ohio-based electronics company . . .

Compass Points

9. Compass points are abbreviated when occurring after street names, though styling varies regarding whether these abbreviations are punctuated and whether they are preceded by a comma. When compass points form essential internal elements of street names, they are usually spelled out in full.

> 2122 Fourteenth Street, NW   *or*   2122 Fourteenth Street NW
>   *or*   2122 Fourteenth Street, N.W.
> 192 East 49th Street
> 1282 North Avenue

Compounds—See section on Plurals, Possessives, and Compounds above.

Computer Terms—See **Scientific Terms** below.

Contractions

10. Some abbreviations resemble contractions by including an apostrophe in place of omitted letters. These abbreviations are not punctuated with a period.

> sec'y for *secretary*   dep't for *department*
> ass'n for *association*

NOTE: This style of abbreviation is usually avoided in formal writing.

Courtesy Titles—See **Titles** below.

Dates

11. The names of days and months are usually not abbreviated in running text, although some publications do abbreviate names of months when they appear in dates that refer to a specific day or days. The names of months are not abbreviated in date lines of business letters, but they may be abbreviated in government or military correspondence.

> the December issue of *Scientific American*
> going to camp in August
> a report due on Tuesday
> a meeting held on August 1, 1985
>   *or*   a meeting held on Aug. 1, 1985
> *general business date line*   November 1, 1985
> *military date line*   1 Nov 1985

NOTE: When dates are used in tables or in notes, the names of days and months are commonly abbreviated.

Degrees

12. Except for a few academic degrees with highly recognizable abbreviations (as *A.B.*, *M.S.*, and *Ph.D.*), the names of degrees and professional ratings are spelled out in full when first mentioned in running text. Often the name of the degree is followed by its abbreviation enclosed in parentheses, so that the abbreviation may be used alone later in running text. When a degree or professional rating follows a person's name it is usually abbreviated.

> Special attention will be devoted to the master of arts in teaching (M.A.T.) degree.
> Julia Ramirez, P.E.

13. Like other abbreviations, abbreviations of degrees and professional ratings are often unpunctuated. In general, punctuated abbreviations are more common for academic degrees, and unpunctuated abbreviations are slightly more common for professional ratings, especially if the latter comprise three or more capitalized letters.

R.Ph.	P.E.	CLA	CMET
Ph.D.	B.Sc.	M.B.A.	BGS

14. The initial letter of each element in abbreviations of all degrees and professional ratings is capitalized. Letters other than the initial letter are usually not capitalized.

D.Ch.E.   M.F.A.
Litt.D.   D.Th.

Division of Abbreviations

15. Division of abbreviations at the end of lines or between pages is usually avoided.

| received an M.B.A. degree | *not* | received an M.B.-A. degree |

Expansions—See **Full Forms** below.

Footnotes

16. Footnotes sometimes incorporate abbreviations.

ibid.   op. cit.   loc. cit.

NOTE: In current practice these abbreviations are usually not italicized.

Full Forms

17. When using an abbreviation that may be unfamiliar or confusing to the reader, many publications give the full form first, followed by the abbreviation in parentheses; in subsequent references just the abbreviation is used.

first reference   At the American Bar Association (ABA) meeting in June . . .
subsequent reference At that particular ABA meeting . . .

Geographical and Topographical Names

18. U.S. Postal Service abbreviations for states, possessions, and Canadian provinces are all-capitalized and unpunctuated, as are Postal Service abbreviations for streets and other geographical features when these abbreviations are used on envelopes addressed for automated mass handling.

addressed for automated handling   1234 SMITH BLVD
                                     SMITHVILLE, MN 56789
regular address styling   1234 Smith Blvd.
                                     Smithville, MN 56789

19. Abbreviations of states are often used in running text to identify the location of a city or county. In this context they are set off with commas, and punctuated, upper- and lowercase state abbreviations are usually used. In other situations within running text, the names of states are usually not abbreviated.

John Smith of 15 Chestnut St., Sarasota, Fla., has won . . .

the Louisville, Ky., public library system

Boston, the largest city in Massachusetts, . . .

20. Terms such as *street* and *parkway* are variously abbreviated or unabbreviated in running text. When they are abbreviated, they are usually punctuated.

> our office at 1234 Smith Blvd. (*or* Boulevard)
> an accident on Windward Road (*or* Rd.)

21. Names of countries are typically abbreviated in tabular data, but they are usually spelled in full in running text. The most common exceptions to this pattern are the abbreviations *U.S.S.R.* and *U.S.* (see paragraph 23 below).

> | | |
> |---|---|
> | *in a table* | Gt. Brit. *or* U.K. *or* UK |
> | *in text* | Great Britain and the U.S.S.R. announced the agreement. |

22. Abbreviations for the names of most countries are punctuated. Abbreviations for countries whose names include more than one word are often not punctuated if the abbreviations are formed from only the initial letters of the individual words.

> | | |
> |---|---|
> | Mex. | U.K. *or* UK |
> | U.S.S.R. *or* USSR | Scot. |
> | Can. | U.S. *or* US |
> | Gt. Brit. | U.A.E. *or* UAE |

23. *United States* is often abbreviated when it is being used as an adjective, such as when it modifies the name of a federal agency, policy, or program. When *United States* is used as a noun in running text, it is usually spelled out, or it is spelled on its initial use and then abbreviated in subsequent references.

> U.S. Department of Justice
> U.S. foreign policy
> The United States has offered to . . .

24. *Saint* is usually abbreviated when it is part of the name of a geographical or topographical feature. *Mount, Point,* and *Fort* are variously spelled out or abbreviated according to individual preference. *Saint, Mount* and *Point* are routinely abbreviated when space is at a premium. (For more on the abbreviation of *Saint,* see paragraph 36 below.)

> | | |
> |---|---|
> | St. Louis, Missouri | Fort Sumter |
> | Mount St. Helens | Mount McKinley |
> | St. Kitts | Point Pelee |

Latin Words and Phrases—See also **Footnotes** above.

25. Words and phrases derived from Latin are commonly abbreviated in contexts where readers can reasonably be expected to recognize them. They are punctuated, not capitalized, and usually not italicized.

etc.	e.g.	et al.
i.e.	viz.	pro tem.

Latitude and Longitude

26. Latitude and longitude are abbreviated in tabular data but written out in running text.

> *in a table*   lat. 10°20′N   *or*   lat. 10-20N
> *in text*   from 10°20′ north latitude to 10°30′ south latitude

Laws and Bylaws

27. Laws and bylaws, when first mentioned, are spelled in full; however, subsequent references to them in a text may be abbreviated.

> *first reference*   Article I, Section 1
> *subsequent reference*   Art. I, Sec. 1

Military Ranks and Units

28. Military ranks are usually given in full when used with a surname only but are abbreviated when used with a full name.

> Colonel Howe
> Col. John P. Howe

29. In nonmilitary publications, abbreviations for military ranks are punctuated and set in capital and lowercase letters. Within the military (with the exception of the Marine Corps) these abbreviations are all-capitalized and unpunctuated. The Marine Corps follows the punctuated, capital and lowercase styling.

> *in the military*   BG John T. Dow, USA
>   LCDR Mary I. Lee, USN
>   Col. S. J. Smith, USMC
> *outside the military*   Brig. Gen. John T. Dow, USA
>   Lt. Comdr. Mary I. Lee, USN
>   Col. S. J. Smith, USMC

30. Abbreviations for military units are capitalized and unpunctuated.

USA	SAC
USAF	NORAD

Number

31. The word *number*, when used with figures such as *1* or *2* to indicate a rank or rating, is usually abbreviated. When it is, the *N* is capitalized, and the abbreviation is punctuated.

> The No. 1 priority is to promote profitability.

32. The word *number* is usually abbreviated when it is part of a set unit (as a contract number), when it is used in tabular data, or when it is used in bibliographic references.

> Contract No. N-1234-76-57
> Policy No. 123-5-X
> Publ. Nos. 12 and 13
> Index No. 7855

Period with Abbreviations—See section on Punctuation above.

Personal Names

33. First names are not usually abbreviated.

> George S. Patterson   *not*   Geo. S. Patterson

34. Unspaced initials of famous persons are sometimes used in place of their full names. The initials may or may not be punctuated.

> FDR   *or*   F.D.R.

35. Initials used with a surname are spaced and punctuated.

> F. D. Roosevelt

Plurals—See section on Plurals, Possessives, and Compounds above.

Possessives—See section on Plurals, Possessives, and Compounds above.

Saint

36. The word *Saint* is often abbreviated when used before the name of a saint or when it is the first element of the name of a city or institution named after a saint. However, when it forms part of a surname, it may or may not be abbreviated, and the styling should be the one used by the person or the institution.

> St. Peter   *or*   Saint Peter
> St. John's University
> Ruth St. Denis
> Augustus Saint-Gaudens
> St. Cloud, Minnesota
> Saint Joseph College

Scientific Terms—See also **Units of Measure** below.

37. In binomial nomenclature, a genus name may be abbreviated with its initial letter after the first reference to it is spelled out. The abbreviation is always punctuated.

> *first reference*   *Escherichia coli*
> *subsequent reference*   *E. coli*

38. Abbreviations for the names of chemical compounds or mechanical or electronic equipment or processes are usually not punctuated.

OCR   CPU
PCB   PBX

39. The symbols for chemical elements are not punctuated.

H   Pb
Cl   Na

Time—See also **A.D. and B.C.** and **Dates** above and **Units of Measure** below.

40. When time is expressed in figures, the abbreviations that follow are most often styled as punctuated lowercase letters; punctuated small capital letters are also common. For more on the use of *a.m.* and *p.m.*, see paragraph 44 in the section on Specific Styling Conventions, on page 145, in Chapter 5, "The Treatment of Numbers."

8:30 a.m.   8:30 A.M.
10:00 p.m.   10:00 P.M.

41. In transportation schedules *a.m.* and *p.m.* are generally styled in capitalized, unpunctuated, unspaced letters.

8:30 AM
10:00 PM

42. Time zone designations are usually styled in capitalized, unpunctuated, unspaced letters.

EST   PST   CDT

Titles—See also **Degrees** and **Military Ranks and Units** above.

43. The only courtesy titles that are invariably abbreviated in written references are *Mr., Ms., Mrs.,* and *Messrs.* Other titles, such as *Doctor, Representative,* or *Senator,* may be either written out or abbreviated.

Ms. Lee A. Downs
Messrs. Lake, Mason, and Nambeth
Doctor Howe   *or*   Dr. Howe
Senator Long   *or*   Sen. Long

44. Despite some traditional injunctions against the practice, the titles *Honorable* and *Reverend* are often abbreviated when used with *the.*

the Honorable Samuel I. O'Leary
   or   the Hon. Samuel I. O'Leary
the Reverend Samuel I. O'Leary   *or*   the Rev. Samuel I. O'Leary

NOTE: There is also a traditional injunction against using the titles *Honorable* and *Reverend* without *the* preceding them. However, in current practice, *Reverend* and *Rev.* are commonly used without *the*.

> Reverend Samuel I. O'Leary   *or*   Rev. Samuel I. O'Leary

45. The designations *Jr.* and *Sr.* may be used in conjunction with courtesy titles, with abbreviations for academic degrees, and with professional rating abbreviations. They may or may not be preceded by a comma according to the writer's preference. They are terminated with a period, and they are commonly only used with a full name.

> Mr. John K. Walker, Jr.
> Dr. John K. Walker, Jr.
> General John K. Walker Jr.
> The Honorable John K. Walker, Jr.
> John K. Walker Jr., M.D.

46. When an abbreviation for an academic degree, professional certification, or association membership follows a name, it is usually preceded by a comma. No courtesy title should precede the name.

> Dr. John Smith   *or*   John Smith, M.D.
>   *but not*   Dr. John Smith, M.D.
> Katherine Derwinski, CLU
> Carol Manning, M.D., FACPS

47. The abbreviation *Esq.* for *Esquire* is used in the United States after the surname of professional persons such as attorneys, architects, consuls, clerks of the court, and justices of the peace. It is not used, however, if *the Honorable* precedes the first name. If a courtesy title such as *Dr., Hon., Miss, Mr., Mrs.,* or *Ms.* is used in correspondence, *Esq.* is omitted. *Esquire* or *Esq.* is frequently used in the United States after the surname of a woman lawyer, although the practice has not yet gained acceptance in all law offices or among all state bar associations.

> Carolyn B. West, Esq.

Units of Measure

48. Measures and weights may be abbreviated in figure plus unit combinations; however, if the numeral is written out, the unit should also be written out.

> 15 cu ft   *or*   15 cu. ft.   *but*   fifteen cubic feet
> How many cubic feet does the refrigerator hold?

49. Abbreviations for metric units are usually not punctuated. In many scientific and technical publications, abbreviations for traditional nonmetric units are also unpunctuated. However, in most general-interest publications, abbreviations for traditional units are punctuated.

14 ml	22 mi.	4 sec.
12 km	8 ft.	20 min.

Versus

50. *Versus* is abbreviated as *v.* in legal contexts; it is either spelled out or abbreviated as lowercase roman letters *vs.* in general contexts. For more on the use of *v.* in legal contexts, see paragraph 35 in the section on Proper Nouns, Pronouns, and Adjectives, beginning on page 65, in Chapter 2, "Capitals, Italics, and Quotation Marks."

in a legal context	*Smith* v. *Vermont*
in a general context	honesty versus dishonesty
	or
	honesty vs. dishonesty

Chapter 5

The Treatment of Numbers

CONTENTS

The styling of numbers presents special difficulties to writers and editors because there are so many conventions to follow, some of which may conflict when applied to particular passages. The writer's major decision is whether to write out numbers in running text or to express them in figures. Usage varies considerably, in part because no single neat formula covers all the categories in which numbers are used. In general, the more formal the writing the more likely that numbers will be spelled out. In scientific, technical, or statistical contexts, however, numbers are likely to be expressed as figures. This chapter explains most of the conventions used in the styling of numbers. A discussion of general principles is followed by detailed information on specific situations involving numbers.

Numbers as Words or Figures

At one extreme of styling, all numbers, sometimes even including dates, are written out. This usage is uncommon and is usually limited to proclamations, legal documents, and some other types of very formal writing. This styling is space-consuming and time-consuming; it can also be ungainly or, worse, unclear. At the other extreme, some types of technical writing, such as statistical reports, contain no written-out numbers except at the beginning of a sentence.

In general, figures are easier to read than the spelled-out forms of numbers; however, the spelled-out forms are helpful in certain circumstances, such as in distinguishing different categories of numbers or in providing relief from an overwhelming cluster of numerals. Most writers follow one or the other of two common conventions combining numerals and written-out numbers. The conventions are described in this section, along with the situations that provide exceptions to the general rules.

Basic Conventions

1. The first system requires that a writer use figures for exact numbers that are greater than nine and words for numbers nine and below (a variation of this system sets the number ten as the dividing point). In this system, numbers that consist of a whole number between one and nine followed by *hundred, thousand, million,* etc. may be spelled out or expressed in figures.

    > She has performed in 22 plays on Broadway, seven of which won Pulitzer prizes.

    > The new edition will consist of 25 volumes which will be issued at a rate of approximately four volumes per year.

    > The cat show attracted an unexpected two thousand entries.

    > They sold more than 2,000 units in the first year.

2. The second system requires that a writer use figures for all exact numbers 100 and above (or 101 and above) and words for numbers from one to ninety-nine (or one to one hundred) and for numbers that consist of a whole number between one and ninety-nine followed by *hundred, thousand, million,* etc.

    > The artist spent nearly twelve years completing these four volumes, which comprise 435 hand-colored engravings.

    > The 145 participants in the seminar toured the area's eighteen period houses.

    > In the course of four hours, the popular author signed twenty-five hundred copies of her new book.

Sentence Beginnings

3. Numbers that begin a sentence are written out, although some make an exception for the use of figures for dates that begin a sentence. Most writers, however, try to avoid spelled-out numbers that are lengthy and awkward by restructuring the sentence so that the number appears elsewhere than at the beginning and may then be styled as a figure.

    > Sixty-two species of Delphinidae inhabit the world's oceans.
    > *or*
    > The Delphinidae consist of 62 ocean-dwelling species.

Twelve fifteen was the year King John of England signed the Magna Carta.
or
1215 was the year King John of England signed the Magna Carta.
or
In 1215 King John of England signed the Magna Carta.

One hundred fifty-seven illustrations, including 86 color plates, are contained in the book.
or
The book contains 157 illustrations, including 86 color plates.

Adjacent Numbers and Numbers in Series

4. Generally, two separate sets of figures should not be written adjacent to one another in running text unless they form a series. So that the juxtaposition of unrelated figures will not confuse the reader, either the sentence is restructured or one of the figures is spelled out. Usually the figure with the written form that is shorter and more easily read is converted. When one of two adjacent numbers is an element of a compound modifier, the first of the two numbers is often expressed in words, the second in figures. But if the second number is the shorter, the styling is often reversed.

original	*change to*
16 ½-inch dowels	sixteen ½-inch dowels
25 11-inch platters	twenty-five 11-inch platters
20 100-point games	twenty 100-point games
78 20-point games	78 twenty-point games
By 1997, 300 more of the state's schools will have closed their doors.	By 1997, three hundred more of the state's schools will have closed their doors.

5. Numbers paired at the beginning of a sentence are usually styled alike. If the first word of the sentence is a spelled-out number, the second, related number is also spelled out. However, some writers and editors prefer that each number be styled independently, even if that results in an inconsistent pairing.

Sixty to seventy-five acres were destroyed.
Sixty to 75 acres were destroyed.

6. Numbers that form a pair or a series referring to comparable quantities within a sentence or a paragraph should be treated consistently. The style of the largest number usually determines the style of the other numbers. Thus, a series of numbers including some which would ordinarily be spelled out might all be styled as figures. Similarly, figures are used to express all the numbers in a series if one of those numbers is a mixed or simple fraction.

> Graduating from the obedience class were 3 corgis, 20 Doberman pinschers, 19 German shepherds, 9 golden retrievers, 10 Labrador retrievers, and 1 Rottweiler.
>
> The three jobs took 5, 12, and 4½ hours, respectively.

Round Numbers

7. Approximate or round numbers, particularly those that can be expressed in one or two words, are often written out in general writing; in technical and scientific writing they are more likely to be expressed as numerals.

> seven hundred people
> five thousand years
> four hundred thousand volumes
> seventeen thousand metric tons
> four hundred million dollars
> *but in technical writing*
> 50,000 people per year
> 20,000 species of fish

8. For easier reading, numbers of one million and above may be expressed as figures followed by the word *million, billion,* and so forth. The figure may include a decimal fraction, but the fraction is not usually carried past the first digit to the right of the decimal point, and it is never carried past the third digit. If a more exact number is required, the whole amount should be written in figures.

> about 4.6 billion years old
> 1.2 million metric tons of grain
> the last 600 million years
> $7.25 million
> $3,456,000,000
> *but* 200,000 years   *not*   200 thousand years

NOTE: In the United Kingdom, the word *billion* refers to an amount that in the United States is called *trillion*. In the American system each of the denominations above 1,000 millions (the American billion) is one thousand times the one preceding (thus, one trillion equals 1,000 billions; one quadrillion equals 1,000 trillions). In the British system the first denomination above 1,000 millions (the British milliard) is one thousand times the preceding one, but each of the denominations above 1,000 milliards (the British billion) is one million times the preceding one (thus, one trillion equals 1,000,000 billions; one quadrillion equals 1,000,000 trillions).

Ordinal Numbers

1. Ordinal numbers generally follow the styling rules for cardinal numbers that are listed above in the section on Numbers as Words or Figures: if a figure would be required for the cardinal form of a number, it should also be used for the ordinal form; if conventions call for a written-out form, it should be used for both cardinal and ordinal numbers. In technical writing, however, as well as in footnotes and tables, all ordinal numbers are written as figure-plus-suffix combinations. In addition, certain ordinal numbers—those specifying percentiles and latitudinal lines are common ones—are conventionally set as figures in both general and technical writing.

> the sixth Robert de Bruce
> the ninth grade
> the 9th and 14th chapters
> his twenty-third try
> the 20th century
> the 98th Congress
> the 12th percentile
> the 40th parallel

2. The forms *second* and *third* may be written with figures as *2d* or *2nd, 3d* or *3rd, 22d* or *22nd, 93d* or *93rd, 102d* or *102nd*. A period does not follow the suffix.

Roman Numerals

Roman numerals, which may be written either in capital or lowercase letters, are conventional in the specific situations described below. Roman numerals are formed by adding the numerical values of letters as they are arranged in descending order going from left to right. If a letter with a smaller numerical value is placed to the left of a letter with a greater numerical value, the value of the smaller is subtracted from the value of the larger. A bar placed over a numeral ($\bar{V}$) multiplies its value by one thousand. A list of Roman numerals and their Arabic equivalents is given in the table on page 128.

1. Roman numerals are traditionally used to differentiate rulers and popes that have identical names.

> Elizabeth II   Innocent X
> Henry VIII   Louis XIV

Arabic and Roman Numerals

Name	Arabic Numeral	Roman Numeral
zero	0	
one	1	I
two	2	II
three	3	III
four	4	IV
five	5	V
six	6	VI
seven	7	VII
eight	8	VIII
nine	9	IX
ten	10	X
eleven	11	XI
twelve	12	XII
thirteen	13	XIII
fourteen	14	XIV
fifteen	15	XV
sixteen	16	XVI
seventeen	17	XVII
eighteen	18	XVIII
nineteen	19	XIX
twenty	20	XX
twenty-one	21	XXI
twenty-two	22	XXII
twenty-three	23	XXIII
twenty-four	24	XXIV
twenty-five	25	XXV
twenty-six	26	XXVI
twenty-nine	29	XXIX
thirty	30	XXX
thirty-one	31	XXXI
thirty-two	32	XXXII
forty	40	XL
fifty	50	L
sixty	60	LX
seventy	70	LXX
eighty	80	LXXX
ninety	90	XC
one hundred	100	C
one hundred one *or* one hundred and one	101	CI
one hundred two *or* one hundred and two	102	CII
two hundred	200	CC
three hundred	300	CCC
four hundred	400	CD
five hundred	500	D
six hundred	600	DC
seven hundred	700	DCC
eight hundred	800	DCCC
nine hundred	900	CM
one thousand	1,000	M
two thousand	2,000	MM
five thousand	5,000	V̄
ten thousand	10,000	X̄
one hundred thousand	100,000	C̄
one million	1,000,000	M̄

2. Roman numerals are used to differentiate related males who have the same name. The numerals are used only with a person's full name and, unlike the similar forms *Junior* and *Senior*, they are placed after the surname with no intervening comma. Ordinals are sometimes used instead of Roman numerals.

James R. Watson II	James R. Watson 2nd *or* 2d
James R. Watson III	James R. Watson 3rd *or* 3d
James R. Watson IV	James R. Watson 4th

NOTE: Possessive patterns for these names are the following:

singular	James R. Watson III's (*or* 3rd's *or* 3d's) house
plural	the James R. Watson IIIs' (*or* 3rds' *or* 3ds') house

3. Roman numerals are used to differentiate certain vehicles and vessels, such as yachts, that have the same name. If the name is italicized, the numeral is italicized also. Names of American spacecraft formerly bore Roman numerals, but Arabic numerals are now used.

> *Shamrock V*
>
> The U.S. spacecraft *Rangers VII, VIII,* and *IX* took pictures of the moon.
>
> On July 20, 1969, *Apollo 11* landed on the moon.

4. Lowercase Roman numerals are often used to number book pages that precede the regular Arabic sequence, as in a foreword, preface, or introduction.

5. Roman numerals are often used in enumerations to list major headings. An example of an outline with Roman-numeral headings is shown on page 140.

6. Roman numerals are sometimes used to specify a particular act and scene of a play or a particular volume in a collection. In this system, capitalized Roman numerals are used for the number of the act, and lowercase Roman numerals for the number of the scene. Arabic numerals are increasingly used for these purposes, however.

Roman style	*Arabic style*
Richard II, Act II, scene i	Act 2, scene 1
Hamlet, I.i.63	Act 1, scene 1, line 63 *or* 1.1.63
II, iii, 13–20	2, 3, 13–20

7. Roman numerals are found as part of a few established technical terms such as blood-clotting factors, quadrant numbers, and designations of cranial nerves. Also, chords in the study of music harmony are designated by capital and lowercase Ro-

man numerals. For the most part, however, technical terms
that include numbers express them in Arabic form.

> blood-clotting factor VII
> quadrant III
> the cranial nerves II, IV, and IX
> Population II stars
> type I error
>   *but*
> adenosine 3′, 5′-monophosphate
> cesium 137
> PL/1 programming language

Punctuation, Spacing, and Inflection

This section explains general rules for the use of commas, hyphens, and spacing in compound and large numbers, as well as
the plural forms of numbers. For the styling of specific categories
of numbers, such as dates, money, and decimal fractions, see the
section on Specific Styling Conventions in this chapter.

Commas and Spaces in Large Numbers

1. In general writing, with the exceptions explained in paragraph 3 below, figures of four digits may be styled with or
   without a comma; the punctuated form is more common. In
   scientific writing, these numerals are usually styled with a
   comma (but see paragraph 4 below). If the numerals form
   part of a tabulation, commas are necessary so that four-digit
   numerals can align with numerals of five or more digits.

   > 2,000 case histories   *or less commonly*   1253 people

2. Whole numbers of five digits or more (but not decimal fractions) use a comma or a space to separate three-digit groups,
   counting from the right. Commas are used in general writing;
   either spaces or commas are used in technical writing.

   > a fee of $12,500
   > 15,000 units   *or*   15 000 units
   > a population of 1,500,000   *or*   1 500 000

3. Certain types of numbers do not conform to these conventions. Decimal fractions and serial and multidigit numbers in
   set combinations, such as the numbers of policies, contracts,
   checks, streets, rooms, suites, telephones, pages, military
   hours, and years, do not contain commas. Numerals used in
   binary notation are also written without commas or spaces.

check 34567
page 209
Room 606
1650 hours
the year 1929
Policy No. 33442
10011
111010

NOTE: Year numbers of five or more digits (as geological or archeological dates) do contain a comma.

The Wisconsin glaciation lasted from approximately 70,000 to 10,000 years B.P.

4. In technical and scientific writing, lengthy figures are usually avoided by the use of special units of measure and by the use of multipliers and powers of ten. When long figures are written, however, each group of three digits may be separated by a space counting from the decimal point to the left and the right. If the digits are separated by a comma instead of a space, neither commas nor spaces are placed to the right of the decimal point. Whichever system is used should be applied consistently to all numbers with four or more digits.

27 483 241
23.000 003
27 483.241 755
27,483,241
23.000003
27,483.241755

Hyphens

5. Hyphens are used with written-out numbers between 21 and 99.

forty-one
forty-first
four hundred twenty-two
the twenty-fifth day

6. A hyphen is used between the numerator and the denominator of a fraction that is written out when that fraction is used as a modifier. A written-out fraction consisting of two words only (as *two thirds*) is usually styled open, although the hyphenated form is common also. Multiword numerators and denominators are usually hyphenated. If either the numerator or the denominator is hyphenated, no hyphen is used between them. For more on fractions, see pages 140–141.

a two-thirds majority of the staff
three fifths of her paycheck

seven and four fifths
forty-five hundredths
four five-hundredths

7. Numbers that form the first part of a compound modifier expressing measurement are followed by a hyphen. An exception to this practice is that numbers are not followed by a hyphen when the second part of the modifier is the word *percent*.

   a 5-foot board
   a 28-mile trip
   a 10-pound weight
   an eight-pound baby
   a 680-acre ranch
   a 75 percent reduction

8. An adjective or adverb made from a numeral plus the suffix *-fold* contains a hyphen, while a similar term made from a written-out number is styled solid. (For more on the use of suffixes with numbers, see page 106 in Chapter 3, "Plurals, Possessives, and Compounds.")

   a fourfold increase
   increased 20-fold

9. Serial numbers, such as social security or engine numbers, often contain hyphens that make lengthy numerals more readable.

   020-42-1691

10. Numbers are usually not divided at the end of a line. If division is unavoidable, the break occurs only after a comma. End-of-line breaks do not occur at decimal points, and a name with a numerical suffix (as *Elizabeth II*) is not divided between the name and the numeral.

Inclusive Numbers

11. Inclusive numbers—those which express a range—are separated either by the word *to* or by an en dash, which serves as an arbitrary equivalent of the phrase "(up) to and including" when used between dates and other inclusive numbers. (The en dash is explained further in the section on Dash, beginning on page 29, in Chapter 1, "Punctuation.") En dashes are used in tables, parenthetical references, and footnotes to save space. In running text, however, the word *to* is more often used.

   pages 40 to 98
   pages 40–98
   pp. 40–98

14–18 months
the years 1960–1965
spanning the years 1915 to 1941
the decade 1920–1930
the fiscal year 1984–1985

NOTE: Inclusive numbers separated by an en dash are not used in combination with the words *from* or *between,* as in "from 1955–60" or "between 1970–90." Instead, phrases like these are written as "from 1955 to 1960" or "between 1970 and 1990."

12. Units of measurement expressed in words or abbreviations are usually used only after the second element of an inclusive number. Symbols, however, are repeated.

> an increase in dosage from 200 to 500 mg
> running 50 to 75 miles every week
> ten to fifteen dollars
> 30 to 35 degrees Celsius
> *but*
> $50 to $60 million
> 45° to 48° F
> 45°–48°
> 3'–5' long

13. Numbers that are part of an inclusive set or range are usually styled alike: figures with figures, spelled-out words with other spelled-out words. Similarly, approximate numbers are usually not paired with exact numbers.

> from 8 to 108 absences
> five to twenty guests
> 300,000 to 305,000   *not*   300 thousand to 305,000

14. Inclusive page numbers and dates that use the en dash may be written in full (1981–1982) or elided (1981–82). Both stylings are widely used. However, inclusive dates that appear in titles and other headings are almost never elided. Dates that appear with era designations are also not elided.

> 467–68   *or*   467–468
> 550–602
> 203–4   *or*   203–204
> 552–549 B.C.
> 1724–27   *or*   1724–1727
> 1463–1510
> 1800–1801

Plurals

15. The plurals of written-out numbers are formed by the addition of *-s* or *-es.*

Back in the thirties these roads were unpaved.
Christmas shoppers bought the popular toy in twos and threes.

16. The plurals of figures are formed by adding -*s*. Some writers and publications prefer to add an apostrophe before the -*s*. For more on the plurals of figures, see the section on Plurals, beginning on page 82, in Chapter 3, "Plurals, Possessives, and Compounds," and the section on Apostrophe, beginning on page 5, in Chapter 1, "Punctuation."

This ghost town was booming back in the 1840s.
The first two artificial hearts to be implanted in human patients were Jarvik-7s.
but also
linen manufacture in France in the 1700's
1's and *7*'s that looked alike

Specific Styling Conventions

The following paragraphs describe styling practices commonly followed for specific types of situations involving numbers. The paragraphs are arranged under the following alphabetical headings:

Addresses
Dates
Degrees of Temperature and Arc
Enumerations and Outlines
Fractions and Decimal Fractions
Money
Percentages
Proper Names
Ratios
Serial Numbers and Miscellaneous Numbers
Time of Day
Units of Measurement

Addresses

1. Arabic numerals are used for all building, house, apartment, room, and suite numbers except for *one,* which is written out.

6 Lincoln Road
1436 Fremont Street
Apt. 281, Regency Park Drive
Room 617, McClaskey Building
but
One Bayside Drive
One World Trade Center

NOTE: When the address of a building is used as its name, the number in the address is written out.

Fifty Maple Street

2. Numbered streets have their numbers written as ordinals. There are two distinct conventions for the styling of numbered street names. The first, useful where space is limited, calls for Arabic numerals to denote all numbered streets above Twelfth; numbered street names from First through Twelfth are written out. A second, more formal, convention calls for the writing out of all numbered street names up to and including One Hundredth.

19 South 22nd Street
167 West Second Avenue
One East Ninth Street
145 East 145th Street
122 East Forty-second Street
36 East Fiftieth
in the Sixties (streets from 60th to 69th)
in the 120s (streets from 120th to 129th)

NOTE: A disadvantage of the first convention is that the direct juxtaposition of the house or building number and the street number may occur when there is no intervening word such as a compass direction. In these cases, a spaced hyphen or en dash may be inserted to distinguish the two numbers, or the second convention may be used and the street number written out.

2018–14th Street
2018 Fourteenth Street

3. Arabic numerals are used to designate interstate, federal, and state highways and, in some states, county roads.

U.S. Route 1   *or*   U.S. 1
Interstate 91   *or*   I-91
Massachusetts 57
Indiana 60
County 213

Dates

4. Year numbers are styled as figures. However, if a number representing a year begins a sentence, it may be written in full or the sentence rewritten to avoid beginning it with a figure. (For additional examples, see paragraph 3 in the section on Numbers as Words or Figures in this chapter.)

in 323 B.C.
before A.D. 40
1888–96

Fifteen eighty-eight marked the end to Spanish ambitions for the control of England.

or

Spanish ambitions for the control of England ended in 1588 with the destruction of their "Invincible Armada."

5. A year number may be abbreviated, or cut back to its last two digits, in informal writing or when an event is so well-known that it needs no century designation. In these cases an apostrophe precedes the numerals. For more on this use of the apostrophe, see the section on Apostrophe, beginning on page 5, in Chapter 1, "Punctuation."

He always maintained that he'd graduated from Korea, Clash of '52.

the blizzard of '88

6. Full dates (month, day, and year) may be styled in one of two distinct patterns. The traditional styling is the month-day-year sequence, with the year set off by commas that precede and follow it. An alternate styling is the inverted date, or day-month-year sequence, which does not require commas. This sequence is used in Great Britain, in U.S. government publications, and in the military.

traditional style
July 8, 1776, was a warm, sunny day in Philadelphia.
the explosion on July 16, 1945, at Alamogordo

military style
the explosion on 16 July 1945 at Alamogordo
Lee's surrender to Grant on 9 April 1865 at Appomattox

7. Ordinal numbers are not used in expressions of full dates. Even though the numbers may be pronounced as ordinals, they are written as cardinal numbers. Ordinals may be used, however, to express a date without an accompanying year, and they are always used when preceded in a date by the word *the*.

December 4, 1829
on December 4th   *or*   on December 4
on the 4th of December
on the 4th

8. Commas are usually omitted from dates that include the month and year but not the day. Alternatively, writers sometimes insert the word *of* between month and year.

in November 1805
back in January of 1981

9. Once a numerical date has been given, a reference to a related date may be written out.

   > After the rioting of August 3 the town was quiet, and by the seventh most troops had been pulled out.

10. All-figure dating (as 6-8-85 or 6/8/85) is inappropriate except in the most informal writing. It also creates a problem of ambiguity, as it may mean either June 8, 1985, or August 6, 1985.

11. References to specific centuries are often written out, although they may be expressed in figures, especially when they form the first element of a compound modifier.

   > the nineteenth century
   > a sixteenth-century painting
   > *but also*
   > a 12th-century illuminated manuscript
   > 20th-century revolutions

12. In general writing, the name of a specific decade often takes a short form. Although many writers place an apostrophe before the shortened word and a few capitalize it, both the apostrophe and the capitalization are often omitted when the context clearly indicates that a date is being referred to.

   > in the turbulent seventies
   > growing up in the thirties
   > *but also*
   > back in the 'forties
   > in the early Fifties

13. The name of a specific decade is often expressed in numerals, usually in plural form. (For more on the formation of plural numbers, see paragraphs 15 and 16 in the section on Punctuation, Spacing, and Inflection in this chapter.) The figure may be shortened with an apostrophe to indicate the missing numerals, but any sequence of such numbers should be styled consistently. (For more on this use of the apostrophe, see the section on Apostrophe, beginning on page 5, in Chapter 1, "Punctuation.")

   > during the 1920s   *or*   during the 1920's
   > the 1950s and 1960s   *or*   the '50s and '60s
   > *but not*
   > the 1950s and '60s
   > the 1930s and forties
   > *and not*
   > the '50's and '60's

14. Era designations precede or follow words that specify centuries or numerals that specify years. Era designations are unspaced and are nearly always abbreviated; they are usually printed as small capitals and typed as regular capitals, and they may or may not be punctuated with periods. Any date that is given without an era designation or context is understood to mean A.D. The two most commonly used abbreviations are B.C. (before Christ) and A.D. (*anno Domini,* "in the year of our Lord"). The abbreviation B.C. is placed after the date, while A.D. is usually placed before the date but after a century designation. (For more on the use of these abbreviations, see page 112 in Chapter 4, "Abbreviations.")

> 1792–1750 B.C.
> between 600 and 400 B.C.
> from the fifth or fourth millennium to c. 250 B.C.
> 35,000 B.C.
> between 7 B.C. and A.D. 22
> c. A.D. 1100
> the second century A.D.
> the seventeenth century

15. Less commonly used era designations include A.H. (*anno Hegirae,* "in the year of [Muhammad's] Hegira," or *anno Hebraico,* "in the Hebrew year"); B.C.E. (before the common era; a synonym for B.C.); C.E. (of the common era; a synonym for A.D.); and B.P. (before the present; often used by geologists and archeologists, with or without the word *year*). The abbreviation A.H. in both its meanings is usually placed before the year number, while B.C.E., CPE., and B.P. are placed after it.

> the tenth of Muharram, A.H. 61 (October 10, A.D. 680)
> the first century A.H.
> from the first century B.C.E. to the fourth century C.E.
> 63 B.C.E.
> the year 200 C.E.
> 5,000 years B.P.
> two million years B.P.

Degrees of Temperature and Arc

16. In technical writing, figures are generally used for quantities expressed in degrees. In addition, the degree symbol (°) rather than the word *degree* is used with the figure. With the Kelvin scale, however, neither the word *degree* nor the symbol is used with the figure.

> a 45° angle
> 6°40′10″N
> 32° F
> 0° C
> Absolute zero is zero kelvins or 0 K.

NOTE: In many technical and scientific publications, the figure, degree symbol, and the *F* or *C* that follows it are usually written without any space between them or with a space before the degree symbol but not after it. Another style followed in some scientific publications is to omit the degree symbol in expressions of temperature.

100°F *or* 100 °F *or* 100F
39°C *or* 39 °C *or* 39C

17. In general writing, the quantity expressed in degrees may or may not be written out, depending upon the styling conventions being followed. A figure is followed by the degree symbol or the word *degree;* a written-out number is always followed by the word *degree.*

latitude 43°19″ N
latitude 43 degrees N
a difference of 43 degrees latitude
The temperature has risen thirty degrees since this morning.

Enumerations and Outlines

18. Both run-in and vertical enumerations are often numbered. In run-in enumerations, each item is preceded by a number (or an italicized letter) enclosed in parentheses. The items in the list are separated by commas if the items are brief and have little or no internal punctuation; if the items are complex, they are separated by semicolons. The entire run-in enumeration is introduced by a colon if it is preceded by a full clause.

We feel that she should (1) increase her administrative skills, (2) pursue additional professional education, and (3) increase her production.

The oldest and most basic word-processing systems consist of the following: (1) a typewriter for keyboarding information, (2) a console to house the storage medium, and (3) the medium itself.

The vendor of your system should (1) instruct you in the care and maintenance of your system; (2) offer regularly scheduled maintenance to ensure that the system is clean, with lubrication and replacement of parts as necessary; and (3) respond promptly to service calls.

19. In vertical enumerations, the numbers are usually not enclosed in parentheses but are followed by a period. Each item in the enumeration begins its own line, which is either flush left or indented. Runover lines are usually aligned with the first word that follows the number, and figures are aligned on the periods that follow them. Each item on the list is usually capitalized if the items on the list are syntactically independent of the words that introduce them; however, style varies on this point, and use of a lowercase style for such items is fairly common. There is no terminal punctuation following the items unless at least one of the items is a complete sentence, in which case a period follows each item. Items that are syntactically dependent on the words that introduce them begin with a lowercase letter and carry the same punctuation marks that they would if they were a run-in series in a sentence.

Required skills include the following:
1. Shorthand
2. Typing
3. Transcription

To type a three-column table, follow this procedure:
1. Clear tab stops.
2. Remove margin stops.
3. Determine precise center of the page. Set a tab stop at center.

The vendor of your system should
1. instruct you in the care and maintenance of your system;
2. offer regularly scheduled maintenance to ensure that the system is clean, with lubrication and replacement parts as necessary; and
3. respond promptly to service calls.

20. Outlines make use of Roman numerals, Arabic numerals, and letters.

   I. Editorial tasks
     A. Manuscript editing
     B. Author contact
       1. Authors already under contract
       2. New authors
  II. Production responsibilities
     A. Scheduling
       1. Composition
       2. Printing and binding
     B. Cost estimates and bids
       1. Composition
       2. Printing and binding

Fractions and Decimal Fractions

21. In running text, fractions standing alone are usually written out. Common fractions used as nouns are usually styled as open compounds, but when they are used as modifiers they are usually hyphenated. For more on written-out fractions, see page 131.

two thirds of the paint
a two-thirds majority

three thirty-seconds
seventy-two hundredths
one one-hundredth

NOTE: Most writers try to find ways to avoid the necessity of writing out complicated fractions (as *forty-two seventy-fifths*).

22. Mixed fractions (fractions with a whole number, such as 3½) and fractions that form part of a unit modifier are expressed in figures in running text. A *-th* is not added to a figure fraction.

waiting 2½ hours
1¼ million population
a ⅞-mile course
a 2½-kilometer race

NOTE: When mixed fractions are typewritten, the typist leaves a space between the whole number and the fraction. The space is closed up when the number is set in print. Fractions that are not on the typewriter keyboard may be made up by typing the numerator, a virgule, and the denominator in succession without spacing.

23. Fractions used with units of measurement are expressed in figures.

$\frac{1}{10}$ km $\qquad\qquad\qquad$ ¼ mile

24. Decimal fractions are always set as figures. In technical writing, a zero is placed to the left of the decimal point when the fraction is less than a whole number. In general writing, the zero is usually omitted.

An example of a pure decimal fraction is 0.375, while 1.402 is classified as a mixed decimal fraction.
0.142857
0.2 gm
received 0.1 mg/kg diazepam i.v.
but
a .40 gauge shotgun

25. A comma is never inserted in the numbers following a decimal point, although spaces may be inserted as described and illustrated in paragraph 4 in the section on Punctuation, Spacing, and Inflection in this chapter.

26. Fractions and decimal fractions are usually not mixed in a text.

5½ lb. 2⅕ oz.
5.5 lb. 2.2 oz.
but not
5½ lb. 2.2 oz.

Money

27. Sums of money are expressed in words or figures, according to the conventions described in the first section of this chapter. If the sum can be expressed in one or two words, it is usually written out in running text. But if several sums are mentioned in the sentence or paragraph, all are usually expressed as figures. When the amount is written out, the unit of currency is also written out. If the sum is expressed in figures, the symbol of the currency unit is used, with no space between it and the numerals.

> We paid $175,000 for the house.
>
> My change came to 87¢.
>
> The shop charged $67.50 for hand-knit sweaters.
>
> The price of a nickel candy bar seems to have risen to more like forty cents.
>
> Fifty dollars was stolen from my wallet.
>
> forty thousand dollars
> fifty-two dollars

28. Monetary units of mixed dollars-and-cents amounts are expressed in figures.

> $16.75
> $307.02
> $1.95

29. Even-dollar amounts are often expressed in figures without a decimal point and zeros. But when even-dollar amounts are used in a series with or are near to amounts that include dollars and cents, the decimal point and zeros are usually added for consistency. The dollar sign is repeated before each amount in a series or inclusive range; the word *dollar* may or may not be repeated.

> The price of the book rose from $7.95 in 1970 to $8.00 in 1971 and then to $8.50 in 1972.
>
> The bids were eighty, ninety, and one hundred dollars.
>
> *or*
>
> The bids were eighty dollars, one hundred dollars, and three hundred dollars.

30. Sums of money given in round units of millions or above are usually expressed in a combination of figures and words, either with a dollar sign or with the word *dollars*. For more on the handling of round numbers, see paragraphs 7 and 8 in the section on Numbers as Words or Figures in this chapter.

> 60 million dollars
> a $10 million building program
> $4.5 billion

31. In legal documents a sum of money is usually written out fully, with the corresponding figures in parentheses immediately following.

twenty-five thousand dollars ($25,000)

Percentages

32. In technical writing and in tables and footnotes, specific percentages are styled as figure plus unspaced percent sign (%). In general writing, the percentage number may be expressed as a figure or spelled out, depending upon the conventions that apply to it. The word *percent* rather than the symbol is used in nonscientific texts.

technical	*general*
15%	15 percent
13.5%	87.2 percent
	Twenty-five percent of the office staff was out with the flu.
	a four percent increase

33. The word *percentage* or *percent,* used as a noun without an adjacent numeral, should never be replaced by a percent sign.

Only a small percentage of the test animals exhibited a growth change.

The clinic treated a greater percentage of outpatients this year.

34. In a series or unit combination the percent sign should be included with all numbers, even if one of the numbers is zero.

a variation of 0% to 10%

Proper Names

35. Numbers in the names of religious organizations and of churches are usually written out in ordinal form. Names of specific ruling houses and governmental bodies may include ordinals, and these are written out if they are one hundred or below. A few ruling houses, however, are traditionally designated by Roman numerals that follow the name.

First Church of Christ, Scientist
Third Congregational Church
Seventh-Day Adventists
Fifth Republic
Third Reich
First Continental Congress
but
Egyptian tombs from Dynasty XI

36. Names of electoral, judicial, and military units may include ordinal numbers that precede the noun. Numbers of one hundred or below may be either written out or styled as numerals.

First Congressional District
Twelfth Precinct
Ninety-eighth Congress   *or*   98th Congress
Circuit Court of Appeals for the Third Circuit
United States Eighth Army   *or*   8th United States Army

At H hour, the 32d would drive forward to seize the 77th Division's position southeast of Maeda.

The assault was led by the 54th Massachusetts, the first black regiment recruited in a free state.

37. Specific branches of labor unions and fraternal organizations are conventionally identified by an Arabic numeral usually placed after the name.

International Brotherhood of Electrical Workers Local 42
Elks Lodge No. 61
Local 98 Operating Engineers

Ratios

38. Ratios expressed in figures use a colon, a hyphen, a virgule, or the word *to* as a means of comparison. Ratios expressed in words use a hyphen, or the word *to*.

a 3:1 chance
odds of 100 to 1
a 6-1 vote
22.4 mi/gal
a ratio of ten to four
a fifty-fifty chance

Serial Numbers and Miscellaneous Numerals

39. Figures are used to refer to things that are numbered serially, such as chapter and page numbers, addresses, years, policy and contract numbers, and so forth.

Serial No. 5274
vol. 5, p. 202
Permit No. 63709
column 2
paragraphs 5–7
Table 16
pages 420–515

40. Figures are also used to express stock market quotations, mathematical calculations, scores, and tabulations.

won by a score of 8 to 2
the tally: 322 ayes, 80 nays
3⅛ percent bonds
$3 \times 15 = 45$

Time of Day

41. In running text the time of day is usually spelled out when expressed in even, half, or quarter hours.

> Quitting time is four-thirty.
> By half past eleven we were all getting hungry.
> We should arrive at a quarter past five.

42. The time of day is also usually spelled out when it is followed by the contraction *o'clock* or when *o'clock* is understood.

> I plan to leave here at eight o'clock.
> He should be here by four at the latest.
> My appointment is at eleven o'clock.
> *or*
> My appointment is at 11 o'clock.

43. Figures are used to delineate a precise time.

> The patient was discharged at 9:15 in the morning.
> Her plane is due in at 3:05 this afternoon.
> The program starts at 8:30 in the evening.

44. Figures are also written when the time of day is used in conjunction with the abbreviations *a.m. (ante meridiem)* and *p.m. (post meridiem)*. The punctuated lowercase styling for these abbreviations is most common, but punctuated small capital letters are also frequently used. These abbreviations should not be used in conjunction with the words *morning* or *evening;* and the word *o'clock* should not be combined with either *a.m.* or *p.m.*

> 8:30 a.m.   *or*   8:30 A.M.
> 10:30 p.m.   *or*   10:30 P.M.
> 8 a.m.   *or*   8 A.M.
> *but*
> 9:15 in the morning
> 11:00 in the evening
> nine o'clock

NOTE: When twelve o'clock is written, it is often helpful to add the designation *midnight* or *noon,* as *a.m.* and *p.m.* sometimes cause confusion.

> twelve o'clock (midnight)   *or*   12:00 midnight
> twelve o'clock (noon)   *or*   12:00 noon

45. For consistency, even-hour times should be expressed with a colon and two zeros, when used in a series or pairing with any odd-hour times.

> He came at 7:00 and left at 9:45.

46. The 24-hour clock system—also called military time—uses no punctuation and is expressed without the use of *a.m., p.m.,* or *o'clock.*

from 0930 to 1100
at 1600 hours

Units of Measurement

47. In technical writing, numbers used with units of measurement—even numbers below ten—are expressed as numerals.

2 liters	12 miles
55 pounds	6 hectares
60 watts	15 cubic centimeters
20 kilometers	35 milligrams

48. General writing, on the other hand, usually treats these numbers according to the basic conventions explained in the first section of this chapter. However, in some cases writers achieve greater clarity by styling all numbers—even those below ten—that express quantities of physical measurement as numerals.

The car was traveling in excess of 80 miles an hour.

The old volume weighed three pounds and was difficult to hold in a reading position.

but also in some general texts
3 hours, 25 minutes
saw 18 eagles in 12 minutes
a 6-pound hammer
weighed 3 pounds, 5 ounces

49. When units of measurement are written as abbreviations or symbols, the adjacent numbers are always figures, in both general and technical texts.

6 cm	67.6 fl oz
1 mm	4′
10 cm^3	98.6°
3 kg	$4.25

50. When two or more quantities are expressed, as in ranges or dimensions or series, an accompanying symbol is usually repeated with each figure.

2′ x 4′
4″ by 6″ cards
temperature on successive days of 30°, 55°, 43°, and 58°
$400–$500

Chapter 6

Composition and Grammar

CONTENTS

No guide to effective communication can ignore the basic components of discourse: the word, the phrase, the clause, the sentence, and the paragraph. Each of these increasingly complex units contributes to the expression of a writer's ideas.

The simplest component of discourse is the word. The treatment of words in this chapter focuses on their grammatical function in a sentence. For a discussion of the ways in which plurals and possessives of words or compound words are formed, see Chapter 3, "Plurals, Possessives, and Compounds." General questions concerning the more complex language components of phrases, clauses, sentences, and paragraphs are also discussed in separate sections in this chapter.

Parts of Speech

Words have traditionally been classified into eight parts of speech: the adjective, adverb, conjunction, interjection, noun, preposition, pronoun, and verb. This classification system is based mainly on a word's inflectional features, its general grammatical functions, and its positioning within a sentence. On the following pages, these parts of speech are listed alphabetically and discussed briefly.

Adjective

An adjective is a word that typically describes or modifies the meaning of a noun. Adjectives serve to point out a quality of a thing named, to indicate its quantity or extent, or to specify a thing as distinct from something else.

Adjectives are often classified by the ways in which they modify or limit the meaning of a noun. The classifications commonly referred to are the following: descriptive adjectives, demonstrative adjectives, indefinite adjectives, interrogative adjectives, possessive adjectives, proper adjectives, relative adjectives, and articles.

A *descriptive adjective* describes something or indicates a quality, kind, or condition ("a *sick* person," "a *brave* soldier," "a *new* dress"). The *demonstrative adjectives,* such as *this* and *that,* point to what they modify in order to distinguish it from others. These two are the only adjectives with plural forms ("*this* child," "*these* children"; "*that* house," "*those* houses"). An *indefinite adjective* designates an unidentified or not immediately identifiable person or thing ("*some* books," "*other* hotels"). An *interrogative adjective* conveys the force of a question ("*Whose* office is this?" "*Which* book do you want?"). A *possessive adjective* is the possessive form of a personal pronoun ("*her* idea," "*his* job," "*my* car," "*our* savings plan," "*their* office," "*your* opinion"). A *proper adjective* is derived from a proper noun and takes its meaning from what characterizes the noun. It is usually capitalized ("*Victorian* furniture," "a *Puerto Rican* product," "*Keynesian* economics"). A *relative adjective* introduces an adjectival clause ("at the April conference, by *which* time the report should be finished") or a clause that functions as a noun ("the uncomfortable position of not knowing *which* course she should follow"). An *article* is one of a small group of words (as *a, an,* and *the*) that are used with nouns to limit or give definiteness to the application of a noun ("*a* condominium," "*an* honor," "*the* jetliner").

The following paragraphs describe some other types of adjectives. They also outline situations involving adjectives that are sometimes troublesome for writers.

1. **Absolute adjectives** Some adjectives (such as *prior, maximum, optimum, minimum,* and *first*) admit no comparison under ordinary circumstances (see paragraphs 4 and 5 below), because they represent ultimate conditions. These adjectives are called *absolute adjectives.* Some writers are careful to modify these adjectives with adverbs such as *almost, near,* or *nearly,* rather than *least, less, more, most,* or *very.*

   an almost fatal dose
   at near maximum capacity
   a more nearly perfect likeness

   NOTE: Many writers do compare and qualify this type of adjective in order to show connotations and shades of meaning they consider less than absolute.

a more perfect union
a less complete account

When in doubt about the comparability of an absolute adjective, one should check the definitions and examples of usage given for the adjective in a dictionary.

2. **Adjective/noun agreement** Most American grammar books insist that demonstrative adjectives used with the words *kind, sort,* and *type* + *of* + noun should agree in number with both nouns.

> these kinds of typewriters   *not*   these kind of typewriters
> those sorts of jobs   *not*   those sort of jobs
> this type of person   *not*   these type of people

This formulation generally accords with most formal American writing; however, in speech and in British English, usage patterns are more varied. In addition, the use of a plural demonstrative adjective with a singular *kind, sort,* or *type* is appearing more regularly in contemporary American writing, especially writing intended to have an informal or speechlike quality.

3. **Compared with adverbs** Both adjectives and adverbs describe or modify other words; however, adjectives can only modify nouns, while adverbs can modify verbs, adverbs, and adjectives. For more on the differences between adjectives and adverbs, see paragraph 14 below and paragraphs 4–6 under Adverb in this section.

4. **Comparison of adjectives** The main structural feature of an adjective is its ability to indicate degrees of comparison (positive, comparative, superlative) by addition of suffixal endings *-er/-est* to the base word, by addition of *more/most* or *less/least* before the base word, or by use of irregular forms.

positive	*comparative*	*superlative*
clean	cleaner	cleanest
meaningful	more meaningful	most meaningful
meaningful	less meaningful	least meaningful
bad	worse	worst

5. The comparative degree is used to show that the thing being modified has more (or less) of a particular quality than the one or ones to which it is being compared. The superlative degree is used to show that the thing being modified has the most (or least) of a quality out of all of the ones to which it is being compared. The superlative degree is most commonly used when there are more than two things being compared.

comparative
prices that were higher than those at other stores
a better report than our last one
the more expensive of the two methods

superlative
the highest prices in the area
the best report so far
the most expensive of the three methods

6. In general, the comparatives and superlatives of one-syllable adjectives are formed by adding -*er*/-*est* to the base word. The comparatives and superlatives of adjectives with more than two syllables are formed by adding *more* and *most* or *less* and *least* before the base word. The comparatives and superlatives of two-syllable adjectives are variously formed by adding -*er*/ -*est* to the base word or using *more* and *most* or *less* and *least* before the base word. When in doubt about the inflection of a particular adjective, one should consult a dictionary.

positive	*comparative*	*superlative*
big	bigger	biggest
loose	looser	loosest
empty	emptier	emptiest
narrow	narrower	narrowest
complex	more complex	most complex
concise	less concise	least concise
important	more important	most important
troublesome	less troublesome	least troublesome

7. Some adjectives are ordinarily not compared, because they are felt to represent ultimate conditions. For more on these adjectives, see paragraph 1, above.

8. **Coordinate and noncoordinate adjectives** Adjectives that share equal relationships to the nouns they modify are called *coordinate adjectives* and are separated from each other by commas.

    a concise, coherent essay
    a hard, flickering light

9. When the first of two adjectives modifies the noun plus a second adjective, the result is a pair of *noncoordinate adjectives*. Noncoordinate adjectives are not separated by commas.

    a low monthly fee
    the first warm day

10. **Double comparisons** Double comparisons are considered nonstandard and should be avoided.

    an easier method   *not*   a more easier method
    the easiest solution   *not*   the most easiest solution

11. **Incomplete or understood comparisons** Some comparisons are left incomplete because the context clearly implies the comparison. These are commonly used especially in advertising. It should be understood, however, that the use of incomplete comparisons is often considered careless or illogical in formal writing.

    > Get better buys here!
    > We have lower prices.

12. **Nouns used as adjectives** Nouns are frequently used to describe other nouns, and in this way they act like adjectives. For more on the use of nouns as modifiers, see paragraph 6 under Noun in this section and the discussion under Compounds That Function as Adjectives, pages 97–102.

13. **Placement within a sentence** Adjectives may occur in the following positions within sentences: (1) preceding the nouns they modify, (2) following the nouns they modify, (3) following the verb *to be* and other linking verbs in the predicate-adjective position, and (4) following some transitive verbs used in the passive voice.

(1) the black hat	a dark, shabby coat
(2) an executive par excellence	painted the room blue
(3) a hat that is black	food that tastes stale
while I felt sick	
(4) a room that was painted blue	
passengers found dead at the crash site	

14. **Predicate adjectives** A predicate adjective modifies the subject of a linking verb (as *be, become, feel, taste, smell, seem*) which it follows.

    > She is happy.
    > The milk tastes sour.
    > The student seems puzzled.

    NOTE: Because some linking verbs (as *feel, look, smell, taste*) can also function as active verbs, which can in turn be modified by adverbs, writers are sometimes confused over whether they should use the adverbial or adjectival form of a modifier after the verb. The answer is that an adjective is used if the subject of the sentence is being modified. If the verb is being modified, an adverb is used. (For more examples, see paragraph 5 under Adverb in this section.)

    > Your report looks good. [adjective]
    > The colors feel right. [adjective]
    > The engine smells hot. [adjective]
    > They looked quickly at each item. [adverb]
    > He felt immediately for his wallet. [adverb]
    > She felt the corners carefully for dampness. [adverb]

Adverb

An adverb is a word or combination of words typically serving as a modifier of a verb, an adjective, another adverb, a preposition, a phrase, a clause, or a sentence and expressing some relation of manner or quality, place, time, degree, number, cause, opposition, affirmation, or denial.

Most commonly, adverbs take the form of an adjective with an -*ly* ending added to it (*actually, congenially, madly, really*). There are many exceptions to this pattern, however. For instance, adverbs based on adjectives ending in -*ly* (*costly, friendly, likely*) do not include an additional -*ly* ending but take the same form as the adjective. In addition, some adverbs do not end in -*ly* (*now, quite, too*).

Adverbs answer such questions as the following: "when?" ("Please reply *at once*"); "how long?" ("This job is taking *forever*"); "where?" ("She works *there*"); "in what direction?" ("Move the lever *upward*"); "how?" ("The staff moved *expeditiously* on the project"); and "to what degree?" ("The book was *very* popular").

1. **Basic uses** Adverbs modify verbs, adjectives, and other adverbs.

    She *carefully* studied the balance sheet.

    She gave the balance sheet *very* careful study.

    She studied the balance sheet *very* carefully.

2. Conjunctive adverbs join clauses or link sentences. (For more on this use of adverbs, see paragraphs 13–15 under Conjunction in this section.)

    You are welcome to join our car pool; *however,* please be ready by 7:00 a.m.

    He thoroughly enjoyed the symposium. *Indeed,* he was fascinated by the presentations.

3. In addition, adverbs may be essential elements of two-word verbs commonly having separate entries in dictionaries.

    Our staff will work *up* the specifications.

    We can work them *up* later.

4. **Compared with adjectives** Adverbs but not adjectives modify action verbs.

    not
    He answered very *harsh.*

    instead
    He answered very *harshly.*

5. Complements referring to the subject of a sentence and occurring after linking verbs conventionally take adjectives but

not adverbs. (For more examples, see paragraph 14 under Adjective in this section.)

not
He looks *badly* these days.
The letter sounded *strongly*.

instead
He looks *bad* these days.
The letter sounded *strong*.

and also
He looks *good* these days.
He looks *well* these days.

NOTE: In the last two examples, either *good* or *well* is acceptable, because both words are here functioning as adjectives in the sense of "healthy."

6. Adverbs but not adjectives modify adjectives and other adverbs.

not
She looked *dreadful* tired.

instead
She looked *dreadfully* tired.

7. **Comparison of adverbs** Most adverbs have three different forms to indicate degrees of comparison (positive, comparative, superlative). The positive form is the same as the base word *(quickly, loudly, near)*. The comparative form is usually shown by the addition of *more* or *less* before the base word *(more quickly, less quickly)*; the superlative form is usually shown by the addition of *most* or *least (most quickly, least quickly)*. However, a few adverbs (such as *fast, slow, loud, soft, early, late,* and *quick*) may be compared in two ways: by the method described above or by the addition of the suffixal endings *-er/-est* to the base word *(quick, quicker, quickest)*. For an explanation of the uses of the comparative and superlative forms, see paragraph 5 under Adjective in this section.

8. As a general rule, one-syllable adverbs use the *-er/-est* endings to show comparison. Adverbs of three or more syllables use *more/most* and *less/least*. Two-syllable adverbs take either form.

fast	faster	fastest
late	later	latest
easy	easier	easiest
madly	more madly	most madly
happily	more happily	most happily

9. Some adverbs (such as *quite* and *very*) cannot be compared.

10. **Double negatives** A combination of two negative adverbs (such as *not, hardly, never,* and *scarcely*) used to express a single negative idea is avoided in all but the most speechlike or informal writing.

> *not*
> We *cannot* see *hardly* any reason why we should buy this product.
>
> *instead*
> We *cannot* see any reason why we should buy this product.
>
> We can see *hardly* any reason why we should buy this product.

NOTE: Double negatives used as a means of understatement appear in all levels of writing, but their overuse can be annoying.

> We were *not unimpressed* by the progress he had made.

11. **Emphasis** Adverbs (such as *just* and *only*) are often used to emphasize other words. A writer should be aware of the various emphases that can result from the positioning of an adverb in a sentence.

> *emphasis on the action itself*
> He *just* nodded to me as he passed.
>
> *emphasis on timing of the action*
> He nodded to me *just* as he passed.

12. In some positions and contexts, these adverbs can be ambiguous.

> They will only tell it to you.

It is not clear whether this writer means that they will only tell it, not put it in writing, or that they will tell no one else. If the latter interpretation is intended, a slight shift of position would remove the uncertainty.

> They will tell it only to you.

13. **Placement within a sentence** Adverbs are generally positioned as close as possible to the words they modify if such a position will not result in misinterpretation.

> *unclear*
> A project that the board would support *completely* occupied her thinking.

It is unclear whether the writer means "would support completely" or "completely occupied her thinking." The adverb may be moved to another position, or the sentence may be recast, depending on intended meaning.

> *clear*
> A *project that the board would completely* support occupied her thinking.

or
Her thinking was *completely* occupied with a project that the board would support.

14. When an adverb separates *to* from the verbal element of an infinitive ("hope to really start"), the result is called a split infinitive. For a discussion of split infinitives, see paragraph 32 under Verb in this section.

15. In some cases, adverbs modify an entire sentence rather than a specific word or phrase within the sentence. Such adverbs are referred to as *sentence adverbs,* and their position can vary according to the emphasis one wishes to use.

    Fortunately they had already placed their order.
    They *fortunately* had already placed their order.
    They had already placed their order, *fortunately.*

16. **Relative adverbs** Relative adverbs (such as *when, where, why*) introduce subordinate clauses. (For more on subordinate clauses, see the section on Clauses, beginning on page 185.)

    They met at a time *when* prospects were good.
    I went into the room *where* they were sitting.
    Everyone knows the reason *why* she did it.

Conjunction

A conjunction is a word or phrase that joins together words, phrases, clauses, or sentences. Conjunctions may occur in many different positions in a sentence, although they ordinarily do not appear at the end of a sentence unless the sentence is elliptical. There are three main types of conjunctions: *coordinating, correlative,* and *subordinating.* In addition to these three types of conjunctions, the English language has transitional adverbs and adverbial phrases called *conjunctive adverbs.* These function as conjunctions even though they are customarily classified as adverbs. A definition and discussion of the three types of conjunctions and of conjunctive adverbs follows. (For information about punctuating sentences with conjunctions, see paragraphs 1–5, 23, and 26–28 under Comma, pages 13–15 and 19–20, and paragraphs 1–5 under Semicolon, pages 48–50.)

Coordinating conjunctions Coordinating conjunctions (such as *and, but, for, or, nor, so,* and *yet*) join together grammatical elements of equal weight. The elements may be words, phrases, subordinate clauses, main clauses, or complete sentences.

1. Coordinating conjunctions are used to join elements, to exclude or contrast, to offer alternatives, or to propose reasons, grounds, or a result.

joining elements
She ordered pencils, pens, *and* erasers.
Sales were slow, *and* they showed no sign of improvement.
excluding or contrasting
He is a brilliant *but* arrogant man.
They offered a promising plan, *but* it had not yet been tested.
alternative
She can wait here *or* go on ahead.
reason or grounds
The report is useless, *for* its information is no longer current.
result
His diction is excellent, *so* every word is clear.

2. A comma is used before a coordinating conjunction linking coordinate clauses, especially when these clauses are lengthy. For more on the use of Commas between clauses, see paragraphs 1–4 under Comma, pages 13–14.

   We encourage applications from all interested persons, *but* we do have high professional standards that the successful applicant must meet.

3. Coordinating conjunctions should link equal grammatical elements—for example, adjectives with other adjectives, nouns with other nouns, participles with other participles, clauses with other equal-ranking clauses, and so on. Combining unequal grammatical elements may result in unbalanced sentences.

   unbalanced (*and* links a participial phrase with an adverbial clause)
   Having become disgusted *and* because he was tired, he left the meeting.
   balanced (*and* links two adjectives)
   Because he was tired *and* disgusted, he left the meeting.
   Having become tired *and* disgusted, he left the meeting.

4. Coordinating conjunctions should not be used to string together excessively long series of elements, regardless of their grammatical equality.

   strung-out
   We have sustained enormous losses in this division, *and* we have realized practically no profits even though the sales figures indicate last-quarter gains, *and* we are therefore reorganizing the entire management structure as well as cutting back on personnel.
   tightened
   Because this division has sustained enormous losses and has realized only insignificant profits even with its last-quarter sales gains, we are totally reorganizing its management. We are also cutting back on personnel.

5. The choice of just the right coordinating conjunction for a particular verbal situation is important: the right word will pinpoint the writer's true meaning and intent and will emphasize the most relevant idea or point of the sentence. The following three sentences show increasingly stronger degrees of contrast through the use of different conjunctions:

neutral
He works hard *and* doesn't progress.

more contrast
He works hard *but* doesn't progress.

stronger contrast
He works hard, *yet* he doesn't progress.

6. The coordinating conjunction *and/or* linking two elements of a compound subject often poses a problem: should the verb that follows be singular or plural? A subject comprising singular nouns connected by *and/or* may be considered singular or plural, depending on the meaning of the sentence.

singular
All loss *and/or* damage is to be the responsibility of the sender. [one or the other and possibly both]

plural
John R. Westlake *and/or* Maria A. Artandi are hereby *appointed* as the executors of my estate. [both executors are to act, or either of them is to act if the other dies or is incapacitated]

Correlative conjunctions Correlative conjunctions are coordinating conjunctions that are regularly used in pairs, although they are not placed adjacent to one another.

7. Correlative conjunctions are used to link alternatives and equal elements.

alternatives
Either you go *or* you stay.
He had *neither* looks *nor* wits.

equal elements
Both typist *and* writer should understand the rules of punctuation.
Not only was there inflation, *but* there was *also* unemployment.

8. Because they link equal grammatical elements, correlative conjunctions should be placed as close as possible to the elements they join.

misplaced (joining clause and verb phrase)
Either I must send a telex *or* make a long-distance call.

repositioned (joining two verb phrases)
I must *either* send a telex *or* make a long-distance call.

9. The most common negative counterpart to *either . . . or* is *neither . . . nor,* although some people use *neither . . . or. Or* may also occur in combination with *no.*

> He received *neither* a promotion *nor* a raise.
> He received *neither* a promotion *or* a raise.
> He received *no* promotion *or* raise.

Subordinating conjunction Subordinating conjunctions join a subordinate or dependent clause to a main clause.

10. Subordinating conjunctions are used to express cause, condition or concession, manner, purpose or result, time, place or circumstance, and alternative conditions or possibilities.

> *cause*
> *Because* she learns quickly, she is doing well in her new job.
> *condition or concession*
> Don't call *unless* you have the information.
>
> *manner*
> He looks *as though* he is ill.
> We'll do it *however* you tell us to.
>
> *purpose or result*
> She routes the mail early *so that* they can read it.
> *time*
> She kept meetings to a minimum *when* she was president.
>
> *place or circumstance*
> I don't know *where* he has gone.
> He tries to help out *wherever* it is possible.
>
> *conditions or possibilities*
> It was hard to decide *whether* I should go or stay.

11. The subordinating conjunction *that* introduces several kinds of subordinate clauses, including those used as noun equivalents (such as a subject or an object of a verb or as a predicate nominative).

> Yesterday I learned *that* he has been sick for over a week.

12. In introducing subordinate clauses, subordinating conjunctions deemphasize less important ideas in favor of more important ideas. The writer must take care that the point he or she wishes to emphasize is in the main clause and that the points of less importance are subordinated. Notice how differently these two versions strike the reader.

> We were just coming out of the door *when* the building burst into flames.
> *As* we were just coming out of the door, the building burst into flames.

Conjunctive adverb Conjunctive adverbs are transitional adverbs and adverbial phrases that express relationships between two units of discourse (as two main clauses, two complete sentences, or two or more paragraphs). Conjunctive adverbs are classed as adverbs, but they function as conjunctions when they are used as connectives. Some common conjunctive adverbs are listed below.

accordingly	incidentally
also	in conclusion
anyhow	indeed
anyway	in fact
as a result	later
besides	likewise
consequently	moreover
e.g.	namely
finally	nevertheless
first	on the contrary
for example	otherwise
for instance	second
furthermore	still
further on	that is (to say)
hence	then
however	therefore
i.e.	to be sure
in addition	too

13. Conjunctive adverbs are used to express addition, to add emphasis, to express contrast or discrimination, to introduce illustrations or elaborations, to express or introduce conclusions or results, or to orient elements of discourse as to time or space.

addition
This employee deserves a substantial raise; *furthermore,* she should be promoted.

emphasis
He is brilliant; *indeed,* he is a genius.

contrast or discrimination
The major responsibility lies with the partners; *nevertheless,* associates should be competent in decision-making.

illustrations or elaborations
Losses were due to several negative factors; *namely,* inflation, foreign competition, and restrictive government regulation.

conclusions or results
Government overregulation in that country reached a prohibitive level in the last quarter. *Thus,* we are phasing out all of our operations there.

time or space
First, we can remind them that their account is long overdue; *second,* we can say that we must consider consulting our attorneys if they do not meet their obligation.

14. Conjunctive adverbs are usually placed at the beginning of a clause or sentence. When they are placed later in the clause or sentence, additional emphasis is placed on them.

> The overdue shipment arrived this morning; *however*, we must point out that it was incomplete.
>
> The overdue shipment arrived this morning; we must point out, *however*, that it was incomplete.

15. The misuse of conjunctive adverbs can lead to a problem known as *comma fault*. When a conjunctive adverb is used to connect two main clauses, a semicolon should be used; a comma will not suffice. (For more on comma fault and punctuation between main clauses, see paragraphs 1–4 under Comma, pages 13–14 and paragraph 5 under Semicolon, pages 49–50.)

> *comma fault*
> The company had flexible hours, *however* its employees were expected to abide by their selected arrival and departure times.
>
> *repunctuated*
> The company had flexible hours; *however*, its employees were expected to abide by their selected arrival and departure times.

Interjection

Interjections are exclamatory or interrupting words or phrases that express an emotion. Interjections are usually independent clauses that lack grammatical connection with the rest of the sentence. They often stand alone.

1. Interjections may be stressed or ejaculatory words, phrases, or even short sentences.

> Absurd!
> No, no!
> Get out!
> Not now!

2. Interjections may also be so-called "sound" words, such as those representing shouts, hisses, or cries:

> Shh! The meeting has begun.
> Pssst! Come over here.
> Ouch! That hurts.
> Ugh! What a horrible flavor.

3. Emphatic interjections expressing forceful emotions use exclamation points.

> Fire!
> What an awful time we had!

4. Mildly stressed words or sentences may be punctuated with commas and periods.

> *Ah,* that's my idea of a terrific deal.
> *Well, well,* so that's the solution.
> *Oh,* you're probably right.

5. Interjections should be sparingly used in discourse, and then only to signal genuine emotion or for strong emphasis.

Noun

A noun is a word that is the name of something (as a person, animal, place, object, quality, concept, or action). Nouns are used in a sentence as the subject or object of a verb, as the object of a preposition, as a predicate after a linking verb, as an appositive name, or as a name in an absolute construction.

Nouns exhibit these characteristic features: they are inflected for possession; they have number (that is, they are either singular or plural); they are often preceded by determiners (as *a, an, the; this, that, these, those; all, every,* and other such qualifiers; *one, two, three,* and other such numerical quantifiers; *his, her, their,* and other such pronominal adjectives); a few of them still show gender differences (as masculine *host, actor,* feminine *hostess, actress*); and many of them are formed by adding a suffix (such as *-ance, -ist, -ness,* and *-tion*).

1. Basic uses Nouns are used as subjects, direct objects, objects of prepositions, indirect objects, retained objects, predicate nominative, objective complements, and appositives and in direct address.

> *subject*
> The *office* was quiet.
> *direct object*
> He locked the *office.*
> *object of a preposition*
> The file is in the *office.*
> *indirect object*
> He gave his *client* the papers.
> *retained object*
> His client was given the *papers.*
> *predicate nominative*
> Mrs. Adams is the managing *partner.*
> *objective complement*
> They made Mrs. Adams managing *partner.*
> *appositive*
> Mrs. Adams, the managing *partner,* wrote that memorandum.
> *direct address*
> *Mrs. Adams,* may I present Mr. Bonkowski.

2. **Compound nouns** Because English is not a static and unchanging entity, many of its words undergo styling variations because of the changing preferences of its users. The styling of compound nouns (whether open, closed, or hyphenated) is especially subject to changing usage. No rigid set of rules can cover every possible variation or combination; however, some consistent patterns of usage can be discerned. For a description of these patterns, see the discussion under Compound Nouns, pages 93–97.

3. **Indefinite articles with nouns** Before a word or abbreviation beginning with a consonant *sound,* the article *a* is used. This is true even if the spelling of the word begins with a vowel.

a BA degree	a human
a hat	a U.S. Senator
a one	a door
a COD package	a union

4. Before *h-* in an unstressed or lightly stressed first syllable, the article *a* is more frequently used, although *an* is more usual in speech whether or not the *h-* is actually pronounced. Either is acceptable in speech or writing.

a historian   *or*   an historian
a heroic attempt   *or*   an heroic attempt
a hilarious performance   *or*   an hilarious performance

5. Before a word or abbreviation beginning with a vowel *sound,* the article *an* is used. This is true even if the spelling (especially of an abbreviation) begins with a consonant.

an icicle	an MIT professor
an hour	an unknown
an FCC report	an nth degree
an orange	an Rh factor

6. **Nominals** Nominals are words or groups of words that function as nouns. Adjectives, gerunds, and infinitives act as nominals. An example of an adjective used as a noun is the word *good* in the phrase "the good die young." Examples of gerunds and infinitives used as nouns are *seeing* in the clause "seeing is believing" and *to see* in the clause "to see is to believe." Noun phrases and noun clauses are also considered to be nominals. For more information about gerunds and infinitives, see paragraphs 12–14 under Verb in this section. For information about noun phrases and noun clauses, see pages 184 and 185–186 respectively.

7. **Nouns used as adjectives** A frequent practice in English is to use a noun as an adjective by placing it before another noun

(in the attributive position), as in *school board* or *office management*. When nouns are frequently combined in this way, they become familiar compounds like *profit margin, systems analysis, money market, box lunch*. Such compounds provide useful verbal shortcuts (e.g., office management = the management of an office or offices). However, care should be taken not to pile up so many of these noun modifiers that the reader has difficulty sorting out their meanings.

> *shorter but unclear*
> Management review copies of the Division II sales department machine parts file should be indexed.

> *longer but clear*
> Copies of the machine parts file from the Division II sales department should be indexed before being sent to management for review.

NOTE: Both of these sentences could be made clearer by hyphenating the compound nouns used as adjectives. For complete information about the treatment of this kind of compound, see the discussion under Compounds That Function as Adjectives, pages 97–102.

> Management-review copies of the Division II sales-department machine-parts file should be indexed.

8. **Plurals** The plurals of nouns are usually indicated by addition of an *-s* or *-es* to the base word, although some nouns (such as those of foreign origin) have irregular plurals. For complete information about the formation of plurals, see the discussion under Plurals, pages 82–88.

9. **Possessives** The possessive case is the only noun case indicated by inflection. Typically, the possessives of nouns are formed by the addition of an apostrophe plus *-s* to singular nouns or just an apostrophe to plural words ending in *-s*. For complete information about the formation of possessives, see the discussion under Possessives, pages 88–92.

10. **Proper nouns** Proper nouns are nouns that name a particular person, place, or thing and distinguish it from other members of the same class. The most obvious feature of proper nouns is that they are almost always capitalized. For complete information about capitalizing proper nouns, see the discussion under Proper Nouns, Pronouns, and Adjectives, pages 56–77.

Preposition

A preposition is a word that combines with a noun, pronoun, or noun equivalent (as a phrase or clause) to form a phrase that usually acts as an adverb, adjective, or noun.

Prepositions are not characterized by inflection, number, case, gender, or identifying suffixes. They can be identified chiefly by their position within sentences and by their grammatical functions. Prepositions may be simple, i.e., composed of only one element (*against, from, near, of, on, out,* or *without);* or they may be compound, i.e., composed of more than one element (*according to, by means of,* or *in spite of).*

1. **Basic uses** Prepositions are chiefly used to link nouns, pronouns, or noun equivalents to the rest of the sentence. A prepositional phrase is usually adverbial or adjectival in function.

> She expected resistance *on* his part.
> He sat down *beside* her.

2. **Conjunctions vs. prepositions** The words *after, before, but, for,* and *since* may function as either prepositions or conjunctions. Their position within the sentence identifies them as conjunctions or prepositions. Conjunctions link two words or sentence elements that have the same grammatical function. Prepositions precede a noun, pronoun, noun phrase, or noun equivalent.

> *conjunction*
> I was a bit concerned *but* not panicky. (*but* links two adjectives)
> *preposition*
> I was left with nothing *but* hope. (*but* precedes a noun)
> *conjunction*
> The device conserves fuel, *for* it is battery-powered. (*for* links two clauses)
> *preposition*
> The device conserves fuel *for* residual heating. (*for* precedes a noun phrase)

3. **Implied or unknown prepositions** If two words combine idiomatically with the same preposition, that preposition need not be used after both.

> We were antagonistic [*to*] and opposed *to* the whole idea.
>   *but*
> We are interested *in* and anxious *for* raises.

4. **Position** Prepositions may occur in the following positions: before nouns or pronouns ("*below* the desk," "*beside* them"); after adjectives ("antagonistic *to*," "insufficient *in*," "symbolic *of*"); and after the verbal elements of idiomatically fixed verb + preposition combinations ("take *for*," "get *after*," "come *across*").

5. There is no reason why a preposition cannot terminate a sentence, especially when it is an integral element in an idiomatically fixed verb phrase.

> His lack of organization is only one of the things I put up *with*.
> What does all this add up to?

6. **Use of** *between* **and** *among* Despite an unfounded notion to the contrary, the preposition *between* can be used of more than two items. It is especially appropriate to denote a one-to-one relationship, regardless of the number of items. *Between* can be used when the number is unspecified, when more than two are enumerated, and even when only one item is mentioned (but repetition is implied).

> Treaties established economic cooperation *between* nations.
> This is *between* you and me and the lamppost.
> He paused *between* every sentence to clear his throat.

Among is more appropriate where the emphasis is on overall distribution rather than individual relationships.

> There was discontent *among* the peasants.

NOTE: When *among* is automatically chosen for more than two, the results can sound strained.

> The author alternates *among* quotes, clichés, and street slang.

Pronoun

A pronoun is a word that is used as a substitute for a noun or noun equivalent, takes noun constructions, and refers to persons or things named or understood in the context. The noun or noun equivalent for which it substitutes is called the *antecedent*.

Pronouns exhibit all or some of the following characteristic features: case (nominative, possessive, objective); number (singular, plural); person (first, second, third person); and gender (masculine, feminine, neuter). Pronouns are divided into seven major categories, each with its own function. Each pronoun category is listed and described alphabetically in this section.

Demonstrative pronouns The words *this, that, these,* and *those* are classified as pronouns when they function as nouns (they are classified as demonstrative adjectives when they modify nouns; see the discussion under Adjective in this section).

1. Demonstrative pronouns point out the person or thing referred to and distinguish it from others of the same type.

> *These* are the best cookies I've ever eaten.
> *Those* are strong words.

2. They also distinguish between a person or thing nearby and one further away.

> *This* is my desk; *that* is yours.

3. A potentially troublesome situation occurs when a demonstrative pronoun introduces a sentence referring back to something previously mentioned. The reference should be clear and not cloudy:

> *cloudy*
> The heir's hemophilia, the influence of an unprincipled faith healer on the royal family, devastating military setbacks, general strikes, mass outbreaks of typhus, and repeated crop failures contributed to the revolution. *This* influenced the course of history.
>
> *clear*
> None of the participants in the political scandal kept records of what they said or did. *That* is most unfortunate, and it should be a lesson for the future.

Indefinite pronouns Indefinite pronouns designate an unidentified or not immediately identifiable person or thing. They are chiefly used as third-person references and do not distinguish gender. Examples of indefinite pronouns are the following: *all, another, any, anybody, anyone, anything, both, each, each one, either, everybody, everyone, everything, few, many, much, neither, nobody, none, no one, other, several, some, somebody, someone, something.*

4. Indefinite pronouns should agree in number with their verb. The following are singular and take singular verbs: *another, anything, each one, everything, much, nobody, no one, one, other, someone, something.*

> *Much is* being done.
> *No one wants* to go.

5. The following indefinite pronouns are plural and take plural verbs: *both, few, many, several.*

> *Many were* called; *few were* chosen.

6. Some indefinite pronouns (such as *all, any, none, some*) present problems because they may be either singular or plural, depending on whether they are used with mass nouns or count nouns (a *mass noun* identifies something not ordinarily thought of in terms of numbered elements; a *count noun* identifies things that can be counted).

> *with mass noun*
> *All* of the *property is* entailed.
> *None* of the *ink was* erasable.
> Not *any* of the *sky was* visible.

with count noun
All of our *bases are* covered.
None of the *clerks were* available.
Not *any* of the *stars were* visible.

7. The following are singular in form, and as such logically take singular verbs. However, because of their plural connotations, informal speech has established the use of plural pronoun references to them: *anybody, anyone, everybody, everyone, somebody.*

    I knew *everybody* by *their* first names.
    Don't tell *anyone; they* might spread the rumor.

8. Even in more formal contexts, expressions such as the following are used increasingly, especially as a result of attempts to avoid sexism in language:

    We called *everyone* by *their* first *names.*
    instead of
    We called *everyone* by *his* first *name.*

For more about avoiding sexism in the use of personal pronouns, see paragraph 22 below.

9. In some constructions an apparently singular indefinite pronoun may take a plural verb if the context makes it seem plural. The following two sentences illustrate how a singular indefinite pronoun may take either a singular or plural verb, depending on how the writer interprets *either*:

    Either of these pronunciations *is* acceptable.
    Either of these pronunciations *are* acceptable.

The conventional choice of verb would be *is*, because the subject of the sentence is the singular pronoun *either*. However, the proximity of the plural word *pronunciations*, together with the possibility of interpreting *either* to mean "one or both," lets the writer or speaker choose either a singular or a plural verb, depending on the interpretation of the subject.

10. The indefinite pronouns *any* and *anyone* are conventionally followed by *other(s)* or *else* when they form part of a comparison of two individuals in the same class.

    not
    Helen has more seniority than *anyone* in the firm.
    instead
    Helen has more seniority than *anyone else* in the firm.
    not
    Our house is older than *any* building on the block.
    instead
    Our house is older than *any other* building on the block.

The addition of *else* and *other* in the preceding sentences avoids the logical impossibility that Helen has more seniority than herself or that our house is older than itself. Likewise, it prevents the possible misreading that Helen is not a member of the firm or that our house is not on the block.

11. The antecedent of an indefinite pronoun should be clearly stated, not implied. A good check for a clear reference is to see if there is an antecedent in the sentence that could be substituted for the pronoun.

> *unclear*
> He's the author of a best-selling book on sailing, despite the fact that he's never set foot on *one*.
>
> *clear*
> He's the author of a best-selling book on sailing, despite the fact that he's never set foot on a sailboat.

12. Interrogative pronouns The interrogative pronouns *what, which, who, whom,* and *whose* as well as combinations of these words with the suffix *-ever* are used to introduce direct and indirect questions.

> *Who* is she?
> He asked me *who* she was.
> *Whom* did the article accuse?
> She asked *whom* the article accused.
> *Whoever* can that be?
> We wondered *whoever* that could be.

Personal pronouns Personal pronouns refer to beings and objects and reflect the person, number, and gender of those antecedents. Examples of personal pronouns are: *he, I, it, she, they, we, you.*

13. Most personal pronouns take different forms for the three cases.

	Nominative	Possessive	Objective
first person singular	I	my, mine	me
first person plural	we	our, ours	us
second person singular	you	your, yours	you
second person plural	you	your, yours	you
third person singular	he	his, his	him
	she	her, hers	her
	it	its, its	it
third person plural	they	their, theirs	them

14. A personal pronoun agrees in person, number, and gender with the word it refers to. However, the case of a pronoun is determined by its function within a sentence. The nominative case is used for a pronoun that acts as a subject of a sentence or as a predicate nominative (but see paragraph 15 below). The possessive case is used for pronouns that express possession or a similar relationship. The objective case is used for pronouns that are direct objects, indirect objects, retained objects, objects of prepositions, or objective complements.

> *You* and *I* thought the meeting was useful.
> My assistant and *I* attended the seminar.
> Our new candidate will be *you.*
> We all had *our* own offices.
> The vice president informed my assistant and *me* about the seminar.
> She gave *me* the papers.
> Just between *you* and *me,* the meeting was much too long.
> I was given *them* yesterday.
> That makes our new candidate *her.*

15. The nominative case after the verb *to be* (as in "It is I" and "This is she") is considered standard English and is preferred by strict grammarians, but the objective case (as in "It's me") also may be used without criticism, especially in spoken English.

> The only candidate left for that job may soon be she.
> *or*
> The only candidate left for that job may soon be her.

16. When a personal pronoun occurs in a construction introduced by *than,* the pronoun can be in the nominative or objective case. In formal writing, the use of the nominative case is the more frequent choice; in speech or informal writing, the objective case is often used.

> He received a bigger bonus than *she.*
> Kathy is ten years younger than *me.*

17. The suffixes *-self* and *-selves* combine only with the possessive case of the first- and second-person pronouns *(myself, ourselves, yourself, yourselves)* and with the objective case of the third-person pronouns *(himself, herself, itself, themselves).* Other combinations (as "hisself" and "theirselves") are considered nonstandard and should not be used.

18. Personal pronouns in the possessive case (such as *your, their, theirs, its*) do not contain apostrophes and should not be confused with similar-sounding contractions (such as *you're, they're, there's, it's*), which do contain apostrophes.

possessive personal pronoun	*contraction*
Put the camera in *its* case.	*It's* an expensive camera.
Whose camera is it?	*Who's* going to go?

19. When one uses the pronoun *I* or *me* with other pronouns or with other people's names, *I* or *me* should be last in the series:

Mrs. Smith and *I* were trained together.

He and *I* were attending the meeting.

The memorandum was directed to Ms. Montgomery and *me*.

20. Some companies prefer that writers use *we* and not *I* when speaking for their companies in business correspondence. *I* is more often used when a writer is referring only to himself or herself. The following example illustrates use of both within one sentence:

We [i.e., the writer speaks for the company] have reviewed the manuscript that you sent to *me* [i.e., the manuscript was sent only to the writer] on June 1, but *we* [a corporate or group decision] feel that it is too specialized a work to be marketable by *our* company.

21. While the personal pronouns *it, you,* and *they* are often used as indefinite pronouns in spoken English, they can be vague or even redundant in some contexts.

vague
They said at the seminar that the economy would experience a third-quarter upturn. (The question is: Who exactly is *they?*)

explicit
The economists on the panel at the seminar predicted a third-quarter economic upturn.

redundant
In the graph *it* says that production fell off by 50%.

lean
The graph indicates a 50% production drop.

22. Forms of the personal pronoun *he* and the indefinite pronoun *one* have been the standard substitutes for antecedents whose genders are mixed or irrelevant:

Present the letter to the executive for *his* approval.

Each employee should check *his* W-2 form.

If *one* really wants to succeed, *one* can.

However, many writers today who are concerned about sexism in language recast such sentences, where possible, to avoid generic use of the masculine pronoun:

Present the letter to the executive for approval.
All employees should check *their* W-2 forms.
Each employee should check *his or her* W-2 form.

The phrase *his or her* should be used sparingly, however, as it seems awkward and could certainly become tiresome if used frequently throughout a text. For more on avoiding the generic use of the masculine pronoun, see paragraph 8 above.

23. Reciprocal pronouns The reciprocal pronouns *each other* and *one another* are used in the object position to indicate a mutual action or cross relationship between the members comprised in a plural or compound subject.

They do not quarrel with *one another*.

Karen and Rachel spelled *each other* at driving on their trip.

24. Reciprocal pronouns may also be used in the possessive case:

The two secretaries borrowed *one another's* stationery.

The president and his vice president depend on *each other's* ideas.

25. Reflexive pronouns Reflexive pronouns express reflexive action or add extra emphasis to the subject of the sentence, clause, or verbal phrase in which they occur. Reflexive pronouns are formed by compounding the personal pronouns *him, her, it, my, our, them,* and *your* with *-self* or *-selves*. Reflexive pronouns are used when an object or subjective complement refers to the same thing as the foregoing noun or noun phrase.

She dressed *herself*.

The baby isn't *himself* this morning.

They asked *themselves* if they were being honest.

I *myself* am not afraid.

The cook told Jim to help *himself*.

Relative pronouns The relative pronouns are *that, what, which, who, whom,* and *whose,* as well as combinations of these with *-ever*. They introduce subordinate clauses acting as nouns or modifiers. While a relative pronoun itself does not exhibit number, gender, or person, it does determine the number, gender, and person of elements that follow it in the relative clause because of its implicit agreement with its antecedent. Consider, for instance, the following sentence:

People *who are* ready to start *their* jobs should arrive at 8:00 a.m.

In this sentence, the relative pronoun "who" refers to the plural subject "People," and it acts as the subject of the relative clause "who are ready to start their jobs." Because it refers to a plural word it acts like a plural word within its clause and therefore calls for the plural verb "are" and the plural pronoun "their."

26. The relative pronoun *who* typically refers to persons and some animals; *which,* to things and animals; and *that,* to both beings and things.

> a man who sought success
> a man whom we can trust
> Seattle Slew, who won horse racing's Triple Crown
> a book which sold well
> a dog which barked loudly
> a book that sold well
> a dog that barked loudly
> a man that we can trust

27. Relative pronouns can sometimes be omitted for the sake of brevity.

> The man *whom* I was talking to is the president.
>   *or*
> The man I was talking to is the president.

28. The relative pronoun *what* may be substituted for the longer and more awkward phrases "that which," "that of which," or "the thing which" in some sentences.

> *stiff*
> He was blamed for *that which* he could not have known.
>
> *easier*
> He was blamed for *what* he could not have known.

29. The problem of when to use *who* or *whom* has been blown out of proportion. The situation is very simple: formal written English makes a distinction between the nominative and objective cases of these pronouns when they are used as relatives or interrogatives.

> *nominative case*
> *Who* is she?
> *Who* does she think she is, anyway?
> She thinks she is the one *who* ought to be promoted.
> Give me a list of the ones *who* you think should be promoted.
>
> *objective case*
> *Whom* are you referring to?
> To *whom* are you referring?
> He's a man *whom* everyone should know.
> He's a man with *whom* everyone should be acquainted.

In speech and less formal writing, case distinctions and boundaries often become blurred, with *who* being freely used for *whom* except in set phrases such as "*To whom* it may concern." In such contexts, then, *who* may be used not only as the subject of the clause it introduces but also as the object of a verb in a clause that it introduces or as an interrogative.

> See the manager, Mrs. Keats, *who* you should be able to find in her office.
>
> *Who* should we tell?

30. *Whom* is commonly used as the object of a preposition in a clause that it introduces; however, the form *who* is commonly used to introduce a question even when it is the object of a preposition:

> Presiding is a judge *about whom* I know nothing.
> He is a man *for whom* I would gladly work.
> > *but*
> *Who* (rarely *whom*) are you going to listen to?
> *Who* (rarely *whom*) do you work for?

31. While the nominative form *who* can be used in the objective case in certain instances, substitution of the objective form *whom* in place of *who* is usually considered to be a hypercorrect, or overcompensating use. One should therefore avoid such usages as "*Whom* do you suppose is coming to the meeting?" which result from a mistaken notion that *whom* is somehow always more correct.

32. The relative pronouns *whoever* and *whomever* follow the same principles as *who* and *whom* in formal writing:

> *nominative*
> Tell *whoever* is going to research the case that . . . .
> He wants to help *whoever* needs it most.
>
> *objective*
> She makes friends with *whomever* she meets.

NOTE: In speech and less formal writing, however, as with *who* and *whom,* case distinctions become blurred, and *whoever* is used without criticism in most sentences:

> *Whoever* did she choose?

Verb

A verb is a word that is characteristically the grammatical center of a predicate and expresses an act, occurrence, or mode of being. Verbs are inflected for agreement with the subject and for mood, voice, or tense. Verbs typically have rather full descriptive meaning and characterizing quality, but they sometimes are almost completely devoid of these, especially when they are used as auxiliary or linking verbs.

Verbs exhibit the following characteristic features: inflection (*help, helps, helping, helped*), person (first, second, third person), number (singular, plural), tense (present, past, future), aspect (time relations other than the simple present, past, and future), voice (active, passive), mood (indicative, subjunctive, imperative), and suffixation (as by the typical suffixal markers *-ate, -en, -ify,* and *-ize*).

Inflection Regular verbs have four inflected forms signaled by the suffixes *-s* or *-es, -ed,* and *-ing.* The verb *help* as shown in the sentence above is regular. Most irregular verbs have four or five forms, as *see, sees, seeing, saw,* and *seen;* and one, the verb *be,* has eight: *be, is, am, are, being, was, were,* and *been.* When one is uncertain about a particular inflected form, one should consult a dictionary that indicates not only the inflections of irregular verbs but also those inflections resulting in changes in base-word spelling.

> blame; blamed; blaming
> spy; spied; spying
> picnic; picknicked; picnicking

A dictionary should also show variant inflected forms.

> bias; biased *or* biassed; biasing *or* biassing
> counsel; counseled *or* counselled; counseling *or* counselling
> diagram; diagramed *or* diagrammed; diagraming *or* diagramming
> travel; traveled *or* travelled; traveling *or* travelling

All of the foregoing forms may be found at their respective main entries in *Webster's Ninth New Collegiate Dictionary.* There are, however, a few rules that will aid one in ascertaining the proper spelling patterns of certain verb forms.

1. Verbs ending in a silent *-e* generally retain the *-e* before consonant suffixes (as *-s*) but drop the *-e* before vowel suffixes (as *-ed* and *-ing*).

> arrange; arranges; arranged; arranging
> hope; hopes; hoped; hoping
> require; requires; required; requiring
> shape; shapes; shaped; shaping

NOTE: A few verbs ending in a silent *-e* retain the *-e* before vowel suffixes in order to avoid confusion with other words.

> dye; dyes; dyed; dyeing (*vs.* dying)
> singe; singes; singed; singeing (*vs.* singing)

2. Monosyllabic verbs ending in a single consonant preceded by a single vowel double the final consonant before vowel suffixes (as *-ed* and *-ing*).

brag; bragged; bragging
grip; gripped; gripping
pin; pinned; pinning

3. Polysyllabic verbs ending in a single consonant preceded by a single vowel and having an accented last syllable double the final consonant before vowel suffixes (as *-ed* and *-ing*).

commit; committed; committing
control; controlled; controlling
occur; occurred; occurring
omit; omitted; omitting

NOTE: The final consonant of such verbs is not doubled when two vowels occur before the final consonant or when two consonants form the ending of the verb.

daub; daubed; daubing
soil; soiled; soiling
help; helped; helping
lurk; lurked; lurking
peck; pecked; pecking

4. Verbs ending in *-y* preceded by a consonant regularly change the *-y* to *-i* before all suffixes except *-ing*.

carry; carried; carrying
marry; married; marrying
study; studied; studying

NOTE: If the final *-y* is preceded by a vowel, it remains unchanged in suffixation.

delay; delayed; delaying
enjoy; enjoyed; enjoying
obey; obeyed; obeying

5. Verbs ending in *-c* add a *-k* when a suffix beginning with *-e* or *-i* is added.

mimic; mimics; mimicked; mimicking
panic; panics; panicked; panicking
traffic; traffics; trafficked; trafficking

NOTE: Words derived from this type of verb also add a *-k* when such a suffix or the suffix *-y* is added to them.

panicky
trafficker

6. **Tense, aspect, voice, and mood** English verbs exhibit their simple present and simple past tenses by use of two single-word grammatical forms.

simple present = do
simple past = did

7. The future tense is expressed by *shall* or *will* followed by the base form of the verb or by use of the simple present or present progressive forms in a revealing context.

> I *shall do* it.
> He *will do* it.
> I *leave* shortly for New York.
> I *am leaving* shortly for New York.

8. Aspect is a property that allows verbs to indicate time relations other than the simple present, past, or future tenses. Aspect covers these relationships:

action occurring in the past and continuing to the present	has seen	*present perfect*
action completed at a past time or before the immediate past	had seen	*past perfect*
action that will have been completed by a future time	will have seen	*future perfect*
action occurring now	is seeing	*progressive*

In contexts that require it, the perfective and the progressive aspects can be combined to yield special verb forms, such as *had been seeing*.

9. Voice enables a verb to indicate whether the subject of a sentence is acting (he *loves* = active voice) or whether the subject is being acted upon (he *is loved* = passive voice).

10. Mood indicates manner of expression. The indicative mood states a fact or asks a question (He *is* here. *Is* he here?). The subjunctive mood expresses condition contrary to fact (I wish that he *were* here). The imperative mood expresses a command or request (*Come* here. Please *come* here).

11. **Transitive and intransitive verbs** Verbs may be used transitively or intransitively. A *transitive* verb acts upon a direct object.

> She *contributed* money.
> He *ran* the store.

An *intransitive* verb does not act upon a direct object.

> She *contributed* generously.
> He *ran* down the street.

NOTE: As in the examples above, many verbs are transitive in one sense and intransitive in another.

Verbals There is another group of words derived from verbs and called *verbals* that deserve added discussion. The members of this group—the gerund, the participle, and the infinitive—exhibit some but not all of the characteristic features of their parent verbs.

12. A gerund is an *-ing* verb form, but it functions mainly as a noun. It has both the active *(seeing)* and the passive *(being seen)* voices. In addition to voice, a gerund's verbal characteristics are as follows: it conveys the notion of a verb—i.e., action, occurrence, or being; it can take an object; and it can be modified by an adverb. In the following sentences, for instance, "Typing" and "driving" are gerunds, "data" and "cars" are their objects, and "daily" and "fast" are adverbs modifying the gerund.

> *Typing* tabular *data daily* is a boring task.
>
> He liked *driving cars fast.*

NOTE: Nouns and pronouns occurring before gerunds usually use the possessive case. However, writers often use objective pronouns or nouns not in the possessive case when they want to put emphasis on the noun or pronoun. In addition, plural nouns are often not expressed in the possessive before gerunds.

> She is trying to improve *her typing.*
>
> We objected to *their telling* the story all over town.
>
> We cannot imagine *him doing* anything less than is required.
>
> Talks began without the negotiating *parties having* any choice about the location.

13. Participles, on the other hand, function as adjectives and may occur alone ("a *broken* typewriter") or in phrases that modify other words ("*Having broken the typewriter,* she gave up for the day"). Participles have active and passive forms like gerunds.

> *active-voice participial phrase modifying "he"*
> *Having failed to pass the examination,* he was forced to repeat the course.
>
> *passive-voice participial phrase modifying "he"*
> *Having been failed* by his instructor, he was forced to repeat the course.

NOTE: Participles, unlike gerunds, are not preceded by possessive nouns or pronouns:

> We saw the *car waiting* outside the door.

14. Infinitives may exhibit active *(to do)* and passive *(to be done)* voices, and they may indicate aspect *(to be doing, to have done, to have been doing, to have been done).* Infinitives may take complements and may be modified by adverbs. In addition, they can function as nouns, adjectives, and adverbs in sentences. Examples:

noun use
To be known is *to be castigated.* (subject and predicate nominative)
He tried everything except *to bypass his superior.* (object of preposition "except")

adjectival use
They had found a way *to increase profits greatly.* (modifies the noun "way")

adverbial use
He was too furious *to speak.* (modifies "furious")

NOTE: Although *to* is the characteristic marker of an infinitive, it is not always stated but may be understood:

He helped [to] complete the marketing report.

15. **Sequence of tenses** If the main verb in a sentence is in the present tense, any other tense or compound verb form may follow it in subsequent clauses, as:

I *realize* that you *are leaving.*
I *realize* that you *will be leaving.*
I *realize* that you *left.*
I *realize* that you *will leave.*
I *realize* that you *were leaving.*
I *realize* that you *will have been leaving.*
I *realize* that you *have been leaving.*
I *realize* that you *can be leaving.*
I *realize* that you *had left.*
I *realize* that you *may be leaving.*
I *realize* that you *had been leaving.*
I *realize* that you *must be leaving.*

16. If the main verb is in the past tense, that tense imposes time restrictions on any subsequent verbs in the sentence, thus excluding use of the present tense, as:

I *realized* that you *were leaving.*
I *realized* that you *would be leaving.*
I *realized* that you *left.*
I *realized* that you *could be leaving.*
I *realized* that you *had left.*
I *realized* that you *might be leaving.*
I *realized* that you *had been leaving.*
I *realized* that you *would leave.*

17. If the main verb is in the future tense, it imposes time restrictions on subsequent verbs in the sentence, thus excluding the possibility of using the simple past tense, as:

He *will see* you because he *is going* to the meeting too.
He *will see* you because he *will be going* to the meeting too.
He *will see* you because he *will go* to the meeting too.
He *will see* you because he *has been going* to the meetings too.
He *will see* you because he *will have been going* to the meetings too.

18. In general, most writers try to maintain an order of tenses throughout their sentences that is consistent with natural or real time, e.g., present tense = present-time matters, past tense = past matters, and future tense = matters that will take place in the future. However, there are two outstanding exceptions to these principles. First, if one is discussing the contents of printed or published material, one conventionally uses the present tense.

> In *Etiquette,* Emily Post *discusses* forms of address.
>
> This analysis *gives* market projections for the next two years.
>
> In his latest position paper on the Middle East, the Secretary of State *writes* that . . . .

Second, if one wishes to add the connotation of immediacy to a particular sentence, one may use the present tense instead of the future.

> I *leave* for Tel Aviv tonight.

19. The sequence of tenses in sentences which express contrary-to-fact conditions is a special problem frequently encountered in writing. The examples below show the sequence correctly maintained.

> If he *were* on time, we *would leave* now.
>
> If he *had been* (not *would have been*) on time, we *would have left* an hour ago.

20. At one time, *shall* was considered the only correct form to use with the first person in simple future tenses *(I shall, we shall),* while *will* was limited to the second and third persons *(you will, it will, they will).* Today, however, either of the following forms is considered correct for the first person:

> We *shall give* your request special attention.
>
> We *will give* your request special attention.

Subject-verb agreement Verbs agree in number and in person with their grammatical subjects. At times, however, the grammatical subject may be singular in form, but the thought it carries—i.e., the notional subject—may have plural connotations. Here are some general guidelines. For discussion of verb agreement with indefinite-pronoun subjects, see paragraphs 4–9 under Pronoun in this section. For discussion of verb number as affected by a compound subject whose elements are joined by *and/or,* see paragraph 6 under Conjunction in this section.

21. Plural and compound subjects take plural verbs even if the subject is inverted.

Both dogs and cats *were* tested for the virus.
Grouped under the heading "fine arts" *are* music, theater, and painting.

22. Compound subjects or plural subjects working as a unit take singular verbs in American English.

Lord & Taylor *has* stores in the New York area.
Cauliflower and cheese *is* my favorite vegetable.
Five hundred dollars *is* a stiff price for a coat.
   but
Twenty-five milligrams of pentazocine *were* administered.

23. Compound subjects expressing mathematical relationships may be either singular or plural.

One plus one *makes* (or *make*) two.
Six from eight *leaves* (or *leave*) two.

24. According to traditional guidelines, singular subjects joined by *or* or *nor* take singular verbs; plural subjects so joined take plural verbs. If one subject is singular and the other plural, the verb agrees with the number of the subject that is closer to it.

A freshman or sophomore *is* eligible for the scholarship.
Neither freshmen nor sophomores *are* eligible for the scholarship.
Either the secretaries or the supervisor *has* to do the job.
Either the supervisor or the secretaries *have* to do the job.

NOTE: Some writers prefer using a plural verb with singular subjects joined by *nor* because they construe *neither . . . nor* as being the negative form of *both . . . and.*

Neither Michael nor his father *were* happy with the solution.

25. Singular subjects introduced by *many a, such a, every, each,* or *no* take singular verbs, even when several such subjects are joined by *and.*

Many an executive *has* gone to the top in that division.
No supervisor and no assembler *is* excused from the time check.
Every chair, table, and desk *has* to be accounted for.

26. The agreement of the verb with its grammatical subject ordinarily should not be skewed by an intervening phrase.

One of my reasons for resigning *involves* purely personal considerations.
The president of the company, as well as members of his staff, *has* arrived.
He, not any of the proxy voters, *has* to be present.

27. The verb *to be* agrees with its grammatical subject and not with its complement.

> His mania *was* fast cars and beautiful women.
> Women in the work force *constitute* a new field of study.

NOTE: The verb *to be* introduced by the word *there* must agree in number with the subject following it.

> There *are* many complications here.
> There *is* no reason to worry about him.

28. Collective nouns—such as *orchestra, team, committee, family*—usually take singular verbs but can take plural verbs if the emphasis is on the individual members of the unit rather than on the unit itself.

> The committee *has agreed* to extend the deadline.
>   *but also*
> The committee *have been* at odds ever since the beginning.

29. The word *number* in the phrase *a number of* usually takes a plural verb, but in the phrase *the number of* it takes a singular verb.

> A number of errors *were* (also *was*) made.
> The number of errors *was* surprising.

30. A relative clause that follows the expression *one of those/these* + plural noun takes a plural or singular verb, depending on whether the singular notion of *one* or the plural notion of *those* or *these* is uppermost in the writer's mind.

> He is one of those executives who *worry* (or *worries*) a lot.
> This is one of those typewriters that *create* (or *creates*) perfect copies.

31. **Linking and *sense* verbs** Linking verbs (as the various forms of *to be*) and the so-called "sense" verbs (as *feel, look, taste, smell,* as well as particular senses of *appear, become, continue, grow, prove, remain, seem, stand,* and *turn*) connect subjects with predicate nouns or adjectives.

> He *is* a vice president.
> He *became* vice president.
> The temperature *continues* cold.
> The future *looks* prosperous.
> I *feel* bad.
> He *remains* healthy.

NOTE: Sense words often cause confusion, in that writers sometimes mistakenly use adverbs instead of adjectives following these words.

not
This perfume smells nicely.
instead
This perfume smells nice.
not
The meat tastes well.
instead
The meat tastes good.

32. **Split infinitives** A split infinitive is an infinitive that has a modifier between the *to* and the verbal (as in "to really care"). In the past, some grammarians disapproved of this construction, and many people still try to avoid it whenever they can. However, the split infinitive has been around a long time and has been used by a wide variety of distinguished English writers. It can be a useful device if a writer wants to stress the verbal element of an infinitive or express a thought that is most clearly shown with *to* + adverb + infinitive. In some cases where special emphasis on a word or a group of words is desirable, that emphasis cannot be achieved with an undivided infinitive construction. For example, in the phrase "to *thoroughly* complete the financial study" the position of the adverb as close as possible to the verbal element of the whole infinitive phrase strengthens the effect of the adverb on the verbal element. This situation is not necessarily true in the following reworded phrases:

    to complete *thoroughly* the financial study
    thoroughly to complete the financial study
    to complete the financial study *thoroughly*

In other instances, the position of the adverb may actually modify or change the entire meaning.

    original
    arrived at the office to *unexpectedly* find a new name on the door
    recast with new meanings
    arrived at the office *unexpectedly* to find a new name on the door
    arrived at the office to find a new name on the door *unexpectedly*

NOTE: Very long adverbial modifiers that interrupt an infinitive are clumsy and should be avoided or recast.

    clumsy
    He wanted to *completely and without mercy* defeat his competitor.
    recast
    He wanted to defeat his competitor *completely and without mercy*.

33. **Dangling participles** Dangling participles are participles occurring in a sentence without a normally expected syntactic rela-

tion to the rest of the sentence. They are best avoided, as they may create confusion for the reader or seem ludicrous.

dangling
Walking through the door, her coat was caught.

recast
While walking through the door, she caught her coat.
Walking through the door, she caught her coat.
She caught her coat while walking through the door.

dangling
Caught in the act, his excuses were unconvincing.

recast
Caught in the act, he could not make his excuses convincing.

dangling
Having been told that he was incompetent and dishonest, the executive fired the man.

recast
Having told the man that he was incompetent and dishonest, the executive fired him.
Having been told by his superior that he was incompetent and dishonest, the man was fired.

NOTE: Participles should not be confused with prepositions that end in *-ing*—like *concerning, considering, providing, regarding, respecting, touching,* etc.

prepositional usage
Concerning your complaint, we can tell you . . . .
Considering all the implications, you have made a dangerous decision.
Touching the matter at hand, we can say that . . . .

Phrases

A phrase is a brief expression that consists of two or more grammatically related words that may contain either a noun or a finite verb (that is, a verb that shows grammatical person and number) but not both, and that often functions as a particular part of speech with a clause or sentence.

Basic Types

There are seven basic types of phrases.

1. An *absolute phrase* consists of a noun followed by a modifier (such as a participle). Absolute phrases act independently within a sentence without modifying a particular element of the sentence. Absolute phrases are also referred to as *nominative absolutes*.

He stalked out, *his eyes staring straight ahead.*

2. A *gerund phrase* is a verbal phrase that includes a gerund and functions as a noun.

Sitting on a patient's bed is bad hospital etiquette.

3. An *infinitive phrase* is a verbal phrase that includes an infinitive and that may function as a noun, adjective, or adverb.

noun
To do that would be stupid.

adjective
This was a performance *to remember.*

adverb
He struggled *to get free.*

4. A *noun phrase* consists of a noun and its modifiers.

The concrete building is huge.

5. A *participial phrase* is a verbal phrase that includes a participle and that functions as an adjective.

Listening all the time with great concentration, she began to line up her options.

6. A *prepositional phrase* consists of a preposition and its object. It may function as a noun, adjective, or adverb.

noun
Out of debt is where we'd like to be!

adjective
Here is the desk *with the extra file drawer.*

adverb
He now walked *without a limp.*

7. A *verb phrase* consists of a verb and any other terms that either modify it or that complete its meaning.

She *will have arrived too late* for you to talk to her.

Usage Problems

1. Usage problems with phrases occur most often when a modifying phrase is not placed close enough to the word or words that it modifies. The phrase "On December 10" in the following sentence, for example, must be repositioned to clarify just what happened on that date.

original
We received your letter concerning the shipment of parts on December 10.

recast
On December 10 we received your letter concerning the shipment of parts.

or
We received your letter concerning the December 10 shipment of parts.

2. A very common usage problem with phrases involves dangling participial phrases. For a discussion of dangling participles, see paragraph 33 under Verb, pages 182–183.

Clauses

A clause is a group of words containing both a subject and a predicate. A clause functions as an element of a compound or a complex sentence. There are two general types of clauses: the *main* or *independent clause* and the *subordinate* or *dependent clause*. The main clause (such as "it is hot") is an independent grammatical unit and can stand alone. The subordinate clause (such as "because it is hot") cannot stand alone. A subordinate clause is either preceded or followed by a main clause.

Basic Types

Like phrases, clauses can perform as particular parts of speech within the total environment of the sentence. There are three basic types of clauses having part-of-speech functions.

1. The *adjective clause* modifies a noun or pronoun and typically follows the word it modifies.

> Her administrative assistant, *who was also a speech writer,* was overworked.
>
> I can't see the reason *why you're upset.*
>
> He is a man *who will succeed.*
>
> Anybody *who opts for a career like that* is crazy.

2. The *adverb clause* modifies a verb, an adjective, or another adverb and typically follows the word it modifies.

> They made a valiant effort, *although the risks were great.*
>
> *When it rains,* it pours.
>
> I'm certain *that he is guilty.*
>
> We accomplished less *than we did before.*

3. The *noun clause* fills a noun slot in a sentence and thus can be a subject, an object, or a complement.

subject
Whoever is qualified should apply.

object of a verb
I do not know *what his field is.*

object of a preposition
Route that journal to *whichever department you wish.*

complement
The trouble is *that she has no ambition.*

Elliptical Clauses

Some clause elements may be omitted if the context makes clear the understood elements:

> I remember the first time [that] we met.
>
> This typewriter is better than that [typewriter is].
>
> When [she is] on the job, she is always competent and alert.

Placement of Clauses

A modifying clause should be placed as close as possible to the word or words it modifies. This placement will give maximum clarity, and it avoids the possibility that the reader will misinterpret written material. If intervening words muddy the overall meaning of a sentence, it should be rewritten or recast.

> *muddy*
> A memorandum is a piece of business writing, less formal than a letter, which serves as a means of interoffice communication.
>
> *recast*
> A memorandum, less formal than a letter, is a means of interoffice communication.

Restrictive and Nonrestrictive Clauses

Clauses that modify are also referred to as *restrictive* or *nonrestrictive*. Whether a clause is restrictive or nonrestrictive has a direct bearing on sentence punctuation. For information about punctuating restrictive and nonrestrictive clauses, see paragraph 10 under Comma, page 16.

1. Restrictive clauses are the so-called "bound" modifiers. They are absolutely essential to the meaning of the word or words they modify, they cannot be omitted without the meaning of the sentences being radically changed, and they are unpunctuated.

   > Women who aren't competitive should not aspire to high corporate office.

   In this example, the restrictive clause "who aren't competitive" limits the classification of women, and thus is essential to the total meaning of the sentence. If, on the other hand, the restrictive clause is omitted as shown below, the classification of women is now not limited at all, and the sentence conveys an entirely different idea.

> Women should not aspire to high corporate office.

2. Nonrestrictive clauses are the so-called "free" modifiers. They are not inextricably bound to the word or words they modify but instead convey additional information about them. Nonrestrictive clauses may be omitted altogether without the meaning of the sentence being radically changed, and they are set off by commas; i.e., they are both preceded and followed by commas when they occur in mid-sentence.

> Our guide, who wore a green beret, was an experienced traveler.

In this example, the nonrestrictive clause "who wore a green beret" does not restrict the classification of the guide; i.e., it does not set him apart from all other guides but merely serves as a bit of incidental detail. Removal of the nonrestrictive clause does not affect the meaning of the sentence:

> Our guide was an experienced traveler.

Tacked-on *Which* Clauses

Many writers try to avoid tacking a *which* clause onto the end of a sentence when the clause actually refers to the total idea of the sentence. It can usually be avoided by recasting the sentence.

> *tacked-on*
> The company is retooling, which I personally think is a wise move.

> *recast*
> The company's decision to retool is a wise move in my opinion.
> *or*
> I believe that the company's decision to retool is wise.

Sentences

A sentence is a grammatically self-contained unit that consists of a word or a group of syntactically related words and that (1) expresses a statement (declarative sentence); (2) asks a question (interrogative sentence); (3) expresses a request or command (imperative sentence); or (4) expresses an exclamation (exclamatory sentence). A sentence typically contains both a subject and a predicate, begins with a capital letter, and ends with a punctuation mark.

Basic Types

Sentences are classified into three main types on the basis of their clause structure.

1. The *simple sentence* is a complete grammatical unit having one subject and one predicate (either or both of which may be compound).

   > Paper is costly.
   > Bond and tissue are costly.
   > Bond and tissue are costly and are sometimes scarce.

2. The *compound sentence* is made up of two or more main clauses.

   > I could arrange to arrive late, or I could simply send a proxy.
   > This commute takes at least forty minutes by car, but we can make it in twenty by train.
   > A few of the executives had Ph.D.'s, even more of them had B.A.'s, but the majority of them had both B.A.'s and M.B.A.'s.

3. The *complex sentence* combines a main clause with one or more subordinate clauses (subordinate clauses are italicized in the examples).

   > The committee meeting began *when the business manager and the secretarial staff supervisor walked in.*
   > *Although the city council made some reforms,* the changes came so late *that they could not prevent these abuses.*

Construction

The construction of grammatically sound sentences can be achieved by following some general guidelines.

1. Sentence coordination should be maintained by the use of connectives linking phrases or clauses of equal rank. When a connective is used to link phrases or clauses that are not equal, the resulting sentence is ineffective at best, and can be confusing.

   > *faulty coordination with improper use of "and"*
   > I was sitting in on a meeting, and he stood up and started a long rambling discourse on a new pollution-control device.
   > *recast (one clause subordinated)*
   > I sat in on a meeting during which he stood up and rambled on about a new pollution-control device.
   > *recast (two sentences)*
   > I sat in on that meeting. He stood up and rambled on about a new pollution-control device.

faulty coordination with improper use of "and"
This company employs a full-time research staff and was founded
in 1945.

recast (one clause subordinated)
This company, which employs a full-time research staff, was
founded in 1945.

recast (one clause reworded into a phrase)
Established in 1945, this company employs a full-time research
staff.

2. Parallel, balanced sentence elements are necessary in order to
   achieve good sentence structure. When clauses having unparallel subjects are linked together, the resulting sentence can be
   unclear.

   unparallel
   The report gives market statistics, but he does not list his sources
   for these figures.

   parallel
   The report gives market statistics, but it does not list the sources
   for these figures.

   unparallel
   We are glad to have you as our client, and please call on us whenever you need help.

   parallel
   We are glad to have you as our client and we hope that you will
   call on us whenever you need help.

   recast into two sentences
   We are glad to have you as our client. Please do call on us whenever you need help.

3. In order for a sentence to read effectively, its elements should
   be tightly linked together. When sentence elements are strung
   together by loose or excessive use of *and*, the sentence as a
   whole can be too lengthy and lacking in logical flow to be
   readily understood.

   faulty coordination/excessive use of "and"
   This company is a Class 1 motor freight common carrier of general commodities and it operates over 10,000 tractors, trailers,
   and city delivery trucks through 200 terminals, and serves 40
   states and the District of Columbia.

   recast into three shorter, more effective sentences
   This company is a Class 1 motor freight common carrier of general commodities. It operates over 10,000 tractors, trailers, and
   city delivery trucks through 200 terminals. The company serves
   40 states and the District of Columbia.

4. The correct choice of a conjunction to link clauses is important in writing an effective sentence. *And* is a general coordinating conjunction which functions to join sentence elements.

If a sentence is expressing more than simple linkage, as when one clause is being contrasted with another, or when a reason or result is being expressed, a more specific conjunction should be used. For more on the specific functions of coordinating and subordinating conjunctions, see paragraphs 1–6 and 10–12 under Conjunction, pages 155–157 and 158 respectively.

> *too general*
> The economy was soft *and* we lost a lot of business.
>
> *specific*
> We lost a lot of business *because* the economy was soft.
> The economy was soft, *so* we lost a lot of business.
>
> *specific*
> The soft economy has cost us a lot of business.

5. Unnecessary or unexpected grammatical shifts in a sentence interrupt the reader's train of thought and needlessly complicate the material. Some unnecessary grammatical shifts are shown below, along with their improvements:

> *unnecessary shifts in verb voice*
> Any information you *can give* us *will be* greatly *appreciated* and we *assure* you that discretion *will be exercised* in its use.
>
> *rephrased* (note the italicized all-active verb voice)
> We *will appreciate* any information that you *can give* us. We *assure* you that we *will use* it with discretion.
>
> *unnecessary shifts in person*
> *One* can use either erasers or correction fluid to remove typographical errors; however, *you* should make certain that *your* corrections are clean.
>
> *rephrased* (note that the italicized pronouns are consistent)
> *One* can use either erasers or correction fluid to eradicate errors; however, *one* should make certain that *one's* corrections are clean.
>   *or*
> *You* can use either erasers or correction fluid to eradicate errors; however, *you* should make certain that *your* corrections are clean.
>
> *unnecessary shift from phrase to clause*
> *Because of the current parts shortage* and *we are experiencing a strike,* we cannot fill any orders now.
>
> *rephrased*
> *Because of a parts shortage and a strike,* we cannot fill any orders now.
>   *or*
> *Because we are hampered by a parts shortage and we are experiencing a strike,* we cannot fill any orders now.

6. A rational, logical ordering of sentence elements is a writer's best guarantee that the material will be understood. Closely related elements, for example, should be placed as close together as possible for the sake of maximum clarity.

related elements separated
We would appreciate your sending us the instructions on copy-editing by mail or cable.

related elements joined
We would appreciate your sending us by mail or by cable the copy-editing instructions.

We would appreciate your mailing or cabling us the copy-editing instructions.

We would appreciate it if you would mail or cable us the copy-editing instructions.

7. Sentences should form complete, independent grammatical units containing both a subject and a predicate. Exceptions are dialogue or specialized copy where fragmentation may be used for particular reasons (as to reflect speech or to attract the reader's attention).

incomplete grammatical units
During the last three years, our calculator sales soared. While our conventional office machine sales fell off.

complete grammatical units
During the last three years, our calculator sales soared, but our conventional office machine sales fell off.

While our conventional office machine sales fell off during the last three years, our calculator sales soared.

sentences fragmented for special effects in advertising
See it now. The car for the Nineties . . . A car you'll want to own.

Sentence Length

Sentence length is directly related to the writer's purpose: there is no magic number of words that guarantees a good sentence. For example, an executive covering broad and yet complex topics in a long memorandum may choose concise, succinct sentences for the sake of clarity, impact, fast dictation, and readability. On the other hand, a writer who wants the reader to reflect on what is being said may employ longer, more involved sentences. Still another writer may juxtapose long and short sentences to emphasize an important point. The longer sentences may build up to a climactic and forceful short sentence.

Sentence Strategy

1. **Coordination and subordination** Either coordination or subordination or a mixture of both can be used to create a variety of stylistic writing effects. Coordination links independent sentences and sentence elements by means of coordinating conjunctions, while subordination transforms elements into dependent structures by means of subordinating conjunctions. Coordination tends to promote rather loose sentence

structure, which can become a fault; subordination tends to tighten the structure and to emphasize a main clause.

coordination
During the balance of 1983, this Company expects to issue $100,000,000 of long-term debt and equity securities *and* may guarantee up to $200,000,000 of new corporate bonds.

subordination
While this Company expects to issue $100,000,000 of long-term debt and equity securities during the balance of 1983, it may also guarantee up to $200,000,000 of new corporate bonds.

2. **Interrupting elements** Interrupting the normal flow of discourse by inserting comments can be a useful device to call attention to an aside, to emphasize a word or phrase, to convey a particular tone (as forcefulness), or to make the prose a little more informal. Interrupting elements should be used with discretion; too many of them may distract the reader and disrupt his or her train of thought. The following are examples of effective interrupted sentences:

an aside
His evidence, if reliable, could send our client to prison.

emphasis
These companies—ours as well as theirs—must show more profits.

forcefulness
This, ladies and gentlemen, is the prime reason for your cost overruns. I trust it will not happen again?

3. **Parallelism and balance** While interruption breaks up the flow of discourse, parallelism and balance work together toward maintaining an even, rhythmic thought flow. Parallelism means a similarity in the grammatical construction of adjacent phrases and clauses that are equivalent, complementary, or antithetical in meaning.

These ecological problems are of crucial concern *to* scientists, *to* businessmen, *to* government officials, and *to* all citizens.

Our attorneys have argued *that* the trademark is ours, *that* our rights have been violated, and *that* appropriate compensation is required.

He was respected not only *for his intelligence* but also *for his integrity.*

Balance is the juxtaposition and equipoise of two or more syntactically parallel constructions (as phrases and clauses) that contain similar, contrasting, or opposing ideas:

To err is human; to forgive, divine.

—Alexander Pope

Ask not what your country can do for you—ask what you can do
for your country.

—John F. Kennedy

And finally, a series can be an effective way to emphasize a
thought and to establish a definite prose rhythm:

> The thing that interested me . . . about New York . . . was the . . .
> contrast it showed between the dull and the shrewd, the strong
> and the weak, the rich and the poor, the wise and the
> ignorant. . . .
>
> —Theodore Dreiser

4. **Periodic and cumulative sentences** Stylistically, there are two basic types of sentences—the periodic and the cumulative or
loose. The periodic sentence is structured so that its main idea
or its thrust is suspended until the very end, thereby drawing
the reader's eye and mind along to an emphatic conclusion. In
the example below, the main point follows the final comma.

> While the Commission would wish to give licensees every encour-
> agement to experiment on their own initiative with new and dif-
> ferent means of providing access to their stations for the
> discussion of important public issues, it cannot justify the imposi-
> tion of a specific right of access by government fiat.
>
> —*Television/Radio Age*

The cumulative sentence, on the other hand, is structured so
that its main point appears first, followed by other phrases or
clauses expanding on or supporting it. In the following example, the main point precedes the first comma.

> The solution must be finely honed, lest strategists err too much
> on the side of sophistication only to find that U.S. military forces
> can be defeated by overwhelming mass.
>
> —William C. Moore

The final phrase or clause in a cumulative sentence theoreti-
cally could be deleted without skewing or destroying the essential meaning of the total sentence. A cumulative sentence
is therefore more loosely structured than a periodic sentence.

5. **Reversal** A reversal of customary or expected sentence order
is another effective stylistic strategy, when used sparingly, because it injects a dash of freshness, unexpectedness, and origi-
nality into the prose.

> *customary or expected order*
> I find that these realities are indisputable: the economy has taken
> a drastic downturn, costs on all fronts have soared, and jobs are
> at a premium.

reversal
That the economy has taken a drastic downturn; that costs on all fronts have soared; that jobs are at a premium—these are the realities that I find indisputable.

6. **Rhetorical questions** The rhetorical question is yet another device to focus the reader's attention on a problem or an issue. The rhetorical question requires no specific response from the reader but often merely sets up the introduction of the writer's own view. In some instances, a rhetorical question works as a topic sentence in a paragraph; in other instances, a whole series of rhetorical questions may spotlight pertinent issues for the reader's consideration.

What can be done to correct the problem? Two things, to begin with: never discuss cases out of the office, and never allow a visitor to see the papers on your desk.

7. **Variety** As a means of keeping the reader's attention, careful writers try to maintain a balance of different kinds of sentences. For example, they may use a combination of simple, compound, and complex sentences in a paragraph, together with a variey of short and long sentences. Writers also vary the beginnings of their sentences so that every sentence in a paragraph does not begin directly with the subject. Any kind of repetitious pattern creates monotony. Through judicious use of combinations of sentence patterns and the sentence strategies discussed in the preceding pragraphs, a writer can attain an interesting, diversified style.

Paragraphs

The underlying structure of any written communication—be it a memorandum, a letter, or a report—must be controlled by the writer if the material is to be clear, coherent, logical in progression, and effective. Since good paragraphing is a means to this end, it is essential that the writer become adept at using techniques of paragraph development and of transition between paragraphs. In order to do this, writers should be able to recognize various kinds of paragraphs and their functions as well as the potential problems that might arise in structuring a logical paragraph system. In this way, they should be able to spot possible discrepancies that might result in misinterpretation by the reader or that might detract from the total effect of the communication.

A paragraph is a subdivision in writing that consists of one or more sentences, that deals with one or more ideas, or that quotes a speaker or a source. The first line of a paragraph is indented in reports, studies, articles, theses, and books. However, the first line of a paragraph in business letters and memorandums may or may not be indented, depending on the style being followed.

Paragraphs should not be considered as isolated entities that are self-contained and mechanically lined up without transitions or interrelationship of ideas. Rather, paragraphs should be viewed as components of larger groups or blocks that are tightly interlinked and that interact in the sequential development of a major idea or cluster of ideas. The overall coherence of a communication depends on this interaction.

Individual paragraphs and paragraph blocks are flexible: their length, internal structure, and purpose vary according to the writer's intention and his own style. For example, one writer may be able to express his point in a succinct, one-sentence paragraph, while another may require several sentences to make his point. Writers' concepts of paragraphing also differ. For instance, some writers think of paragraphs as a means of dividing their material into logical segments with each unit developing one particular point in depth and in detail. Others view paragraphs as a means of emphasizing particular points or adding variety to long passages.

Development of Paragraphs

Depending on the writer's intentions, paragraph development may take any of the following directions:

1. The paragraph may move from the general to the specific.

2. The paragraph may move from the specific to the general.

3. The paragraph may exhibit an alternating order of comparison and contrast.

4. The paragraph may chronicle events in a set temporal order—e.g., from the beginning to the end, or from the end to the beginning.

5. The paragraph may describe something (as a group of objects) in a set spatial order—e.g., the items being described may be looked at from near-to-far, or vice versa.

6. The paragraph may follow a climactic sequence with the least important facts or examples described first followed by a buildup of tension leading to the most important facts or examples then followed by a gradual easing of tension. Other material can be so ordered for effectiveness; for example, facts or issues that are easy to comprehend or accept may be

set forth first and followed by those that are more difficult to comprehend or accept. In this way the easier material prepares the reader to comprehend or accept the more difficult points.

7. Anticlimactic order is also useful when the writer's intent is to persuade the reader. With this strategy, the writer sets forth the most persuasive arguments first so that the reader, having been influenced in a positive way by that persuasion, moves along with the rest of the argument with a growing feeling of assent.

Effective Paragraphing

The following material outlines some ways of building effective paragraphs within a text.

A topic sentence—a key sentence to which the other sentences in the paragraph are related—may be placed either at the beginning or at the end of a paragraph. A lead-in topic sentence should present the main idea in the paragraph and should set the initial tone of the material that follows. A terminal topic sentence should be an analysis, a conclusion, or a summation of what has gone before it.

A single-sentence paragraph can be used to achieve easy transition from a preceding to a subsequent paragraph (especially when the paragraphs are long and complex) if it repeats an important word or phrase from the preceding paragraph, if it contains a pronoun reference to a key individual mentioned in a preceding paragraph, or if it is introduced by an appropriate conjunction or conjunctive adverb that connects the paragraphs.

1. Since the very first paragraph sets initial tone, introduces the subject or topic under discussion, and leads into the main thrust of a communication, it should be worded so as to immediately attract the reader's attention and arouse interest. These openings can be effective:

   A. a succinct statement of purpose or point of view
   B. a concise definition (as of a problem)
   C. a lucid statement of a key issue or fact

2. These openings, by contrast, can blunt the point of the rest of the material:

   A. an apology for the material to be presented
   B. a querulous complaint or a defensive posture
   C. a detailed account of material presented earlier
   D. a presentation of self-evident facts
   E. a group of sentences rendered limp and meaningless because of clichés

3. The last paragraph ties together all of the ideas and points that have been set forth earlier and reemphasizes the main thrust of the communication. These can be effective endings:

   A. a setting forth of the most important conclusion or conclusions drawn from the preceding discussion
   B. a final analysis of the main problem or problems under discussion
   C. a lucid summary of the individual points brought up earlier
   D. a final, clear statement of opinion or position
   E. concrete suggestions or solutions if applicable
   F. specific questions asked of the reader if applicable

4. The following endings, by contrast, can reduce the effectiveness of a communication:

   A. apologies for a poor presentation
   B. qualifying remarks that blunt or negate incisive points made earlier
   C. insertion of minor details or afterthoughts
   D. a meaningless closing couched in clichés

5. The following are tests of good paragraphs:

   A. Does the paragraph have a clear purpose? Is its utility evident, or is it there just to fill up space?
   B. Does the paragraph clarify rather than cloud the writer's ideas?
   C. Is the paragraph adequately developed, or does it merely raise other questions that the writer does not attempt to answer? If a position is being taken, does the writer include supporting information and statistics that are essential to its defense?
   D. Are the length and wording of all the paragraphs sufficiently varied, or does the writer employ the same types of locutions again and again?
   E. Is the sentence structure coherent?
   F. Is each paragraph unified? Do all the sentences really *belong* there; or does the writer digress into areas that would have been better covered in another paragraph or that could have been omitted altogether?
   G. Are the paragraphs coherent so that one sentence leads clearly and logically to another? Is easy, clear transition between paragraphs effected by a wise selection of transitional words and phrases which indicate relationships between ideas and signal the direction in which the writer's presentation is moving?
   H. Does one paragraph simply restate in other terms what has been said before?

Chapter 7

Notes and Bibliographies

CONTENTS

Writers and editors often need to provide readers with documentation of the source of a quotation or a piece of information. Authors may also wish to provide additional information and commentary or cross-references. This type of information is usually included in a note, which may take the form of a footnote at the bottom of a page, an endnote at the end of a chapter or at the end of a work, or a note in parentheses.

Authors and editors use various methods to indicate the source of a given quotation or piece of information. In works related to the social and natural sciences, writers have relied on a system of parenthetical references within the text that refer readers to a list of sources at the end of the work or one of its divisions. In works related to the humanities, the footnote form has traditionally been preferred. In recent years, however, the footnote form has become slightly less popular, as some style books have urged writers in the humanities to adopt parenthetical references.

This chapter describes both the footnote or endnote system and the system of parenthetical references. For both of these systems, the examples in this chapter illustrate generally acceptable ways of styling references. However, writers and editors should be aware that many professions and academic disciplines have developed their own systems for documenting sources, and some of these systems differ from the stylings illustrated in this chapter.

Footnotes and Endnotes

A footnote or an endnote keys full bibliographical information about a source, including author, title, place of publication, publisher, date, and page number, to a specific text passage making use of that source. The text passage is marked with a number, and all such notes are set aside from the rest of the text. Notes that appear at the bottom of the page are called *footnotes*. Notes that appear at the end of the chapter or at the end of an entire work are called *endnotes*.

Some recently published style manuals have discouraged the use of footnotes and endnotes for providing readers with bibliographical information about sources. Among the obvious difficulties with footnotes is that they are troublesome for typists to type and expensive for typesetters to set. The problem is that it is necessary to reserve sufficient space at the bottom of each page to allow for the notes that go with the text on that page. While the last note on a page may go over to the next page, each note should begin on the same page on which its number appears in the text. If there are many notes on a page, the result can be an unattractive page with more space given to footnotes than to text. And in some cases, there may be no way to get each footnote to begin on the same page as its text reference without rewriting some portion of the main text or the footnote or both.

The disadvantage of endnotes is primarily one of inconvenience for the reader, who has to flip back and forth in the book from the main text to the notes. This can be especially frustrating when the note contains no more than a page reference to a work already cited.

The use of parenthetical references to document sources does not guarantee that writers and readers will be saved entirely from these disadvantages. However, it does usually result in fewer footnotes or endnotes, and it does allow authors to treat notes that provide strictly bibliographical information—the details of which readers are often willing to do without—differently from notes that provide commentary, cross-references, or additional information. For more on the styling of parenthetical references, see the section on Parenthetical References in this chapter.

Placement of the Elements

Footnotes and endnotes to a text are indicated by unpunctuated Arabic superior numbers (or reference symbols, discussed later in this section) placed immediately after the quotation or information with no intervening space. The number is usually placed at the end of a sentence or clause, or at some other natural break in the sentence when the reference material is not a quotation. The number follows all marks of punctuation except the dash. If a terminal quotation mark appears (as at the end of a short quotation that is included in the running text), the numeral is placed outside the final quotation mark with no space intervening (see the sample on page 200). The numbering may be consecutive throughout

According to Lesikar, if a "quoted passage is four lines or less in length, it is typed with the report text and is distinguished from the normal text by quotation marks."[17] However, a different procedure is used for longer quotations:

> But if a longer quotation (five lines or more) is used, the conventional practice is to set it in from both left and right margins (about five spaces) but without quotation marks. . . . The quoted passage is further distinguished from the report writer's work by single spacing. . . .[18]

A series of usually three periods called ellipsis is used to indicate omissions of material from a passage.[19]

Footnotes may be placed "at the bottom of the page . . . separated from the text by a horizontal line. If a line is used, it is typed a single space below the text and followed by one blank line."[20] Lesikar prefers the separation line to be one and one-half or two inches.[21] Generally, typewriting textbooks state that a two-inch line is adequate (20 pica strokes; 24 elite strokes). The line is constructed by striking the underscore key.

From a typing standpoint, reserve three lines of blank typing space per footnote at the bottom of the page.

---

17. _Report Writing for Business_ (Homewood, Ill.: Richard D. Irwin, Inc., 1981), p. 187.

18. Ibid.

19. Ibid., p. 188.

20. Ruth I. Anderson et al., _The Administrative Secretary: Resource_ (New York: McGraw-Hill Book Company, 1970), p. 391.

21. Lesikar, op. cit., p. 189.

Figure 7.1. A typewritten page with footnotes

the work or, as in the case of book-length works, it may begin again with each new chapter. Footnote numbers like 7a and 7b, which usually result from last-minute revisions in the manuscript, are to be avoided, even if it means renumbering all the notes in the copy.

The text of the note itself is introduced with the applicable Arabic numeral or reference symbol. The numeral may be a superior numeral, unpunctuated and separated from the first word of the footnote by one space, or it may be set on the line and followed by a period and one or two spaces. The latter styling has become more popular recently and is much easier to type.

traditional styling
[7] Ibid., p. 223.

newer styling
7. Ibid., p. 223.

The indention of footnote and endnote text varies according to individual preference. Indenting the first line of the footnote to a paragraph indent with runover lines returning to flush left (as shown on pages 202 and 206) is probably the most common styling. However, the flush-left styling and the flush-and-hang styling, in which the first line is set flush left and succeeding lines are indented, are also common. The following examples reproduce the first three footnotes on page 202. In these examples, the reference number is set on the line in the flush-left styling and is raised in the flush-and-hang styling; however, either of the positions for reference numbers may be used with any of the indention styles.

flush left
1. Jennie Mason, *Introduction to Word Processing* (Indianapolis: Bobbs-Merrill, 1981), p. 55.
2. John E. Warriner and Francis Griffith, *English Grammar and Composition* (New York: Harcourt Brace Jovanovich, 1977), p. 208.
3. Ruth I. Anderson et al., *The Administrative Secretary: Resource* (New York: McGraw-Hill, 1970), p. 357.

flush and hang
[1] Jennie Mason, *Introduction to Word Processing* (Indianapolis: Bobbs-Merrill, 1981), p. 55.
[2] John E. Warriner and Francis Griffith, *English Grammar and Composition* (New York: Harcourt Brace Jovanovich, 1977), p. 208.
[3] Ruth I. Anderson et al., *The Administrative Secretary: Resource* (New York: McGraw-Hill, 1970), p. 357.

In typewritten publications, the notes themselves are usually single-spaced, but double spacing is used between notes. When a

NOTES

1. Jennie Mason, *Introduction to Word Processing* (Indianapolis: Bobbs-Merrill, 1981), p. 55.

2. John E. Warriner and Francis Griffith, *English Grammar and Composition* (New York: Harcourt Brace Jovanovich, 1977), p. 208.

3. Ruth I. Anderson et al., *The Administrative Secretary: Resource* (New York: McGraw-Hill, 1970), p. 357.

4. Simone de Beauvoir, *The Second Sex,* trans. and ed. H. M. Parshley (New York: Alfred A. Knopf, 1953), p. 600.

5. Alfred H. Markwardt, *American English,* ed. J. L. Dillard (New York: Oxford University Press, 1980), p. 94.

6. Martha L. Manheimer, *Style Manual: A Guide for the Preparation of Reports and Dissertations,* Books in Library and Information Science, vol. 5 (New York: Marcel Dekker, 1973), p. 14.

7. Charles T. Brushaw, Gerald J. Alred, and Walter E. Oliu, *Handbook of Technical Writing,* 2d ed. (New York: St. Martins Press, 1982), pp. 182–184.

8. National Micrographics Association, *An Introduction to Micrographics,* rev. ed. (Silver Spring, Md.: National Micrographics Association, 1980), p. 42.

9. *The World Almanac and Book of Facts* (New York: Newspaper Enterprises Association, Inc., 1985), p. 310.

10. *Rules for Alphabetical Filing as Standardized by ARMA* (Prairie Village, Kans.: Association of Records Managers and Administrators, 1981), p. 14.

11. Peggy F. Bradbury, ed., *Transcriber's Guide to Medical Terminology* (New Hyde Park, N.Y.: Medical Examination Publishing Co., 1973), p. 446.

12. Kemp Malone, "The Phonemes of Current English," *Studies for William A. Read,* ed. Nathaniel M. Caffee and Thomas A. Kirby (Baton Rouge: Louisiana State University Press, 1940), p. 133–165.

13. Robert Chambers, *Cyclopaedia of English Literature,* 2 vols. (New York: World Publishing House, 1875), vol. 1, p. 45.

Figure 7.2. A page of endnotes illustrating footnote and endnote style for references to books manuscript is being typed prior to typesetting, however, the notes should be double-spaced internally with triple spacing between the notes. In typeset material, footnotes and endnotes are usually set in type that is one or two points smaller than the text type. Extra space may or may not be placed between the notes according to individual preference.

When endnotes rather than footnotes are being used, all of the notes are gathered together in a single list (as shown on page 202) either at the end of a chapter or other section or at the end of an entire work. When a book uses a single note section at the end of the entire work, the section is usually divided with chapter headings to indicate where the notes of a particular chapter begin and end. An endnote may be styled in any of the ways that a footnote is styled.

Content and Styling for First References

Both footnotes and endnotes provide full bibliographical information for a source the first time it is cited; however, in subsequent references, this information is provided in an abbreviated manner. The following paragraphs describe the content and style used for first references. Subsequent references are discussed later in this section. Examples of the stylings described in this section are shown on pages 202 and 206. (The content and style for entries in bibliographies and lists of references are given in the section on Bibliographies and Lists of References later in this chapter.)

Books A footnote or endnote that refers to a book contains as many of the following elements as are relevant. Examples of each of the elements described below can be found in the references on page 202.

1. *Author's name* In footnotes and endnotes, the author's first name comes first and the last name after. If there are more than three authors, the first author's name is followed by the phrase *et al.,* which is an abbreviation for the phrase *et alii* or *et aliae,* meaning "and others." (For examples of notes describing books with multiple authors, see notes 2, 3, and 7 on page 202.) If a publication is issued by a group or organization and no individual is mentioned on the title page, the name of the group or organization may be used in place of an author's name; in this case, the group or organization is thought of as being the corporate author. (For an example of a note describing a work with a corporate author, see note 8 on page 202.) In footnotes and endnotes, the author's name is followed by a comma.

2. *Title of the work* The title is underlined in typewritten manuscript and italicized in type. Each word of the title is capitalized except for articles and short prepositions other than the first word. In cases in which no author's name is used in the note, the title comes first. This is commonly the styling for well-known reference books and for publications that have corporate authors but are more likely to be known by their titles. (For examples of notes in which the title comes first, see notes 9 and 10 on page 202.)

3. *Portion of the book* If a reference is to one portion of a book (as an essay within a collection), the name of the portion should be included. The titles of chapters within nonfiction works by a single author are usually not part of a footnote reference. The titles of parts of books, such as short poems, short stories, and essays, are enclosed in quotation marks. (For an example of a reference to a work within a collection, see note 12 on page 202.)

4. *Editor, compiler, or translator* The name of an editor, compiler, or translator is preceded by the abbreviation *ed., comp.,* or *trans.* or some combination of them joined by *and.* The abbreviation is separated from the title that precedes it by a comma. (For examples of notes describing a book with a translator or editor, see notes 4, 5, and 12 on page 202.) If there is no author mentioned on the title page of the book, the name of the editor, compiler, or translator is placed first in the note, followed by the abbreviation *ed., comp.,* or *trans.* (For an example of a note in which the editor's name comes first, see note 11 on page 202.)

5. *Name of the series* If a book is part of a series, the name of the series should be included. If the book corresponds to a specific volume in that series, the volume number is also included. The volume number is separated from the title by a comma. The name of the series is separated from the title of the volume by a comma and is capitalized as a title, but it is not underlined or italicized. (For an example of a note describing a book that is part of a series, see note 6 on page 202.)

6. *Edition* If a work is other than the first edition, the number or the nature of the edition should be indicated. (For examples of notes describing books that are not first editions, see notes 7 and 8 on page 202.)

7. *Volume number* If a work has more than one volume, the total number of volumes is given after the title and edition data.

In addition, the number of the particular volume cited should precede the page number. In traditional footnote styling, a *vol.* or *vols.* precedes the volume number, but many authors now omit these abbreviations. (For an example of a note referring to a multivolume work, see note 13 on page 202.)

8. *Publishing data* The city of publication, the name of the publisher, and the year of publication should all be included. These items are usually placed within parentheses; a colon separates the city from the publisher's name. Names of states may be abbreviated, but not names of cities. A comma separates the publisher's name from the year of issue.

9. *Page number* The number of the page on which the quotation or piece of information can be found should be included. In traditional footnote styling a *p.* or *pp.* precedes the page number or numbers; however, many authors now omit those abbreviations.

Periodicals A footnote or endnote describing an article in a periodical should include all of the following information that is relevant. Examples of each of the elements described below can be found in the sample references on the next page.

1. *Author's name* The author's name is treated in the same way as described above for a reference to a book. The names of writers of letters to a periodical and contributors of signed book reviews are treated like names of authors. (For examples of references to a letter and to a signed review, see notes 6 and 7 in figure 7.3 on page 206.)

2. *Title of the article* The title of the article is enclosed in quotation marks. The words of the title are capitalized as in a book title. The title of the article is followed by a comma that is placed inside the quotation marks.

3. *Name of the periodical* The name of the periodical is treated in the way described above for the title of a book.

4. *Volume and number of the periodical* If a periodical uses both volume and number designations to identify an issue, both should be used. If a periodical uses some other system for identifying issues (as the month and year of issue), that system should be used. Note 1 on page 206 illustrates a reference to a periodical in which pages are numbered consecutively through a volume, and therefore only a volume number is required. Note 2 illustrates a reference to a periodical that uses a seasonal designation as well as volume and number designa-

NOTES

1. John Heil, "Seeing is Believing," *American Philosophical Quarterly* 19 (1982): 229–239.

2. Donald K. Ourecky, "Cane and Bush Fruits," *Plants & Gardens* 27, No. 3 (Autumn 1971): pp. 13–15.

3. Xan Smiley, "Misunderstanding Africa," *Atlantic* (Sept. 1982); pp. 70–79.

4. Shiva Naipaul, "A Trinidad Childhood," *New Yorker* (17 Sept. 1984): pp. 63–64.

5. Gail Pitts, "Money Funds Holding Own," *Morning Union* [Springfield, Mass.] (Aug. 23, 1982): p. 6.

6. Jeremy C. Rosenberg, "Letters," *Advertising Age* (7 June, 1982): p. M–1.

7. M. O. Vassell, rev. of *Applied Charged Particle Optics,* ed. A. Septier, *American Scientist* 70 (1982): 229.

8. Joyce A. Velasquez, "The Format of Formal Reports," report prepared for the Southern Engineering Company, Johnson City, Miss. (May 29, 1985).

9. Clive Johnson, letter to Elizabeth O'Hara, 9 Nov. 1916, Johnson Collection, item 5298, California State Historical Society, San Marino, Calif.

Figure 7.3. Sample notes showing footnote and endnote styling for references to periodicals and unpublished sources

tions for each issue, and which paginates each issue independently of the volume. Note 3 illustrates a reference to a monthly magazine. Most monthly magazines have a volume and number designation somewhere in them, but they are more commonly referred to by month and year.

5. *Issue date* Periodicals variously use months, days, and years to identify issues. The date is written in whatever form the periodical uses, but the names of the months may be abbreviated.

6. *Page number* The number of the page on which the quotation or piece of information can be found is included. The varying use and omission of the abbreviation *p.* or *pp.* as described above for books hold true for references to periodicals as well. One situation in which the abbreviation is almost always

dropped occurs when the reference is to a volume number and page number only. In that case, the volume number and page number are separated by a colon, and neither is identified with an abbreviation. Notes 1 and 7 on page 206 illustrate this styling.

NOTE: In making the decision of whether or not to include the abbreviation, writers and editors should keep in mind the needs of their readers. If most of the readers are well acquainted with footnote style, the abbreviation can be safely dropped. However, if a significant number of the readers of a text are unfamiliar with footnote styling, including the identifying abbreviation will help lessen the chances of confusion.

Unpublished materials A footnote referring to a work that is unpublished should include as many of the following elements as are known or are relevant. The elements described below are illustrated in notes 8 and 9 on page 206.

1. *Author's name* The author's name is treated in the same way as described above for a book.

2. *Title of the work* The title is enclosed in quotation marks and capitalized like a book title.

3. *The nature of the material* The reference should include a description of the document (as "letter" or "dissertation").

4. *Date* Include the date of the material if it is known.

5. *Folio number or other identification number* Include whatever kind of identification number is conventionally used with the material.

6. *Geographical location of the material* Include the name of the institution where the materials can be found and the city where the institution is located.

Style and Content for Subsequent References

There are two systems that are currently used to refer to a source that has already been cited. One makes use of a shortened footnote styling; the other uses Latin abbreviations. Both systems are described below.

Shortened footnotes When the same source is cited repeatedly with intervening footnotes, shortened footnotes may be used as space-saving devices. The following styling is generally acceptable for most publications.

1. If the author's name occurs in the running text, it need not be repeated in footnote references to the work after the first one.

   first reference
      1. Albert H. Marckwardt, *American English* (New York: Oxford University Press, 1980), p. 94.

   repeated reference
      2. *American English,* p. 95.

2. If the author's name does not appear in the running text prior to a repeated reference, either of the following stylings may be used. The styling of footnote 3 should be followed if more than one work by the same author is cited within the text.

   repeated reference
      3. Marckwardt, *American English,* p. 95.
      or
      4. Marckwardt, p. 95.

3. In repeated references to books by more than one author, the authors' names may be shortened. The styling of footnote 6 should be followed if more than one work by the same authors is cited within the text.

   first reference
      5. De Witt T. Starnes and Gertrude E. Noyes, *The English Dictionary from Cawdrey to Johnson 1604–1775* (Chapel Hill: University of North Carolina Press, 1946), p. 120.

   repeated reference
      6. Starnes and Noyes, *The English Dictionary from Cawdrey to Johnson 1604–1775,* p. 126.
      or
      7. Starnes and Noyes, p. 126.

4. A long title may be shortened if it has already been given in full in an earlier footnote.
      8. Starnes and Noyes, *The English Dictionary,* p. 126.

5. A shortened reference to an article in a periodical that has been cited earlier should include the author's last name; the title of the article, which can be shortened if it is a long one, and if no similar title by the same author is being cited; and the page number.
      9. Goldman, "Warren G. Harding," p. 45.

Latin abbreviations While the simplified and shortened footnote stylings described above have gained wide currency, some writers still prefer to use the traditional Latin abbreviations *ibid., loc. cit.,* and *op. cit.* as space-savers in repeated references to sources cited earlier. Current usage indicates that these abbreviations need no longer be typed with underscoring or italicized in type; however, some writers still prefer this traditional styling. When a page reference follows one of these abbreviations, it may or may not be set off with a comma.

> 10. Ibid. pp. 95–98.
> *or*
> 11. Ibid., pp. 95–98.

These Latin abbreviations are capitalized when they appear at the beginning of a footnote or endnote, but not otherwise.

The abbreviation *ibid.* (for *ibidem,* "in the same place") is used when the writer is referring to the work cited in the immediately preceding footnote. The abbreviation may be used several times in succession.

> *first reference*
> 12. Simone de Beauvoir, *The Second Sex,* trans. and ed. H. M. Parshley (New York: Alfred A. Knopf, 1953), p. 600.
>
> *repeated reference* (immediately following note 12)
> 13. Ibid., p. 609.
>
> *repeated reference* (immediately following note 13)
> 14. Ibid.

When *ibid.* is used without a page number, it indicates that the same page of the same source is being cited as in the footnote immediately preceding. Thus, note 14 above cites page 609 of *The Second Sex.*

The abbreviations *loc. cit.* (for *loco citato,* "in the place cited") and *op. cit.* (for *opere citato,* "in the work cited") may be used only in conjunction with the author's name, which may occur in the running text or at the beginning of the first reference. When the writer cites a book or periodical, its complete title should be included the first time it is referred to in a footnote. In subsequent references, *loc. cit.* or *op. cit.* with or without page numbers may be substituted for the title, depending on the type of citation.

The difference between *loc. cit.* and *op. cit.* is that *loc. cit.* is used only when referring to the same page or pages of the same source cited earlier with footnotes intervening, while *op. cit.* is used to refer to a source cited earlier but not to the same page or pages of that source.

> *first reference*
> 15. De Witt T. Starnes and Gertrude E. Noyes, *The English Dictionary from Cawdrey to Johnson 1604–1775* (Chapel Hill: University of North Carolina Press, 1946), pp. 119–133.

repeated reference (with other footnotes intervening)
>   18. Starnes and Noyes, loc. cit.
>   21. Starnes and Noyes, loc. cit., p. 119.

The note without a page number indicates that pages 119–133 are being cited again.
>   Examples of the use of *op. cit.* are as follows:

first reference
>   22. Albert H. Marckwardt, *American English* (New York: Oxford University Press, 1980), p. 94.

repeated reference
>   24. Marckwardt, op. cit., p. 98.

The title of the work rather than the Latin abbreviation should be used if the writer is using material from more than one work by the same author.

Nonbibliographical Footnotes and Endnotes

Nonbibliographical notes provide additional information, commentary, or cross-references that the author does not want to include in the main text. They are keyed to the text in the same way as bibliographical notes. In texts in which bibliographical notes are keyed with superior numerals, nonbibliographical notes are included in the same sequence, as in the examples below.

>   1. Lyon Richardson, *A History of Early American Magazines* (New York: Thomas Nelson and Sons, 1931), p. 8.
>   2. Total average circulation per issue of magazines reporting to the Bureau of Circulation rose from 96.8 million in 1939 to 147.8 million in 1945.
>   3. For a particularly compelling account of this episode, see James P. Wood, *Magazines in the United States* (New York: The Ronald Press Company, 1949), pp. 92–108.
>   4. Richardson, op. cit., p. 42.
>   5. For more details, see Appendix.

Texts that rely on parenthetical references for bibliographical notes can still include footnotes or endnotes for other notes. When a nonbibliographical note mentions the name of a book or article that is not the source of a quotation or piece of information in the text, footnote styling is used to describe the reference.

In some publications, there are certain nonbibliographical notes that are not keyed to the text with any kind of symbol. These include notes that an editor places at the beginning of each part of a collection of works by different authors and that identify each author. They also include notes that an author uses to acknowledge those who gave assistance or contributed to the writing of the work. One reason that these notes are not keyed is that the only logical place to put the reference mark (described below) or number would be following the title of the work or the name of the author (both of which are often set in a larger distinctive type style), and some editors and designers are reluctant to use footnote symbols in this position. These unnumbered notes are conventionally placed in the footnote position on the first page.

Reference Marks

In texts that have only a limited number of footnotes or endnotes, writers sometimes substitute reference marks for reference numbers. The traditional footnote reference symbols are listed below in the order in which they are usually used.

* asterisk
† dagger
‡ double dagger
§ section mark
‖ parallels
¶ paragraph mark
# number sign

The sequence of these symbols can begin anew with each page or with each chapter. If more than seven notes are needed in a sequence, the reference marks are doubled, as **, ††, etc.; however, if such a large number of footnotes is needed, reference numbers rather than reference symbols should probably be used. A common alternative to using the full set of symbols when only a few footnotes are needed is to use an asterisk for the first note, a double asterisk for the second, and so on without using the dagger or other marks. A variation on this that works for up to four footnotes in a sequence is to use the asterisk and dagger in the following order: *, **, †, ††.

Parenthetical References

Parenthetical references present very abbreviated bibliographical information (typically the name of the author followed by a page number, but sometimes just a page number) enclosed in parentheses. They are placed in the main body of the text, and they refer the reader to a list of references that is found at the end of the article, chapter, or book. A list of references is simply a bibliography, and details regarding its content and styling are presented in the section on Bibliographies and Lists of References, later in this chapter. For purposes of convenience, a sample list of

references is included on page 213, and all parenthetical references in this section refer to it.

Parenthetical formats have the advantage of providing essential and useful information within the text, without providing so
much information that reading the text is impeded. They can
help the reader decide whether to turn to the list of references
for further information.

The practice of using parenthetical references originated in
the social and natural sciences; however, its adoption for writing
in the humanities, and for all general writing that includes numer-
ous bibliographical references, is being encouraged more and
more. Most systems of parenthetical references are similar, but
differences in details of styling do exist among the systems used
by various academic disciplines and professional organizations.
The examples in this section of the book are styled in accordance
with the precepts of the *MLA Handbook for Writers of Research Papers*, second edition, to which readers of this book are referred for
more details regarding parenthetical references. A discussion of a
different parenthetical reference system used in the sciences follows at the end of this section.

Placement of the Reference

Parenthetical references are placed immediately after the quotation or piece of information whose source they refer to. The sample on page 214 reproduces the text of the sample on page 200
and shows how the same text would appear using parenthetical
references instead of footnotes. Note especially that sentence
punctuation (that is, punctuation not associated with a quotation)
is placed after the reference. This means that periods and commas are placed outside of quotation marks and that run-in quoted
sentences that end in an omission are styled with three spaced ellipsis points before the reference and a terminal period closed-up
after the reference. If the final sentence of the extract quotation
on page 214 had been set as a run-in quotation, it would appear
as follows:

> Lesikar says, "The quoted passage is further distinguished from
> the report writer's work by single spacing . . ." (187).

Content and Style of Parenthetical References

The content and style are determined by two factors: (1) the style
and content of the first element of the entry in the list of references to which it refers and (2) the bibliographical information
that is included in the text around it.

These general principles are illustrated in the example on
page 214. For instance, in the third paragraph, the parenthetical
reference "(Anderson et al. 391)" is given because, in the list of

List of References

Anderson, Ruth I., et al. *The Administrative Secretary: Resource.* New York: McGraw-Hill, 1970.

"Aristotle." *Webster's New Biographical Dictionary.* Springfield, Mass.: Merriam-Webster Inc., 1983.

Brushaw, Charles T., Gerald J. Alred, and Walter E. Oliu. *Handbook of Technical Writing.* 2d ed. New York: St. Martin's Press, 1982.

Chambers, Robert. *Cyclopaedia of English Literature.* 2 vols. New York: World Publishing House, 1875.

Lesikar, Raymond V. *Report Writing for Business.* Homewood, Ill.: Richard D. Irwin, Inc., 1981.

National Micrographics Association. *An Introduction to Micrographics.* Rev. ed. Silver Spring, Md.: National Micrographics Association, 1980.

Rules for Alphabetical Filing as Standardized by ARMA. Prairie Village, Kans.: Association of Record Managers and Administrators, 1981.

Figure 7.4. A sample list of references

references, the full reference to this source begins "Anderson, Ruth I., et al."

The way that bibliographical information in the text determines the styling of the parenthetical reference is illustrated in the first sentence of the first paragraph. The parenthetical reference "(187)" is sufficient, because it is clear that Lesikar is the author of the source that is being quoted. In the second paragraph, the full parenthetical reference "(Lesikar 188)" is required because it is not clear from the sentence who is the source of the information being provided.

Sometimes a reference is supported by citations to two separate sources; the two citations are enclosed in the same parentheses but are separated by a semicolon, as "(Lesikar 189; Anderson et al. 390)." Lengthy parenthetical references should be avoided because they interrupt the flow of text. Authors can avoid unwieldy parenthetical references by incorporating as much of the bibliographical information within the text as can be smoothly absorbed.

According to Lesikar, if a "quoted passage is four lines or
less in length, it is typed with the report text and is distinguished from the normal text by quotation marks" (187). However,
a different procedure is used for longer quotations:

> But if a longer quotation (five lines or more) is used,
> the conventional practice is to set it in from both
> left and right margins (about five spaces) but without
> quotation marks. . . . The quoted passage is further
> distinguished from the report writer's work by single
> spacing. . . . (187)

A series of usually three periods called ellipsis is used to
indicate omissions of material from a passage (Lesikar 188).

Footnotes may be placed "at the bottom of the page . . .
separated from the text by a horizontal line. If a line is used,
it is typed a single space below the text and followed by one
blank line" (Anderson et al. 391). Lesikar prefers the separation
line to be one and one-half or two inches (189). Generally, typewriting textbooks state that a two-inch line is adequate (20 pica
strokes; 24 elite strokes). The line is constructed by striking
the underscore key.

From a typing standpoint, reserve three lines of blank typing
space per footnote at the bottom of the page.

The first line of a footnote is indented from one to six (but
usually two or five) spaces from the left margin, depending on the
writer's preference or the style manual being followed. The footnote may be introduced with the applicable superscript Arabic numeral, unpunctuated and separated from the first letter of the
author's first name by one space; or it may be introduced by the

Figure 7.5. A typewritten page with parenthetical references

Matching the list of references The name in a parenthetical reference must correspond to a name that begins an entry in the list of references. In general, the last name of the author is usually sufficient within a parenthetical reference, as it was in the case of the references to Lesikar's book in the sample on page 214. However, if there had been another author with the last name Lesikar in the list of references, it would have been necessary to include both first and last name, as "(Lesikar, Raymond, 188)." Alternatively, if the list of references had included two different books both of which were by Raymond Lesikar, it would have been necessary to include both the author's name and the book's title (which may be shortened) in the parenthetical reference, as "(Lesikar, *Report Writing* 188)." The following paragraphs explain some other special cases.

1. *A work with two or three authors* The list of references on page 213 includes an entry for a book by Charles T. Brushaw, Gerald J. Alred, and Walter E. Oliu. A parenthetical reference to that work would take the following form:

   (Brushaw, Alred, and Oliu 182–184)

2. *A work with more than three authors* A work with more than three authors is listed in the list of references under the name of the first author, followed by the phrase *et al*. The reference to Anderson et al. in the third paragraph of the sample on page 214 illustrates this style.

3. *A work by a corporate author* The list of references on page 213 includes an entry in which National Micrographics Association is given as the author. A parenthetical reference to that work would also use National Micrographics Association as its author, although the name may be abbreviated.

   (National Micrographics 42)
   or
   (Natl. Micrographics 42)

4. *A work listed by its title* The list of references on page 213 includes an entry for a book *Rules for Alphabetical Filing as Standardized by ARMA*. A parenthetical reference to that work should also refer to it by its title, which may be shortened for convenience.

   (*Rules for Alphabetical Filing* 14)
   or
   (*Rules* 14)

Locators Usually the only locator that is required in a parenthetical reference is a page number. However, sometimes additional or alternate information is needed to help the reader find the original source. The following paragraphs describe some of these special situations. Note that in all cases no punctuation separates the author's name or the title from the locator and that no abbreviation is used to identify the nature of the locator unless confusion would result from its omission (but see the note following paragraph 1 below).

1. *A multivolume work* The list of references on page 213 includes a reference to Robert Chambers's two-volume *Cyclopaedia of English Literature*. A reference to that work would have to include a volume designation as well as a page number. The volume number and the page number are separated by an unspaced colon.

    (Chambers 1:45)

    NOTE: If an entire volume of a multivolume work is being referred to, the abbreviation *vol.* is used to make it clear that the number is a volume number and not a page number.

    (Chambers, vol. 1)

2. *A reference book* A reference to an entry in a reference book often begins with the name of the entry being cited, as in the entry for "Aristotle" on page 213. A parenthetic reference need only mention the name of the entry, as no page number is included in the list of references. The name of the reference book should be mentioned in the text preceding such a reference; otherwise, the reader must consult the list of references to know what source is being cited.

    ("Aristotle")

3. *Literary works* Parenthetical references to literary works often include references to stanzas, lines, verses, chapters, books, parts, and the like. This is often very useful to readers trying to find a particular passage, because they may be using an edition of the work whose pagination differs from that of the edition used by the author of the note. For more on giving references to literary works, see the section on Special Cases later in this chapter.

References to unpublished sources Parenthetical references are also used to cite unpublished sources that are not listed in a bibliography, such as letters to the author or telephone interviews. The following information should be included: the name of the person providing the information, the type of source, and the date, as "(Paul Roberts, letter to the author, Sept. 1984)." Any of these elements may be omitted from the parenthetical reference if included in the text.

Parenthetical Reference Styling in the Sciences

Another system of parenthetical citation that is used mostly in the social and natural sciences is the author-date system (also called the name-year system). In the author-date system the parenthetical reference contains the author's last name and the date of publication with no intervening punctuation. A third element, a page number, is optional. If the author's name is mentioned in the introductory text, only the date and possibly the page number are needed within the parentheses. By referring to the list of references, the reader can find complete bibliographical information about the work. However, lists of references written in connection with the author-date system must also follow the scientific styling of placing the date after the author's name in each entry.

A book or article by two or more authors would be represented by the following stylings:

(Martin and Zim 1951)

(Martin, Zim, and Nelson 1951)

(Martin et al. 1951)

A corporate author name or a title may be substituted when there are no individual authors. An editor's last name may also be substituted, but the name is not followed by the abbreviation *ed.*

A page number or other number indicating a division of the work is often added to the date with a comma (a colon in some stylings) between date and page numbers. For citations to the short articles so prevalent in the scientific literature, page numbers are unnecessary, but for books, page references are certainly helpful to the reader.

(Martin et al. 1951, 147–149) *or* (Martin et al. 1951:147–149)

Volumes are indicated by Arabic numerals. Thus, "(1.147–149)" denotes volume 1, pages 147–149.

More than one work by the same author can be readily shown with the listing of a second date that follows the first with a comma between them, as "(Martin et al. 1951, 1958)." Two or more separate citations can also be included within one parenthesis if they are separated by a semicolon.

More than one work published in the same year by the same author can be indicated by adding an *a, b,* or *c* to the date. The same letters should be added to the dates in the entries in the list of references.

(Martin and Zim 1952a)

Bibliographies and Lists of References

A bibliography differs from a list of references in that it lists all of the works that a writer has found relevant in writing the text. A list of references, on the other hand, includes only those works that are specifically mentioned in the text or from which a particular quotation or piece of information was taken. In all other respects, however, bibliographies and lists of references are quite similar. They both appear at the end of an article, chapter, or book, where they list sources of information that are relevant to the text. They differ from a section of bibliographical endnotes in that their entries are arranged alphabetically (as in the sample on page 213), and they use different patterns of indention, punctuation, and capitalization, as explained in the paragraphs that follow. Bibliographies and lists of references are punctuated and capitalized in the same way, and hereafter in this chapter, references to bibliographies should be understood to be inclusive of lists of references as well.

Additional detail regarding the styling of bibliographical entries is provided in the following paragraphs. For each of the kinds of entries that are described below, two examples are given. The first example is in a style used in the humanities, which is also the style used in most general writing and the style that is familiar to most writers. The second example is in a style that is representative of the social and natural sciences.

In general, bibliographical stylings used in the sciences differ from those used in general writing in that (1) the author's first and middle names are expressed with initials only, (2) the date, which is important in scientific writings, is often placed near the beginning instead of at the end of the entry, (3) less capitalization is used, (4) titles of articles are not enclosed in quotation marks, (5) book titles are not underlined or italicized, (6) dates are usually written as day-month-year, which results in less punctuation, and (7) more abbreviations are used. In content, however, the two stylings are much the same, and both rely on periods to separate each element of the bibliographical entry.

The examples used in this section by no means exhaust the possible variations on these two basic stylings. Different combinations of the styles illustrated here, as well as other alternatives, are found in print. Several of these variations are recommended by various professional organizations and academic disciplines within the social and natural sciences. The entries in this section that illustrate scientific style are based on the style described in the *CBE Style Manual*, fifth edition, published by the Council of Biology Editors. (NOTE: Some entries in this section may differ somewhat from preferred CBE style. Writers who need to style their bibliographies in strict accordance with CBE style should consult that manual.) Other style manuals that give details of bibliographical styling used in specialized fields within the social and natural sciences are published by professional organizations in those fields.

Books

Style and content of entries A bibliographical entry that refers to a book includes as many of the following elements as are relevant. The order of elements listed here is the order in which they appear in entries written in the styling of the humanities. Each of these elements is illustrated in the examples that begin on page 221.

1. *Author's name* The author's name or authors' names come first, whether the author is a single individual, or a group of individuals, or an organization. Names of coauthors are arranged in the order in which they are found on the title page. A work without an author but with an editor is styled with the editor's name first, followed by a comma and *ed.* (see paragraph 4 below). The name of the first author is inverted so that the surname comes first and can be alphabetized. In bibliographies that follow the style of the humanities, the author's name is written as it appears on the title page. In many stylings used in the social and natural sciences, the last name and first two initials are always used, regardless of how the author's name is printed on the title page. This is the style followed in this section for examples of bibliographical entries in the social and natural sciences; however, authors should remember that some confusion can result if more than one writer in the relevant subject area has the same initials and last name. The best way to avoid this difficulty is to include first names whenever there is a chance of confusion.

    In the humanities and in some stylings in the social and natural sciences, if there are more than three authors the first author's name is followed by *et al.*, which is an abbreviation for the Latin phrase *et alii* or *et aliae*, meaning "and others." In other stylings, the names of all the authors are included.

2. *Title of the work* In the humanities, the title is underlined in typewritten manuscript and italicized in type. In the social and natural sciences, the title may follow this styling or it may be left without underlining or italicization. Capitalization is either headline-style (that is, all words are capitalized except for internal articles and prepositions) or sentence-style (that is, only the first word and proper nouns and adjectives are capital-

ized). In the humanities, headline-style capitalization is used; in the social and natural sciences, both styles of capitalization are used. The titles of references in the sciences that appear as examples in this chapter are unitalicized and use sentence-style capitalization. Another difference between the two stylings is that titles in the humanities include any subtitles, whereas subtitles are often omitted in bibliographies for the sciences. Subtitles are italicized and capitalized to match the styling of the titles that precede them.

3. *Portion of the book* Some bibliography entries cite only one portion of a book, as an essay within a collection or an article within a symposium. For these entries, the name of that portion is given first as a title. It is either italicized or enclosed in quotation marks, depending on its nature, or it is left alone as in stylings for the sciences. The title of the book is given next. The titles of chapters within nonfiction works by a single author are usually not included in the entry.

4. *Editor, compiler, or translator* In entries for books that have an author, the name of an editor, compiler, or translator comes after the title and is preceded or followed by the abbreviation *ed.*, *comp.*, or *trans.* or some combination of these. If no author is listed, the name of the editor, compiler, or translator is placed first in the entry—styled like an author's name but followed by a comma and the lowercase abbreviation *ed.*, *comp.*, or *trans.*

5. *Edition* If a book is other than the first edition, the number (as "2d ed." or "1986 ed.") or other description of the edition is written after the title. If the edition is identified by a word instead of a numeral, the first letter in that word is capitalized, as "Rev. ed."

6. *Volume number or number of volumes* In a bibliography entry that cites a multivolume work, the total number of volumes in that work is written before the publication information as, for example, "9 vols." There is no need to cite the volumes actually used, since this information will be in a note or in a parenthetical reference. On the other hand, if only one volume of a multivolume work was consulted, that volume alone is listed as an entry, so that the text references need cite only page numbers, not volume numbers as well.

7. *Name of the series* If the book is part of a series, the name of the series should be included, as well as the book or volume number if the book represents a specific numbered volume in that series. The series name is not italicized.

8. *Publication data* The city of publication (with the state abbreviation if the city is not well known), the name of the publisher, and the year of publication of the particular edition used—together these form the grouping called the publication data. A colon usually follows the city name, a comma follows the name of the publisher, and a period after the date ends the bibliographical entry if the styling is that used in the humanities. In stylings used in the sciences, the date often appears after the author's name.

All of this information comes from the title page and the copyright page. If the title page lists more than one city, only the first is mentioned in the bibliography. Some books are published under a special imprint name, which is usually printed on the title page above the publisher's name. In a bibliographical entry, the imprint name is joined to the publisher's name with a hyphen, as *Golden Press-Western Publishing Co.* Short forms of publisher's names are often used in bibliographies. This usage is acceptable if consistently applied. Also the word *and* and the ampersand are equally acceptable within a publisher's name if they are used consistently.

For a multivolume work that is published over a period of several years, inclusive numbers are given for those years. The phrase *in press* is substituted for the date in works that are about to be published.

9. *Locators* Page numbers are added to book entries in a bibliography only when the entry cites a portion of a book such as a story or essay in an anthology or an article in a collection. If that portion is in a volume of a multivolume work, both volume and page number are given.

Examples The following examples illustrate how each of the elements described above is styled in a number of different situations. In each case, the first example illustrates a typical style in the humanities and general publications; the second illustrates a representative style used in the social and natural sciences.

1. *Book with a single author*

    Chapman, R. F. *The Insects.* New York: American Elsevier, 1969.

    Chapman, R. F. 1969. The insects. New York: American Elsevier.

2. *Book with two or three authors*

    Starnes, De Witt T., and Gertrude E. Noyes. *The English Dictionary from Cawdrey to Johnson 1604–1775.* Chapel Hill: University of North Carolina Press, 1946.

    Starnes, D. T.; Noyes, G. E. 1946. The English dictionary from Cawdrey to Johnson 1604–1775. Chapel Hill: University of North Carolina Press.

3. *Book with more than three authors*

> Allee, W. C., et al. *Principles of Animal Ecology*. Philadelphia: W. B. Saunders Co., 1949.

> Allee, W. C.; Emerson, A. E.; Park, O.; Park, S.; Schmidt, K. D. 1949. Principles of animal ecology. Philadelphia: W. B. Saunders Co.

4. *Book with a corporate author*

> National Micrographics Association. *An Introduction to Micrographics*. Rev. ed. Silver Spring, Md.: National Micrographics Association, 1980.

> National Micrographics Association. 1980. An introduction to micrographics. Rev. ed. Silver Spring, Md.: National Micrographics Association.

5. *Book without an author listed*

> *The World Almanac & Book of Facts*. New York: Newspaper Enterprises Association, Inc., 1985.

> The world almanac & book of facts. 1985. New York: Newspaper Enterprises Association.

6. *Book with editor listed and no author*

> Bradbury, Peggy F., ed. *Transcriber's Guide to Medical Terminology*. New Hyde Park, N.Y.: Medical Examination Publishing Co., 1973.

> Bradbury, P. F., editor. 1973. Transcriber's guide to medical terminology. New Hyde Park, N.Y.: Medical Examination Publishing Co.

7. *Book with author and editor-translator*

> Beauvoir, Simone de. *The Second Sex*. Trans. and ed. H. M. Parshley. New York: Alfred A. Knopf, 1953.

> Beauvoir, S. 1953. The second sex. Parshley, H. M., translator and editor. New York: Alfred A. Knopf.

8. *Multivolume book*

> Farrand, John Jr., ed. *The Audubon Society Master Guide to Birding*. 3 vols. New York: Alfred A. Knopf, 1983.

> Farrand, J. Jr., editor. 1983. The Audubon Society master guide to birding. New York: Alfred A. Knopf, 3 vol.

9. *Multivolume book only one volume of which was consulted*

> Chambers, Robert. Vol. 1 of *Cyclopaedia of English Literature*. 2 vols. New York: World Publishing House, 1875.

> Chambers, R. 1875. Cyclopaedia of English literature. Vol. 1. New York: World Publishing House.

10. *Portion of a book*

> Malone, Kemp. "The Phonemes of Current English." *Studies for William A. Read.* Ed. Nathaniel M. Caffee and Thomas A. Kirby. Baton Rouge: Louisiana State University Press, 1940. pp. 133–165.
>
> Malone, K. 1940. The phonemes of current English. In: Caffee, N. M.; Kirby, T. A., eds. Studies for William A. Read. Baton Rouge: Louisiana State University Press: p. 133–165.

11. *Book in a series*

> Manheimer, Martha L. *Style Manual: A Guide for the Preparation of Reports and Dissertations.* Vol. 5 of Books in Library and Information Science. New York: Marcel Dekker, 1973.
>
> Manheimer, M. L. 1973. Style manual. New York: Marcel Dekker. (Books in library and information science; vol. 5.)

Articles in Journals or Other Periodicals

Style and Content of Entries A bibliography entry for an article in a journal or other periodical or in a newspaper includes as many of the following elements as are relevant. Examples of each of these elements can be found in the reference samples beginning on page 225. The elements are listed here in the order in which they appear in entries styled on the humanities pattern.

1. *Author's name* The author's name is written as it appears on the printed page and is styled in the way described above for an entry that refers to a book. Names of people who write letters to a periodical or who contribute signed reviews are treated like names of authors.

2. *Title of the article* The title of the article is written in full as it appears in the printed article. In most bibliography stylings used in the humanities, the title and subtitle are enclosed in quotation marks (with a period before the closing quotation mark) and capitalized headline-style. Titles of articles styled for use in the social and natural sciences tend to omit the quotation marks, use sentence-style capitalization, and omit subtitles.

3. *Name of the periodical* The name of the periodical is treated in the same way as described above for a book: underlined to indicate italics in bibliographies for the humanities but not italicized in bibliographies for the sciences. However, unlike book titles, periodical titles are fully capitalized in bibliographies in both the humanities and the sciences. In addition, there are special principles for the styling of periodical names in both categories. One is the omission of an initial article. Whereas

the initial article is included in a book title but ignored in alphabetizing, the initial article of a journal title is dropped completely. Another is the use of abbreviations for journal titles of more than one word. These abbreviations are widely used in technical writing. Each discipline has its own set of abbreviations for the journals that tend to be used in that discipline. For general writing, however, these titles are written in full for the reader's convenience, and the examples that follow show journal titles in unabbreviated form. Journal titles that begin with the words *Transactions, Proceedings,* and *Annals* are often reversed for the purpose of alphabetizing so that these words come last.

Names of newspapers are treated as they appear on the masthead, except that initial articles are omitted. Also, a place name is added in brackets after the newspaper's name if it is necessary to distinguish that particular paper.

4. *Volume and number of the periodical* This information comes after the name of the periodical and identifies the particular issue cited. An issue that is identified by both volume and number should be identified in that way in a bibliography entry, as "3(2):25–37" for volume 3, number 2, pages 25–37. If the issue is identified in some other manner, as by a full date, that method is used in the bibliography entry. Issue numbers are not commonly used, however, unless the issue is paginated independently of the volume as a whole and the number is needed to identify the issue. Examples 1 and 5 below illustrate entries for a periodical in which pages are numbered consecutively through a volume and which therefore needs only a volume number. If the volume number corresponds to a particular year, as in the examples, the year in parentheses follows the volume number—but not, of course, in the scientific stylings, where the year is placed after the author's name.

Example 2 on page 225 illustrates a reference to a periodical that uses a seasonal designation in addition to a volume and number designation; the pages in this issue are numbered independently of the volume as a whole. Example 3 illustrates a popular monthly magazine, issues of which are commonly referred to by date rather than by volume or issue number. Newspapers are always identified by date.

5. *Issue date* Periodicals issued daily, weekly, monthly, and bimonthly are usually designated by date of issue. The date follows the unpunctuated day-month-year order (27 May 1984) rather than the punctuated month-day-year order (May 27, 1984). Names of months that are spelled with more than four letters are usually abbreviated.

6. *Page numbers* Inclusive pages for the whole article are written at the end of the entry. For newspaper entries, it may be necessary to add a section number or edition identification number as well, as "p. B6." Articles that are continued on later pages are styled thus: "38–41, 159–160." The use of the abbreviations *p.* or *pp.* in bibliographies is the same as it is in footnotes (see pages 206–207).

Examples The following examples illustrate how each of the elements described above is styled in a number of different situations. The first example of each group illustrates a style used in the humanities and in general publications; the second illustrates a style used in the social and natural sciences.

1. *Article in journal with continuous pagination of volume*

   > Heil, John. "Seeing is Believing." *American Philosophical Quarterly* 19 (1982): 229–239.
   >
   > Heil, J. 1982. Seeing is believing. American Philosophical Quarterly 19:229–239.

2. *Article in journal that paginates each issue separately*

   > Ourecky, Donald K. "Cane and Bush Fruits." *Plants & Gardens* 27, No. 3 (Autumn 1971): pp. 13–15.
   >
   > Ourecky, D. K. 1971. Cane and bush fruits. Plants & Gardens 27(3):13–15.

3. *Articles in periodicals issued by date*

   > Smiley, Xan. "Misunderstanding Africa." *Atlantic,* Sept. 1982, pp. 70–79.
   >
   > Smiley, X. 1982. Misunderstanding Africa. Atlantic, Sept.:70–79.
   >
   > Rosenberg, Jeremy C. "Letters." *Advertising Age,* 7 June 1982, p. M–1.
   >
   > Rosenberg, J. C. 1982. Letters. Advertising Age, 7 June: M–1.

4. *Article in newspaper*

   > Pitts, Gail. "Money Funds Holding Own." *Morning Union* [Springfield, Mass.], 23 Aug. 1982, p. 6.
   >
   > Pitts, G. 1982. Money funds holding own. Morning Union [Springfield, Mass.] 23 Aug.:6.

5. *Signed review*

   > Vassell, M. O. Rev. of *Applied Charge Particle Optics,* ed. A. Septier. *American Scientist* 70 (1982): 229.
   >
   > Vassell, M. O. 1982. Rev. of A. Septier, ed., Applied charge particle optics. American Scientist 70:229.

6. *Anonymous article*

> "Education at Home: A Showdown in Texas." *Newsweek,* 25 March 1985, p. 87.
>
> Anonymous. 1985. Education at home. Newsweek 25 March:87.

Unpublished Materials

Bibliography entries for unpublished materials include as many of the following elements as are known or are relevant.

1. *Author's name* The author's name is treated in the same way as described above for a book.

2. *Title of the work* If there is an official title, it is copied as it appears on the work. It is enclosed in quotation marks and capitalized like a book title in a bibliography using a styling from the humanities. If the work has no official title, a descriptive title is used, as in example 2 below, but it is not enclosed in quotation marks.

3. *The nature of the material* The entry should include a description of the document, such as "letter to the author" or "doctoral dissertation." For works without official author or title, this element is the first part of the entry.

4. *Date* The date must be included if it is known. If the date is known but is not written on the document, it is enclosed in brackets.

5. *Name of collection and identification number* Whatever information is necessary to completely identify the document is included.

6. *Geographical location* The name of the institution and the city where the materials can be located are often listed last in this kind of bibliographical entry.

Examples

1. *Unpublished report*

> Velasquez, Joyce A. "The Format of Formal Reports." Report prepared for the Southern Engineering Company. Johnson City, Miss., May 29, 1985.
>
> Velasquez, J. A. 1985. The format of formal reports. Report prepared for the Southern Engineering Company. 29 May. Johnson City, Miss.

2. *Letter in a collection*

> Johnson, Clive. Letter to Elizabeth O'Hara. 9 Nov. 1916. Johnson

Collection, item 5298. California State Historical Society, San Marino, Calif.

Johnson, C. 1916. Letter to Elizabeth O'Hara. 9 Nov. Located at California State Historical Society, San Marino, Calif.

Format of a Bibliography

Bibliographies are always typed beginning on a new page. Most are alphabetically arranged and indented flush-and-hang to set off the alphabetical sequence. Initial articles that are included in a title that begins an entry are ignored in determining the alphabetical order. All the entries are usually listed together in a single alphabetical arrangement, whether the first word is an author's surname or the title of an anonymous work. It is possible to divide a bibliography into categories by date of publication or by subject matter, but such divisions are not recommended unless the single-list form proves unmanageable.

More than one work by an author After the first listing of an entry by an author or group of coauthors who have more than one work listed in the bibliography, that person's name is replaced in succeeding, adjacent entries by a dash. In typewritten bibliographies, the dash is usually represented by three typed hyphens. The author is not usually expected to type this dash or its equivalent in hyphens; instead, the editor substitutes the dash for the author's names as needed on the copyedited page. The dash is followed by a period, just as a name would be, or by a comma and an abbreviation such as *ed.*

The dash substitutes for the author's full name (or the full names of the set of coauthors) but no more. Thus, the dash may be used only when the names are exactly the same in adjacent entries. For example, if an entry for a work by Kemp Malone is followed by an entry for a work coauthored by Malone and someone else, the second entry would be spelled out. But if Malone and his coauthor wrote more than one book together, the dash would be used to replace both names in the second reference. A work by a single author precedes a work by that author and another; and works edited by an author usually follow works written by the same person.

In the general bibliographical stylings, the various works by a single author or group of coauthors are arranged alphabetically by title. In bibliographies in the social and natural sciences, however, where the date appears after the author's name, these multiple entries are arranged by date of publication. Occasionally an author publishes more than one article during a year. In these cases, the work is identified by a letter (often italicized) that follows the year. Thus, an author's works may be listed as 1977, 1979a, 1979b, 1980, and so on.

Headings Depending on their scope as explained at the beginning of this section, bibliographies may be headed *Bibliography* or *List of References*. Writings in the sciences often list bibliographical entries under the heading *Literature Cited*. If this heading is used, then only "literature"—that is, published works—and only works actually cited can be included on the list. Unpublished works that are referred to in the text must carry information such as the author's name and the title and where the work can be located, as well as the word *unpublished,* within the text or within parentheses. To avoid having to refer to an unwieldy number of unpublished works in the text, the author or editor may head the reference list *References Cited,* which allows the inclusion of unpublished works. Works in press are usually listed under *Literature Cited* heads even though they are not yet published. In lieu of the date, the entry contains the phrase *in press.*

Annotated bibliographies Annotated bibliographies are those in which the entries are written as for a regular bibliography but are then followed by a sentence or paragraph of description. Annotated bibliographies are designed to lead the reader to the most useful works for further study. Comments may be added to all or just some of the entries. The descriptive part may be run in with the bibliographical entry, or it may be set off typographically by lines of space, indention, italics, or smaller type.

Special Cases

Lists of references frequently contain items that do not fit neatly into any of the categories described in the previous sections of this chapter. Some are printed items like government publications, others are nonprint items. These special references are styled, as far as possible, in formats similar to those used for the published and unpublished works described and illustrated in the previous sections. They are arranged and punctuated in a way that corresponds to whatever styling has been chosen for the publication's notes, parenthetical references, and bibliography entries.

In the following paragraphs there are several references to the styling of titles in quotation marks or italics. These statements refer only to the documentation styles used in the humanities and in general-purpose writing. As was pointed out in the preceding section, titles have no special styling in the documentation formats used in the social and natural sciences. Also the date of publication, which occurs near the end of the references discussed here, is set after the author's name in the bibliographical stylings used in the sciences.

Nonprint Sources

Many sources in the following categories are often not cited in bibliographies and lists of references. When they are not, however, full documentation should be supplied within the text or in a note.

Personal communications The name of the person who supplied information in a personal communication is listed first in this kind of reference; the name is styled like an author's name. A descriptive word or phrase (like *personal communication* or *telephone interview*) follows, unitalicized and without quotation marks. The place, if applicable, and date of the communication are also given. This type of source is rarely included in a list of references. In scientific publications a form like the following is often found as a parenthetical reference: "(J. Scott, pers. comm. 1985)."

Speeches Lectures and other addresses are listed with the speaker's name first, then the title of the speech in quotation marks (or a descriptive term if the speech has no title), the name of the meeting or sponsoring organization or the occasion, then the place and date.

Radio and television programs The title of the program is usually listed first and is underlined or italicized. However, if the program is an episode of a multipart series, the episode title is placed in quotation marks and the name of the series follows without underlining or italics. If the reference in the text is to a particular performer, composer, or other person, that person's name may be listed before the title. Following the title are the names of the network, the local station and city (in a bibliography entry these two are separated by a comma not a period), and the date of the broadcast. Depending on its relevance, additional information may be given after the title, such as the names of the performers, the composer, or the director.

Sound recordings, films, and videotapes Sound recordings, films and filmscripts, and videotapes are usually documented according to their titles. If the name of a particular writer, composer, or performer is stressed in the text, and especially if the source is a recording, that person's name may be listed first. The italicized title is usually followed by whatever names are needed to identify the work, such as writers, performers, and others. Some programs may need to be further identified by a descriptive term like *filmstrip, slide program,* or *videocassette*. The director's name follows, preceded by the abbreviation *dir*. Finally, the name of the distributor, the year, the catalog number, and other information is added as needed to complete the identification of the work. The following example illustrates a bibliography entry for a recording.

> Brahms, Johannes. *A German Requiem (Ein deutsches Requiem)*, Op. 45. Cond. Erich Leinsdorf. Boston Symphony Orchestra. RCA, LSC-7054, 1969.

Works of art References to works of art include the artist's name, which is styled like an author's name, an italicized title, the name of the proprietary institution, and the city.

Computer software References to computer software contain the following elements: the name of the program's writer, if known; the title of the program, which is italicized; the descriptive term *computer software;* the name and location of the distributor; and the year of publication. Additional information, such as the machines or the operating systems the software is designed for, may be added at the end of the note or bibliographical entry.

Microforms Materials in microform are documented in whatever styling is appropriate for their contents—as periodical articles, unpublished reports, etc.—except that to the end of the note or the bibliography entry is added a term that describes the form (as *microfiche*) and also the name and location of the commercial service that supplied the form. However, regular published material that has been microfilmed and preserved in a library is cited as if the actual works had been handled, and there is no mention of the microform process.

Material from an information service Sources from an information service are documented like books, articles, reports, and other printed materials, but at the end of the note or bibliography entry is added the name of the service, its location, and any identification numbers for the material.

Government Publications

If a publication by a government agency has a named author, that name may go first in a note or bibliography entry. Most government publications, however, are authored by an agency. The name of the government (as United States, Montana, or Chicago) often comes first, then the name of the department if applicable, then the name of the specific agency responsible for the publication. These names are not abbreviated when they precede the title of the work.

Next is the title, italicized like a book title and further identified as needed by series or publication numbers or by whatever format the agency uses to identify the work. As with other kinds of documentation, publication data is also included. Most U.S.

government publications are published by the Government Print-
ing Office, which is usually referred to in notes and bibliographies
as *GPO*. References to congressional documents usually omit the
GPO publication data, because it is understood. Standardized abbreviations are often used in these references, but names may also
be spelled out, especially in writings for the general public.

> United States. Department of Labor. Employment and Training
> Administration. *Dictionary of Occupational Titles.* 4th ed. Wash-
> ington: GPO, 1977.

Congressional documents are often attributed first to the
"U.S. Congress" in notes and bibliography entries but not in parenthetical references. The name of the appropriate house follows
(the short forms *House* and *Senate* are used), and then the name
of the committee, if applicable. The document title is listed next
in the reference, followed by the number and session of Congress.
The year is listed next, then the number or other description of
the document. The *Congressional Record* needs to be identified only
by date and page number, as in the following bibliography entry:

> *Congressional Record.* 96th Cong., 2d sess., 1976. Vol. 5, pt. 7, pp.
> 13–27.

Bills in Congress are identified in a special way. *H.R.* is the
conventional abbreviation for the House of Representatives in this
case, and *S.* for the Senate. Thus, bills are referred to as "H.R.
93" or "S. 120." In citations to congressional reports, however, the
House is abbreviated *H.* (as in "H. Rept. 1303"), while a Senate
report would be styled "S. Rept. 671." In each case, the number
and session of the congress follow the document title.

Laws and constitutions References to laws and constitutions are
documented in notes and bibliography entries unless full information is provided in the text. These citations are not italicized. In
legal writing, a large number of standard abbreviations is used,
but in most writing for a general audience the abbreviations are
limited to those which can be readily understood by the public.
Roman numerals are traditionally used to denote certain sections
of constitutions, as shown in the first two examples below.

> U.S. Constitution, Amendment XIII.
> Indiana Constitution, Art. III, sec. 2, cl. 4.
> Trade Agreements Act, Public Law 96–39, sec. 32, 96th Cong.,
> 1st sess., July 26, 1979.
> 90 Stat. 1113 (1976).

The fourth reference in the list above is an example of the abbreviated form that is typical of legal citations. It is also typical in that
the volume number comes *before* the name of a multivolume work.

The reference points to a statute that is found in volume 90 of
the *U.S. Statutes at Large* beginning on page 1113. Inclusive numbers are not used in legal references. The examples below illustrate a reference to a federal statute that has been codified in the
U.S. Code and that can be found in volume 28, section 17 of that
work, together with its supplement.

> 28 U.S.C. sec. 17. (1964).
> 28 U.S.C. sec. 17 (1964), as amended (Supp. II, 1966).

Regulations of the federal government also conform to official citation form. Like codified statutes, regulations codified in
the *Code of Federal Regulations* or the *Federal Register* are identified
first by volume number, then by section or page number and
date.

> 33 C.F.R. sec. 403.2 (1980).
> 43 Fed. Reg. 54221 (1978).

Court Cases

Titles of court cases are italicized within the text, whether they involve two opposing parties (as *Surner* v. *Kellogg*) or whether they
have titles like *In re Watson* or *In the matter of John Watson.* When
these cases are listed in a bibliography, however, they are not italicized. The *v.* (for versus) within a case title is usually set roman in
printed matter, but on a typewritten page the underscore is usually extended throughout the case title. A citation to a court case
gives the name of the case, the number, title, and page of the volume in which it is recorded, and the date.

> *A Minor* v. *State,* 85 Nev. 323, 454 P. 2d 895 (1969).

The example above refers the reader to two sources in one
reference: volume 85 of *Nevada Reports* on page 323, and also volume 454 of the second series of the *Pacific Reporter,* on page 895.
Frequently the name of the court that decided the case is listed
before the date.

Literary Works

Since literary works are printed in so many different editions,
each of which is paginated differently, documentation of such
works as poems, stories, plays, and novels does not always involve
page numbers. Instead, reference is frequently made to the divisions of the work, such as chapter, book, part, act, scene, or line.
Page numbers are referred to, however, in prose works if the edition used is clearly identified in a list of references or in a note;
but in poetry and verse plays, where each line has a number, documentation refers to lines rather than to pages.

In cases where the author wishes to lead the reader to a particular chapter or part of a work of prose, the page number may

be given in a reference, followed by a semicolon and the appropriate location, as "22; ch. 2" or "433; pt. 7."

Numerals alone, without accompanying terms like *chapter, verse, act, scene,* or *line,* are used in footnotes and endnotes and especially in parenthetical references, where they take up little space. Numerals are used wherever they can be easily understood without accompanying words or abbreviations. Frequently two numerals are used together, one that indicates a large division of the work and another that indicates a smaller division, as "4.122" for book 4, line 122. The two numerals are separated by a period or sometimes by a comma. Some stylings use capital and lowercase Roman numerals to denote the act and scene of a play, as "*Hamlet* III.ii" for act 3, scene 2; but the Arabic form 3.2 is also found, as in "*Hamlet* 3.2."

A single numeral is generally not used in a reference without an identifying word or abbreviation because it could be confusing. Thus, parenthetical references such as the following should include an identifying term: (*Hamlet,* Act 3) and ("The Waste Land," part 4). The abbreviations for line and lines (*l.* and *ll.*) should be used with great care, since they are easily confused with the numbers 1 and 11.

The Bible

Biblical references are not usually listed in a bibliography unless a particular version or edition is specified in the text. A text reference includes the name of the book, which is not italicized and which is often abbreviated, followed by Arabic numerals representing chapter and verse. Chapter and verse numerals are traditionally separated by a colon, but a period is a common alternative. A book with two or more parts is styled with an Arabic numeral before the name of the book, as "2 Chron. 2:18." Page numbers are never used to refer to biblical material.

Chapter 8

The Treatment of Quotations

CONTENTS

Authors rely on two common conventions to indicate that a passage of prose or poetry is being quoted from another source. Short quotations are most commonly run in with the rest of the text and set off with quotation marks. Longer passages are most commonly indented as separate paragraphs without enclosing quotation marks. These paragraphs are usually referred to as *extracts, excerpts,* or *block quotations*. This chapter tells how authors decide which format to use. It also explains the conventions that apply to the treatment of long quotations set as extracts and specifies the conditions under which authors are allowed to alter the original source.

   Most of the information needed to punctuate short run-in passages can be found in Chapter 1, "Punctuation," especially in the section on Quotation Marks, Double, beginning on page 43, but also in the sections on Brackets, Colon, Comma, Ellipsis Points, and Virgule. Information about the capitalization of run-in quotations can be found in the section on Beginnings, starting on page 53, in Chapter 2, "Capitals, Italics, and Quotation Marks."

Choosing between Run-in and Block Quotations

The length of a quotation usually determines whether it is run into the text or set as a block quotation. For prose quotations, length can be assessed in terms of the number of words, the number of typewritten or typeset lines, or the number of sentences in the passage. Authors who consider the number of words in making this decision usually run in quotations of less than 100 words and set off quotations of more than 100 words. Authors who base their decisions on the number of lines in the passage use cutoff points ranging from four to ten lines. When the number of sentences is the criterion, passages of one sentence in length are run in; passages of two or more sentences are set off as extracts, although some authors add the condition that the quotation must also run to at least four lines.

Each of these approaches relies on an arbitrary cutoff, and no matter which approach is used, the writer will want to make exceptions for certain sentences. For instance, writers who want to make a passage read more smoothly may prefer to run in the longer quotations, even if the system they are using would dictate that the quotations be set as extracts. Alternatively, writers who want to emphasize quoted passages to make them easier for the reader to locate will set even short quotations as extracts.

For quotations of poetry, different criteria are used. Full lines of poetry are usually set as extracts, although it is also common to run one or two lines into the text.

Styling Block Quotations

Block quotations are set off from the text that precedes and follows them by a number of devices, including (1) the addition of extra space between the quotation and the text; (2) indenting each line of the quoted matter—on the left only or on both right and left margins; (3) setting the quotation in smaller type; and (4) leaving less space between the lines of quoted material than there is between lines of the main text. Most often some combination of these devices is used, as in the examples below.

> *typeset passage with extra space between text and quotation, smaller type for the quotation, and each line indented*

> He took the title for his biography of Henry David Thoreau from a passage in *Walden*, one of Thoreau's most well-known books:
>
> > I long ago lost a hound, a bay horse, and a turtle-dove, and am still on their trail. . . . I have met one or two who had heard the hound, and the tramp of the horse, and even seen the dove disappear behind a cloud, and they seemed as anxious to recover them as if they had lost them themselves.
>
> However, the title *A Hound, a Bay Horse, and a Turtle-dove* probably puzzled some readers.

typewritten passage with less space between lines of the quotation and each line indented

```
He took the title for his biography of Henry David

Thoreau from a passage in Walden, one of Thoreau's most

well-known books:

    I long ago lost a hound, a bay horse, and a
    turtle-dove, and am still on their trail. . . . I
    have met one or two who had heard the hound, and the
    tramp of the horse, and even seen the dove disappear
    behind a cloud, and they seemed as anxious to recover
    them as if they had lost them themselves.

However, the title A Hound, a Bay Horse, and a

Turtle-dove probably puzzled some readers.
```

Introductory Punctuation, Capitalization, and Indention

Typically, block quotations are preceded by a full sentence ending with a colon, and they begin with a full sentence whose first word is capitalized. However, if the opening words of the quoted passage can be made to flow with the syntax of an incomplete sentence that precedes the quotation, then no punctuation is required to introduce the extract, and the quotation can begin with a lowercase letter. (For an explanation of the conditions under which authors can alter the original capitalization of a quoted passage, see the section on Alterations, Omissions, and Interpolations in this chapter.)

> The chapter begins with a general description of interoffice memorandums:
>
> > The interoffice memorandum or memo is a means of informal communication within a firm or organization. Its special arrangement replaces the salutation, complimentary close, and written signature of the letter with identifying headings.
>
> They describe the interoffice memorandum as
>
> > a means of informal communication within a firm or organization. Its special arrangement replaces the salutation, complimentary close, and written signature of the letter with identifying headings.

If the sentence that precedes the quotation does not introduce it or refer directly to it, the sentence ends in a period.

> As of the end of April she believed that the product had been introduced well and that it stood a good chance of success.
>
> > Unit sales are strong, revenues are better than forecast, shipments are being made on schedule, and inventory levels are stable.

A block quotation is sometimes introduced by a sentence that includes words or sentence fragments quoted from the same source as the quotation that follows.

The report spoke of a "sense of direction" and "newfound optimism" in the community.

> This community is building for its future. New institutions are being created, and existing ones are being strengthened. Civic, cultural, and social events are once again well attended.

When the beginning of a block quotation is also the beginning of a paragraph in the original, the first line of the quotation begins with extra indention.

> The first chapter includes a statement that should be encouraging to secretaries:
>
> > In the past, many secretaries have been placed in positions of responsibility without being delegated enough authority to carry out the responsibility. The current pressures affecting managers have caused them to rethink the secretarial function and to delegate more responsibility and authority to their secretaries.

Quotations that include two or more consecutive paragraphs follow the paragraphing form of the original; each new paragraph is indented.

Quotations within an Extract

If a block quotation itself contains quoted material, that material is enclosed in double quotation marks.

> The authors of the book recommend the following procedures for handling reports:
>
> > The presiding officer will call for the appropriate report from an officer, a board member, a standing committee, or a special committee by saying, "Will the chairperson of the Ways and Means Committee please present the committee's report?" After the report is presented, a motion is heard to accept the report.

Dialogue in a block quotation is enclosed in quotation marks. The beginning of each speech is also marked by extra indention. If a speech runs to more than one paragraph, open quotation marks appear at the beginning of each paragraph of the extract; closing quotation marks appear only at the end of the final paragraph.

> Marion makes her invitation at the end of the first chapter, but Richard's reply is at least somewhat tentative.
>
> > "Would you like to come visiting again on your next vacation?" she asked.
> >
> > "Yes, I would," I replied, "but I don't know when that will be. It's becoming harder and harder for me to find the time to get away.
> >
> > "By the way," I went on, "I want to thank you for introducing me to those people last night."
> >
> > "It was my pleasure," she said.
> >
> > "I really appreciate it."
> >
> > "I do hope you will come again."
> >
> > "I'd like to."

Alterations, Omissions, and Interpolations

Although absolute accuracy is always of first importance when quoting from another source, there are certain kinds of alterations, omissions, and additions that authors and editors are traditionally allowed to make. Most of these alterations occur at the beginning or end of the quotation. The following paragraphs explain the kinds of changes that authors and editors may make and how these changes are indicated. All of the conventions described in this section are illustrated with block quotations; however, the conventions are equally applicable to run-in quotations. Examples of alterations, omissions, and interpolations occurring in run-in quotations can be found in the section on Brackets, beginning on page 6, and in the section on Ellipsis Points, beginning on page 30, in Chapter 1, "Punctuation."

Changing Capital or Lowercase Letters

If the opening words of a quotation act as a sentence within the quotation, the first word is capitalized, even if that word did not begin a sentence in the original version. (In the following example, the full version of the passage being quoted appears in the example on page 237.)

> The authors make exactly this point in the first chapter:
>
>> Many secretaries have been placed in positions of responsibility without being delegated enough authority to carry out the responsibility. The current pressures affecting managers have caused them to rethink the secretarial function and to delegate more responsibility and authority to their secretaries.

In situations in which meticulous handling of original source material is required, the capital *M* would be placed in square brackets to indicate that it was not capitalized in the source.

> The authors make exactly this point in the first chapter:
>
>> [M]any secretaries have been placed in positions of responsibility without being delegated enough authority to carry out the responsibility.

When the opening words of a quoted passage are joined syntactically to the sentence that precedes the quotation, the first word is generally not capitalized, even if it was capitalized in the original version. A few writers, however, retain the capital letter of the original in these circumstances. (Once again, the full version of the passage quoted below appears on page 237.)

> The author of this chapter knows full well that
>
>> in the past, many secretaries have been placed in positions of responsibility without being delegated enough authority to carry out the respon-

sibility. The current pressures affecting managers have caused them to rethink the secretarial function and to delegate more responsibility to their secretaries.

Omissions at the Beginning or End of a Quotation

If an omission is made from the beginning of a quotation, no ellipsis points are required. However, style varies somewhat on this point, and some writers will use ellipsis points for this kind of omission, although usually only in very formal contexts.

> They describe an interoffice memorandum as

> ... a means of informal communication within a firm or organization. Its special arrangement replaces the salutation, complimentary close, and written signature of the letter with identifying headings.

but more commonly

> They describe an interoffice memorandum as

> a means of informal communication within a firm or organization. Its special arrangement replaces the salutation, complimentary close, and written signature of the letter with identifying headings.

A quoted passage that is cut off before a period in the original may be concluded with a period and a set of three ellipsis points to show that the last part of the original sentence was omitted. Any original punctuation at the end of the quotation—with the exception of question marks and exclamation points, which are discussed in the next paragraph—may then be dropped. In the example given below, the quoted passage ended with a comma in the original version. In the extract, the first of the four periods at the end of the passage marks the end of the sentence; the periods that follow are ellipsis points that indicate the omission of material.

> The book offers this advice about overseas calls:

> Give the Overseas Operator the same information that you would give to the regular Long-distance Operator. There may be a delay, but it is possible to call practically every telephone in the world by this method. Direct dialing is also available to many countries. . . .

If the final sentence in the original version ends in an exclamation point or a question mark, that mark of punctuation is retained and is preceded by three ellipsis points. In the example given below, words that immediately precede the question mark in the original version are omitted.

> The authors recommend that secretaries take the following steps to improve their working environment:

> You could think of ways to improve the flow of paperwork: Where do backlogs occur, for example, and where and why do most errors occur? Can you design a new rubber stamp or sticker to help speed the flow of paper? Are there ways to reduce interruptions to your work . . . ?

Omissions within Quotations

Omission of a full paragraph   If a full paragraph or more is omitted from a block quotation, the omission is indicated by ellipsis points at the end of the paragraph that comes before the omission. In the example that follows, the quoted passage includes text from two different paragraphs in the original version and omits entirely an intervening paragraph.

> The chapter offers the following advice regarding preconference preparations:
>
>> After the cutoff date for preregistration, and usually one week before the meeting, the rooming list of conference participants should be sent to the conference manager. . . .
>>   Whenever possible, the conference name tags or badges should be prepared ahead of time and arranged in a system that will facilitate easy distribution. These items are often included in the conference packets. All convention- or conference-related materials should be assembled in packets for the participants. These items include the convention program, appropriate brochures, relevant reports, minutes, and other materials.

Omission at the beginning of a paragraph   If text is omitted from the beginning of any paragraph other than the first paragraph of the extract, the omission is marked by three ellipsis points at the beginning of the paragraph from which the omission has been made. Regular paragraph indention precedes the ellipsis points. The example that follows shows how the preceding example would look if the writer doing the quoting decided to omit the first two sentences of the final paragraph.

> The chapter offers the following advice regarding preconference preparations:
>
>> After the cutoff date for preregistration, and usually one week before the meeting, the rooming list of conference participants should be sent to the conference manager. . . .
>>   . . . All convention- or conference-related materials should be assembled in packets for the participants. These items include the convention program, appropriate brochures, relevant reports, minutes, and other materials.

Omission within a sentence   Omissions from quoted material that fall within a sentence are indicated by three ellipsis points.

> The chapter offers the following advice regarding preconference preparations:
>
>> Whenever possible, the conference name tags should be . . . arranged in a system that will facilitate easy distribution.

Punctuation used in the original that falls on either side of the ellipsis points is often omitted; however, it may be retained, especially if such retention helps clarify the meaning or structure of the sentence.

> The chapter offers the following advice regarding preconference preparations:
>
> > After the cutoff date for preregistration . . . the rooming list of conference participants should be sent to the conference manager. . . .
> > Whenever possible, . . . badges should be prepared ahead of time and arranged in a system that will facilitate easy distribution.
> >
> > *or*
> >
> > After the cutoff date . . . , the rooming list of conference participants should be sent to the conference manager. . . .

Omission of a full sentence   If an omission comprises an entire sentence or the beginning or end of a sentence within a paragraph, the end punctuation preceding or following the omission is retained and followed by three periods.

> The chapter offers the following advice regarding preconference preparations:
>
> > Whenever possible, conference name tags or badges should be prepared ahead of time and arranged in a system that will facilitate easy distribution. . . . All convention- or conference-related materials should be assembled in packets. . . . These items include the convention program, appropriate brochures, relevant reports, minutes, and other materials.
>
> On pages 234–235 we presented the following description of how authors choose between block and run-in formats for prose quotations:
>
> > The length of a quotation usually determines whether it is run into the text or set as a block quotation. . . . Length can be assessed in terms of the number of words, the number of typewritten or typeset pages, or the number of sentences in the passage.

The capitalization of the word *Length* in the second example is generally acceptable, although in some situations in which meticulous handling of original source material is required, the capital *L* would be placed in square brackets. For an example of this use of square brackets, see the second example on page 238.

Other Minor Alterations

Archaic spelling and punctuation   Archaic spellings and styles of punctuation should be preserved in direct quotations if they do not interfere with a reader's comprehension. If they occur frequently in a quotation, the author may wish to modernize them. An explanation to this effect should be placed in the text, in a note, or in a general statement within the preface if such modernizing has been done throughout the work. On the other hand, obvious typographical errors in modern works may be corrected without explanation.

Insertions   Sometimes an author wishes to insert into a quotation a brief explanation, clarification, summary of omitted material, or correction. These insertions (also called *interpolations*) are enclosed in square brackets. This use of brackets is explained and illustrated in the section on Brackets, beginning on page 6, in Chapter 1, "Punctuation."

Italics added   Words that were not italicized in the original version of a text may be italicized in the quoted passage in order to give emphasis to a particular word or phrase if the author informs the reader of the change. Any of several notations may be used. The notation may appear in the quoted passage, following the italicized portion, or at the end of the passage.

In works that include footnotes or other kinds of source notes, the notation may be set as a footnote or added to a source note. Common examples of notations are "italics mine," "emphasis added," and "italics added."

> The first chapter includes a statement that should be encouraging to secretaries:
>
>> In the past, many secretaries have been placed in positions of responsibility *without being delegated enough authority to carry out the responsibility.* The current pressures affecting managers have caused them to rethink the secretarial function and to delegate more responsibility and authority to their secretaries. [Italics mine.]
>
> The chapter offers the following advice regarding preconference preparations:
>
>> Whenever possible, conference name tags or badges should be prepared ahead of time and arranged in a system for early distribution. These items are often included in the conference packets. *All convention- or conference-related materials should be assembled in packets for the participants.* [Emphasis added.] These items include the convention program, appropriate brochures, relevant reports, minutes, and other materials.

If the note is placed at the end of the passage, parentheses may be used in place of brackets.

Footnote or endnote reference symbols or numbers are usually omitted from short quotations. In their place, authors often insert their own references.

Quoting Verse

The major difference between quotations of prose and poetry is that lines of poetry keep their identity as separate lines when set as extracts and also when run in with the text. When more than one line is run in, the poetic lines are separated by a virgule.

When poetic lines are set as extracts, the lines are divided exactly as in the original.

> When Gerard Manley Hopkins wrote that "Nothing is so beautiful as spring— / When weeds, in wheels, shoot long and lovely and lush," he probably had my yard in mind.

> The experience was one that reminded them of the wisdom of Pope's observation:
>
>> A little learning is a dang'rous thing;
>> Drink deep, or taste not the Pierian spring:
>> There shallow draughts intoxicate the brain,
>> And drinking largely sobers us again.

Style varies regarding spacing around the virgule. Some authors and publishers put no space on either side; others prefer a word space on each side. The virgule is sometimes omitted when each line of the original begins with a capital letter and the quotation contains no other capitals. Up to three or four lines of poetry are sometimes run in if they are closely integrated with the text. However, quotations of as few as two lines of poetry are commonly set off from the text as extracts.

> It was a fatalistic view of life that seemed to say, as James Payn did, "I never had a piece of toast / Particularly long and wide; / But fell upon the sanded floor, / And always on the buttered side."

> Some lines from Wordsworth seemed to express their attitude:
>
>> Bliss was it in that dawn to be alive,
>> But to be young was very heaven!

Horizontal Spacing

In typeset material, poetry quoted as an extract is usually arranged so that the longest line is centered on the page and the first word of all other flush-left lines align above or below the first word of the longest line. If the poem includes varied line lengths and indention, the alignment in the original version should be preserved. In typewritten material, authors will frequently choose a uniform indention for all lines that are flush left in the original version rather than center each poetry extract separately. Authors using this approach still indent lines that are not flush left in such a way as to preserve the alignment in the original.

> Consider these excerpts from Edgar Allen Poe, the first from "Annabel Lee," the second from "The Bells."
>
>> She was a child and I was a child,
>>> In this Kingdom by the sea,
>> But we loved with a love that was more than love—
>>> I and my Annabel Lee—
>> With a love that the wingèd seraphs of Heaven
>>> Coveted her and me.

> Hear the sledges with the bells—
>   Silver bells!
> What a world of merriment their melody foretells!
>   How they tinkle, tinkle, tinkle,
>   In the icy air of night!
> While the Stars that oversprinkle
> All the heavens seem to twinkle
>   With a crystalline delight;
>   Keeping time, time, time,
>   In a sort of Runic rhyme
> To the tintinnabulation that so musically wells
>   From the bells, bells, bells, bells,
>   Bells, bells, bells—
> From the jingling and the tinkling of the bells.

If the quotation does not start at the beginning of the line, the alignment in the quotation should still follow the original.

> He praised her with words taken from Shelley:

>> Wit and sense,
>> Virtue and human knowledge, all that might
>> Make this dull world a business of delight,

For an explanation of how to style poetry quotations that do not end in a period, see page 245.)

Sometimes the lines of a poem are too long to center. In these cases, the quotation may be set using a standard indention; run-over lines are indented further.

> They were asked to comment on the following lines by Walt Whitman:

> You flagg'd walks of the cities! you strong curbs at the edges!
> You ferries! you planks and posts of wharves! you
>   timber-lined sides! you distant ships!
> You rows of houses! you window-pierc'd façades! you roofs!
> You porches and entrances! you copings and iron guards!
> You windows whose transparent shells might expose so much!
> You doors and ascending steps! you arches!
> You gray stones of interminable pavements! You trodden crossings!
> From all that had touch'd you I believe you have imparted to yourselves
>   and now impart the same secretly to me,
> From the living and the dead you have peopled your impassive sur-
>   faces, and the spirits thereof would be evident and amicable with
>   me

Quotation Marks in Poetry

If a quotation mark occurs at the beginning of a line of poetry, it should be aligned with the first letter of other lines. In a speech that extends over several lines, quotation marks are placed at the beginning of the speech and at the beginning of each stanza within the speech as well as at its conclusion.

> They based their comments on the following lines from Matthew Arnold's "Stanzas from the Grande Chartreuse":

O children, what do ye reply? —
"Action and pleasure, will ye roam
Through these secluded dells to cry
And call us? — but too late ye come!
Too late for us your call ye blow,
Whose bent was taken long ago.

"Long since we pace this shadowed nave,
We watch those yellow tapers shine,
Emblems of hope over the grave,
In the high altar's depth divine;
The organ carries to our ear
Its accents of another sphere.

"Fenced early in this cloistral round
Of reverie, of shade, of prayer,
How should we grow in other ground?
How can we flower in foreign air?
—Pass, banners, pass, and bugles, cease;
And leave our desert to its peace!"

Omissions from Poetry

When a full line or several consecutive lines of poetry are omitted
from a quotation, the omission is indicated by a line of spaced
points. The lines of points extend the length of the preceding line
or of the missing line.

> Whitman's attitude on the subject is revealed in these lines from
> "When I Heard the Learned Astronomer":
>
>> When I heard the learned astronomer,
>> . . . .
>> How soon unaccountable I became tired and sick,
>> Til rising and gliding out I wandered off by myself,
>> In the mystical moist night-air, and from time to time,
>> Looked up in perfect silence at the stars.

Style varies regarding the treatment of poetry quotations that
do not end in a period. Sometimes authors indicate an omission
with ellipsis points, sometimes they prefer not to use ellipsis points
but rather to reproduce the text exactly as it appeared in the original version.

> Whitman's attitude on the subject is revealed in these lines from
> "When I Heard the Learned Astronomer":
>
>> When I heard the learned astronomer,
>> . . . .
>> How soon unaccountable I became tired and sick, . . .

> *or*

> Whitman's attitude on the subject is revealed in these lines from
> "When I Heard the Learned Astronomer":
>
>> When I heard the learned astronomer,
>> . . . .
>> How soon unaccountable I became tired and sick,

Attribution of Sources

The ways in which authors acknowledge the sources of quotations vary with the kind of publication they are writing for and the kind of system that they are using to document sources of information throughout the work. In some cases, simply including the author's name is sufficient; in other cases, full bibliographical information is required, including publisher's name, date of publication, and page number of the passage quoted. The following paragraphs describe some of the alternative methods that are available to authors. For more on the details of styling such documentation, see Chapter 7, "Notes and Bibliographies."

In Works without Notes or a Bibliography

In works that do not include footnotes, endnotes, or a bibliography, authors often include all necessary information in the body of the text preceding the quotation.

> Levin summarizes these points in an article entitled "The Office in the Electronic Age" on page 46 of the March, 1982, issue of *The Office*:
>
>> The quality of work in general, whether involving electronic equipment or not, is based on the manager's knowing the responsibilities of each worker, careful assignment of tasks, effective written and oral communication, and periodic evaluation and modification of procedures.

An alternative method used in books that do not include notes or a bibliography is to run in all bibliographical information in a parenthetical note that follows the quotation. If the quotation is a run-in quotation the note comes between the closing quotation mark and the terminal punctuation of the sentence. If the quotation is set as an extract, the note follows the terminal punctuation.

> Levin makes the same points when she says, "The quality of work in general, whether involving electronic office equipment or not, is based on the manager's knowing the responsibilities of each worker, careful assignment of tasks, effective written and oral communication, and periodic evaluation and modification of procedures" ("The Office in the Electronic Age," *The Office*, March 1982, 46).

> Levin has summarized these points as follows:
>
>> The quality of work in general, whether involving electronic office equipment or not, is based on the manager's knowing the responsibilities of each worker, careful assignment of tasks, effective written and oral communication, and periodic evaluation and modification of procedures. ("The Office in the Electronic Age," *The Office*, March 1982, 46)

In each of these examples, it is assumed that the author's full

name has already been given in the text and therefore does not
need to be repeated.

In Works with Footnotes or Endnotes

In works that include footnotes or endnotes, the source of a quotation can be indicated by a raised reference number or reference
mark that is placed at the end of the quoted passage after any terminal punctuation. For a full description of how to style footnotes
and endnotes, see the section on Footnotes and Endnotes, beginning on page 198, in Chapter 7, "Notes and Bibliographies."

> Levin makes the same point when she says, "The quality of work
> in general, whether involving electronic office equipment or not,
> is based on the manager's knowing the responsibilities of each
> worker, careful assignment of tasks, effective written and oral
> communication, and periodic evaluation and modification of pro-
> cedures."[17]

> Levin has summarized these points as follows:

>> The quality of work in general, whether involving electronic office
>> equipment or not, is based on the manager's knowing the responsibili-
>> ties of each worker, careful assignment of tasks, effective written and
>> oral communication, and periodic evaluation and modification of pro-
>> cedures.[17]

If a work with footnotes and endnotes includes more than
one quotation from the same source, reference to full bibliographical information is required only at the first quotation. The
usual practice is to include an explanation with the footnote to the
first quotation that all subsequent references to that work in the
text are from the same source. Having done that, one needs only
to mention the page number at subsequent references.

> Levin makes the same point when she says, "The quality of work
> in general, whether involving electronic office equipment or not,
> is based on the manager's knowing the responsibilities of each
> worker, careful assignment of tasks, effective written and oral
> communication, and periodic evaluation and modification of pro-
> cedures" (p. 46).

> Levin has summarized these points as follows:

>> The quality of work in general, whether involving electronic office
>> equipment or not, is based on the manager's knowing the responsibili-
>> ties of each worker, careful assignment of tasks, effective written and
>> oral communication, and periodic evaluation and modification of proce-
>> dures. (p. 46)

In a Work with Parenthetical References

In a work utilizing parenthetical references to provide bibliographical information, the parenthetical reference is either in-

cluded in the sentence that precedes the quotation or placed after
the quotation, as were the page references in the preceding examples. Note that these references are placed before the terminal
punctuation of a run-in quotation, but after the terminal punctuation of an extract. For more on the placement of parenthetical
references, see the section on Parenthetical References, beginning
on page 211, in Chapter 7, "Notes and Bibliographies."

In Other Contexts

In a context in which only the author's name or the author's name
and the title of the work quoted are required, the attribution can
be placed on its own line following the quotation. The attribution
is usually set flush right and either enclosed in parentheses or preceded by an em dash. In a variation on this arrangement, the attribution may be run in with the quotation and either enclosed in
parentheses or preceded by a dash.

> I went to the woods because I wished to live deliberately, to front only
> the essential fact of life, and see if I could not learn what it had to teach,
> and not, when I came to die, discover that I had not lived.
> —Henry David Thoreau, *Walden*

> That things always collapse into the *status quo ante* three weeks after a
> drive is over, everybody knows and apparently expects. . . . And yet
> many managements fail to draw the obvious conclusion. . . .
> (Peter F. Drucker)

> Winter lies too long in country towns; hangs on until it is stale and
> shabby, old and sullen. —Willa Cather, *My Ántonia*

When an attribution line follows a passage of poetry, the line
may be set flush right, or it may be centered on the longest line
in the quotation, or it may be indented a standard distance from
the right margin.

> If this belief from heaven be sent,
> If such be Nature's holy plan,
> Have I not reason to lament
> What Man has made of Man?
> —William Wordsworth,
> "Lines Written in Early Spring"

> The sun descending in the west,
> The evening star does shine;
> The birds are silent in their nest,
> And I must seek for mine.
> —William Blake, "Night"

> Happy the man whose wish and care
> A few paternal acres bound,
> Content to breathe his native air
> In his own ground.
> —Alexander Pope, "Ode on Solitude"

Chapter 9

Style in Business Correspondence

CONTENTS

The word *style* as applied to business-letter writing encompasses the format of the letter; the punctuation, capitalization, and other mechanical aspects of the writing; grammar and word usage; and the traditional conventions relating to the etiquette of letter-writing, such as proper salutations, closings, and forms of address. This chapter, however, focuses solely on questions of format and general punctuation patterns. For more on punctuation and the details relating to capitalization and other mechanics of writing, see Chapter 1, "Punctuation," and Chapter 2, "Capitals, Italics, and Compounds." For a discussion of grammar and word usage, see Chapter 6, "Composition and Grammar." For a list of forms of address, see Chapter 10, "Forms of Address."

Style in business correspondence, like language itself, is not a static entity. It has changed over the years to meet the varying needs of its users, and it continues to do so. For example, the open-punctuation pattern and the Simplified Letter have recently gained wide popularity, while the closed-punctuation pattern and the Indented Letter, once considered standard formats, are now little used in the United States. In many cases, this process of change had led to the situation in which writers have a range of alternatives available to them regarding aspects of letter-writing style. This chapter and the ones that follow have been written with these alternative acceptable stylings in mind, and, whenever such alternative stylings exist, they are presented and described. If there are reasons to prefer one over another, the reasons are explained; however, in many cases, the choice will be a question of individual taste, and writers will have to use their own judgment to choose among the acceptable styles.

The Business Letter as Image-Maker

All of the elements of business-letter style come together in a letter to produce a tangible reflection on paper not only of the writer's ability and knowl-
edge and the typist's competence, but also of an organization's total image.
For example, well-prepared business letters reflect a firm's pride and its concern for quality. On the other hand, poorly prepared correspondence can
create such a negative impression on its recipients that they may have second thoughts about pursuing business relationships with the writer or the
writer's organization. This is a special consideration for small businesses.
The business letter, then, is actually an indicator of overall organizational
style, regardless of the size of the firm. Thus, the impression created by at-
tractively and accurately typed, logically oriented, and clearly written letters
can be a crucial factor in the success of any business.

A businessperson may devote as much as 50 percent or more of his or
her workday to correspondence. This includes planning and thinking out
the directions, tone, and content of outgoing letters or reading and acting
on incoming letters. Secretaries spend an even higher proportion of their
time on correspondence. And all this time costs money. However, if both
writer and typist keep in mind the following simple aids to good letter production, the time and money involved will have been well spent:

1. Stationery should be of high-quality paper having excellent correcting
   or erasing properties.
2. Typing should be neat and accurate with any corrections or erasures
   rendered invisible.
3. The essential elements of a letter (such as the date line, inside address,
   message, and signature block) and any other included parts should conform in page placement and format with one of the generally acceptable, up-to-date business-letter stylings (such as the Simplified Letter,
   the Block Letter, the Modified Block Letter, the Modified Semi-block
   Letter, or the Hanging-indented Letter).
4. The language of the letter should be clear, concise, grammatically correct, and devoid of padding and clichés.
5. The ideas in the message should be logically oriented, with the writer
   always keeping in mind the reader's reaction.
6. All statistical data should be accurate and complete.
7. All names should be checked for accuracy of spelling and style.

Letter Balance and Letterhead Design

It has often been said that an attractive letter should look like a symmetri-
cally framed picture with even margins working as a frame for the typed

lines that are balanced under the letterhead. But how many letters really do look like framed pictures? Planning ahead before starting to type is the key to letter symmetry. The following steps will help the writer or typist achieve the desired appearance:

1. Estimate the approximate number of words in the letter or the general length of the message by looking over the writer's rough draft or one's shorthand notes, or by checking the length of a dictated source.
2. Make mental notes of any long quotations, tabular data, long lists or footnotes or of the occurrence of scientific names and formulas that may require margin adjustments, a different typeface, or even hand-work within the message.
3. Set the left and right margin stops according to the estimated letter length: about one inch for very long letters (300 words or more, or at least two pages), about one and one-half inches for medium-length ones (about 100–300 words), and about two inches for very short ones (100 words or less).
4. Remember that the closing parts of a letter take 10–12 lines (two inches) or more and that the bottom margin will be at least six lines (one inch). Thus you will want to allow at least three inches from the last line of the message to the bottom of the page.
5. Use the scale on the typewriter's page-end indicator or a guide sheet that numbers each line in the margin as a bottom margin warning; or lightly pencil a warning mark on the paper.
6. Single-space within paragraphs; double-space between paragraphs. Very short letters (up to three sentences) may be double-spaced throughout.
7. Set continuation-sheet margins to match those of the first sheet, and carry over at least three lines of the message to the continuation sheet.

With experience, a secretary can easily estimate the overall length of a letter. An inexperienced secretary should refer to a letter placement table such as Table 1 on page 252. As the table suggests, short letters may be typewritten on half-sheets, on Executive-size stationery, or on full-size stationery with wide margins. Some offices, however, use a standard six-inch typing line for all letters on full-size stationery, regardless of length, because it eliminates the need to reset tabs.

Very short letters typed on full-size stationery may create spacing problems. There are three simple ways to handle the extra space involved in these letters:

1. Use the six-inch line but lengthen the space between the date and the inside address, between the complimentary close and the signature, and between the signature and the transcriber's initials or enclosure notations.
2. Use the six-inch line but double-space. Double spacing should be used only in very short letters (about six lines or less, or up to three sentences). If a double-spaced letter contains more than one paragraph, an

Table 1
Letter Placement Table
Three Sizes of Stationery

Lines in Letter Body	Words in Letter Body	Number of Blank Lines between Date and Inside Address*	Typewriter Marginal Stops Elite/Pica	Length of Typing Line	
				Inches	Spaces Elite/Pica
Half-sheet Stationery: Assume Letterhead takes 7 vertical lines.					
(Baronial—center No. 33 for Elite; No. 28 for Pica)					
9–10	60–66	7	15–60/10–50	4	48/40
11–12	67–73	6	15–59/10–50	4	48/40
13–14	74–80	5	15–60/10–50	4	48/40
15–16	81–87	4	15–60/10–50	4	48/40
17–18	88–94	3	15–60/10–50	4	48/40
19–20	95–100	2	15–60/10–50	4	48/40
Executive-size Stationery: Assume Letterhead takes 8 lines.					
(Monarch—center No. 43, Elite; No. 36, Pica)					
13–14	95–115	8	15–75/10–60	5	60/50
15–16	116–135	7	15–75/10–60	5	60/50
17–18	136–155	6	15–75/10–60	5	60/50
19–20	156–175	5	15–75/10–60	5	60/50
Full-size Stationery: Assume Letterhead takes 9 lines.					
(Standard—center No. 51, Elite; No. 42, Pica)					
3–5	under 100	7–12	25–75/22–62	4	48/40
6–10	100–200	4–8	20–80/17–67	5	60/50
11–14	175–200	7	15–87/12–72	6	72/60
15–18	201–225	6	15–87/12–72	6	72/60
19–22	226–250	5	15–87/12–72	6	72/60
23–26	251–275	4	15–87/12–72	6	72/60
27–30	276–300**	3	15–87/12–72	6	72/60

*Assume that the date is typed three lines below the last line of the letterhead on all letters.
**Letters consisting of more than 300 words should be two-page letters.

indented-paragraph format should be used to help distinguish the paragraphs.
3. Use a four-inch or five-inch typing line, setting margins as suggested in Table 1 above.

Letterhead Design

Letterhead designs vary. Some letterheads are positioned at the center of the top of the page, others are laid out across the top of the page from the left to the right margin, and still others are more heavily balanced right or left of the center. Sometimes a company's name and logo appear at the top of the page, while its address and other data are printed at the bottom.

Regardless of layout and design, a typical business letterhead contains all or some of the following elements, with items 2, 3, 5, and 6 being essential:

1. logo
2. full name of the firm, company, corporation, institution, or group
3. full street address
4. suite, room, or building number, if needed—post office box number, if applicable
5. city, state, and zip code
6. area code and telephone number(s)
7. other data (as telex or cable references, branch offices, or products or services offered)

The names of particular departments, plants, groups, or divisions may be printed on the letterhead of extremely large or diversified companies or institutions. Other organizations such as large law firms may have the full names of their partners and staff attorneys all listed on the letterhead. Elaborate letterhead layouts require especially careful letter planning to avoid an unbalanced look. For example, a letterhead with a long list of names on the left side might be best balanced by use of the Modified Block Letter, where the date, reference numbers, and signature appear on the right side of the page.

High corporate officers frequently use a personalized or executive letterhead. Here the standard company letterhead design is supplemented with the name of the office (as "Office of the President") or with the full name and business title of the officer (as "John M. Jones, Jr., President") printed or engraved in small letters one or two lines beneath the letterhead at or near the left margin. The officer's business title may appear on the same line as his or her name if space permits and if both name and title are short, or it may be blocked directly below the name. Executive stationery is often not printed but instead engraved on a better grade of paper than that of the standard, printed company stationery. Executive stationery is also smaller than the standard, as shown in Table 2 on page 7. Envelopes match the paper and are printed with the executive's name and return address.

If you are writing a business letter for an organization that does not have letterhead stationery, you can create a typewritten letterhead. The typewritten letterhead can include all of the elements included in the printed letterhead (listed above) except for the logo; and, as with the printed letterhead, the essential items are (1) the full name of the company, institution, or group; (2) the full street address; (3) the city, state, and zip code; and (4) the area code and telephone number. The elements are centered, each on its own line.

In writing your own personal correspondence, a letterhead, whether printed or typewritten is not required. In this type of correspondence, a three-line heading replaces the letterhead. The correct form for the heading is to put the street address or post-office box number on line 1, the city,

```
                BEDFORD FALLS HISTORICAL ASSOCIATION

                        324 Sycamore Street

                      Bedford Falls, ST 56789

                         (215)-555-7654

                                                    May 9, 1988
```

Figure 9.1.   Typewritten letterhead

state, and zip code on line 2, and the date on line 3. The heading may be positioned six lines from the top of the edge of the paper (or higher or lower) to achieve a good balance and with the longest line flush with the right margin (see Figure 1.38).

Choosing the Right Paper

Paper and envelope size, quality, and basis weight vary according to application. Table 2 on page 255 lists various paper and envelope sizes along with their uses.

Good-quality paper is an essential element in the production of attractive, effective letters. Paper with rag content is considerably more expensive than sulfite bonds. Nevertheless, many business firms use rag-content paper because it suggests the merit and stature of the company. Since the cost of paper has been estimated at less than five percent of the total cost of the average business letter, it is easy to understand why some companies consider high-quality paper to be worth the added expense—at least for certain types of correspondence. In choosing a good grade of paper, one should look for paper that meets the following standards:

1. The paper withstands corrections and erasures without pitting, buckling, or tearing.
2. The paper accepts even and clear typed characters.
3. The paper permits smooth written signatures.
4. The paper performs well with carbons and in copying machines.
5. The paper withstands storage and repeated handling, and its color wears well over a long time.
6. The paper folds easily without cracking or rippling.
7. The paper holds typeset letterhead without bleed-through.

An important characteristic of paper is its fiber direction or grain. Paper grain should be parallel to the direction of the typewritten lines, thus pro-

Table 2
Stationery and Envelope Sizes and Applications

Stationery	Stationery Size	Application	Envelope	Envelope Size
Standard	8½″ × 11″ *also* 8″ × 10½″	general business correspondence	*commercial* No. 6¾ No. 9 No. 10	3⅝″ × 6½″ 3⅞″ × 8⅞″ 4⅛″ × 9½″
			window No. 6¾ No. 9 No. 10	3⅝″ × 6½″ 3⅞″ × 8⅞″ 4⅛″ × 9½″
			airmail No. 6¾ No. 10	3⅝″ × 6½″ 4⅛″ × 9½″
Executive *or* Monarch	7¼″ × 10½″ *or* 7½″ × 10″	high-level corporate officers' correspon- dence; usually personalized	*regular* *window*	3⅞″ × 7½″ 3⅞″ × 7½″
Half-sheet *or* Baronial	5½″ × 8½″	extremely brief notes	*regular*	3⅝″ × 6½″

viding a smooth surface for clear and even characters, an easy erasing or correcting surface, and a smooth fit of paper against the typewriter platen. Every sheet of paper has a *felt* side, which is the top side of the paper from which a watermark may be read. It is on this side of the sheet that the letterhead should be printed or engraved.

The weight of the paper must also be considered when ordering stationery supplies. *Basis weight,* also called *substance number,* is the weight in pounds of a ream of paper cut to a basic size. Basis 24 is heaviest for stationery; basis 13 is lightest. Table 3 on page 256 illustrates various paper weights according to their specific uses in the office.

The paper used for carbon copies is lighter in weight and is available as inexpensive *manifold* paper, a stronger and more expensive *onionskin,* or a lightweight letterhead with the word COPY printed on it.

Continuation sheets, although blank, must match the letterhead sheet in color, basis weight, texture, size, and quality. Envelopes should match both the first and continuation sheets. Therefore, these materials should be ordered along with the letterhead to ensure a good match.

Letterhead and continuation sheets as well as envelopes should be stored in their boxes to prevent soiling. A small supply of these materials may be kept in the typist's stationery drawer, but it should be arranged carefully so as to protect the materials from wear and tear.

Table 3
Weights of Letter Papers and Envelopes
For Specific Business Correspondence Applications

Application	Basis Weight
Standard (*i.e., corporate correspondence*)	24 *or* 20
Executive	24 *or* 20
Airmail (*for overseas correspondence*)	13
Branch-office *or* salesmen's stationery	20 *or* 16
Form letters	20 *or* 24
Continuation sheets	match basis weight of first sheet
Half-sheets	24 *or* 20

General Punctuation Patterns in Business Correspondence

Like letterhead designs, the choice of general punctuation patterns in business correspondence is usually determined by the organization. However, it is important that specific punctuation patterns be selected for designated letter stylings and that these patterns be adhered to for the sake of consistency and fast output. The two most common patterns are *open punctuation* and *mixed punctuation*. Their increased popularity in recent years is a reflection of the marked trend toward streamlining correspondence, for these patterns have all but totally replaced the older and more complex *closed punctuation* requiring a terminal mark at the end of each element of a business letter—a pattern that was used most often with the now little-used Indented Letter styling.

Open-Punctuation Pattern

Letters using an open-punctuation pattern exhibit the following characteristics:

1. The end of the date line is unpunctuated, although the comma between day and year is retained.
2. The ends of the lines of the inside address are unpunctuated, unless an abbreviation such as *Inc.* terminates a line, in which case the period after the abbreviation is retained.
3. The salutation if used is unpunctuated.
4. The complimentary close if used is unpunctuated.
5. The ends of the signature block lines are unpunctuated.
6. This pattern is always used with the Simplified Letter (see pages 288–289) and is often used with the Block Letter (see pages 290–291).

Mixed-Punctuation Pattern

Letters using a mixed-punctuation pattern exhibit the following characteristics:

The Simplified Letter   **The Block Letter**

Figure 9.2.   Open-punctuation pattern

1. The end of the date line is unpunctuated, although the comma between the day and year is retained.
2. The ends of the lines of the inside address are unpunctuated unless an abbreviation such as *Inc.* terminates a line, in which case the period after the abbreviation is retained.
3. The salutation is punctuated with a colon.
4. The complimentary close is punctuated with a comma.
5. The end(s) of the signature block line(s) are unpunctuated.
6. This pattern is used with either the Block, the Modified Block, the Modified Semi-block, or the Hanging-indented Letters. (See pages 290–295 and page 287 for facsimiles of these letters.)

As suggested at the beginning of this section, virtually all American business offices today use either the mixed or the open puntuation pattern.

Closed-Punctuation Pattern

Although the closed-punctuation pattern is rarely used in the United States today, it is still employed in some European business correspondence. This pattern exhibits the following characteristics:

1. A period terminates the date line.
2. A comma terminates each line of the inside address except the last, which is ended by a period.

The Block Letter

The Modified Block Letter

- letterhead
- date line
- inside address
- salutation with colon

- message

- complimentary close with comma
- signature block
- typist's initials
- other notations

The Modified Semi-block Letter

The Hanging-indented Letter

- letterhead
- date line
- inside address
- salutation with colon

- message

- complimentary close with comma
- signature block
- typist's initials
- other notations

Figure 9.3. Mixed-punctuation pattern illustrated in four letter stylings

3. A colon punctuates the salutation.
4. A comma punctuates the complimentary close.
5. A comma terminates each line of the signature block except the last, which is terminated by a period.
6. This pattern is used chiefly with the Indented Letter.

It should be pointed out that the illustration of the closed-punctuation pattern is the only description given in this book of the Indented Letter. It is shown here only as a point of information for those who may occasionally encounter it, especially in foreign correspondence.

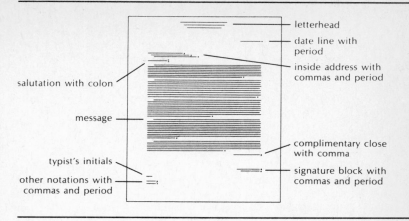

Figure 9.4.   Closed-punctuation pattern with the Indented Letter

The Individual Parts of a Business Letter

The various elements of a business letter are listed below in the order of their occurrence. While asterisked items are essential elements of any letter regardless of its general styling, those items that are unmarked may or may not be included, depending on general styling (as the Simplified Letter or the Block Letter) and on the nature of the letter itself (as general or confidential correspondence):

*date line	attention line	identification initials
reference line	salutation	enclosure notation
special mailing notations	subject line	carbon copy notation
on-arrival notations	*message	postscript
*inside address	complimentary close	
	*signature block	

For a discussion of typewritten letterheads and return addresses, see pages 253–254.

Date Line

The date line may be typed two to six lines below the last line of the printed letterhead; however, three-line spacing is recommended as a standard for most letters. Some office manuals specify a *fixed date line,* positioned three lines below the letterhead in all instances, with extra space added as needed below the date line and elsewhere on the page. Other offices prefer to use a *floating date line,* which may be typed two to six lines below the letterhead, depending on the letter length, space available, and letterhead design. The date line consists of the month, the day, and the year (January 1, 19--), all on one line. Ordinals (such as 1st, 2d, or 24th) should not be used, and the months should not be represented with abbreviations or Arabic numerals. However, the day and the month may be reversed and the comma dropped in United States government correspondence or in British correspondence, where the styling is common (1 January 19--). The date line should never overrun the margin.

The date line is commonly placed in one of four positions, and all are acceptable. The choice depends on the general letter styling or the letter-head layout. Placing the date line *flush with the left margin* is appropriate when using the Block Letter format (see the letter facsimile on pages 290–291 for a full-page view). Placing the date line *flush with the right margin* is appropriate for Hanging-indented, Modified Block, and Modified Semi-block Letters (see pages 287, 292–293, and 294–295). In order to align a date at the right margin, move the typewriter carriage to the right margin and then backspace once for each keystroke (including spaces) that will be required in the typed date. You can then set the tab stops if you are typing several letters that will bear the same date. Centering the date line *directly under the letterhead* or positioning it about *five spaces to the right of center* are other positions that are appropriate when using the Modified Block or Modified Semi-block formats.

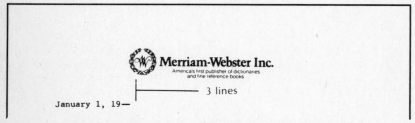

Figure 9.5.   Date line blocked flush with the left margin

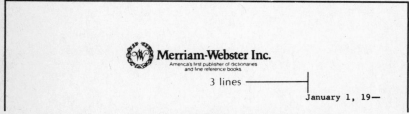

Figure 9.6.   Date line blocked flush with the right margin

Reference Line

A reference line with file, correspondence, control, order, invoice, or policy numbers is included in a letter when the addressee has specifically requested that correspondence on a subject contain a reference, or when it is needed

Figure 9.7. Date line centered directly under the letterhead

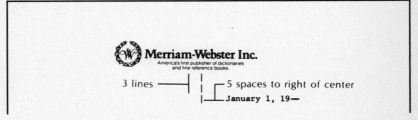

Figure 9.8. Date line positioned about five spaces to the right of dead center

for filing. It may be centered and typed one to four lines below the date, although some offices require that it be typed and single-spaced directly above or below the date to make it less conspicuous. With the Block Letter, the reference line should be aligned flush left. With the Modified Block and the Modified Semi-block Letters, the reference line may be centered on the page or blocked under or above the date line.

reference line blocked left	*reference line blocked right*
January, 1, 19--	January 1 19--
X-123-4	X-123-4
or	*or*
X-123-4	X-123-4
January 1, 19--	January 1, 19--

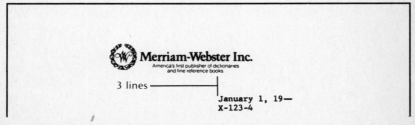

Figure 9.9. Reference line blocked with date line to right of dead center

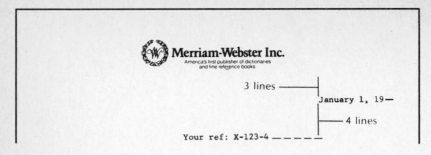

Figure 9.10.   Reference number centered on page, four lines beneath date line

Reference lines on the first sheet must be carried over to the heading of a continuation sheet or sheets. The styling of the date line and the reference line on a continuation sheet should match the one on the first page as closely as possible. For example, if the reference line appears on a line below the date on the first sheet, it should be typed that way on the continuation sheet. The first setup below illustrates a continuation-sheet reference line as used with the Simplified or Block Letter.

> Mr. John B. Jones
> January 1, 19--
> X-123-4
> Page 2

The second example illustrates the positioning of a reference line on the continuation sheet of a Modified Block, a Modified Semi-block, or a Hanging-indented Letter.

> Mr. John B. Jones   -2-   January 1, 19--
>   X-123-4

See Figures 9.18 and 9.19 for continuation-sheet facsimiles.

Special Mailing Notations

If a letter is to be sent by any method other than by regular mail, that fact may be indicated on the letter itself and on the envelope (see pages 297–305 for details on envelope styling). The all-capitalized special mailing notation such as CERTIFIED MAIL, SPECIAL DELIVERY, or AIRMAIL (for foreign mail only) in all letter stylings is aligned flush left about four lines below the line on which the date appears, and about two lines above the first line of the inside address. While some organizations prefer that this notation appear on the original and on all copies, others prefer that the notation be typed only on the original. And in many organizations, this notation is omitted no matter how the letter is mailed.

Vertical spacing (such as between the date line and the special mailing notation) may vary with letter length; i.e., more space may be left for short or medium letter lengths.

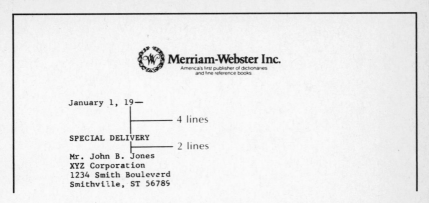

Figure 9.11.   Special mailing notation vis-à-vis inside address and date line

On-arrival Notations

The on-arrival notations that may be included in the letter itself are PERSONAL and CONFIDENTIAL. The first indicates that the letter may be opened and read only by its addressee; the second, that the letter may be opened and read by its addressee and/or any other person or persons authorized to view such material. These all-capitalized notations are usually positioned four lines below the date line and usually two but not more than four lines above the first line of the inside address. They are blocked flush left in all letter stylings. If a special mailing notation has been used, the on-arrival notation is blocked one line beneath it. Spacing between the date line and the on-arrival notation may be increased to as much as six lines if the letter is extremely brief.

If either PERSONAL or CONFIDENTIAL appears in the letter, it must also appear on the envelope (see pages 299–301 for envelope styling).

Inside Address

An inside address typically includes the following elements if it is directed to a particular individual:

1. addressee's courtesy title and full name
2. addressee's business title if required
3. full name of addressee's business affiliation
4. full geographical address

If the letter is addressed to an organization in general, the inside address typically includes the following elements:

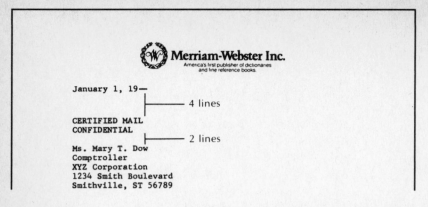

Figure 9.12.   On-arrival notation vis-à-vis date line, special mailing notation, and inside address

1. full name of the firm, company, corporation, or institution
2. individual department name if required
3. full geographical address

The inside address is placed about three to eight but not more than 12 lines below the date. The inside address in the Simplified Letter is typed three lines below the date. Inside-address page placement in relation to the date may be expanded or contracted according to letter length or organization policy. The inside address is always single-spaced internally. In most of the letters discussed in this book, the inside address is blocked flush with the left margin. See pages 285–296 for full-page views.

Figure 9.13.   Inside address styling used with the Block Letter

A courtesy title (as *Mr., Ms., Mrs., Miss, Dr.,* or *The Honorable*) should be typed before the addressee's full name, even if a business or professional title (as *Treasurer* or *Chief of Staff*) follows the surname. No courtesy title, however, should ever precede the name when *Esquire* or an abbreviation for a degree follows the name.

Before typing the addressee's full name, the secretary should, if possible, refer to the signature block of previous correspondence from that individual to ascertain the exact spelling and styling of the person's name. This information may also be obtained from printed executive letterhead. A business or professional title, if included, should also match the styling in previous correspondence or in official literature (such as an annual report or a business directory). If an individual holds more than one office (as *Vice President* and *General Manager*) within an organization, the title shown in the signature block of previous correspondence should be copied, or the title of the individual's highest office (in this case, *Vice President*) may be selected. Business and professional titles should not be abbreviated. If a title is so long that it might overrun the center of the page, it may be typed on two lines with the second line indented two spaces.

Mr. John P. Hemphill, Jr.
Vice President and Director
   of Research and Development

Special attention should be paid to the spelling, punctuation, and official abbreviations of company names. Note, for example, whether an ampersand is used for the word *and,* whether series of names are separated by commas, and whether the word *Company* is spelled in full or abbreviated.

The addressee's title may be typed on the same line as the name, separated by a comma. Alternatively, the title may be typed on the second line either by itself or followed by a comma and the name of the organization. Care should be taken, however, to choose a style that will enhance and not detract from the total balance of the letter on the page. The following are acceptable inside-address stylings for business and professional titles:

Mr. Arthur O. Brown
News Director
Radio Station WXYZ
1234 Peters Street
Jonesville, ZZ 56789

Ms. Ann B. Lowe, Director
Apex Community Theater
67 Smith Street
North Bend, XX 12345

Dr. Joyce A. Cavitt, Dean
School of Business and Finance
Stateville University
Stateville, ST 98765

Mrs. Joyce A. Cavitt
President, C & A Realty
Johnson Beach, ZZ 56789

If an individual addressee's name is unknown or irrelevant and the writer wishes to direct a letter to an organization in general or to a unit within that organization, the organization name is typed on line 1 of the inside address, followed on line 2 by the name of a specific department if required. The full address of the organization is then typed on subsequent lines.

> XYZ Corporation
> Consumer Products Division
> 1234 Smith Boulevard
> Smithville, ST 56789

On the other hand, if an addressee's address is unknown and the writer wishes to send a letter to him or her in care of a third party, the phrase *In care of* (or *c/o*) is used on line 2 before the name of the third party. The percentage sign (%) is a shortcut symbol that can be used, but it is usually not used in formal correspondence.

Street addresses should be typed in full and not abbreviated unless window envelopes are being used (see page 298). Numerals are used for all building, house, apartment, room, and suite numbers except for *One*, which is written out.

> One Bayside Drive   6 Link Road   1436 Fremont Avenue

However, when the address of a building is used as its name, the number in the address is written out.

> Fifty Maple Street

Numerals are usually used for all numbered street names above *Twelfth*, but numbered street names from *First* through *Twelfth* are usually written out.

> 19 South 22nd Street   167 West Second   One East Ninth Street
>   Avenue

An alternative, more formal convention calls for writing out all numbered streets up to and including *One Hundredth*.

> 122 East Forty-second Street   36 East Fiftieth Street

An apartment, building, room, or suite number if required follows the street address on the same line with a comma separating the two.

> 62 Park Towers, Suite 9   Rosemont Plaza Apartments,
>   Apartment 117

Note that neither the word *Number* nor its abbreviation *No.* is used between the words *Suite, Apartment,* or *Building* and a following numeral.

Names of cities (except those including the word *Saint,* such as *St. Louis* or *St. Paul*) should be typed out in full, as *Fort Wayne* or *Mount Prospect*. The name of the city is followed by a comma and then by the name of the state and the zip code. Names of states may or may not be abbreviated (the District of Columbia is always styled *DC* or *D.C.*). If a window envelope is being used, the all-capitalized, unpunctuated two-letter Postal Service abbreviation followed by one space and the zip code should be used. If a regular envelope is being used, the name of the state may be typed out in full followed by one space and the zip code, or the two-letter Postal Service abbreviation may be used. Most firms now use the two-letter Postal Service abbreviations on all inside and envelope addresses. See Table 5 on page 300 for a list of these abbreviations.

An inside address should comprise no more than five typed lines. No line should overrun the center of the page. Lengthy organizational names, however, like lengthy business titles, may be carried over to a second line and indented two spaces from the left margin.

Sometimes a single letter will have to be sent to two persons at different addresses, both of whom should receive an original. In these cases, the inside address should consist of two complete sets of names and addresses separated by a line of space. The names should be in alphabetical order unless one person is obviously more important than the other. For salutations used in letters to multiple addressees, see pages 325–333.

For information about styling foreign addresses, see pages 301–303.

Attention Line

If the writer wishes to address a letter to an organization in general but at the same time bring it to the attention of a particular individual, an attention line may be typed two lines below the last line of the inside address and two lines above the salutation if there is one. The attention line is usually blocked flush with the left margin; it must be so blocked in the Simplified and Block Letters. On the other hand, some organizations prefer that the attention line be centered on the page. This placement is acceptable with all letters except the Simplified and the Block. This line should be neither underlined nor entirely capitalized; only its main elements are capitalized. The word *Attention* is not abbreviated. Placement of a colon after the word *Attention* is optional unless the open punctuation pattern is being followed throughout the letter, in which case the colon should be omitted:

    Attention Mr. John P. Doe   Attention: Mr. John P. Doe

The salutation appearing beneath the attention line should be "Gentlemen" or "Ladies and Gentlemen" even though the attention line routes the letter to a particular person. Such a letter is actually being written to the organization, so a collective-noun salutation should be used.

Salutation

The salutation—used with all letter stylings except the Simplified—is typed flush with the left margin, two lines beneath the last line of the inside address or two lines below the attention line if there is one. Additional vertical lines of space may be added after the inside address of a short letter which is to be enclosed in a window envelope. The first letter of the first word of the salutation is capitalized, as are the first letters of the addressee's courtesy title and surname. If the mixed-punctuation pattern is being followed in the letter, the salutation is followed by a colon; if open punctuation is being observed, the salutation is unpunctuated. Only in informal, personal correspondence is the salutation followed by a comma.

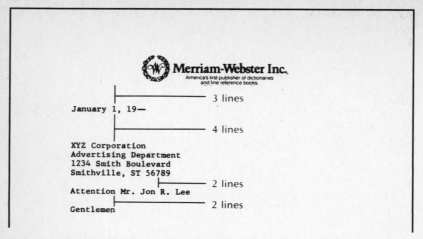

Figure 9.14.   Page placement of an attention line in a Block Letter with open punctuation

One of the most frequently asked questions today is what salutation to use when addressing an organization or when addressing a person whose name and gender are unknown to the letter-writer. Unfortunately, there are no universally accepted forms to use in these situations. Traditionally the salutation "Dear Sir" has been used when the recipient of the letter is to be a particular individual, and "Gentlemen" has been used when the recipient is to be an organization or a group of people within it. However, as it has become more and more likely that the recipients of these letters may be women, many writers—both male and female—have looked for more appropriate salutations. Most commonly, these writers have adopted "Dear Sir or Madam" and "Ladies and Gentlemen" as substitutes for "Dear Sir" and "Gentlemen" respectively; however, these forms do sound awkward to some people. Some writers have used the salutations "Dear People," "Dear Person," "Gentlepeople," "Gentlepersons," and "Dear Sir, Madam, or Ms."; however, there is little evidence that these forms are catching on.

The salutation "To whom it may concern" is another way to begin such a letter; however, it is extremely impersonal and is usually used only when the writer is unfamiliar with both the person and the organization that is being addressed, as when one is addressing a letter of recommendation. In other instances, when a specific organization is being addressed, most writers try to find an alternate salutation.

A different type of salutation now being used to solve the problem of addressing a company or a company officer whose name and sex are unknown is that which simply names the company ("Dear XYZ Company") or states the title or department of the intended recipient, as in the following examples:

Dear Personnel Supervisor
Dear Personnel Department
Dear XYZ Engineers

The use of this type of salutation has increased markedly in the past several years and is considered acceptable by most businesspeople.

When a letter is addressed to an all-female organization, the salutations "Ladies" or "Mesdames" may be used.

Occasionally a letter writer is faced with an addressee's name that gives no clue as to the addressee's sex. Traditionally in these uncertain cases, convention has required the writer to use the masculine courtesy title in the salutation, as *Mr. Lee Schmidtke, Mr. T. A. Gagnon*. However, some writers prefer to express their uncertainty by using such forms as the following:

Dear Mr. or Ms. Schmidtke
Dear Lee Schmidtke

The most convenient way of avoiding the problem of sexual semantics is to use the Simplified Letter styling (see the facsimile on pages 288–289), which eliminates the salutation altogether.

The salutation for a married couple may be styled in the following ways:

Dear Mr. and Mrs. Hathaway
Dear Dr. and Mrs. Simpson
Dear Dr. Smith and Mr. Smith

For more information about choosing appropriate salutations, including salutations for two or more persons and for people with specialized titles, see Chapter 10, "Forms of Address."

Subject Line

A subject line gives the gist of a letter. Its phrasing is necessarily succinct and to the point: it should not be so long as to require more than one line. The subject line serves as an immediate point of reference for the reader as well as a convenient filing tool for the secretaries at both ends of the correspondence.

In the Simplified Letter, which does not include a salutation, the subject line (an essential element) is positioned flush left, three lines below the last line of the inside address. The subject line may be entirely capitalized and not underlined. As an alternative, the main words in the subject line may be capitalized and every word underlined.

If a subject line is included in a letter featuring a salutation, it is frequently positioned flush left, two lines beneath the salutation, and may be entirely capitalized. With the Modified Block and Modified Semi-block styles, however, the subject line may be centered or even indented to match

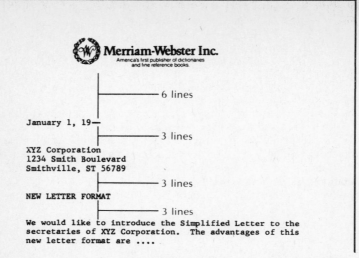

Figure 9.15.   Page placement of the subject line in the Simplified Letter

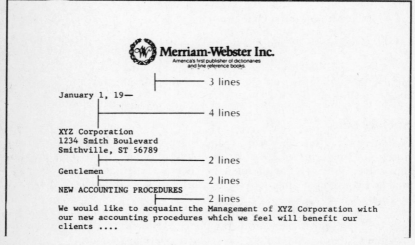

Figure 9.16.   Page placement of the subject line in a Block Letter with open punctuation

the indention of the paragraphs. Legal correspondence uses the subject line in a variety of positions. Legal correspondence based on letter styles other than the Simplified or Block frequently centers the subject line or positions it at the right. A growing number of law offices prefer to position the subject line two lines above the salutation rather than below it.

The subject line may be entirely capitalized, and the word *subject* may be used to introduce the line. When the word *subject* is used, the subject line may also be capitalized headline-style—that is, with the initial letter of the first word capitalized and with the initial letter of all other words except co-ordinating conjunctions, articles, and short prepositions also capitalized. The word *reference* is sometimes also used.

> SUBJECT: CHANGES IN TRAFFIC ROUTE
> Subject: Changes in Traffic Route
> Reference: Changes in Traffic Route

The subject-line headings *In re* and *Re* are now seldom used for general office letters; however, they are often used in legal correspondence. Headings should not be used if one is following the Simplified Letter styling.

Care should be taken not to confuse the subject line with the reference line (see pages 260–262). The subject line differs not only in position but also in styling and purpose: the reference line indicates a numerical classification; the subject line identifies the content of the letter.

Message

The body of the letter—the message—should begin two lines below the salutation or two lines below the subject line, if there is one, in all letter stylings except the Simplified Letter, where the message is typed three lines below the subject line.

Paragraphs are single-spaced internally. Double spacing is used to separate paragraphs. If a letter is extremely brief, it may be double-spaced throughout. Paragraphs in such letters should be indented so that they will be readily identifiable.

The first lines of indented paragraphs (as in the Modified Semi-block Letter) should begin five or ten spaces from the left margin; however, the five-space pattern is the most common. With the Hanging-indented Letter, the first lines of the paragraphs are blocked flush left, while subsequent lines are indented five spaces from the left margin. All other letter stylings require flush-left paragraph alignment.

Long quotations should be indented and blocked five to ten spaces from the left and right margins with internal single spacing and top-and-bottom double spacing so that the material will be set off from the rest of the message. Long enumerations should also be indented: enumerations with items requiring more than one line apiece may require single-spacing within each item, followed by double-spacing between items. Tabular data should be centered on the page.

Additional rules for typing letters that have traditionally been observed include the following:

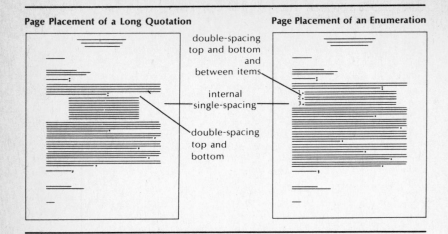

Figure 9.17.   Page placement of items inset within the message

1. Do not divide a word at the end of the first line.
2. Do not divide a word at the end of the last full line of a letter.
3. Do not divide a person's name from his or her courtesy title.

If a letter is long enough to require a continuation sheet or sheets, at least three message lines must be carried over to the next page. The complimentary close and/or typed signature block should never stand alone on a continuation sheet. The last word on a page should not be divided. Continuation-sheet margins should match those of the first sheet. At least six blank lines equaling one inch should be maintained at the top of the continuation sheet.

At the top of every continuation sheet there should be a continuation-sheet heading. The two most common continuation-sheet headings are illustrated in Figures 9.18 and 9.19. The format shown in Figure 9.18 is used with the Simplified and Block Letters. It features a flush-left heading beginning with the page number, followed on the next line by the addressee's courtesy title and full name, and ending with the date on the third line. Some companies prefer that the page number appear as the last line of the continuation-sheet heading, especially if a reference number is included.

Another way to type the heading of a continuation sheet is illustrated in Figure 9.19. In this format, the material is laid out across the page, six lines down from the top edge of the sheet. The addressee's name is typed flush with the left margin, the page number in Arabic numerals is centered on the same line and enclosed with spaced hyphens, and the date is aligned flush with the right margin—all on the same line. This format is often used with the Modified Block, the Modified Semi-block, and the Hanging-indented Letters.

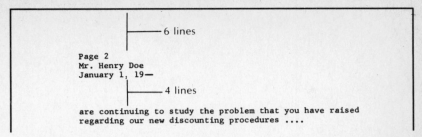

```
              ┌────── 6 lines
              │
    Page 2    │
    Mr. Henry Doe
    January 1, 19—
              ┌────── 4 lines
              │
    are continuing to study the problem that you have raised
    regarding our new discounting procedures ....
```

Figure 9.18. Continuation-sheet heading for Simplified and Block Letters

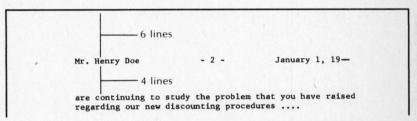

```
              ┌────── 6 lines
              │
    Mr. Henry Doe            - 2 -            January 1, 19—
              ┌────── 4 lines
              │
    are continuing to study the problem that you have raised
    regarding our new discounting procedures ....
```

Figure 9.19. Continuation-sheet heading for Modified Block, Modified Semi-block, and Hanging-indented Letters

Complimentary Close

There is no complimentary close in the Simplified Letter. However, a complimentary close is used with all other letter styles. It is typed two lines below the last line of the message. Its page placement depends on the general letter styling being used. With the Block Letter, the complimentary close is blocked flush with the left margin.

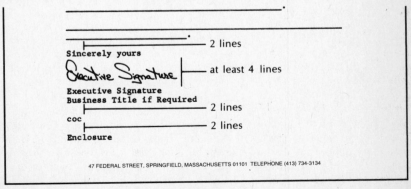

Figure 9.20. Open-punctuation pattern shown in Block Letter format for complimentary close

With the Modified Block, the Modified Semi-block, and the Hanging-indented Letter, the complimentary close may begin at the center or may be aligned directly under the date line (e.g., about five spaces to the right of center, or flush with the right margin) or under some particular part of the printed letterhead. It should never overrun the right margin.

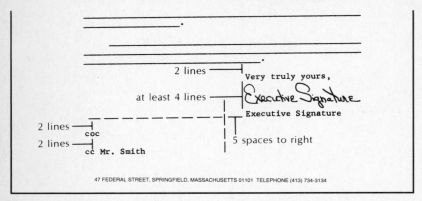

Figure 9.21.   Complimentary close five spaces to right of center as in a Modified Block Letter with mixed punctuation

Only the first word of the complimentary close is capitalized. If the open-punctuation pattern is being followed, the complimentary close is un-punctuated. If the mixed-punctuation pattern is being followed, a comma terminates the complimentary close.

The typist should always use the complimentary close that is dictated, because the writer may have a special reason for the choice of phrasing. If the writer does not specify a particular closing, the typist may wish to select the one that best reflects the general tone of the letter and the state of the writer-reader relationship. Table 4 on page 275 lists the most commonly used complimentary closes and groups them according to general tone and degree of formality.

Complimentary closes on letters written over a period of time to a particular person may become gradually more informal and friendly, but they should not revert to a more formal style once an informal pattern has been established.

Signature Block

The first line of the signature block indicates responsibility for the letter. Either the name of the writer or the name of the organization may appear on the first line of the signature block. In the former case, the writer's name is typed at least four lines below the complimentary close; in the latter, the organization name is typed all in capital letters two lines below the complimentary close and the writer's name at least four lines below the organization name.

Table 4
Complimentary Closes Common in Business Correspondence

General Tone & Degree of Formality	Complimentary Close
highly formal—usually used in diplomatic, governmental, or ecclesiastical correspondence to show respect and deference to a high-ranking addressee	Respectfully yours Respectfully Very respectfully
politely neutral—usually used in general correspondence	Very truly yours Yours very truly Yours truly
friendly and less formal—usually used in general correspondence	Most sincerely Very sincerely Very sincerely yours Sincerely yours Yours sincerely Sincerely
more friendly and informal—often used when writer and reader are on a first-name basis but also often used in general business correspondence	Most cordially Yours cordially Cordially yours Cordially
most friendly and informal—usually used when writer and reader are on a first-name basis	As ever Best wishes Best regards Kindest regards Kindest personal regards Regards
British	Yours faithfully Yours sincerely

With the Simplified Letter, the name of the writer is typed entirely in capitals flush left at least five lines below the last line of the message. If the writer's business title is not included in the printed letterhead, it may be typed on the same line as the name entirely in capitals and separated from the last element of the name by a spaced hyphen. Some organizations, however, prefer to use a comma in place of the hyphen. A combination of the two may be used if the title is complex.

> JOHN P. HEWETT - DIRECTOR
> JOHN P. HEWETT, DIRECTOR
> JOHN P. HEWETT - DIRECTOR, TECHNICAL INFORMATION
> *or*
> JOHN P. HEWETT - DIRECTOR
> TECHNICAL INFORMATION CENTER

With the Block Letter, the signature block is aligned flush left at least four lines below the complimentary close. Only the first letter of each element of the writer's name is capitalized, and only the first letter of each major element of the writer's business title and department name is capitalized

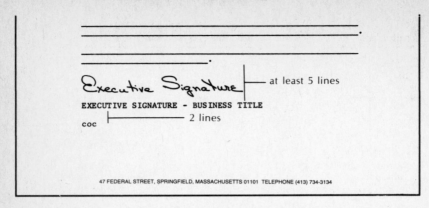

Figure 9.22.   Page placement of signature block in the Simplified Letter

if they are included. The business title and the department name may be omitted if they appear in the printed letterhead:

if title and department name are needed for identification	John D. Russell, Director Consumer Products Division
if department name is already printed on the letterhead	John D. Russell Director
if both title and department name appear in printed letterhead	John D. Russell

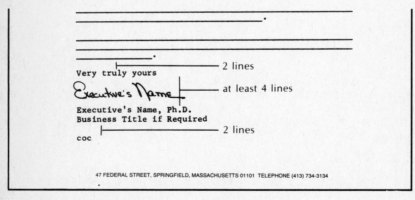

Figure 9.23.   Signature block in the Block Letter

With the Modified Block, the Modified Semi-block, and the Hanging-indented Letters, the signature block begins with the name of the writer typed at least four lines below the complimentary close. The first letter of the first element of each line in the signature block is aligned directly below the first letter of the first element of the complimentary close, unless this alignment will result in an overrunning of the right margin. In that case the signature block may be centered under the complimentary close, as shown in Figure 9.26. Only the first letter of each of the major elements of the writer's name, title (if used), and department name (if used) is capitalized:

Mrs. Joy L. Tate, Director   Mrs. Joy L. Tate   Mrs. Joy L. Tate
Marketing Division   Director

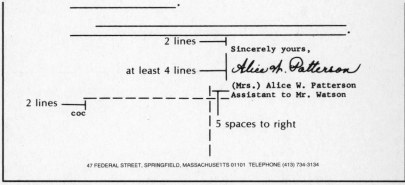

Figure 9.24.   Signature block five spaces to right of center as in a Modified Block Letter with mixed punctuation

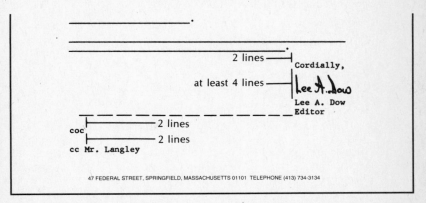

Figure 9.25.   Complimentary close and signature block flush right as in the Modified Block Letter

If printed letterhead stationery is being used, the name of the firm should not appear below the complimentary close. If printed letterhead is not being used, the name of the firm may be typed in capitals two lines beneath the complimentary close with the first letter of the firm's name aligned directly underneath and the writer's name typed in capitals and lowercase at least four lines below the firm's name. The writer's title if needed is typed in capitals and lowercase on a line directly underneath the signature line.

If the company name is long enough to overrun the right margin, it may be centered beneath the complimentary close in the Modified Block and the Modified Semi-block Letters.

Very truly yours,

AJAX VAN LINES, INC.

Samuel O. Lescott

Samuel O. Lescott
Dispatcher

Very truly yours,

JOHNSON AEROSPACE ENGINEERING ASSOCIATES

Sidney C. Johnson

Sidney C. Johnson, Ph.D.
President

Figure 9.26.   Signature block when a printed letterhead is not being used

Regardless of page placement and letter styling, the name of the writer should be typed exactly as it appears in his or her signature. The only exceptions to this rule are the use of *Ms./Mrs./Miss* (as explained in the next paragraph) and the signature of a married woman over the typewritten name of her husband preceded by *Mrs.* If applicable, any academic degrees (as *Ph.D.*) or professional ratings (as *P.E.*) that the writer holds should be included after the surname so that the recipient of the letter will know the proper form of address to use in his or her reply.

Typed Signature	*Salutation in Reply*
Francis E. Atlee, M.D.	Dear Dr. Atlee
Ellen Y. Langford, Ph.D.	Dear Dr. Langford
Dean of Women	*or*
	Dear Dean Langford
Carol I. Etheridge, C.P.A.	Dear Ms. Etheridge
or	
Mrs. Carol I. Etheridge, C.P.A.	Dear Mrs. Etheridge

These academic and professional degrees and ratings need not be repeated in the signature line if they are already included in the printed letterhead, and they are never included in the written signature.

The only titles that may precede a typed signature are *Ms., Mrs.,* and *Miss.* These titles, which may be enclosed in parentheses, are blocked flush left in the Simplified and the Block Letters, and they are aligned with or centered under the complimentary close in the Modified Block, the Modified Semi-block, and the Hanging-indented Letters.

The use of the courtesy title *Ms.* (which usually includes a period even though it is not an abbreviation of any word) has become so widespread that it is now the standard form to use with the name of a woman whose marital status is irrelevant or in doubt. For this reason, there is a marked trend for a woman to omit a courtesy title altogether in the signature line, on the assumption that the recipient will address the reply to "Ms. _____." Only if the writer wishes to show her preference for *Miss* or *Mrs.* will she usually include a courtesy title before her typewritten signature. On the other hand, if the woman's name might be confused with a man's name (as Lee, Lynn, Terry, or Leslie), it is thoughtful to include one of the courtesy titles to help the recipient address a reply. The examples in Figures 9.27 through 9.32 show alternate stylings of the courtesy title with and without the optional parentheses.

Sincerely yours	Sincerely yours	Sincerely yours
Joan Conti	*Joan Conti*	*Joan Conti*
Joan Conti	Miss Joan Conti	Ms. Joan Conti
Vice President	Vice President	Vice President

	Sincerely yours	Sincerely yours
	Joan Conti	*Joan Conti*
	(Miss) Joan Conti	(Ms.) Joan Conti
	Vice President	Vice President

Figure 9.27. Signature sylings for unmarried women

Sincerely yours	Sincerely yours	Sincerely yours
Joan Conti	*Joan Conti*	*Joan Conti*
Joan Conti	Ms. Joan Conti	(Ms.) Joan Conti
Vice President	Vice President	Vice President

Figure 9.28. Signature stylings for women who consider their marital status irrelevant

Sincerely yours	Sincerely yours	Sincerely yours
Joan M. Conti	*Joan M. Conti*	*Joan M. Conti*
Joan M. Conti	Mrs. Joan M. Conti	Ms. Joan M. Conti

	Sincerely yours	Sincerely yours
	Joan M. Conti	*Joan M. Conti*
	(Mrs.) Joan M. Conti	(Ms.) Joan M. Conti

Figure 9.29. Signature stylings for married women using given name + maiden name initial + husband's surname

Sincerely yours

Joan Conti

Mrs. Robert A. Conti
Vice President

Sincerely yours

Joan Conti

(Mrs. Robert A. Conti)
Vice President

Figure 9.30.   Signature stylings for married women using husband's full name

A widow may use either her first name and her maiden name initial and her late husband's surname with the courtesy title *Mrs.* or *Ms.* enclosed in optional parentheses. She may also use her social signature—her husband's full name with *Mrs.*—although the social signature is not commonly used in business correspondence.

Sincerely yours

Joan M. Conti

Ms. Joan M. Conti

Sincerely yours

Joan M. Conti

(Ms.) Joan M. Conti

Sincerely yours

Joan Conti

Mrs. Robert A. Conti

Figure 9.31.   Signature stylings for widows

A divorcée may use her maiden name if it has been legally regained, along with the courtesy title *Ms.* or *Miss* enclosed in optional parentheses or she may omit the title. She may also use her maiden name and her former husband's surname with *Mrs.*

Sincerely yours

Joan M. Conti

Miss Joan M. Conti

Sincerely yours

Joan M. Conti

Joan M. Conti

Sincerely yours

Joan Conti

Mrs. Matthews Conti

Figure 9.32.   Signature stylings for divorcées

Many married women today use both their maiden and married names in hyphenated form, as "Joan Matthews-Dunn" (or "Mrs. Robert Matthews-Dunn"), with the maiden name usually as the first element of the hyphenated compound. In these cases the handwritten signature may not always match the typewritten name. However, the signature should match the hyphenated name when the signer belongs to a Hispanic culture that traditionally combines maternal and paternal family names with a hyphen, as "Carla Monteiro-Lopez."

On rare occasions a letter may be written and signed by two individuals. In these cases, it is generally best to place the names side by side, with the first name flush left in block styles or beginning slightly left of center in other letter styles in order to leave enough room for two horizontally aligned signatures. If horizontal positioning is not feasible, the names may be placed one under the other.

Martin J. Kirchoff   *Sarah K. Wong*
Martin J. Kirchoff   Sarah K. Wong
President   Treasurer

Figure 9.33.   Signature block when two people sign a letter

If the secretary signs a letter for the writer, that person's name is followed by the secretary's initials immediately below and to the right of the surname, or centered under the full name. If the secretary signs a letter in his or her own name for someone else, that individual's courtesy title and surname only are typed directly below.

David R. Robins   *David R. Robins*
      lc   lc

Figure 9.34.   Signature when secretary signs the writer's name

---

Sincerely yours   Sincerely yours   Sincerely yours

Janet A. Smith   *Lee L. Linden*   *Seymour T. Barnes*
(Miss) Janet A. Smith   Lee L. Linden   Seymour T. Barnes
Assistant to Mr. Wood   Secretary to Ms. Key   Assistant to Senator Ross

---

Figure 9.35.   Signature block when secretary signs as a representative

Identification Initials

The initials of the typist and sometimes those of the writer are placed two lines below the last line of the signature block and are aligned flush left in all letter stylings. Most offices prefer that three capitalized initials be used for the writer's name and two lowercase initials be used for the typist's. There is a marked trend towards complete omission of the writer's initials if the name is already typed in the signature block or if it appears in the printed letterhead. In the Simplified Letter, the writer's initials are usually omitted, and the typist's initials if included on the original are typed in lowercase. Many organizations indicate the typist's initials only on carbons for record-keeping purposes, and they do not show the writer's initials unless another individual signs the letter. The following are common stylings:

FCM/HL	FCM:hl	Franklin C. Mason:
FM/hl	FCM:hol	HL
hol	fcm:hol	
hl	FCM:HL	Franklin C. Mason
	FCM:HOL	HL

A letter dictated by one person (as an administrative secretary), typed by another (as a corresponding secretary), and signed by yet another person (as the writer) may show (1) the writer/signer's initials entirely in capitals followed by a colon and (2) the dictator's initials entirely in capitals followed by a colon and (3) the transcriber/typist's initials in lowercase, as AWM:COC:ds

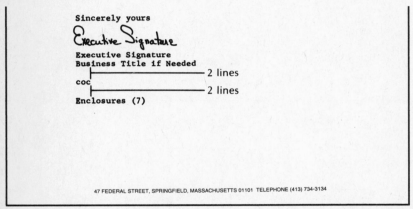

Figure 9.36. Page placement of identification and enclosure notations

Enclosure Notation

If a letter is to be accompanied by an enclosure or enclosures, one of the following expressions should be aligned flush left and typed one to two lines beneath the identification initials, if there are any, or one to two lines beneath the last line of the signature block, if there is no identification line. The unabbreviated form *Enclosure* is usually preferred.

Enclosure   *or if more than one*   Enclosures (3)
enc.   *or*   encl.   *or if more than one*   3 encs.   *or*   Enc. 3

If the enclosures are of special importance, each of them should be numerically listed and briefly described with single-spacing between each item.

Enclosures: 1. Annual Report (19—), 2 copies
 2. List of Major Accounts
 3. Profit and Loss Statement (19—)

The following type of notation then may be typed in the top right corner of each page of each of the enclosures:

Enclosure (1) to Johnson Associates letter No. 1-234-X,
dated January 1, 19—, page 2 of 8

If the enclosure is bound, a single notation attached to its cover sheet will
suffice.

When additional material is being mailed separately, a notation such as
the following may be used:

Separate mailing: 50th Anniversary Report

Carbon Copy Notation

Carbon copies are now often called *courtesy copies* in view of the widespread
use of photocopies; in some offices *c* for *copy* or *pc* for *photocopy* is used instead of the traditional *cc* for *carbon copy.*

A carbon copy notation showing the distribution of courtesy copies to
other individuals should be aligned flush left and typed two lines below the
signature block if there are no other notations or initials, or two lines below
any other notations. If space is very tight, the courtesy copy notation may
be single-spaced below the above-mentioned items.

cc   cc: Copy to   Copies to

Multiple recipients of copies should be listed alphabetically. Sometimes only
their initials are shown.

cc: WPB
       TLC
       CNR

More often, the individuals' names are shown and sometimes also their addresses, especially if the writer feels that such information can be useful to
the addressee.

cc: William L. Carton, Esq.   cc   Ms. Lee Jamieson
       45 Park Towers, Suite 1
       Smithville, ST 56789   Copy to Mr. John K. Long

       Dr. Daniel I. Maginnis   Copies to Mr. Houghton
       1300 Dover Drive   Mr. Ott
       Jonesville, ZZ 12345   Mr. Smythe

To save space, the carbon copy notation may group the recipients.

cc Regional Sales Managers

If the recipient of the copy is to receive an enclosure or enclosures as well,
that individual's full name and address as well as a description of each enclosure and the total number of enclosed items should be shown in the courtesy
copy notation.

cc: Ms. Barbara S. Lee (2 copies, Annual Report)
       123 Jones Street
       Smithville, ST 56789

       Mrs. Sara T. Tufts
       Mrs. Laura E. Yowell

If the first names or initials are given along with the last names, courtesy titles (as *Mr., Mrs., Miss,* and *Ms.*) may be omitted.

cc: William L. Carton   cc: W.L. Carton
     Daniel I. Maginnis   D.I. Maginnis

Typists usually leave either one or two spaces between the *cc:* and the names that follow. However, if only one name follows the *cc:* and it is given in all initials, the space or spaces may be omitted.

cc:JBH

If the writer wishes that copies of the letter be distributed without the list of recipients being shown on the original, the blind carbon copy notation *bcc* or *bcc:* followed by an alphabetical list of the recipients' initials or names may be typed on the copies in the same page position as a regular carbon copy notation. The *bcc* notation may also appear in the upper left-hand corner of the copies.

Carbon or courtesy copies are not usually signed. The secretary may type the signature, preceded by the symbol */S/* or */s/*, to indicate that the writer signed the original copy.

Postscript

A postscript is aligned flush left and is typed two to four lines (depending on space available) below the last notation. If the letter's paragraphs are strict-block, the postscript reflects this format. If the paragraphs within the letter are indented, the first line of the postscript is also indented. If the Hanging-indented Letter styling is used, the first line of the postscript is flush left and all subsequent lines are indented five spaces. All postscripts are single-spaced. Their margins conform with those maintained in the letters themselves. The writer should initial a postscript. While it is not incorrect to head a postscript with the initials *P.S.* (for an initial postscript) and *P.P.S.* (for subsequent ones), these headings are redundant and can be omitted.

Letter Styles for Business Correspondence

The following pages contain full-page letter facsimiles of the five most often used business-letter formats—the Simplified Letter, the Block Letter, the Modified Block Letter, the Modified Semi-block Letter, and the Hanging-indented Letter. In addition, the section contains facsimiles of the following letters: the Official Letter Styling on Executive letterhead, the Official Letter Styling on plain bond, and the Half-sheet. Each facsimile contains a detailed description of letter format and styling. At the end of the section is a discussion of time- and money-saving correspondence methods that have gained acceptance in many of today's business offices.

Merriam-Webster Inc.
America's first publisher of dictionaries
and fine reference books.

Office of the President

January 1, 19—

Dear Ms. Peterson:

This is a facsimile of the Official Letter Styling often used for personal letters written by an executive, or for letters typed on his own personalized company stationery. The paper size is either Executive or Monarch.

The Official Letter Styling is characterized by the page placement of the inside address: It is typed flush left, two to five lines below the last line of the signature block or below the written signature.

The typist's initials if included are typed two lines below the last line of the inside address. An enclosure notation if needed appears two lines below the typist's initials, or two lines below the last line of the inside address. These notations are also flush left.

A typed signature block is not needed on personalized Executive or Monarch stationery; however, if the writer's signature is either difficult to decipher or if it might be unfamiliar to the addressee, it may be typed four lines below the complimentary close.

Open punctuation and blocked paragraphs may also be used in this letter.

Sincerely,

Executive Signature

Ms. Martha Peterson
490 Jones Street
Smithville, ST 56789

47 FEDERAL STREET, SPRINGFIELD, MASSACHUSETTS 01101 TELEPHONE (413) 734-3134

Figure 9.37.   The Official Letter Styling with printed Executive letterhead

```
                              4400 Ambler Boulevard
                              Smithville, ST 56789
                              January 1, 19—

Dear Bob

This is a facsimile of a letter typed on plain
Executive or Monarch stationery.  The basic
format is the same as that of the Official Let-
ter Styling.  The block paragraphs and the open
punctuation pattern are illustrated here.

The heading which includes the writer's full
address and the date may be positioned six lines
from the top edge of the page and flush with the
right margin as shown here.  Approximately six
vertical lines may be placed after the date line
down to the salutation.

The complimentary close is typed two lines be-
low the last line of the message.  The inside
address is flush left, two to five lines below
the last line of the signature block or below
the written signature.

Typist's initials, if included, should be posi-
tioned two lines beneath the last line of the
inside address.  An enclosure notation or any
other notation if required should be typed two
lines below the typist's initials or two lines
below the last line of the inside address if
there are no initials.

                              Sincerely

                              Executive Signature


Mr. Robert Y. Owens
123 East Second Avenue
Jonesville, ST 45678
```

Figure 9.38.   The Official Letter Styling with plain stationery

Merriam-Webster Inc.
America's first publisher of dictionaries
and fine reference books

January 1, 19—

Mrs. Althea Nance
Assistant to the President
XYZ Corporation
1234 Smith Boulevard
Smithville, ST 56789

Dear Mrs. Nance:

This is a facsimile of the Hanging-indented Letter which is not ordinarily used
    in general business correspondence but rather in advertising letters as an
    attractive way of catching the reader's eye. Its main feature is the para-
    graph alignment: The first line of each paragraph is aligned flush left,
    but all subsequent lines are indented five spaces from the left margin.
    The paragraphs are single-spaced internally and double-spaced between each
    other. Either the open or the mixed punctuation pattern may be used in the
    Hanging-indented Letter: This facsimile illustrates the mixed pattern.

The date line, usually typed three lines below the last line of the letterhead,
    is aligned flush right. The inside address and salutation are blocked
    flush left. Spacing between these elements parallels that used in the Mod-
    ified Block and the Modified Semi-block Letters.

Continuation sheets must contain at least three message lines, and the last word
    on the first sheet must not be divided. Continuation-sheet headings may be
    blocked left as in the Block Letter or laid out across the top of the page
    as in the Modified Semi-block Letter. Six blank lines are left from the
    top edge of the page to the first line of the heading and four blank lines
    are left before typing the message. Margins and paragraph alignment paral-
    lel those of the first sheet.

The complimentary close and the signature block are aligned under the date.
    Double-spacing is needed between the last message line and the complimenta-
    ry close. At least four lines should be left for the written signature.

Identification initials and enclosure and carbon copy notations are blocked
    flush left at least two lines below the last line of the signature block.
    Postscripts, if needed, are also hanging-indented.

                                          Cordially,

                              Executive Signature

hg

47 Federal Street, P.O. Box 281, Springfield, MA 01101
Telephone (413) 734-3134

Figure 9.39.   The Hanging-indented Letter

Merriam-Webster Inc.
America's first publisher of dictionaries
and fine reference books.

January 1, 19—

Ms. Sarah H. Smith
Director of Marketing
XYZ Corporation
1234 Smith Boulevard
Smithville, ST 56789

SIMPLIFIED LETTER

Ms. Smith, this is the Simplified Letter recommended by the Administrative Management Society. Its main features—block format,
open punctuation, and fewer internal parts—reduce the number of
keystrokes and typewriter adjustments your secretary must make,
thus cutting costs, saving time, and increasing overall letter
output.

The date line is typed six lines below the last letterhead line.
The inside address, also flush left, appears three lines below the
date line. Since the placement of the inside address is designed
for window envelopes, it is suggested that the all-capitalized,
unpunctuated Postal Service State abbreviation be typed after the
city name, followed by one space and the ZIP Code.

The traditional salutation has been dropped and replaced by an un-
headed, all-capitalized subject line typed flush left, three lines
beneath the last inside-address line. The subject line summarizes
the message.

The first message line begins three lines below the subject line.
The first sentence serves as a greeting to the reader. The addressee's name should appear in the first paragraph, preferably in
the first sentence as shown above. Inclusion of the name adds a
personal touch. All paragraphs are blocked flush left, single-
spaced internally, and double-spaced between each other. Tabular
data and numbered lists are also blocked flush left but are set
off from the rest of the message by double-spacing. Long quotations and unnumbered lists should be indented five to ten spaces
from the left and right margins and set off from the rest of the
message by top and bottom double-spacing.

47 FEDERAL STREET, SPRINGFIELD, MASSACHUSETTS 01101 TELEPHONE (413) 734-3134

Figure 9.40.   The Simplified Letter

Ms. Smith
Page 2
January 1, 19—

If a continuation sheet is required, at least three message lines must be carried over. Continuation-sheet format and margins match those of the first sheet. At least six blank lines are left from the top edge of the page to the first line of the heading which is blocked flush left, single-spaced internally, and typically composed of the addressee's courtesy title and name, the page number, and the applicable date. The rest of the message begins four lines beneath the last heading line.

There is no complimentary close in the Simplified Letter, although closing sentences such as "You have my best wishes," and "My best regards are yours" may end the message. The writer's name (and business title if needed) is aligned flush left and typed all in capitals at least five lines below the last message line. Although the Administrative Management Society uses a spaced hyphen between the writer's surname and his business title, some companies prefer a comma. The writer's department name may be typed flush left all in capitals, one line below the signature line.

The identification initials, flush left and two lines below the last line of the signature block, comprise the typist's initials only. An enclosure notation may be typed one line below the identification initials and aligned flush left. Carbon copy notations may be typed one or two lines below the last notation, depending on available space. If only the signature block and/or typist's initials appear before it, the carbon copy notation is typed two lines below.

[signature]

EXECUTIVE SIGNATURE - BUSINESS TITLE

coc
Enclosures (12)

cc Dr. Alice L. Barnes

January 1, 19—
X-123-4

XYZ Corporation
Sales Department
1234 Smith Boulevard
Smithville, ST 56789

Attention Mr. John Doe

Gentlemen

SUBJECT: BLOCK LETTER

This is a facsimile of the Block Letter, whose structural parts
are flush left. It may feature either the open or the mixed punctuation pattern: The open pattern is shown here.

The date line is typed two to six lines below the last letterhead
line. Here, it is placed three lines below the letterhead. Account or policy numbers if required are single-spaced and blocked
either above or below the date line.

Placement of the inside address varies by letter length. Here, it
is typed four lines below the date line. If window envelopes are
used, the all-capitalized, unpunctuated Postal Service state abbreviations should be employed. One space intervenes between the
state abbreviation and the ZIP Code. If regular envelopes are to
be used, state names may be typed out in full or abbreviated, depending on organization preference. An attention line if required
is typed two lines below the last inside-address line.

The salutation is typed two lines below the attention line, or two
to four lines below the last inside-address line. The salutation
is "Gentlemen" if the letter is addressed to an organization, even
if there is an attention line directing the letter to a particular
individual within that organization. If the letter is addressed
to an individual whose name is on line 1 of the inside address,
the salutation is "Dear Mr. (or Ms. or Mrs. or Miss) + surname" or
"Dear + first name" depending on the writer/reader relationship.
A subject line, typically all in capitals, may be typed two lines
below the salutation. The subject line is optional.

The first message line is typed two lines below the salutation, or
two lines below the subject line if there is one. The message is

47 FEDERAL STREET, SPRINGFIELD, MASSACHUSETTS 01101 TELEPHONE (413) 734-3134

Figure 9.41.   The Block Letter

XYZ Corporation
Sales Department
January 1, 19—
X-123-4
Page 2

single-spaced internally and double-spaced between paragraphs.
At least three message lines must be carried over to a continuation sheet: At no time should the complimentary close and the
signature block stand alone. The last word on a sheet should not
be divided. The continuation-sheet heading is typed six lines
from the top edge of the page. Account or policy numbers if used
on the first sheet must be included in the continuation-sheet
headings. The message begins four lines below the last line of
the heading.

The complimentary close is typed two lines below the last message
line, followed by at least four blank lines for the written signature, followed by the writer's name in capitals and lowercase.
The writer's business title and/or name of his department may be
included in the typed signature block, if they do not appear in
the printed letterhead.

Identification initials may comprise only the typist's initials if
the same person dictated and signed the letter. These initials
are typed two lines below the last signature-block line. The enclosure notation if used is typed one line below the identification line. The carbon copy notation if needed is placed one or
two lines below any other notations, depending on available space.

Sincerely yours

Executive Signature

Executive Signature
Business Title

ccc
Enclosures (2)

cc Mr. Howard T. Jansen

Merriam-Webster Inc.
America's first publisher of dictionaries
and fine reference books.

January 1, 19—

REGISTERED MAIL
PERSONAL

Mr. John Z. Teller
Treasurer
XYZ Corporation
1234 Smith Boulevard
Smithville, ST 56789

Dear Mr. Teller:

This is a facsimile of the Modified Block Letter. It differs from the Block
Letter chiefly in the page placement of its date line, its complimentary close,
and its signature block that are aligned at center, toward the right margin, or
at the right margin. Either the open or the mixed punctuation pattern may be
used: The mixed pattern is illustrated here.

While the date line may be positioned from two to six lines below the last line
of the letterhead, its standard position is three lines below the letterhead,
as shown above. In this facsimile, the date line is typed five spaces to the
right of dead center. If an account or policy number is required, it is blocked
and single-spaced on a line above or below the date.

Special mailing notations and on-arrival notations such as the two shown above
are all-capitalized, aligned flush left, and blocked together two lines above
the first line of the inside address. If used singly, either of these notations
appears two lines above the inside address.

The first line of the inside address is typed about four lines below the date
line. This spacing can be expanded or contracted according to the letter length.
The inside address, the salutation, and all paragraphs of the message are aligned
flush left. The salutation, typed two to four lines below the last line of the
inside address, is worded as it would be in the Block Letter. A subject line if
used is typed two lines below the salutation in all-capital letters and is either
blocked flush left or centered on the page. Underscoring the subject line is also acceptable, but in this case, only the first letter of each word would be capitalized.

The message begins two lines below the salutation or the subject line if there is
one. Paragraphs are single-spaced internally and double-spaced between each other; however, in very short letters, the paragraphs may be double-spaced internally and triple-spaced between each other.

47 Federal Street, P.O. Box 281, Springfield, MA 01101
Telephone (413) 734-3134

Figure 9.42.   The Modified Block Letter

Mr. Teller   - 2 -   January 1, 19—

Continuation sheets should contain at least three message lines. The last
word on a sheet should not be divided. The continuation-sheet heading may be
blocked flush left as in the Block Letter or it may be laid out across the top
of the page as shown above. This heading begins six lines from the top edge
of the page, and the message is continued four lines beneath it.

The complimentary close is typed two lines below the last line of the message.
While the complimentary close may be aligned under some portion of the letterhead, directly under the date line, or even flush with but not overrunning the
right margin, it is often typed five spaces to the right of dead center as
shown here.

The signature line is typed in capitals and lowercase at least four lines below the complimentary close. The writer's business title and department name
may be included if they do not already appear in the printed letterhead. All
elements of the signature block must be aligned with each other and with the
complimentary close.

Identification initials need include only those of the typist, providing that
the writer and the signer are the same person. These initials appear two
lines below the last line of the signature block. An enclosure notation is
typed one line below the identification line, and the carbon copy notation if
required appears one or two lines below any other notations, depending on
space available.

                              Sincerely yours,

                              Executive Signature

                              Executive Signature
                              Business Title

hg
Enclosures (5)

cc Dr. Doe
   Dr. Franklin
   Dr. Mason
   Dr. Watson

Merriam-Webster Inc.
America's first publisher of dictionaries
and fine reference books

January 1, 19—

Mr. Carroll D. Thompson
Sales Manager
XYZ Corporation
1234 Smith Boulevard
Smithville, ST 56789

Dear Mr. Thompson:

MODIFIED SEMI-BLOCK LETTER

This is a facsimile of the Modified Semi-block Letter. It features a date line aligned either slightly to the right of dead center or flush right (as shown above). Its inside address and salutation are aligned flush left, while the paragraphs of the message are indented five or ten spaces. Its complimentary close and signature block are aligned under the date, either slightly to the right or dead center, or flush right. Identification initials, enclosure notations, and carbon copy notations are aligned flush left.

A special mailing notation or an on-arrival notation if required would have been typed flush left and two lines above the first line of the inside address. An account or policy number if needed would have been blocked with the date, one line above or below it. The page placement of these elements parallels their positioning in the Modified Block Letter. An attention line if required is aligned flush left, two lines below the last line of the inside address. A subject line may be typed in all-capitals two lines below the salutation and is typically centered on the page.

The paragraphs are single-spaced internally and double-spaced between each other unless the letter is extremely short, in which case the paragraphs may be double-spaced internally and triple-spaced between each other. Continuation sheets should contain at least three message lines, and the last word on a sheet should never be divided. The heading for a continuation sheet begins at least six lines from the top edge of the page and follows the format shown in this letter.

47 FEDERAL STREET, SPRINGFIELD, MASSACHUSETTS 01101 TELEPHONE (413) 734-3134

Figure 9.43. The Modified Semi-block Letter

Mr. Thompson   - 2 -   January 1, 19—

   The complimentary close is typed at two lines below
the last line of the message. The signature line, four
lines below the complimentary close, is aligned with it
if possible, or centered under it if the name and title
will be long. In this case, it is better to align both
date and complimentary close about five spaces to the
right of dead center to ensure enough room for the signature block which should never overrun the right margin.
The writer's name, business title and department name (if
not already printed on the stationery) are typed in capitals and lowercase.

   Although open punctuation may be followed, the mixed
punctuation pattern is quite common with the Modified
Semi-block Letter, and it is the latter that is shown
here.

                         Sincerely yours,

                         Executive Signature

                         Executive Signature
                         Business Title

jml

Enclosures: 2

cc: Dr. Bennett P. Oakley
     Addison Engineering Associates
     91011 Jones Street
     Smithville, ST 56789

   A postscript if needed is typically positioned two
to four lines below the last notation. In the Modified
Semi-block Letter, the postscript is indented five to ten
spaces to agree with message paragraphing. It is not
necessary to head the postscript with the abbreviation
P.S. The postscript should be initialed by the writer.

                              ES

Merriam-Webster Inc.
America's first publisher of dictionaries
and fine reference books

January 1, 19—

Mr. Ken T. Row
123 Key Place
Smithville, ST   56789

Dear Ken:

    This is a facsimile of the half
sheet which is used for the briefest
of notes—those containing one or
two sentences or two very short paragraphs.

    The Block, Modified Block, or
Modified Semi-block Letters may be
used, and open or mixed punctuation
may be followed.

              Sincerely yours,

              Executive Signature

jml

47 Federal Street, P.O. Box 281, Springfield, MA 01101
Telephone (413) 734-3134

Figure 9.44.   The Half-sheet

Time-saving Correspondence Methods

An increasing number of business offices rely on time-saving and cost-cutting measures for sending out and replying to routine correspondence. Among these methods are the use of form letters and form paragraphs, memorandum forms with detachable reply sections, postal cards, and the writing of marginal notations directly on letters received.

Postal cards Brief messages may be typewritten on standard size (5½ by 3½ inches) postal cards. A message can be fitted on the card if you follow these suggestions:

1. Set the margins for a 4½-inch writing line, which allows half-inch margins at each side. Plan to leave a half-inch margin at the bottom.
2. Type the date on the third line from the top.
3. Omit the inside address.
4. Leave one line of space before the salutation.
5. Leave one line of space before the message.
6. Leave one line of space before the complimentary close and the signature.
7. If necessary, omit one or more of the following: salutation, complimentary close, handwritten signature, identification initials.

Pre-addressed postal cards may also be enclosed with a letter of inquiry to encourage and speed an answer back to your office. You may even type various responses so that the recipient can simply check the appropriate response and mail the card.

Marginal notations The procedure described here is used in many business offices to answer routine queries. The answer to an incoming letter is written at the bottom of the letter, a copy is made for the files, and the original is returned to the sender with the reply written directly on it. Frequently a stamped message or sticker is attached explaining that this speedy reply method is for the customer's convenience.

One variation of this procedure is to stamp on your own letter of inquiry, "Reply here to save time. Photocopy for your files." Or you can enclose a photocopy of your original letter with a request that the recipient simply answer in the margin of the copy and return it to you.

Marginal notations save time and cut costs, and they also reduce the number of file copies. However, they should be used only when such informality is appropriate.

Stylings for Envelope Addresses

The following information may appear on any envelope regardless of its size. Asterisked items are essential and those that are unmarked are optional, depending on the requirements of the particular letter:

*1. The addressee's full name and full geographical address typed approximately in the vertical and horizontal center
2. Special mailing notation or notations typed below the stamp
3. On-arrival notation or notations typed about nine lines below the top left
*4. Sender's full name and geographical address printed or typed in the upper left corner.

The typeface should be block style. The Postal Service does not recommend unusual or italic typefaces.

The address block on a regular envelope should take up no more than $1\frac{1}{2}'' \times 3\frac{3}{4}''$ of space. There should be $\frac{5}{8}''$ of space from the bottom line of the address block to the bottom edge of the envelope. The entire area from the right and left bottom margins of the address block to the right and left bottom edges of the envelope as well as the area under the center of the address block to the bottom center edge of the envelope should be free of print. With regular envelopes, most address blocks are begun about five spaces to the left of horizontal center to admit room for potentially long lines. The address block should be single-spaced. Block styling should be used throughout.

If a window envelope is being used, all address data must appear within the window space, and at least $\frac{1}{4}''$ margins must be maintained between the address and the right, left, top, and bottom edges of the window space.

Position of Elements

Address-block elements should be styled and positioned as described in the following paragraphs:

First Line If the addressee is an individual, that person's courtesy title and full name are typed on the first line.

> Mr. Lee O. Idlewild

If an individual addressee's business title is included in the inside address, it may be typed either on the first line of the address block with a comma separating it from the addressee's name, or it may be typed alone on the next line, depending on the length of title and name.

> Mr. Lee O. Idlewild, President

> Mr. Lee O. Idlewild
> President

If the addressee is an organization, its full name is typed on the first line. If a particular department within an organization is specified, its name is typed on a line under the name of the organization.

> XYZ Corporation
> Sales Department

Next line The full street address should be typed out (although it is accept-able to abbreviate such designations as *Street, Avenue, Boulevard,* etc.). In mass mailings that will be presorted for automated handling (see pages 302–305), it is correct to capitalize all elements of the address block and to use the unpunctuated abbreviations for streets and street-designations that are recommended by the U.S. Postal Service. Room, suite, apartment, and building numbers are typed immediately following the last element of the street address and are positioned on the same line with it. Building names, if used, are listed on a separate line just above the street address.

A post-office box number, if used, is typed on the line immediately above the last line in order to assure delivery to this point. (The box number precedes the station name when a station name is included.) Both street ad-dress and post-office box number may be written in the address, but the let-ter will be delivered to the location specified on the next-to-last line.

Last line The last line of the address block contains the city, state, and the zip code number. Only one space intervenes between the last letter of the state abbreviation and the first digit of the zip code. The zip code should never be on a line by itself. The zip code is mandatory, as are the all-capital-ized, unpunctuated, two-letter Postal Service abbreviations. It is correct, however, to spell the name of a state in full on the letter while using the Postal Service abbreviation on the envelope.

> Mr. John P. Smith
> 4523 Kendall Place, Apt. 8B
> Smithville, ST 56789
>   *or*
> Mr. John P. Smith
> 4523 Kendall Pl., Apt. 8B
> Smithville, ST 56789

When both post-office box number and street address are included in an address, the zip code should correctly match the location (usually the post-office box) specified in the line just above the last line of the address.

> XYZ Corporation
> 1234 Smith Boulevard
> P. O. Box 600
> Smithville, ST 56788

If the addressee has indicated a 9-digit zip code on correspondence to you, use the full number to speed delivery to that address.

> Cameron Corporation
> 765 Bay Street, Room III
> Smithville, ST 56789-1234

Other elements On-arrival notations such as PERSONAL or CONFIDEN-TIAL must be typed entirely in capital letters, about nine lines below the

Table 5
Two-letter State Abbreviations for the United States and its Dependencies

Alabama	AL	Kentucky	KY	Oklahoma	OK
Alaska	AK	Louisiana	LA	Oregon	OR
Arizona	AZ	Maine	ME	Pennsylvania	PA
Arkansas	AR	Maryland	MD	Puerto Rico	PR
California	CA	Massachusetts	MA	Rhode Island	RI
Colorado	CO	Michigan	MI	South Carolina	SC
Connecticut	CT	Minnesota	MN	South Dakota	SD
Delaware	DE	Mississippi	MS	Tennessee	TN
District of		Missouri	MO	Texas	TX
Columbia	DC	Montana	MT	Utah	UT
Florida	FL	Nebraska	NE	Vermont	VT
Georgia	GA	Nevada	NV	Virginia	VA
Guam	GU	New Hampshire	NH	Virgin Islands	VI
Hawaii	HI	New Jersey	NJ	Washington	WA
Idaho	ID	New Mexico	NM	West Virginia	WV
Illinois	IL	New York	NY	Wisconsin	WI
Indiana	IN	North Carolina	NC	Wyoming	WY
Iowa	IA	North Dakota	ND		
Kansas	KS	Ohio	OH		

left top edge of the envelope. Any other on-arrival instructions such as *Hold for Arrival* or *Please Forward* may be typed in capitals and lowercase, underlined, and positioned about nine lines from the left top edge of the envelope.

If an attention line is used in the letter itself, it too must appear on the envelope. The attention line must be placed in the address block so that it is directly above the next-to-last line.

> XYZ Corporation
> Sales Department
> Attention Mr. E. R. Bailey
> 1234 Smith Boulevard
> Smithville, ST 56789

A special mailing notation (as CERTIFIED, REGISTERED MAIL, or SPECIAL DELIVERY) is typed entirely in capitals just below the stamp or about nine lines from the right top edge of the envelope. It should not overrun a ½″ margin.

The printed return address (as of a company) may be supplemented by the name of the writer typed in at the top. The return address on a plain envelope should be styled as follows, with the least two blank lines between the return address and the left and top edges of the envelope:

> Stephen P. Lemke
> 123 Ann Street
> Jonesville, XX 12345

See Table 2 on page 255 for a chart showing stationery and envelope sizes and applications.

PEREZ & MILBANK, P.C.
99 Main Street
Centerville, ST 34567

─────────────── CONFIDENTIAL   ┌─ SPECIAL DELIVERY

                              Mr. Joseph P. Brown
                              President
                              WQR Corporation
                              123 Fontaine Street
                              Anywhere, ST 44678

| on-arrival notation on line 9 | address block typed about 5 spaces left of center | one space | no typed material in lower right corner |

no typed material in lower left corner

special mailing notation under stamp

Figure 9.45. Commercial envelope showing on-arrival and special mailing notations

Foreign Addresses

When typing a foreign address, the secretary should refer first to the return address on the envelope of previous correspondence to ascertain the correct ordering of the essential elements of the address block. Letterhead stationery of previous correspondence may also be checked if an envelope is not available. If neither of these sources is available, the material should be typed as it appears in the inside address of the dictated letter. The following guidelines may be of assistance.

1. All foreign addresses should be typed in English or in English characters. If an address must be in foreign characters (as Russian), an English translation should be inserted between the lines in the address block.
2. Foreign courtesy titles may be substituted for the English, but they are not necessary.
3. The name of the country should be typed in full and in all-capital letters by itself on the last line. Canadian addresses always carry the name CANADA, even though the name of the province is also given.
4. When applicable, foreign postal district numbers should be included. These are positioned either before or after the name of the city, never after the name of the country.

Canadian addresses should adhere to the form requested by the Canada Post for quickest delivery through its automated handling system. As shown in the examples below, the name of the city, fully capitalized, is followed by the name of the province, spelled in full, on one line; the Postal Code follows on a separate line. For mail originating in the United States, CANADA is added on a final line. (Note that capitalization and punctuation differ slightly in French-language addresses.)

Mr. F. F. MacManus	Les Entreprises Optima Ltée
Fitzgibbons and Brown	6789, rue Principale
5678 Main Street	OTTAWA (Ontario)
HALIFAX, Nova Scotia	K1A 0B3
B3J 2N9	CANADA
CANADA	

The Canadian Postal Code consists always of letter-numeral-letter, space, numeral-letter-numeral. Failure to include the correct code number may result in considerable delay in the delivery of mail. When space is limited, the Postal Code may be typed on the same line with the province. In this case, it must be separated from the name of the province by at least two character spaces. The two-letter provincial and territorial abbreviations listed in Table 6 below may also be used when space is limited.

OTTAWA, Ontario K1A 0B3   *or*   OTTAWA, ON K1A 0B3

Table 6
Two-letter Abbreviations for Canadian Provinces

Alberta	AB	Newfoundland	NF	Quebec	PQ
British Columbia	BC	Northwest Territories	NT	Saskatchewan	SK
Labrador	LB	Nova Scotia	NS	Yukon Territory	YT
Manitoba	MB	Ontario	ON		
New Brunswick	NB	Prince Edward Island	PE		

Some samples of foreign corporate abbreviations are shown in Table 7 on page 303.

Addressing for Automation

So that the secretary can take full advantage of the post office's computerized sorting equipment (including new optical character readers that can scan and sort many thousands of pieces of mail an hour), the United States Postal Service recommends that *all* envelopes be addressed properly for automation. All typescript should be clear and easy to read. The basic procedures in addressing envelopes are as follows:

1. Use rectangular envelopes no smaller than $3\frac{1}{2}'' \times 5''$ and no larger than $6\frac{1}{8}'' \times 11\frac{1}{2}''$. There should be good color contrast between the paper and the type impressions.
2. The address should be single-spaced and blocked (straight left margin). The address must be at least $1''$ from the left edge of the envelope and

Table 7
Foreign Corporate Abbreviations

A Brief Sampling of Commonly Used Terms

Language	Type of Business	Abbreviation
Danish	Partnership	I/S
	Limited Partnership	K/S
	Limited-liability Company	A/S
	Private Limited-liability Company	Ap/S
Dutch	Private Company	B.V.
	Public Corporation	N.V.
French	Limited-liability Company	SARL
	Corporation	SA
German	Partnership	OHG
	Limited Partnership	KG
	Limited-liability Company	G.m.b.H.
	Corporation	AG
Italian	Corporation	S.p.A.
	Limited-liability Company	S.r.l.
Portuguese	Corporation	SARL
Spanish	Stock Company	SA
	Corporation	S/A
	Company	CIA
Swedish	Joint Stock Company	SA

at least ⅝″ up from the bottom. There should be no print to the right of or below the address.

3. Additional data (as the attention line, account number, or date) should be part of the blocked address. These data should be positioned above the second line from bottom. Envelope addresses should be typed entirely in capital letters without punctuation marks. Use type fonts other than script, italic, or proportionally-spaced fonts. Do not type the address at a slant.

        C REEVES CORP
        ATTN MR R C SMITH
        XXX XXXX XX XXX XXX
        XXXXXXXX XX XXXXX

4. If mail is addressed to occupants of multi-unit buildings, the unit number should appear after the street address on the same line.

        C REEVES CORP
        ATTN MR R C SMITH
        186 PARK ST ROOM 960
        XXXXXXXX XX XXXXX

5. The bottom line of the address should contain the city, state, and zip code number (see Table 5 on page 300).

> C REEVES CORP
> ATTN MR R C SMITH
> 186 PARK ST ROOM 960
> HARTFORD CT 06106

6. A post-office box number is typed on the line above the last to assure delivery to this point. (Use the zip code for the box number, not for the street address.) The box number precedes the station name.

> C REEVES CORP
> 186 PARK ST
> PO BOX 210 LINCOLN STA
> HARTFORD CT 06106

7. At least ¼″ should be left between the address and the sides and bottom edges of the opening on window envelopes.

A maximum of 22 strokes or positions is allowed on the last line of an envelope address. The Postal Service suggests the following maximum number of positions:

> 13 positions for the city
> 1 space between the city and state
> 2 positions for the state
> 1 space between the state and zip code number
> 5 positions for the zip code number
> _____
> 22 total positions allowed

Many cities exceed the suggested maximum number of 13 positions. The Postal Service suggests that the abbreviations listed in Table 8 below be used to facilitate mail processing.

Table 8
Abbreviations for Street Designators and for Words that Appear Frequently in Place Names

Academy	ACAD	Black	BLK	Causeway	CSWY
Agency	AGNCY	Bluff	BLF	Center	CTR
Airport	ARPRT	Bottom	BTM	Central	CTL
Alley	ALY	Boulevard	BLVD	Church	CHR
Annex	ANX	Branch	BR	Churches	CHRS
Arcade	ARC	Bridge	BRG	Circle	CIR
Arsenal	ARSL	Brook	BRK	City	CY
Avenue	AVE	Burg	BG	Clear	CLR
Bayou	BYU	Bypass	BYP	Cliffs	CLFS
Beach	BCH	Camp	CP	Club	CLB
Bend	BND	Canyon	CYN	College	CLG
Big	BG	Cape	CPE	Corner	COR

Corners	CORS	Island	IS	Rural	R
Court	CT	Islands	IS	Saint	ST
Courts	CTS	Isle	IS	Sainte	ST
Cove	CV	Junction	JCT	San	SN
Creek	CRK	Key	KY	Santa	SN
Crescent	CRES	Knolls	KNLS	Santo	SN
Crossing	XING	Lake	LK	School	SCH
Dale	DL	Lakes	LKS	Seminary	SMNRY
Dam	DM	Landing	LNDG	Shoal	SHL
Depot	DPO	Lane	LN	Shoals	SHLS
Divide	DIV	Light	LGT	Shode	SHD
Drive	DR	Little	LTL	Shore	SHR
East	E	Loaf	LF	Shores	SHRS
Estates	EST	Locks	LCKS	Siding	SDG
Expressway	EXPY	Lodge	LDG	South	S
Extended	EXT	Lower	LWR	Space Flight	
Extension	EXT	Manor	MNR	Center	SFC
Fall	FL	Meadows	MDWS	Spring	SPG
Falls	FLS	Meeting	MTG	Springs	SPGS
Farms	FRMS	Memorial	MEM	Square	SQ
Ferry	FRY	Middle	MDL	State	ST
Field	FLD	Mile	MLE	Station	STA
Fields	FLDS	Mill	ML	Stream	STRM
Flats	FLT	Mills	MLS	Street	ST
Ford	FRD	Mines	MNS	Sulphur	SLPHR
Forest	FRST	Mission	MSN	Summit	SMT
Forge	FRG	Mound	MND	Switch	SWCH
Fork	FRK	Mount	MT	Tannery	TNRY
Forks	FRKS	Mountain	MTN	Tavern	TVRN
Fort	FT	National	NAT	Terminal	TERM
Fountain	FTN	Neck	NCK	Terrace	TER
Freeway	FWY	New	NW	Ton	TN
Furnace	FURN	North	N	Tower	TWR
Gardens	GDNS	Orchard	ORCH	Town	TWN
Gateway	GTWY	Palms	PLMS	Trail	TRL
Glen	GLN	Park	PK	Trailer	TRLR
Grand	GRND	Parkway	PKY	Tunnel	TUNL
Great	GR	Pillar	PLR	Turnpike	TPKE
Green	GRN	Pines	PNES	Union	UN
Ground	GRD	Place	PL	University	UNIV
Grove	GRV	Plain	PLN	Upper	UPR
Harbor	HBR	Plains	PLNS	Valley	VLY
Haven	HVN	Plaza	PLZ	Viaduct	VIA
Heights	HTS	Point	PT	View	VW
High	HI	Port	PRT	Village	VLG
Highlands	HGLDS	Prairie	PR	Ville	VL
Highway	HWY	Ranch	RNCH	Vista	VIS
Hill	HL	Ranches	RNCHS	Water	WTR
Hills	HLS	Rapids	RPDS	Wells	WLS
Hollow	HOLW	Resort	RESRT	West	W
Hospital	HOSP	Rest	RST	White	WHT
Hot	H	Ridge	RDG	Works	WKS
House	HSE	River	RIV	Yards	YDS
Inlet	INLT	Road	RD		
Institute	INST	Rock	RK		

Chapter 10

Forms of Address

CONTENTS

It has already been emphasized that the initial impression created by a letter is vital to the letter's ultimate effectiveness. It follows that the proper use of the conventional forms of address is essential, especially since these forms appear in conspicuous areas of the letter: on the envelope, in the inside address, and in the salutation.

Forms of Address Chart

The following pages contain a chart of alphabetically grouped and listed forms of address for individuals where offices, ranks, or professions warrant special courtesy. (For information about choosing complimentary closes, see page 275.) The main categories in the chart are listed below in the order of their appearance.

Clerical and Religious Orders
College and University Faculty
    and Officials
Consular Officers
Diplomats
Foreign Heads of State

Government Officials—Federal
Government Officials—Local
Government Officials—State
Military Ranks
Miscellaneous Professional Titles
United Nations Officials

A special chart headed "Multiple Addressees" immediately follows the Forms of Address Chart, and a more detailed discussion of special titles and abbreviations (such as *Doctor, Esquire, Honorable,* etc.) begins on page 326. For information about the use of gender-neutral salutations, see pages 268–269.

When two or more stylings are shown in the Forms of Address Chart, it should be understood by the reader that the most formal styling appears first. It should also be understood that if the formal address shown for a man in "Sir," the formal address for a woman is "Madam," and vice versa, and that if the informal address for a man is "Mr.," the informal address for a woman is "Mrs.," "Miss," or "Ms.," and vice versa. In cases where this simple equation does not apply, examples for both male and female addresses are given. In all of the examples for female addresses, the courtesy title *Ms.* has been shown; however, the titles *Mrs.* and *Miss* may be freely substituted in all of these cases according to the preference of the recipient if it is known.

Readers will note that approximately half of the positions and ranks in this chart are illustrated with a man's name and half with a woman's name. This is not meant to suggest that any position or rank in this chart is more likely to be held by a man or a woman. On the contrary, it has been assumed that, except in the category of Clerical and Religious Orders, either a man or woman may hold any position or rank included in this chart; however, space limitations in the chart preclude showing examples of both male and female addresses in every instance.

Lack of space has also resulted in the exclusion from the chart of lower-ranking officials such as city water commissioners. Addressing these minor officials should be no problem, however. An official's title appears in the address only if the official *heads* an agency or department; otherwise, only the name of the agency or department is included.

Mrs. Joan R. White, Chairman   Mrs. Joan R. White
Smithville School Board   Smithville School Board

Mrs. Joan R. White
Sheriff, Rockland County

Salutations on letters to minor officials consist of courtesy title + surname. The substitution of a professional title (as "Dear Justice Smith") for the courtesy title is correct only for high-ranking officials such as governors and judges; for military officers; and for certain police and fire officers.

Dear Governor Roy   Dear Chief Roberts
Dear Senator Scott   Dear Sheriff Roberts
Dear Judge Dow   *but also*
Dear Major Smith   Dear Mr. Roberts

Military officers retain their highest rank upon retirement and are addressed in the same way as active officers.

Inside Address Styling	· Salutation Styling

Clerical and Religious Orders

abbot
The Right Reverend John R. Smith, O.S.B.
Abbot of _____

Right Reverend and dear Father
Dear Father Abbot
Dear Father

archbishop
The Most Reverend Archbishop of _____
or
The Most Reverend John R. Smith
Archbishop of _____

Your Excellency

Your Excellency
Dear Archbishop Smith

archdeacon
The Venerable The Archdeacon of _____
or
The Venerable John R. Smith
Archdeacon of _____

Venerable Sir

Venerable Sir
My dear Archdeacon

bishop, Catholic
The Most Reverend John R. Smith
Bishop of _____

Your Excellency
Dear Bishop Smith

bishop, Episcopal
The Right Reverend The Bishop of _____
or
The Right Reverend John R. Smith
Bishop of _____

Right Reverend Sir

Right Reverend Sir
Dear Bishop Smith

bishop, Episcopal, Presiding
The Most Reverend John R. Smith
Presiding Bishop

Most Reverend Sir
Dear Bishop
Dear Bishop Smith

bishop, Protestant (excluding Episcopal)
The Reverend John R. Smith

Reverend Sir
Dear Bishop Smith

brotherhood, member of
Brother John, S.J. *(or other initials for the order)*

Dear Brother John

canon
The Reverend John R. Smith
Canon of _____ Cathedral

Dear Canon Smith

cardinal
His Eminence John Cardinal Smith

Your Eminence
Dear Cardinal Smith

or
His Eminence Cardinal Smith

Your Eminence
Dear Cardinal Smith

or if also an archbishop
His Eminence John Cardinal Smith
Archbishop of _____
or
His Eminence Cardinal Smith
Archbishop of _____

Your Eminence
Dear Cardinal Smith

Your Eminence
Dear Cardinal Smith

Inside Address Styling	Salutation Styling
chaplain, college or university—see COLLEGE AND UNIVERSITY FACULTY AND OFFICIALS	
clergyman, Protestant	
The Reverend Amelia R. Smith	Dear Ms. Smith
or if having a doctorate	
The Reverend Dr. Amelia R. Smith	Dear Dr. Smith
dean (of a cathedral)	
The Very Reverend John R. Smith	Very Reverend Sir
_____ Cathedral	Dear Dean Smith
or	
Dean John R. Smith	Very Reverend Sir
_____ Cathedral	Dear Dean Smith
monsignor, domestic prelate	
The Right Reverend Monsignor John R. Smith	Right Reverend and dear Monsignor Smith
or	
The Rt. Rev. Msgr. John R. Smith	Dear Monsignor Smith
monsignor, papal chamberlain	
The Very Reverend Monsignor John R. Smith	Very Reverend and dear Monsignor Smith
or	
The Very Rev. Msgr. John R. Smith	Dear Monsignor Smith
mother superior (of a sisterhood)	
The Reverend Mother Superior	Reverend Mother
Convent of _____	Dear Reverend Mother
	My dear Reverend Mother Mary Angelica
or	
Reverend Mother Mary Angelica, O.S.D.	Reverend Mother
(or other initials of the order)	Dear Reverend Mother
Convent of _____	My dear Reverend Mother Mary Angelica
or	
Mother Mary Angelica, Superior	Reverend Mother
Convent of _____	Dear Reverend Mother
	My dear Reverend Mother Mary Angelica
patriarch (of an Eastern Orthodox Church)	
His Beatitude the Patriarch of _____	Most Reverend Lord
pope	
His Holiness the Pope	Your Holiness
	Most Holy Father
or	
His Holiness Pope John	Your Holiness
	Most Holy Father
president, Mormon	
The President	My dear President
Church of Jesus Christ of Latter-day Saints	Dear President Smith
priest, Catholic	
The Reverend Father Smith	Dear Father Smith
or	
The Reverend John R. Smith	Dear Father Smith

Inside Address Styling	Salutation Styling

priest, president (of a college or university)—see COLLEGE AND UNIVERSITY FACULTY
   AND OFFICIALS

rabbi
Rabbi John R. Smith   Dear Rabbi Smith
   or if having a doctorate
Rabbi John R. Smith, D.D.   Dear Dr. Smith

sisterhood, member of
Sister Mary Angelica, S.C. *(or other initials*   Dear Sister
   of the order)   Dear Sister Mary Angelica

College and University Faculty and Officials

chancellor (of a university)
Dr. Amelia R. Smith   Dear Dr. Smith
Chancellor

chaplain (of a college or university)
The Reverend John R. Smith   Dear Chaplain Smith
Chaplain   Dear Mr. Smith
                                             Dear Father Smith

dean (of a college or university)
Dean Amelia R. Smith   Dear Dr. Smith
                                             Dear Dean Smith
   or
Dr. Amelia R. Smith   Dear Dr. Smith
Dean   Dear Dean Smith

instructor
Mr. John R. Smith   Dear Mr. Smith
Instructor

president
Dr. Amelia R. Smith   Dear Dr. Smith
President
   or
President Amelia R. Smith   Dear President Smith

president, priest
The Very Reverend John R. Smith   Dear Father Smith
President

professor, assistant or associate
Dr. Amelia R. Smith   Dear Dr. Smith
Assistant Professor of _____   Dear Professor Smith
                                             Dear Ms. Smith
   or
Dr. Amelia R. Smith   Dear Dr. Smith
Associate Professor of _____   Dear Professor Smith
                                             Dear Ms. Smith

professor, full
Professor John R. Smith   Dear Professor Smith
   or
Dr. John R. Smith   Dear Dr. Smith
Professor of _____

Inside Address Styling	Salutation Styling

Consular Officers

consulate, American
The American Consulate	Gentlemen
(foreign city, country)	Ladies and Gentlemen
or if in Latin America or Canada	
The Consulate of the United States of	Gentlemen
America	Ladies and Gentlemen

consul, American (covers all consular grades such as *Consul, Consul General, Vice-Consul,* and *Consular Agent*)
The American Consul	Sir
(foreign city, country)	Sir or Madam
or if in Latin America or Canada	
The Consul of the United States of America	Sir
	Sir or Madam
or if individual name is known	
Amelia R. Smith, Esq.	Madam
American Consul	Dear Ms. Smith
or if in Latin America or Canada	
Amelia R. Smith, Esq.	Madam
Consul of the United States of America	Dear Ms. Smith

consulate, foreign
The _____ Consulate	Gentlemen
(U.S. city, state, zip code)	Ladies and Gentlemen
or	
The Consulate of _____	Gentlemen
(U.S. city, state, zip code)	Ladies and Gentlemen

consuls, foreign (covers all consular grades)
The _____ Consul	Sir
(U.S. city, state, zip code)	Sir or Madame
or	
The Consul of _____	Sir
(U.S. city, state, zip code)	Sir or Madame
or if individual name is known	
The Honorable John R. Smith	Sir
_____ Consul	Dear Mr. Smith

Diplomats

ambassador, American
The Honorable Amelia R. Smith	Madam
American Ambassador	Dear Madam Ambassador
or if in Latin America or Canada	
The Honorable Amelia R. Smith	Madam
Ambassador of the United States of America	Dear Madam Ambassador
or	
The Honorable John R. Smith	Sir
American Ambassador	Dear Mr. Ambassador
or if in Latin America or Canada	
The Honorable John R. Smith	Sir
Ambassador of the United States of America	Dear Mr. Ambassador

Inside Address Styling	Salutation Styling
ambassador, foreign	
His Excellency John R. Smith	Excellency
Ambassador of _____	Dear Mr. Ambassador
or	
Her Excellency Amelia R. Smith	Excellency
Ambassador of _____	Dear Madame Ambassador
chargé d'affaires ad interim, American	
Amelia R. Smith, Esq.	Madam
American Chargé d'Affaires ad Interim	Dear Ms. Smith
or if in Latin America or Canada	
Amelia R. Smith, Esq.	Madam
United States Chargé d'Affaires ad Interim	Dear Ms. Smith
chargé d'affaires ad interim, foreign	
Mr. John R. Smith	Sir
Chargé d'Affaires ad Interim of _____	Dear Mr. Smith
or	
Ms. Amelia R. Smith	Madame
Chargé d'Affaires ad Interim of _____	Dear Ms. Smith
chargé d'affaires (de missi), foreign	
Ms. Amelia R. Smith	Madame
Chargé d'Affaires of _____	Dear Ms. Smith
or	
Mr. John R. Smith	Sir
Chargé d'Affaires of _____	Dear Mr. Smith
minister, American	
The Honorable John R. Smith	Sir
American Minister	Dear Mr. Minister
or if in Latin America or Canada	
The Honorable John R. Smith	Sir
Minister of the United States of America	Dear Mr. Minister
or	
The Honorable Amelia R. Smith	Madam
American Minister	Dear Madam Minister
or if in Latin America or Canada	
The Honorable Amelia R. Smith	Madam
Minister of the United States of America	Dear Madam Minister
minister, foreign	
The Honorable Amelia R. Smith	Madame
Minister of _____	Dear Madame Minister
or	
The Honorable John R. Smith	Sir
Minister of _____	Dear Mr. Minister

Foreign Heads of State: A Brief Sampling

premier	
His Excellency John R. Smith	Excellency
Premier of _____	Dear Mr. Premier
or	
Her Excellency Amelia R. Smith	Excellency
Premier of _____	Dear Madame Premier

Inside Address Styling	Salutation Styling

president of a republic
Her Excellency Amelia R. Smith
President of _____
  or
His Excellency John R. Smith
President of _____

Excellency
Dear Madame President

Excellency
Dear Mr. President

prime minister
His Excellency John R. Smith

  or
Her Excellency Amelia R. Smith

Excellency
Dear Mr. Prime Minister

Excellency
Dear Madame Prime Minister

Government Officials—Federal

---

attorney general
The Honorable Amelia R. Smith
The Attorney General
  or
The Honorable John R. Smith
The Attorney General

Dear Madam Attorney General

Dear Mr. Attorney General

cabinet officer (other than attorney general)
The Honorable John R. Smith
Secretary of _____
  or
The Secretary of _____
  or
The Honorable Amelia R. Smith
Secretary of _____

Sir
Dear Mr. Secretary

Sir
Dear Mr. Secretary
Madam
Dear Madam Secretary

cabinet officer, former
The Honorable Amelia R. Smith

Dear Ms. Smith

chairman of a (sub) committee, U.S. Congress (stylings shown apply to House of Representatives & Senate)
The Honorable John R. Smith
Chairman
Committee on _____
United States Senate
  or
The Honorable Amelia R. Smith
Chairman
Committee on _____
United States Senate

Dear Mr. Chairman
Dear Senator Smith

Dear Madam Chairman
Dear Senator Smith

chief justice—see SUPREME COURT, FEDERAL; STATE

commissioner
  if appointed
The Honorable Amelia R. Smith
Commissioner
  or
The Honorable John R. Smith
Commissioner
  if career
Ms. Amelia R. Smith
Commissioner

Dear Madam Commissioner
Dear Ms. Smith

Dear Mr. Commissioner
Dear Mr. Smith

Dear Ms. Smith

Inside Address Styling	Salutation Styling

congressman—see REPRESENTATIVE, U.S. CONGRESS

director (as of an independent federal agency)
The Honorable John R. Smith   Dear Mr. Smith
Director
———— Agency

district attorney
The Honorable Amelia R. Smith   Dear Ms. Smith
District Attorney

federal judge
The Honorable John R. Smith   Sir
Judge of the United States District   My dear Judge Smith
   Court of the ———— District   Dear Judge Smith
   of ————

justice—see SUPREME COURT, FEDERAL; STATE

librarian of congress
The Honorable Amelia R. Smith   Madam
Librarian of Congress   Dear Ms. Smith

postmaster general
The Honorable John R. Smith   Sir
The Postmaster General   Dear Mr. Postmaster General
   or
The Honorable Amelia R. Smith   Madam
The Postmaster General   Dear Madam Postmaster General

president of the United States
The President   Mr. President
The White House   My dear Mr. President
                                       Dear Mr. President
   or
The Honorable Amelia R. Smith   Madam President
President of the United States   My dear Madam President
The White House   Dear Madam President

president of the United States (former)
The Honorable John R. Smith   Sir
(local address)   Dear Mr. Smith

president-elect of the United States
The Honorable Amelia R. Smith   Dear Madam
President-elect of the United States   Dear Ms. Smith

press secretary to the President of the United States
Mr. John R. Smith   Dear Mr. Smith
Press Secretary to the President
   of the United States

Inside Address Styling	Salutation Styling
representative, United States Congress	
The Honorable Amelia R. Smith	Madam
United States House of Representatives	Dear Representative Smith
or for local address	
The Honorable Amelia R. Smith	Dear Ms. Smith
Representative in Congress	
representative, United States Congress (former)	
The Honorable John R. Smith	Dear Mr. Smith
(local address)	
senator, United States Senate	
The Honorable Amelia R. Smith	Madam
United States Senate	Dear Senator Smith
senator-elect	
The Honorable John R. Smith	Dear Mr. Smith
Senator-elect	
(local address)	
senator (former)	
The Honorable Amelia R. Smith	Dear Senator Smith
(local address)	
speaker, United States House of Representatives	
The Honorable	Sir
The Speaker of the House of Representatives	
or	
The Honorable Speaker of the House	Sir
of Representatives	
or	
The Honorable John R. Smith	Sir
Speaker of the House of Representatives	Dear Mr. Speaker
	Dear Mr. Smith
speaker, United States House of Representatives (former)	
The Honorable Amelia R. Smith	Madam
(local address)	Dear Madam Speaker
special assistant to the President of the United States	
Mr. John R. Smith	Dear Mr. Smith
supreme court, associate justice	
Mr. Justice Smith	Sir
The Supreme Court of the United States	Mr. Justice
	My dear Mr. Justice
	Dear Mr. Justice Smith
or	
Ms. Justice Smith	Madam
The Supreme Court of the United States	Madam Justice
	My dear Madam Justice
	Dear Madam Justice

Inside Address Styling	Salutation Styling
supreme court, chief justice	
The Chief Justice of the United States	Sir
The Supreme Court of the United States	My dear Mr. Chief Justice
	Dear Mr. Chief Justice
	or
	Madam
	My dear Madam Chief Justice
	Dear Madam Chief Justice
or	
The Chief Justice	Sir
The Supreme Court	My dear Mr. Chief Justice
	Dear Mr. Chief Justice
	or
	Madam
	My dear Madam Chief Justice
	Dear Madam Chief Justice
supreme court, retired Justice	
The Honorable Amelia R. Smith	Madam
(local address)	Dear Justice Smith
territorial delegate	
The Honorable Amelia R. Smith	Dear Ms. Smith
Delegate of _____	
House of Representatives	
undersecretary of a department	
The Honorable John R. Smith	Dear Mr. Smith
Undersecretary of _____	
vice president of the United States	
The Vice President of the United States	Madam
United States Senate	My dear Madam Vice President
	Dear Madam Vice President
or	
The Honorable John R. Smith	Sir
Vice President of the United States	My dear Mr. Vice President
Washington, DC (zip code)	Dear Mr. Vice President

Government Officials—Local

alderman	
The Honorable John R. Smith	Dear Mr. Smith
	Dear Alderman Smith
or	
Alderman John R. Smith	Dear Mr. Smith
	Dear Alderman Smith
city attorney (includes city counsel, corporation counsel)	
The Honorable Amelia R. Smith	Dear Ms. Smith
councilman—see ALDERMAN	
county clerk	
The Honorable John R. Smith	Dear Mr. Smith
Clerk of _____ County	

Inside Address Styling	Salutation Styling

county treasurer—see COUNTY CLERK

judge
The Honorable Amelia R. Smith   Dear Judge Smith
Judge of the _____ Court of _____

mayor
The Honorable John R. Smith   Sir
Mayor of _____   Dear Mayor Smith

selectman—see ALDERMAN

Government Officials—State

assemblyman—see REPRESENTATIVE, STATE

attorney (as commonwealth's attorney, state's attorney)
The Honorable Amelia R. Smith   Dear Ms. Smith
(title)

attorney general
The Honorable John R. Smith   Sir
Attorney General of the State of _____   Dear Mr. Attorney General
  or
The Honorable Amelia R. Smith   Madam
Attorney General of the State of _____   Dear Madam Attorney General

clerk of a court
Amelia R. Smith, Esq.   Dear Ms. Smith
Clerk of the Court of _____

delegate—see REPRESENTATIVE, STATE

governor
The Honorable John R. Smith   Sir
Governor of _____   Dear Governor Smith
  or in some states
His Excellency, the Governor of _____   Sir
                                       Dear Governor Smith

governor (acting)
The Honorable Amelia R. Smith   Madam
Acting Governor of _____   Dear Ms. Smith

governor-elect
The Honorable John R. Smith   Dear Mr. Smith
Governor-elect of _____

governor (former)
The Honorable Amelia R. Smith   Dear Ms. Smith

judge, state court
The Honorable John R. Smith   Dear Judge Smith
Judge of the _____ Court

judge/justice, state supreme court—see SUPREME COURT, STATE

Inside Address Styling	Salutation Styling

lieutenant governor
The Honorable Lieutenant Governor of _____   Madam
  or
The Honorable Amelia R. Smith   Madam
Lieutenant Governor of _____   Dear Ms. Smith

representative, state (includes assemblyman, delegate)
The Honorable John R. Smith   Sir
House of Representatives (or The State   Dear Mr. Smith
  Assembly or The House of Delegates)

secretary of state
The Honorable Secretary of State of _____   Madam
  or
The Honorable Amelia R. Smith   Madam
Secretary of State of _____   Dear Madam Secretary
  or
The Honorable John R. Smith   Sir
Secretary of State of _____   Dear Mr. Secretary

senate, state, president of
The Honorable John R. Smith   Sir
President of the Senate of the State   Dear Mr. Smith
  (or the Commonwealth) of _____   Senator

senator, state
The Honorable Amelia R. Smith   Madam
The Senate of _____   Dear Senator Smith

speaker, state assembly, house of delegates, or house of representatives
The Honorable John R. Smith   Sir
Speaker of _____   Dear Mr. Smith

supreme court, state, associate justice
The Honorable Amelia R. Smith   Madam
Associate Justice of the Supreme Court   Dear Justice Smith
  of _____

supreme court, state, chief justice
The Honorable John R. Smith   Sir
Chief Justice of the Supreme Court of _____   Dear Mr. Chief Justice
  or
The Honorable Amelia R. Smith   Madam
Chief Justice of the Supreme Court of _____   Dear Madam Chief Justice

supreme court, state, presiding justice
The Honorable Amelia R. Smith   Madam
Presiding Justice _____ Division   Dear Madam Justice
Supreme Court of _____
  or
The Honorable John R. Smith   Sir
Presiding Justice   Dear Mr. Chief Justice
_____ Division
Supreme Court of _____

Inside Address Styling	Salutation Styling
Military Ranks	

admiral (coast guard, navy)—see also REAR ADMIRAL, VICE ADMIRAL

Admiral John R. Smith, USCG (or USN)	Dear Admiral Smith
or	
ADM John R. Smith, USCG (or USN)	Dear Admiral Smith

airman

AMN Amelia R. Smith, USAF	Dear Airman Smith

airman basic

AB John R. Smith, USAF	Dear Airman Smith

airman first class

A1C Amelia R. Smith, USAF	Dear Airman Smith

brigadier general (air force, army, marine corps)

Brigadier General John R. Smith, USAF (or USMC)	Dear General Smith
or	
BG John R. Smith, USAF (or USA)	Dear General Smith
or	
Brig. Gen. John R. Smith, USMC	Dear General Smith

cadet (U.S. Air Force Academy, U.S. Military Academy)

Cadet Amelia R. Smith	Dear Cadet Smith

captain (air force, army, coast guard, navy, marine corps)

Captain John R. Smith, USAF (or USA or USCG or USN or USMC)	Dear Captain Smith
or	
CPT John R. Smith, USAF (or USA)	Dear Captain Smith
or	
CAPT John R. Smith, USCG (or USN)	Dear Captain Smith
or	
Capt. John R. Smith, USMC	Dear Captain Smith

chief petty officer (coast guard, navy)

Chief Petty Officer Amelia R. Smith, USCG (or USN)	Dear Petty Officer Smith
or	
CPO Amelia R. Smith, USCG (or USN)	Dear Petty Officer Smith

chief warrant officer W4 (army)

Chief Warrant Officer W4 John R. Smith	Dear Mr. Smith
or	
CWO4 John R. Smith	Dear Mr. Smith

colonel (air force, army, marine corps)

Colonel Amelia R. Smith, USAF (or USA or USMC)	Dear Colonel Smith
or	
COL Amelia R. Smith, USAF (or USA)	Dear Colonel Smith
or	
Col. Amelia R. Smith, USMC	Dear Colonel Smith

Inside Address Styling	Salutation Styling

commander (coast guard or navy)
Commander John R. Smith, USCG (or USN)   Dear Commander Smith
or
CDR John R. Smith, USCG (or USN)   Dear Commander Smith

corporal (army)—see also LANCE CORPORAL
Corporal Amelia R. Smith, USA   Dear Corporal Smith
or
CPL Amelia R. Smith, USA   Dear Corporal Smith

ensign (coast guard, navy)
Ensign John R. Smith, USCG (or USN)   Dear Ensign Smith
Dear Mr. Smith

or
ENS John R. Smith, USCG (or USN)   Dear Ensign Smith
Dear Mr. Smith

first lieutenant (air force, army, marine corps)
First Lieutenant Amelia R. Smith, USAF   Dear Lieutenant Smith
(or USA or USMC)
or
1LT Amelia R. Smith, USAF (or USA)   Dear Lieutenant Smith
or
1st. Lt. Amelia R. Smith, USMC   Dear Lieutenant Smith

first sergeant (army, marine corps)
First Sergeant John R. Smith, USA (or USMC)   Dear Sergeant Smith
or
1SG John R. Smith, USA   Dear Sergeant Smith
or
1st. Sgt. John R. Smith, USMC   Dear Sergeant Smith

general (air force, army, marine corps)—see also BRIGADIER GENERAL, LIEUTENANT
GENERAL, MAJOR GENERAL
General Amelia R. Smith, USAF (or USA   Dear General Smith
or USMC)
or
GEN Amelia R. Smith, USAF (or USA)   Dear General Smith
or
Gen. Amelia R. Smith, USMC   Dear General Smith

gunnery sergeant (marine corps)
Gunnery Sergeant John R. Smith, USMC   Dear Sergeant Smith
or
Gy. Sgt. John R. Smith, USMC   Dear Sergeant Smith

lance corporal (marine corps)
Lance Corporal Amelia R. Smith, USMC   Dear Corporal Smith
or
L/Cpl. Amelia R. Smith, USMC   Dear Corporal Smith

lieutenant (coast guard, navy)—see also FIRST LIEUTENANT, SECOND LIEUTENANT
Lieutenant John R. Smith, USCG (or USN)   Dear Mr. Smith
or
LT John R. Smith, USCG (or USN)   Dear Mr. Smith

Inside Address Styling	Salutation Styling

lieutenant colonel (air force, army, marine corps)

Lieutenant Colonel Amelia R. Smith, USAF (or USA or USMC)
Dear Colonel Smith

or

LTC Amelia R. Smith, USAF (or USA)
Dear Colonel Smith

or

Lt. Col. Amelia R. Smith, USMC
Dear Colonel Smith

lieutenant commander (coast guard, navy)

Lieutenant Commander John R. Smith, USCG (or USN)
Dear Commander Smith

or

LCDR John R. Smith, USCG (or USN)
Dear Commander Smith

lieutenant general (air force, army, marine corps)

Lieutenant General Amelia R. Smith, USAF (or USA or USMC)
Dear General Smith

or

LTG Amelia R. Smith, USAF (or USA)
Dear General Smith

or

Lt. Gen. Amelia R. Smith, USMC
Dear General Smith

lieutenant junior grade (coast guard, navy)

Lieutenant (j.g.) John R. Smith, USCG (or USN)
Dear Mr. Smith

or

LTJG John R. Smith, USCG (or USN)
Dear Mr. Smith

major (air force, army, marine corps)

Major Amelia R. Smith, USAF (or USA or USMC)
Dear Major Smith

or

MAJ Amelia R. Smith, USAF (or USA)
Dear Major Smith

or

Maj. Amelia R. Smith, USMC
Dear Major Smith

major general (air force, army, marine corps)

Major General John R. Smith, USAF (or USA or USMC)
Dear General Smith

or

MG John R. Smith, USAF (or USA)
Dear General Smith

or

Maj. Gen. John R. Smith, USMC
Dear General Smith

master sergeant (air force, army)

Master Sergeant Amelia R. Smith, USAF (or USA)
Dear Sergeant Smith

or

MSGT Amelia R. Smith, USAF
Dear Sergeant Smith

or

MSG Amelia R. Smith, USA
Dear Sergeant Smith

midshipman (coast guard and naval academies)

Midshipman John R. Smith
Dear Midshipman Smith

Inside Address Styling	Salutation Styling
petty officer (coast guard, navy)	
Petty Officer Amelia R. Smith, USCG (or USN)	Dear Ms. Smith
or	
PO Amelia R. Smith, USCG (or USN)	Dear Ms. Smith
private (army, marine corps)	
Private John R. Smith, USA (or USMC)	Dear Private Smith
or	
PVT John R. Smith, USA	Dear Private Smith
or	
Pvt. John R. Smith, USMC	Dear Private Smith
private first class (army)	
Private First Class Amelia R. Smith, USA	Dear Private Smith
or	
PFC Amelia R. Smith, USA	Dear Private Smith
seaman (coast guard, navy)	
Seaman John R. Smith, USCG (or USN)	Dear Seaman Smith
or	
SMN John R. Smith, USCG (or USN)	Dear Seaman Smith
second lieutenant (air force, army, marine corps)	
Second Lieutenant John R. Smith, USAF (or USA or USMC)	Dear Lieutenant Smith
or	
2LT John R. Smith, USAF (or USA)	Dear Lieutenant Smith
or	
2nd Lt. John R. Smith, USMC	Dear Lieutenant Smith
senior master sergeant (air force)	
Senior Master Sergeant Amelia R. Smith, USAF	Dear Sergeant Smith
or	
SMSGT Amelia R. Smith, USAF	Dear Sergeant Smith
sergeant (air force, army)—see also FIRST SERGEANT, GUNNERY SERGEANT, MASTER SERGEANT, SENIOR MASTER SERGEANT, SERGEANT MAJOR, STAFF SERGEANT, TECHNICAL SERGEANT	
Sergeant John R. Smith, USAF (or USA)	Dear Sergeant Smith
or	
SGT John R. Smith, USAF (or USA)	Dear Sergeant Smith
sergeant major (army, marine corps)	
Sergeant Major Amelia R. Smith, USA (or USMC)	Dear Sergeant Major Smith
or	
SGM Amelia R. Smith, USA	Dear Sergeant Major Smith
or	
Sgt. Maj. Amelia R. Smith, USMC	Dear Sergeant Major Smith
specialist (army; covers all classes of specialists)	
Specialist Fourth Class John R. Smith, USA	Dear Specialist Smith
or	
S4 John R. Smith, USA	Dear Specialist Smith

Inside Address Styling	Salutation Styling
staff sergeant (air force, army)	
Staff Sergeant Amelia R. Smith, USAF (or USA)	Dear Sergeant Smith
or	
SSGT Amelia R. Smith, USAF	Dear Sergeant Smith
or	
SSG Amelia R. Smith, USA	Dear Sergeant Smith
technical sergeant (air force)	
Technical Sergeant John R. Smith, USAF	Dear Sergeant Smith
or	
TSGT John R. Smith, USAF	Dear Sergeant Smith
vice admiral (navy)	
Vice Admiral Amelia R. Smith, USN	Dear Admiral Smith
or	
VADM Amelia R. Smith, USN	Dear Admiral Smith
warrant officer (army; covers all classes of warrant officers)	
Warrant Officer W1 John R. Smith, USA	Dear Mr. Smith
or	
WO1 John R. Smith, USA	Dear Mr. Smith
any rank not listed	
full title + full name + comma + abbreviation of branch of service	Dear + rank + surname

Miscellaneous Professional Titles

Inside Address Styling	Salutation Styling
attorney	
Ms. Amelia R. Smith, Attorney-at-Law	Dear Ms. Smith
or	
Amelia R. Smith, Esq.	Dear Ms. Smith
certified public accountant	
Amelia R. Smith, C.P.A.	Dear Ms. Smith
dentist	
John R. Smith, D.D.S.	Dear Dr. Smith
or	
Dr. John R. Smith	Dear Dr. Smith
physician	
Amelia R. Smith, M.D.	Dear Dr. Smith
or	
Dr. Amelia R. Smith	Dear Dr. Smith
veterinarian	
John R. Smith, D.V.M.	Dear Dr. Smith
or	
Dr. John R. Smith	Dear Dr. Smith

Inside Address Styling	Salutation Styling
United Nations Officials	

representative, American (with ambassadorial rank)

The Honorable Amelia R. Smith
United States Permanent Representative to
the United Nations
or
The Honorable John R. Smith
United States Permanent Representative to
the United Nations

Madam
Dear Madam Ambassador

Sir
Dear Mr. Ambassador

representative, foreign (with ambassadorial rank)

His Excellency John R. Smith
Representative of _____ to the United
Nations
or
Her Excellency Amelia R. Smith
Representative of _____ to the United
Nations

Excellency
My dear Mr. Ambassador
Dear Mr. Ambassador
Excellency

My dear Madame Ambassador
Dear Madame Ambassador

secretary-general

Her Excellency Amelia R. Smith
Secretary-General of the United Nations

or
His Excellency John R. Smith
Secretary-General of the United Nations

Excellency
My dear Madam (*or* Madame)
Secretary-General
Dear Madam (*or* Madame) Secretary-
General

Excellency
My dear Mr. Secretary-General
Dear Mr. Secretary-General

undersecretary

The Honorable John R. Smith
Undersecretary of the United Nations

Sir
Dear Mr. Smith

Multiple Addressees (See also discussion on pages 326–333.)

Inside Address Styling	Salutation Styling
two or more men with same surname Mr. Arthur W. Jones Mr. John H. Jones *or* Messrs. A. W. and J. H. Jones *or* The Messrs. Jones	Gentlemen *or* Dear Messrs. Jones
two or more men with different surnames Mr. Angus D. Langley Mr. Lionel P. Overton *or* Messrs. A. D. Langley and L. P. Overton *or* Messrs. Langley and Overton	Gentlemen *or* Dear Mr. Langley and Mr. Overton *or* Dear Messrs. Langley and Overton
two or more married women with same surname Mrs. Arthur W. Jones Mrs. John H. Jones *or* Mesdames A. W. and J. H. Jones *or* The Mesdames Jones	Mesdames *or* Dear Mesdames Jones
two or more unmarried women with same surname Miss Alice H. Danvers Miss Margaret T. Danvers *or* Misses Alice and Margaret Danvers *or* The Misses Danvers	Ladies *or* Dear Misses Danvers
two or more women with same surname but whose marital status is unknown or irrelevant Ms. Alice H. Danvers Ms. Margaret T. Danvers	Dear Ms. Alice and Margaret Danvers
two or more married women with different surnames Mrs. Allen Y. Dow Mrs. Lawrence R. Frank *or* Mesdames Dow and Frank	Dear Mrs. Dow and Mrs. Frank *or* Mesdames *or* Dear Mesdames Dow and Frank
two or more unmarried women with different surnames Miss Elizabeth Dudley Miss Ann Raymond *or* Misses E. Dudley and A. Raymond	Ladies *or* Dear Miss Dudley and Miss Raymond *or* Dear Misses Dudley and Raymond
two or more women with different surnames but whose marital status is unknown or irrelevant Ms. Barbara Lee Ms. Helen Key	Dear Ms. Lee and Ms. Key

Special Titles, Designations, and Abbreviations

Doctor

If *Doctor* or its abbreviation *Dr.* is used before a person's name, academic degrees (as *D.D.S., D.V.M., M.D.,* or *Ph. D.*) are not included after the surname. The title *Doctor* may be typed out in full or abbreviated in a salutation, but it is usually abbreviated in an envelope address block and in an inside address in order to save space. When *Doctor* appears in a salutation, it must be used in conjunction with the addressee's surname.

> Dear Doctor Smith   *not*   Dear Doctor
> *or*
> Dear Dr. Smith

If a woman holds a doctorate, her title should be used in business-related correspondence even if her husband's name is also included in the letter.

> Dr. Ann R. Smith and Mr. James O. Smith
> Dear Dr. Smith and Mr. Smith

If both husband and wife are doctors, one of the following patterns may be followed.

> Dr. Ann R. Smith and   Ann R. Smith, M.D.
>   Dr. James O. Smith   James O. Smith, M.D.
>
> The Drs. Smith   Drs. Ann R. and James O. Smith
>
> The Doctors Smith
>
> *formal salutation*   *informal salutation*
> My dear Doctors Smith   Dear Drs. Smith
>   Dear Doctors Smith

Address patterns for two or more doctors associated in a joint practice are:

> Drs. Francis X. Sullivan and   Francis X. Sullivan, M.D.
>   Philip K. Ross   Philip K. Ross, M.D.
>
> *formal salutation*   *informal salutation*
> My dear Drs. Sullivan and Ross Dear Drs. Sullivan and Ross
>   Dear Doctors Sullivan and Ross
>   Dear Dr. Sullivan and Dr. Ross
>   Dear Doctor Sullivan and
>   Doctor Ross

Esquire

The abbreviation *Esq.* for *Esquire* is often used in the United States after the surnames of professional persons such as attorneys, architects, professional engineers, and consuls, and also of court officials such as clerks of court and justices of the peace. *Esquire* may be written in addresses and signature lines but not in salutations. It is used regardless of sex. Some people, however, object to the use of *Esquire* as a title for a woman professional, and one should follow the recipient's wishes, if they are known, in this regard. Alternative forms may then be used, such as "Amy Lutz, Attorney at Law" or "Amy Lutz, P.E."

In Great Britain *Esquire* is generally used after the surnames of people who have distinguished themselves in professional, diplomatic, or social circles. For example, when addressing a letter to a British surgeon or to a high corporate officer of a British firm, one should include *Esq.* after his surname, both on the envelope and in the inside address. Under no circumstances should *Esq.* appear in a salutation. This rule applies to both American and British correspondence. If a courtesy title such as *Dr., Hon., Miss, Mr., Mrs., or Ms.* is used before the addressee's name, *Esquire* or *Esq.* is omitted.

The plural of *Esq.* is *Esqs.* and is used with the surnames of multiple addressees.

Carolyn B. West, Esq. American Consul	Dear Ms. West
Samuel A. Sebert, Esq. Norman D. Langfitt, Esq. *or* Sebert and Langfitt, Esqs. *or* Messrs. Sebert and Langfitt Attorneys-at-Law	Gentlemen Dear Mr. Sebert and Mr. Langfitt Dear Messrs. Sebert and Langfitt
Simpson, Tyler, and Williams, Esqs. *or* Scott A. Simpson, Esq. Annabelle W. Tyler, Esq. David I. Williams, Esq.	Dear Ms. Tyler and Messrs. Simpson and Williams
British Jonathan A. Lyons, Esq. President	Dear Mr. Lyons

Honorable

In the United States, *The Honorable* or its abbreviated form *Hon.* is used as a title of distinction (but not rank) and is accorded elected or appointed (but not career) government officials such as judges, justices, congressmen, and cabinet officers. Neither the full form nor the abbreviation is ever used by its recipient in written signatures, letterhead, business or visiting cards, or in typed signature blocks. While it may be used in an envelope address block and in an inside address of a letter addressed to him or her, it is never used in a salutation. *The Honorable* should never appear before a surname standing alone: there must always be an intervening first name, an initial or initials, or a courtesy title. A courtesy title should not be added, however, when *The Honorable* is used with a full name.

The Honorable John R. Smith	*not* The Honorable Smith
The Honorable J. R. Smith	
The Honorable J. Robert Smith	*and not* The Honorable Mr. John R.
The Honorable Mr. Smith	Smith
The Honorable Dr. Smith	

The Honorable may also precede a woman's name:

The Honorable Jane R. Smith
The Honorable Mrs. Smith

However, if the woman's full name is given, a courtesy title should not be added. When an official and his wife are being addressed, his full name should be typed out.

The Honorable John R. Smith   *or* The Honorable and Mrs. John R.
   and Mrs. Smith   Smith
                                        Dear Mr. and Mrs. Smith

The stylings "Hon. and Mrs. Smith" and "The Honorable and Mrs. Smith" should *never* be used. If, however, the official's full name is unknown, the styling is:

The Honorable Mr. Smith and Mrs. Smith

If a married woman holds the title and her husband does not, her name appears first on business-related correspondence addressed to both persons. However, if the couple is being addressed socially, the woman's title may be dropped unless she has retained her maiden name for use in personal as well as business correspondence.

business correspondence
The Honorable Harriet M. Johnson   Dear Mrs. (*or* Governor, etc.)
   and Mr. Johnson   Johnson and Mr. Johnson

social correspondence
Mr. and Mrs. Robert Y. Johnson   Dear Mr. and Mrs. Johnson

business correspondence and maiden name retained
The Honorable Harriet A. Ott   Dear Ms. Ott and Mr. Johnson
   and Mr. Robert Y. Johnson

social correspondence
Ms. Harriet A. Ott   Dear Ms. Ott and Mr. Johnson
Mr. Roger Y. Johnson

If space is limited, *The Honorable* may be typed on the first line of an address block, with the recipient's name on the next line.

The Honorable
John R. Smith
 and Mrs. Smith

When *The Honorable* occurs in a running text or in a list of names in such a text, the *T* in *The* is then lowercased.

> A speech by the Honorable Charles H. Patterson, the American Consul in Athens

In informal writing such as newspaper articles, the plural forms *the Honorables* or *Hons.* may be used before a list of persons accorded the distinction. However, in official or formal writing either *the Honorable Messrs.* placed before the entire list of surnames or *the Honorable* or *Hon.* repeated before each full name in the list may be used.

> *formal*
> . . . was supported in the motion by the Honorable Messrs. Clarke, Goodfellow, Thomas, and Harrington.
> . . . met with the Honorable Albert Y. Langley and the Honorable Frances P. Kelley.
> *informal*
> . . . interviewed the Hons. Jacob Y. Stathis, Samuel P. Kenton, William L. Williamson, and Gloria O. Yarnell—all United States Senators.

Jr. and Sr.

The designations *Jr.* and *Sr.* may or may not be preceded by a comma, depending on office policy or writer preference; however, one styling should be selected and adhered to for the sake of uniformity.

> John K. Walker Jr.   *or*   John K. Walker, Jr.

Jr. and *Sr.* may be used in conjunction with courtesy titles, academic degree abbreviations, or professional rating abbreviations.

> Mr. John K. Walker[,] Jr.   John K. Walker[,] Jr., Esq.
> General John K. Walker[,] Jr.   John K. Walker[,] Jr., M.D.
> The Honorable John K. Walker[,]   John K. Walker[,] Jr., C.A.M.
>   Jr.

Madam and Madame

The title *Madam* should be used only in salutations of highly impersonal or high-level governmental and diplomatic correspondence. The title may be used to address women officials in other instances only if the writer is certain that the addressee is married. The French form *Madame* is recommended for salutations in correspondence addressed to foreign diplomats and heads of state. See Forms of Address Chart for examples.

Mesdames

The plural form of *Madam, Madame,* or *Mrs.* is *Mesdames,* which may be used before the names of two or more married women associated together in a professional partnership or in a business. It may appear with their names on an envelope and in the inside address, and it may appear with their names or standing alone in a salutation. (See also the Multiple Addressees Chart, page 325.)

Mesdames T. V. Meade and P. A. Tate	Dear Mesdames Meade and Tate
Mesdames Meade and Tate	Mesdames
Mesdames V. T. and A. P. Stevens	Dear Mesdames Stevens
The Mesdames Stevens	Mesdames

Messrs.

The plural abbreviation of *Mr.* is *Messrs.* It is used before the surnames of two or more men associated in a professional partnership or in a business. *Messrs.* may appear on an envelope, in an inside address, and in a salutation when used in conjunction with the surnames of the addressees; however, this abbreviation should never stand alone.

Messrs. Archlake, Smythe, and Dabney	Dear Messrs. Archlake, Smythe, and Dabney
Attorneys-at-law	Gentlemen
Messrs. K. Y. and P. B. Overton	Dear Messrs. Overton
Architects	Gentlemen

Messrs. should never be used before a compound corporate name formed from two surnames such as *Lord & Taylor* or *Woodward & Lothrup,* or from a corporate name like *H. L. Jones and Sons.* For correct use of *Messrs. + The Honorable* or *+ The Reverend,* see pages 329 and 332–333, respectively.

Misses

The plural form of *Miss* is *Misses,* and it may be used before the names of two or more unmarried women who are being addressed together. It may appear on an envelope, in an inside address, and in a salutation. Like *Messrs., Misses* should never stand alone but must occur in conjunction with a name or names. (For a complete set of examples in this category, see the Multiple Addressees Chart, page 325.)

Misses Hay and Middleton	Dear Misses Hay and Middleton
Misses D. L. Hay and H. K. Middleton	Ladies
Misses Tara and Julia Smith	Dear Misses Smith
The Misses Smith	Ladies

Professor

If used only with a surname, *Professor* should be typed out in full; however, if used with a given name and initial or a set of initials as well as a surname, it may be abbreviated to *Prof.* It is, therefore, usually abbreviated in envelope address blocks and in inside addresses, but typed out in salutations. *Professor* should not stand alone in a salutation.

Prof. Florence C. Marlowe Department of English	Dear Professor Marlowe Dear Dr. Marlowe Dear Miss Marlowe Mrs. Marlowe Ms. Marlowe *but not* Dear Professor

When addressing a letter to a professor and his wife, the title is usually written out in full unless the name is unusually long.

Professor and Mrs. Lee Dow Prof. and Mrs. Henry Talbott- Smythe	Dear Professor and Mrs. Dow Dear Professor and Mrs. Talbott- Smythe

Letters addressed to couples of whom the wife is the professor and the husband is not may follow one of these patterns:

business correspondence Professor Diana Goode and Mr. Goode	Dear Professor Goode and Mr. Goode
business or social correspondence Mr. and Mrs. Lawrence F. Goode	Dear Mr. and Mrs. Goode
if wife has retained her maiden name Professor Diana Falls Mr. Lawrence F. Goode	Dear Professor (*or* Ms.) Falls and Mr. Goode

When addressing two or more professors—male or female, whether having the same or different surnames—type *Professors* and not *"Profs."*:

Professors A. L. Smith and C. L. Doe	Dear Professors Smith and Doe Dear Drs. Smith and Doe Dear Mr. Smith and Mr. Doe Dear Messrs. Smith and Doe Gentlemen
Professors B. K. Johns and S. T. Yarrell	Dear Professors Johns and Yarrell Dear Drs. Johns and Yarrell Dear Ms. Johns and Mr. Yarrell
Professors G. A. and F. K. Cornett The Professors Cornett	*acceptable for any combination* Dear Professors Cornett Dear Drs. Cornett *if males* Gentlemen *if females* Ladies *or* Mesdames *if married* Dear Mr. and Mrs. Cornett Dear Professors Cornett Dear Drs. Cornett

Reverend

In formal or official writing, *The* should precede *Reverend;* however, *The Reverend* is often abbreviated to *The Rev.* or just *Rev.*, especially in unofficial or informal writing, and particularly in business correspondence where the problem of space on envelopes and in inside addresses is a factor. The typed-out full form *The Reverend* must be used in conjunction with the clergyman's full name, as in the following examples:

> The Reverend Philip D. Asquith
> The Reverend Dr. Philip D. Asquith
> The Reverend P. D. Asquith

The Reverend may appear with just a surname only if another courtesy rule intervenes:

> The Reverend Mr. Asquith
> The Reverend Professor Asquith
> The Reverend Dr. Asquith

The Reverend, The Rev., or *Rev.* should not be used in the salutation, although any one of these titles may be used on the envelope and in the inside address. In salutations, the following titles are acceptable for clergymen: *Mr.* (or *Ms., Miss, Mrs.*), *Father, Chaplain,* or *Dr.* See the Forms of Address Chart under the section entitled "Clerical and Religious Orders" for examples. The only exceptions to this rule are salutations in letters addressed to high prelates of a church (as bishops, monsignors, etc.). See the Forms of Address Chart. When addressing a letter to a clergyman and his wife, the typist should follow one of the following stylings:

> The Rev. and Mrs. P. D. Asquith
> The Rev. and Mrs. Philip D. Asquith
> The Reverend and Mrs. P. D. Asquith
> The Reverend and Mrs. Philip D. Asquith
> Dear Mr. (*or, if having a doctorate,* Dr.) and Mrs. Asquith
> *but never*
> Rev. and Mrs. Asquith

Two clergymen having the same or different surnames should not be addressed in letters as "The Reverends" or "The Revs." or "Revs." They may, however, be addressed as *The Reverend* (or *The Rev.*) *Messrs.* or *The Reverend* (or *The Rev.*) *Drs.*, or the titles *The Reverend, The Rev.,* or *Rev.* may be repeated before each clergyman's name.

> The Reverend Messrs. S. J. and
>   D. V. Smith
> The Rev. Messrs. S. J. and
>   D. V. Smith
> The Reverend Messrs. Smith
> The Rev. Messrs. Smith

> The Rev. S. J. Smith and
>   The Rev. D. V. Smith
> Rev. S. J. Smith and
>   Rev. D. V. Smith

When writing to two or more clergymen having different surnames, the following patterns are acceptable:

> The Reverend Messrs. P. A. Francis
>   and F. L. Beale
> The Rev. Messrs. P. A. Francis
>   and F. L. Beale
> The Rev. P. A. Francis
> The Rev. F. L. Beale

In either situation, the following salutations are acceptable:

> Gentlemen
> Dear Mr. and Mrs. Smith
> Dear Messrs. Smith
> Dear Mr. Francis and Mrs. Beale
> Dear Father Francis and Father Beale

In formal texts, "The Reverends," "The Revs.," and "Revs." are not acceptable as collective titles (as in lists of names). *The Reverend* (or *Rev.*) *Messrs.* (or *Drs.* or *Professors*) may be used, or *The Reverend* or *The Rev.* or *Rev.* may be repeated before each clergyman's name. If the term *clergyman* or the expression *the clergy* is mentioned in introducing the list, a single title *the Reverend* or *the Rev.* may be added before the list to serve all of the names. While it is true that "the Revs." is often seen in newspapers and in catalogs, this expression is still not recommended for formal, official writing.

> . . . were the Reverend Messrs. Jones, Smith and Bennett, as well
>   as . . .
> Among the clergymen present were the Reverend John G. Jones,
>   Mr. Smith, and Dr. Doe.
> Prayers were offered by the Rev. J. G. Jones, Rev. Mr. Smith,
>   and Rev. Dr. Doe.

Second, Third

These designations after surnames may be styled as Roman numerals (I, III, IV) or as ordinals (2nd / 2d, 3rd / 3d, 4th). Such a designation may or may not be separated from a surname by a comma, depending on office policy or writer preference.

> Mr. Jason T. Johnson III (*or* 3rd *or* 3d)
> Mr. Jason T. Johnson, III (*or* 3rd *or* 3d)

Sequence of Abbreviations and Initials

The proper order of occurrence of initials representing academic degrees, religious orders, and professional ratings that may appear after a name and that are separated from each other by commas is as follows: (1) religious orders (as *S.J.*); (2) theological degrees (as *D.D.*); (3) academic degrees (as *Ph.D.*); (4) honorary degrees (as *Litt.D.*) (5) professional ratings (as *C.P.A.*).

Initials that represent academic degrees (with the exception of *M.D.*, *D.D.S.*, and other medical degrees) are not commonly used in addresses, and two or more sets of such letters appear even more rarely. Only when the initials represent achievements in different fields that are relevant to one's profession should more than one set be used. On the other hand, initials that represent earned professional achievements (such as *C.P.A.*, *C.A.M.*, *C.P.S.*, or *P.E.*) are often used in business addresses. When any of these sets of initials follow a name, however, the courtesy title *(Mr., Mrs., Ms., Miss, Dr.)* is omitted.

Nancy Robinson, P.L.S.
Mary R. Lopez, C.P.A.
John R. Doe, M.D., Ph.D.
Chief of Staff
Smithville Hospital

John R. Doe, J.D., C.M.C.
The Rev. John R. Doe, S.J., D.D.,
   LL.D.
Chaplain, Smithville College

Chapter 11

Composing Letters: Guidelines and Samples

CONTENTS

Many of the details concerning business correspondence are routine. The impact that a well-written business letter can have, however, is far from routine. A well-thought-out, precisely expressed letter delivers a positive impression on the reader and encourages cooperation.

The Writing of Letters: General Pointers

Getting Ready to Write

Good, clear business correspondence is not an accident. It is the result of careful planning and usually requires some pre-writing preparations. The following five steps can serve as a checklist for achieving optimum results with maximum efficiency.

1. **Assemble needed materials** Frequently previous correspondence must be referred to before a meaningful or accurate reply can be sent. Tabular information, reports, printouts, catalogs, manuals, and other items also may have to be located and arranged for easy reference.

2. **Make marginal notes** It is helpful to make marginal notes on letters to be answered. Jotting down information such as conference dates, appointments, and titles of brochures in advance will ensure a speedier reply.

3. **Underscore important facts** It is useful to employ a yellow felt-tip pen or a red auditor's pen to underscore the significant facts in a letter which are pertinent to the reply. Color will highlight this information and make it easy to identify when the response is later being written.

4. **Outline reply letter content**   Before beginning to draft a letter, put all the facts together. Have a clear-cut idea of what you want to say, jot down the topics that will be treated in the letter, and examine examples of previous correspondence for guidance in drafting the reply.

5. **Compose the letter**   If careful plans and preparations are made before writing begins, the actual composition of the reply should be easier.

The Makeup of a Good Letter

The construction of good business correspondence is built on three key elements: creating the right opening, sending the right cues to the reader, and devising a friendly close to the letter. Each of these elements is discussed in the following paragraphs.

1. **Creating the opening**   The first paragraph should not only set the tone for the entire letter, it should capture the reader's attention. Openings that take into account the reader's point of view will elicit pleasure, satisfaction, and personal involvement in the matters being discussed. The following is an example of a good opening paragraph:

> We feel very fortunate that you have accepted our invitation to appear before a group of new secretaries at our annual "Get-Acquainted Day" on Thursday, October 1. I had the pleasure of hearing you address the CPS meeting last April, and I'm convinced that we couldn't find a better, more interesting speaker.

The reverse is also true. A stilted, cliché-ridden opening such as the following can create a negative impression on the recipient of the letter:

> Enclosed please find information regarding details of our annual "Get-Acquainted Day" on Thursday, October 1. We have noted with pleasure your acceptance to deliver a speech at the meeting as per our request.

2. **Cues to the reader**   The writer should regard every business-communication reader as a knowledgeable critic of corporate letter production. Thus, each communication to a client or to a potential customer provides an opportunity to epitomize the very best in company service, goodwill, and helpfulness. Here are some ways to create a positive impression on the reader:

A. Use tactful, easy-to-understand language. Short words, clear-cut and direct, are easier to read and to understand than lengthy words. Write as you speak, using natural, everyday expressions.

> It is a real pleasure to know that you will lead our Transactional Analysis Seminar on May 14.

B. Organize your language carefully and concisely. Time is a precious commodity, and the busy reader wants to get the gist of the message on the first reading. Interesting messages contain sequences that vary in length and in internal structure. Coherence and continuity are other prime requisites of modern communications.

C. Construct sentences correctly. Technical correctness in writing is a worthy goal for any writer. In order to attain it, proofread the material and make sure that none of the following infelicities is present: misplaced commas, misspelled words, incorrect word division, numbers written incorrectly, hackneyed and stilted expressions, a lack of agreement between subjects and verbs, and other such grammatical and stylistic pitfalls.

D. Give accurate, precise, and complete information. The omission of one important detail can spell the difference between order and confusion in the reader's mind.

E. Write clearly to avoid any hint of double meaning. It has often been said that if a statement can be misunderstood, it will be! By going over all written messages for unintended hidden meanings, the writer can avoid many problems. Keep the reader's reaction always in mind. For example, the following statement raises several questions:

One and two-page photos are needed for this year's annual report.

The questions raised by this statement include the following: How many photos are actually needed? (The statement doesn't say.) Is the need for one one-page photo and one two-page photo? (The statement is ambiguous.) Is the reader expected to supply all of the photos needed? (The statement doesn't say.) The following rewording prevents misunderstanding:

Please prepare one full-page photo and one double-page photo for use in this year's annual report.

F. Respond to questions raised. It is frustrating to a correspondent when a question posed in a previous letter goes unanswered. The omission is also poor business practice, as it creates the need for more correspondence. Double-check to see that no such omissions have been made, by rereading relevant previous correspondence and then comparing it with your response.

G. Introduce an unfavorable comment with a favorable one. It is helpful to present positive aspects of a situation first and then to lead into any negative or unfavorable comments. Mention points of agreement before talking about an unfavorable aspect.

Your complimentary copy of *Modular Office Units* is on its way to you. Your kind comments about this brochure are greatly appreciated.

Popular demand for the brochure has depleted our supply, unfortunately. However, please feel free to reproduce copies for use by your staff. When our new shipment arrives, we'll speed a dozen copies to you.

3. **Devising a friendly way to close a letter**   Give the reader a pleasant closing thought in the final paragraph of the letter.

> Again, thank you for giving us permission to reprint the article on
> your company's research in the field of pollution control. This infor-
> mation will provide excellent material for next month's issue of *The
> Executive*.

Avoid thanking someone for something in advance. It is a little impertinent
to assume beforehand that a request will be honored. Wait until the service
is rendered; then, make an appropriate acknowledgment for it.

The recipient of a letter of request should know exactly what is expected of him or her by the end of the letter. If a certain action is expected,
it should be stated or restated in a clear and friendly manner in the last
paragraph.

Composing Form Letters and Memorandums

Form Letter Construction

An expedient way to handle routine mail is through the use of guide letters
or form letters to standardize responses. A ring binder might be used to cat-
egorize certain types of letters that are frequently written. By the use of appropriate index tabs on the various divisions of the ring binder, information
can be quickly located. Thus, when such letters as those of announcement,
acknowledgment, or apology must be written, the writer may refer to similar
or prototypical letters—a shortcut that expedites composition. The notebook
might also contain a stock of ready-made insertable paragraphs labeled as
A, B, C, D, and so on. By referring to these, a writer might delegate to a
secretary the responsibility of constructing certain letters. Form letters are
often printed in advance. The secretary then adds the date and the inside
address; sometimes other data are also added to the body of the form letter.
When preprinted form letters are used, try to match the typeface as closely
as possible. Automated letter production or word processing is a popular
way to reproduce a form letter because it gives the letter the appearance of
an original.

The Writing Of Office Memorandums

The office memorandum is another type of routine communication. Written
for interoffice circulation only, it may include general messages (as notices,
announcements, or inquiries). Memorandums are usually circulated freely
among corporate branch offices located in distant cities. Large companies
have standardized memorandum forms. There is a wide variety in the
printed styling of memorandums; however, the basic parts of most memo-

randums are the headings (TO, FROM, SUBJECT, DATE) and the body (message). A memorandum has neither salutation nor complimentary close. It is not usually signed but it may be initialed by the author.

Preparing the heading of the memorandum The memorandum is a fast, economical, and efficient way to relay important news that should reach all or a significant fraction of the corporate staff. Today an office copier can, in a few minutes, reproduce multiple copies of a memorandum, thus making it ready for wide distribution to a large readership. On the other hand, a memorandum may also be addressed solely to one person. The TO line may be addressed to one individual, to several individuals, or to a group.

    TO: Frances Rummel, Customer Services Supervisor
    TO: Customer Services Personnel
    TO: Administrative Staff, School of Business

Typically, the other heading components consist of the following: the FROM line, which includes the name of the writer and his or her title or position; the DATE line; the SUBJECT line; and the optional LOCATION (floor, extension, or branch) line.

The subject line of the memorandum The SUBJECT line in the heading of the memorandum is very important, for it gives the reader an overview of the message content. A good SUBJECT line encapsulates the message, which makes it useful for filing purposes. Examples of typical SUBJECT lines are as follows:

    SUBJECT: April Meeting of the Advisory Council
    SUBJECT: NEED FOR A NEW ELECTRIC TYPEWRITER
    SUBJECT: Transportation Rates on Iron or Steel Bars

Composing the message (or body) of the memorandum Brevity, courtesy, factualness, and tact are four requisites of message content in office memorandums. The main idea of the message is usually contained in the first paragraph, while additional or supporting data may be added in succeeding paragraphs. The final part of a memorandum may close with a courteous request for action or further information. In some instances the request for service, action, or specific information may be found in the opening paragraph with supporting data located in subsequent paragraphs.

Sample Letters

This section includes sample business letters that are appropriate for a wide range of situations and occasions. In each case the letter is preceded by a description of a situation in which it would be written and by a description of its elements.

Acceptance of an Invitation

SITUATION: Kathleen Simons, president of a small but fast-growing software-development company has been invited by a professor at a nearby university to speak to his marketing class. The professor particularly wants her to speak at this time because the subject his students are studying at present is one in which she has considerable expertise. She writes to the professor to accept the speaking engagement.

LETTER ELEMENTS: In writing a letter of acceptance to the professor, Simons does the following:

1. She opens by acknowledging the professor's request and by unambiguously accepting the invitation.
2. She repeats all of the details regarding the invitation. This serves as a way of confirming that the details have been communicated accurately.
3. She mentions the enclosed materials.
4. She closes by expressing appreciation for the invitation and her expectation that the event will be enjoyable.

DATAWARE Consultants

1287 West Liberty Avenue
Fort Caroline, ST 85348
406-937-1212

January 2, 19--

Dr. John C. Thomas
Associate Professor of Marketing
Department of Business Administration
State University
Stateville, ST 85364

Dear Dr. Thomas:

    Thank you very much for the kind invitation to lead an
upcoming session of your senior seminar. I will be happy to
do so. I understand that the seminar will be held from 2:30
to 5:30 p.m. on March 23, 19--, in Milton Hall, Room 1289.
The topic—as you suggested in your letter—will be "Marketing the Services of the Emerging Growth Company."

    I am enclosing a list of references to recent articles
on the subject that your students may want to acquaint themselves with before the seminar. Since your students are
currently studying this topic, I think that these references
will be valuable aids to them.

    I appreciate your thinking of me, and I look forward
to working with your students.

                Sincerely,

                Kathleen C. Simons

                Kathleen C. Simons
                President

KCS/hg

Acknowledgment during an Employer's Absence

SITUATION: Barbara O'Toole is secretary to Arthur C. Roebling, president of Communications Media Corporation. Mr. Roebling has just received an invitation from Nancy Voelker, president of the Advertisers Club, to speak at the club's annual awards dinner. However, Mr. Roebling is in Europe on a business trip and therefore cannot reply promptly to the invitation. O'Toole has been instructed to reply to such letters with an acknowledgment letter that is friendly but noncommittal.

LETTER ELEMENTS;   In writing her acknowledgment letter, O'Toole does the following:

1.   She acknowledges receipt of the letter and thanks Ms. Voelker for it.
2.   She explains the reason for the delay, and she gives Ms. Voelker some idea of when she can expect a reply from Mr. Roebling.
3.   She closes in a courteous manner.

Communications Media Corporation/Hawthorne Building/Pierce and Fremont Streets/Houston, TX 77001

CMC

Telephone (713) 898-7642
898-2746

February 15, 19--

Ms. Nancy Voelker
President, Advertisers Club
Post Office Box 1234
Southfield, ST 77078

Dear Ms. Voelker:

Thank you for your gracious invitation to Mr.
Arthur Roebling to be the speaker at the annual
awards dinner of the Advertisers Club on May 26,
19--.

Mr. Roebling will be returning from a business
trip in Europe next week. On his return, you can
be sure that your letter will receive his prompt
attention.

Cordially yours,

Barbara O'Toole

Barbara O'Toole
Secretary to Mr. Roebling

Adjustment Letter

—granting a claim

SITUATION: Thomas Sagarino is president of Sagarino Flower Company. A longtime customer of the company, Mrs. Katz, has just written to say that a shipment of roses she had recently received from the company included some that were noticeably wilted. Sagarino believes that Mrs. Katz has a legitimate complaint. He wants to rectify the current situation, and he wants to secure Mrs. Katz's goodwill and sense of confidence in the company.

LETTER ELEMENTS: In writing his reply to Mrs. Katz, Sagarino does the following:

1. He begins on a friendly and appreciative note by thanking her for calling the situation to his attention.
2. He acknowledges the error and explains the measures that will be taken to rectify the situation. He will send her a full refund.
3. He explains the reason for the error, extends an apology, and reassures her that it will not happen again.
4. He expresses appreciation for having her as a customer, and he closes with a friendly offer of future service.

Sagarino Flower Company
One Maywell Street
Palm Sands Beach, ST 56790
Telephone: 507-414-5252

August 15, 19--

Mrs. Richard Katz
425 Belmont Street
Smithville, ST 56789

Dear Mrs. Katz:

Thank you for letting us know about the roses that arrived at your home in less than perfect condition. We
have enclosed a check refunding your full purchase price.

An unexpected delay in the repair of our loaded delivery
van, coupled with an unusual rise in temperatures last
Thursday, caused the late delivery of your roses. Please
accept our apology and our assurance that steps will be
taken to prevent a repetition of such an occurrence.

During the past fifteen years, it has been our pleasure to
number you among our valued customers. Customer satisfaction is the goal we strive to achieve.

Please let us know how we may be of greater service to
you.

Yours sincerely,

Thomas Sagarino
President

jml

Enclosure: Check

Adjustment Letter

—refusing a claim

SITUATION: The Gem House sells high-quality jewelry through a mail-order catalog. A repeat customer, Ms. Wrightson, has returned an expensive pair of tourmaline earrings for pierced ears, because the stones' color did not match that pictured in the catalog. The Gem House's policy prohibits the return of earrings for pierced ears for hygienic reasons. The office manager, Lillian Ayala, must refuse the return without alienating the customer.

LETTER ELEMENTS: In writing the letter refusing this claim, Ayala does the following:

1. She reminds the customer in a pleasant way that the Gem House's return policy is clearly printed on every page of the catalog.
2. She acknowledges the fact that there is a slight difference between the shade of color of the earrings and the catalog's photograph.
3. She suggests a way that such a problem can be avoided in the future.
4. She expresses her regret that company policy prevents her from carrying out the customer's wishes. She concludes with the positive expectation that the customer will understand her decision without being alienated by it.

The Gem House

June 18, 19--

Ms. Emila Wrightson
123 Ambler Road
Everett, ST 56789

Dear Ms. Wrightson:

We are sending back to you the filigree tourmaline earrings ordered
through the Gem House catalog last month. We are happy to explain
the company's policy on returning earrings for pierced ears. Because we want our customers to be aware that for hygienic reasons
pierced earrings cannot be returned, we print a statement to that
effect at the top of each page in every catalog we print. We have
no intention of springing hidden or trick policies on our customers.

Since the Gem House is a mail-order company, our catalog is, in a
sense, our sales staff. Because of this, we expend a great deal of
time and effort on it. The colors of the gemstones pictured in the
catalog represent as accurately as possible the colors of our gems
in stock. However, colors are notoriously difficult to reproduce
exactly; and, in addition, the colors of gemstones do vary somewhat
from stone to stone. Because of these factors, it is true that the
tourmalines in your earrings do differ somewhat from the color
shown in our catalog.

If you are ordering jewelry to complement a specific garment, and
the exact shade is important, why not send us a sample of the material? Just a small swatch would be enough. Then a member of our
staff could match the color precisely.

I wish it were not necessary to return these earrings to you, but
unfortunately our company policy dictates that we must. I'm sure
that you can understand this necessity, and I hope we can serve you
in a less inconvenient way in the future.

Cordially,

Lillian Ayala

Lillian Ayala
Office Manager

LA:hg

Powder River Boulevard/P.O. Box 4439/Prairie Grove, ST 79462/Tel. 803-141-2000

Adjustment Letter
—granting a discount

SITUATION: Longville Art House, a wholesale art-supply store, has been running a promotional sale on a new line of brushes. A buyer, Mr. Arnaud, who has just received his invoiced order has called the store to complain about his total bill. His usual trade discount is 25%. However, he has been billed for a total that has been discounted 20%, the promotional-sale discount. He had thought, and hadn't been told otherwise by the sales staff of the store, that he would be getting a 45% discount. Since that appears to have been wrong, the buyer wants the trade discount of 25% instead of the promotional discount of 20%. The customer-service manager, William Moore, thinks the buyer has a legitimate complaint, and responds.

LETTER ELEMENTS: In composing his letter to the buyer, the customer-service manager does the following:

1.   He begins by telling the buyer that the store was in the wrong. This is good news for the buyer, so Moore leads off with it.
2.   He explains the situation without overdramatizing the store's error.
3.   He tells the buyer precisely what adjustments will be made.
4.   He closes on a positive note, without excessive apology.

multi-art suppliers

1440 Palmerstown Road : Haywood, ST 23555 : Telephone 416-835-1212

June 18, 19--

Mr. David P. Arnaud
Arnaud Arts
1100 Main Street
Longville, ST 23456

Dear Mr. Arnaud:

The invoiced order you were sent is indeed incorrect. Your order should have been discounted 45%, instead of 20%.

Perhaps we've done our promotional job on those brushes too well. Our billing staff is now so used to allowing the 20% discount that in your case they forgot to add on the 25% trade discount.

We're in the process of recalculating your order with the correct 45% discount. The new invoice should be processed and on its way to you by the end of this week. The new invoice replaces the original, incorrect one in our files. Simply disregard your copy of the original.

We do regret this slip, and are happy to have the chance to set the matter straight. This month our store is featuring a promotion on a new line of acrylics, and I can assure you that it will be offered to you at a 45% discount, which we will make sure you'll get!

Sincerely,

William T. Moore

William T. Moore
Customer-Service Manager

sgg

Adjustment Letter

—refusing a discount

SITUATION: Brandon-Rupert Inc. manufactures wall maps. They hold an annual January sale. They have just received a letter from James Maloney, the principal of Oak Hill School, and a good customer. He has complained that the six maps he ordered for the school were invoiced at the regular price. Oak Hill's order is found to have been received at Brandon-Rupert on February 19; the school is not entitled to the sale price.

LETTER ELEMENTS: In responding to Mr. Maloney, the president of Brandon-Rupert does the following:

1. He opens by thanking Mr. Maloney in a friendly way for bringing the matter to the company's attention. He does not immediately give his decision; a negative answer at the beginning of the letter may make Mr. Maloney ignore the rest.
2. He reviews the facts of the sale, and then, without assigning blame, compares them with his company's sales policy.
3. He states that while Brandon-Rupert is lenient in its policies, particularly when a good customer is involved, the discrepancy in this case between sales policy and the date of Oak Hill School's order is too great.
4. He concludes on a conciliatory note, promising that Brandon-Rupert's treatment of all its customers will be fair.

Brandon-Rupert Inc.

15519 Waterloo Road, Versailles, ST 44736
Telephone (514) 387-1551

March 3, 19--

Mr. James Maloney
Oak Hill School
P.O. Box 100
Manchester, ST 34679

Dear Mr. Maloney:

We can understand your distress when the maps that Oak Hill School ordered
from Brandon-Rupert Inc. arrived at the school invoiced at a price considerably higher than what you had anticipated. We appreciate your taking the
time to provide us with all the facts in this matter, and we welcome the
opportunity to explain this company's sale policy.

Oak Hill School ordered six wall maps from us in February. The order is
dated February 12, and it was received at Brandon-Rupert on February 19.
The maps were priced at $99.50 each, resulting in a total price of $597.00.
Oak Hill requested the January sale discount of 50%, which would have resulted in a total bill of $298.50. Instead, your school has been billed
for the full price of $597.00. Our problem here has to do with the date of
Oak Hill's order, both when it was written and when it was received here.
As the brochure advertising our annual January sale states, sale prices are
given on orders received here before February 1.

We do occasionally honor sale-price orders that reach us a few days after
February 1. We particularly try to give long-standing customers such as
Oak Hill School as much consideration as possible. Unfortunately, Oak Hill's
order wasn't made out until February 12, and we just can't fit it into this
extension period.

We hope you can understand our position. If we extend our February 1 cutoff
date to the middle of February or beyond, we would not only shortchange some
other customers, we would be creating a problematic precedent. We must abide
by guidelines that allow us to be as fair as possible to as many as possible.

Sincerely yours,

Harrison Takington
President

HT/hg

Application Letter
—for a franchise

SITUATION: Perretta and Sons Hardware Store wants to expand the variety of merchandise they offer. The store's president, Howard Perretta, has recently been to a trade show where he saw and was impressed by the Harkins Company line of gardening tools. Having decided that this would be a product line that the store could sell successfully, he writes to the credit manager, David Lindberg, to apply for a franchise to sell Harkins products.

LETTER ELEMENTS: In writing a letter of application for a new franchise, Perretta does the following:

1. He opens with a compliment to the manufacturer, and then he presents his request.
2. He provides the necessary supportive data.
3. He closes in an appreciative and courteous manner.

PERRETTA AND SONS HARDWARE STORE
1510 Long Street
Kansas City, ST 56777
Telephone (507) 877-3447

October 19, 19--

Mr. David Lindberg
Credit Manager
The Harkins Company
100 Lake Street
Smithville, ST 56789

Dear Mr. Lindberg:

After inspecting your recent exhibit of fine hardware
at the International Hardware Convention in San
Francisco last week, we should like to add your line
of merchandise.

Please consider this letter an application for a
charge account within the $1,000 to $1,200 range.
Credit references will be supplied upon request.

We should appreciate the opportunity to handle the
Harkins franchise in Kansas City.

Very truly yours,

Howard Perretta

Howard Perretta
President

jml

Appreciation

SITUATION: The Chen Lumber Company has received an order from Mr. and Mrs. Parent for all the lumber needed to build a new house. The order is considerable, and the president of the company writes a letter of appreciation to the Parents.

LETTER ELEMENTS: In writing to express his appreciation, Chen does the following:

1. He first focuses on the Parents, connecting with the excitement they must be feeling at the prospect of building a new house.
2. He expresses his appreciation for the order.
3. He reinforces the Parents' self-esteem with a compliment.
4. He offers further services that his company might provide.
5. He closes in a friendly but not overly effusive manner.

CHEN LUMBER COMPANY

650 Main Street
Manchester, ST 56717
Telephone (507) 643-2101

August 6, 19--

Mr. and Mrs. George Parent
68 Cottage Street
Smithville, ST 56789

Dear Mr. and Mrs. Parent:

Congratulations on your decision to become a new home
owner! Thank you for the confidence you have shown
in us through opening an account and placing your
order at the Chen Lumber Company.

It will be a pleasure to supply all the lumber and
millwork needs for your beautiful home. You can
build with confidence knowing that only quality lumber
materials and supplies are being used.

Mr. Ralph Fu will be glad to be of service to you in
any aspect of planning or designing your new home.

Please let us know if there is any way in which we
may be of further assistance.

Sincerely,

Larry Chen

Larry Chen
President

jml

Collection Letter
—reminder

SITUATION: Joseph Thomas has purchased a new car from Jamestown Auto Dealers. Up to now, he has been on time with his payments. At present, however, he is two months behind. Francine Hopkins, the credit manager, writes to remind him of the fact and to urge him to attend to his overdue payments.

LETTER ELEMENTS: In writing what is in essence a collection letter, Hopkins does the following:

1. She begins her letter in an unusual way, one that will catch her reader's attention immediately.
2. Before bringing up the problem, she mentions something positive, the fact that Mr. Thomas, up to now, has always met his payment deadlines.
3. She points out the problem tactfully but firmly.
4. She suggests possible alternatives, without being threatening.
5. She closes by asking politely for a response.

Jamestown Auto Dealers

36 Whipple Avenue
Jamestown, ST 58281
Telephone 303-666-2321 or 686-4897

November 5, 19--

Mr. Joseph R. Thomas
46 West Lincoln Street
Comptonville, ST 58201

Dear Mr. Thomas:

Have you ever had to write a reminder letter? We find
ourselves in that position now.

You have been sending your monthly installments to us
promptly for almost a year. However, we find that your
Jamestown Auto Dealers car payments of $215.00 for Sep-
tember 1 and October 1 have not as yet arrived here.

Perhaps your overdue payments are already on their way
to us. If this is the case, please overlook this letter. On the other hand, in the event that some difficulty has arisen, let us know. Perhaps we can offer
some helpful suggestions.

Won't you let us hear from you soon?

Sincerely yours,

Francine Hopkins

Francine Hopkins
Credit Manager

FH/jc

Collection Letter
—request for payment

SITUATION: Carol Derwinski is the treasurer for the advertising agency of Douglas and Alward. One of their clients is Quick Shop, Inc., which runs a chain of convenience stores and advertises on television and in the newspapers. Quick Shop's account with Douglas and Alward is now 90 days past due, and several reminders have already been sent. Quick Shop has been a client for many years and has always paid its bills promptly in the past; however, it now seems clear to Derwinski that failure to pay is no mere oversight. She writes to George Sebastian, director of advertising for Quick Shop, and once again requests payment. Her request to this valued client must be firm but still friendly and polite.

LETTER ELEMENTS: In writing to Quick Shop to request the overdue payment, Derwinski does the following:

1. She summarizes the situation and expresses her concern about it. Her opening is somewhat indirect, since she could have simply begun, "Your account with us is now more than 90 days past due." However, in light of this client's past history with the agency, she is trying to be as tactful as she can.
2. She makes a clear and simple request for immediate payment, and she reminds the client that his company's credit record is at risk. She is well within her rights to be doing this, so she employs no indirection at this point. Her praise for the client's past credit history is a polite gesture, but it is also a reminder that his company has something to lose.
3. She ends with a series of friendly gestures. She wants to maintain good relations with this company, especially if its failure to pay is the result of a temporary problem. However, she needs to know what the situation is, so her final request to Mr. Sebastian is that he make contact with her if something is still preventing payment.

Douglas and Alward

666 Euclid
New Pekin, ST 56151
Tel: 407-996-1438

October 6, 19--

Mr. George Sebastian
Advertising Director
Quick Shop, Inc.
7800 Stateville Road
Portland, ST 56891

Dear Mr. Sebastian:

Our records indicate that your account with us is
now more than 90 days past due. We are very concerned
that we have not yet heard from you about when we may
receive payment, even though we have sent you three
separate reminders about this matter.

We are requesting that you send your payment to
us today. In this way you can preserve your excellent
credit record with us.

Quick Shop has always been one of our best clients,
and we value your business very much. If some special
circumstances are preventing you from making payment,
please call us now so we can discuss the situation with
you.

Sincerely,

Carol Derwinski

Carol Derwinski
Treasurer

CD/hm

Collection Letter
—final notice

SITUATION: Anthony Legere is credit manager for Tri-State Building Supply Company, which sells hardware and building materials to retail customers and contractors. One of these contractors is Kirchoffer and Sons, and their account with Tri-State is now 120 days past due. Legere has written several times to Andrew Kirchoffer, requesting payment, and none of these letters has elicited a response. Legere has already suspended credit for Kirchoffer and Sons, and he now writes one last letter, with a stern ultimatum, before turning the account over to a collection agency.

LETTER ELEMENTS: In writing this final letter, Legere does the following:

1. He states the situation, and he delivers the ultimatum. This kind of ultimatum should never be an empty threat that the writer cannot go through with. In this case, Legere is completely prepared to call in a collection agency.
2. He explains some of the thinking that has gone into his decision. In doing this, he is trying to avoid alienating Mr. Kirchoffer any more than necessary. After all, he would still like to do business with him on a cash basis.
3. He makes one more attempt to try persuasion. He addresses Mr. Kirchoffer by name. This is a technique that should be used sparingly, but it usually does serve to get the reader's attention and add emphasis to a sentence. He ends by reminding Mr. Kirchoffer what can be gained and avoided by making a prompt payment.

Tri-State Building Supply Company
1264 Beaver Ruin Road
West Highlands, ST 09803
(111) 432-1236

February 20, 19--

Mr. Andrew N. Kirchoffer
President
Kirchoffer and Sons
P.O. Box 1200
East Highlands, ST 09809

Dear Mr. Kirchoffer:

Your account with us is now 120 days overdue. If payment
in full is not received by March 2, 19--, we will be forced to
turn your account over to a collection agency.

Up until now, we have been reluctant to take this step, as
it will undoubtedly damage your credit rating. However, you have
been given ample time to pay this bill, and since you have not
responded to any of our reminders or letters to you, we feel we
have no choice but to take this step.

Mr. Kirchoffer, I strongly urge you to settle this account
with us immediately. In this way you can restore your credit
standing with us and avoid any future unpleasantness.

Sincerely,

Anthony T. Legere
Credit Manager

ATL/jm

Collection Letter

—granting an extension

SITUATION: Albert Terranova, credit manager of Kelley Electrical Supply Shop, recently wrote a collection letter to Sarah Finnegan, owner of Modern Design Company, reminding her of her overdue account and requesting payment. In his letter, Terranova held out the offer that Kelley Electrical would be as cooperative as possible if Ms. Finnegan would get in touch with them and discuss the overdue payment. Ms. Finnegan has done so and has requested a 60-day extension, at the end of which time she has promised payment. Because Ms. Finnegan is a long-time customer who has always paid promptly in the past, Terranova agrees to the extension.

LETTER ELEMENTS: In writing this letter granting an extension, Terranova does the following:

1. He tells her that her request for an extension has been granted.
2. He lets her know that he understands and sympathizes with her situation.
3. He tells her the reasons why the extension is being granted. In doing so, he reminds her of the claims and commitments she has made.
4. He states the terms of the extension.
5. In a very polite way, he reminds her that this extension is an exception and she should not expect to receive any further extensions.
6. He closes in a friendly manner.

Kelley Electrical Supply Shop
6802 Eastern Highway
Smithville, ST 56789
Telephone (507) 841-3841

September 15, 19--

Ms. Sarah Finnegan
Modern Design Company
39 Harris Street
Marshaltown, ST 56759

Dear Ms. Finnegan:

I am happy to say that we have agreed to your request for a 60-day
extension to pay the $875.60 due on your account.

We understand that you are currently having problems with your own
collections, and we can certainly sympathize with that problem. We
are pleased to hear you say that these conditions are temporary
and that you feel certain that you will be able to meet the extended payment date of November 15, 19--. We are agreed that you will
settle your account in full on or before that date.

We want to emphasize that granting this extension constitutes an
exception to our usual credit terms. We are granting this exception because MDC has been a good and valued customer for many years,
and we want to do whatever we reasonably can to maintain that good
relationship; however, you should not expect that we will be able
to grant any additional extensions in the future.

We thank you for your cooperation, and we wish you well.

Very sincerely,

Albert Terranova

Albert Terranova
Credit Manager

AT:jml

Complaint

SITUATION: Helen Davison owns and manages a small marina where she offers repair services to her docking guests. Recently she ordered a bilge pump from her usual parts supplier to replace one in the cabin cruiser of a guest who was staying at her marina. Although the supplier assured her the pump would arrive in seven working days, the pump did not actually arrive for more than three weeks, by which time the guest had left. Now Davison has discovered that the mounting arms are so badly bent that the pump would be very difficult to install. She writes to Barry Jacobs, the manager of the parts-supply house, to tell him why she is returning the pump and why she wants a full refund.

LETTER ELEMENTS: In making her complaint to the parts-supply house, Davison does the following:

1. Without being insulting or overly hostile, she gets directly to the point. The details will wait until the next paragraph. She uses the opening to tell the credit manager what he can expect, and why.
2. She goes on to explain the sequence of events, all of which lead in an orderly way to her demand that she receive a full refund for the pump.
3. She does not belabor her disappointment at not being able to complete the repairs for her guest. She does make clear, however, that she considers the supplier's performance below par in this instance and that she hopes they will try to improve their service.

DAVISON'S MARINA
5100 Harbor Drive
East Bay City, ST 76820
(505)-333-1111

July 28, 19--

Mr. Barry Jacobs
Manager
Oceanside Supply Company
129 Fulton Boulevard
Kingston Beach, ST 76842

Dear Mr. Jacobs:

You will soon be receiving via UPS the Johnson II Bilge Pump
I ordered last month. This pump is being returned by me both because it is defective and because it arrived too late to be used
in a repair for a customer.

On June 30, three weeks prior to my guest's scheduled departure I telephoned Oceanside Supply and ordered the Johnson Pump
and was assured that the pump would arrive within seven working
days. The pump actually arrived only after 16 working days, one
day after my guest's departure. I had considered keeping the pump
in stock for a future repair, but the pump arrived with bent mounting arms that would make installation very difficult and time-
consuming, leading to a labor cost that would have to be absorbed
by me or my customer. Under these circumstances, I cannot accept
this pump, and I am returning it to you with the request that the
amount of the purchase price be removed from my account.

Davison's Marina has been a regular customer of Oceanside Supply for several years, and I must say that we have been quite happy
with your service up to now. I hope that in the future you will
pay a bit more attention both to customers' needs and your own as-
surances. Then we all can avoid disappointment.

Sincerely,

Helen Davison

Helen Davison
Proprietor

Condolence Letter

—personal

SITUATION: James Artandi is the buyer for a furniture store. The wife of one of the manufacturer's representatives he works with has passed away after a long illness. The representative, Steve O'Donnell, is an acquaintance, not a close personal friend. Artandi writes to express his sympathy. The letter is on his own personal stationery, not on company stationery; and it is handwritten, not typed.

LETTER ELEMENTS: In writing a letter of sympathy that does not express an inappropriate degree of intimacy, Artandi does the following:

1. He gives his condolence right away. He avoids being maudlin, and he is careful to choose appropriate words. (Under these circumstances, for instance, it would be inappropriate to use the word *grief* to describe his feelings.)
2. He mentions the occasion when he met the deceased, recalling details that will be pleasant for Steve to remember.
3. He avoids closing the letter with an all-too-easy and not very meaningful expression such as "If there is anything I can do, don't hesitate to call." Instead, he suggests something specific that he can do for Steve.
4. He ends on a cheerful note and does not reiterate the condolence.

James Artandi
14 East Old Shakopee Road
Owen, ST 14398

June 8

Dear Steve,

I was very sorry to hear of Eileen's death. I extend to you my heartfelt sympathy.

I well remember meeting Eileen the evening you and she hosted a swimming party for local furniture buyers. I was new to the area at that time, and felt more than a little like an outsider. Eileen took the time to perform introductions and make me feel at home (she even provided me with a towel when George Harkness's four children and the basset hound were discovered playing tug-of-war with my own). I've never forgotten her way of making a stranger feel welcome.

You probably haven't made any definite plans yet, but if you should decide that you would like to get away for a while, I would be happy to keep an eye on the house for you. It would be no trouble at all to stop by each day, and I'd welcome the chance to come admire your garden.

Best personal regards,

Jim

Condolence Letter

—less personal

SITUATION: Randolph Parker, president of a textile mill, has heard that Gunnar Caroleen, president of a company that does business with Parker's firm, was recently widowed. The two men have met on business occasions, but not socially. Parker writes a short letter of sympathy which is typed on Executive-size company statinery.

LETTER ELEMENTS: In writing a letter of condolence to his business associate, Parker does the following:

1. He begins by offering sympathy simply and straightforwardly. He does so on behalf of both himself and his staff since others in his company have dealt with Mr. Caroleen in their work.
2. He offers business-related assistance that Mr. Caroleen might find helpful.
3. He ends on a less business-like, more comforting note.

PARKER MILLS
2605 Commerce Boulevard
Vestavia, ST 06548
Telephone 502-241-7425

Office of the President

September 9, 19--

Dear Gunnar:

My staff and I wish to extend our heartfelt sympathy to you
during this period of your bereavement since the passing
of your wife, Helen.

Your many friends here at Parker Mills join me in offering
assistance with special scheduling of your orders at this
time. Please do not hesitate to let us know how we may
help.

It must be a comfort to have your family so near. May the
memories of your years together sustain you all and bring you
strength and peace.

Sincerely,

Randolph Parker

Mr. Gunnar Caroleen
President
Universal Products, Inc.
Everett, ST 06789

Confirmation

—of oral information

SITUATION: Raymond Weese is the principal at Plainville Middle School. In the course of a telephone conversation, Charlene Rice, a textbook sales representative, has told him of an upcoming promotional sale her company is planning for the following month. A new science textbook that the school needs will be part of the promotion. Weese understood her to say that the books can be ordered from the company now, using a special ordering number, even though the promotion will not officially begin for 30 days. The principal wishes to confirm this information, and he writes to do so.

LETTER ELEMENTS: In writing to the sales representative to confirm oral information, Weese does the following:

1.   He goes over the telephone conversation he held with the representative. He states the facts as he understands them.
2.   He continues by asking in a friendly way if his information is correct. Without putting himself or the sales representative on the spot, he gives her an opening to tell him, if it is necessary, that his understanding is wrong.
3.   He ends on a courteous and friendly note.

Plainville Middle School
Plainville Regional School District
1400 Olive Street
Plainville, ST 70707
(619) 135-7911

March 15, 19--

Ms. Charlene Rice
Charter Oaks Publishers,
 Educational Division
997 Hinsdale Road
Springfield, ST 65802

Dear Charlene:

     When you and I spoke together on the telephone last Friday,
you described a promotional sale that Charter Oaks is planning for
next month. I pricked up my ears when I heard the titles that will
be featured in that sale, because one of them is a science text
that has been chosen by our science department. When I told you
I'd like to order the books as soon as possible so the text can be
used this semester, you gave me an ordering number (3507) for preferred customers. As I understand it, use of this number will allow me to order the text at the promotional-sale price now, even
though the sale will not begin until next month.

     I'm about to order the science texts, but first I'd like to
check with you and make sure that my understanding of the situation
is correct. I'd also appreciate confirmation of the preferred-
customer ordering number.

     I'm very pleased to have information of this sale in advance.
Buying the science texts on sale will be a big help to our budget,
and getting the books for next semester will be a big help to our
science department.

                              Sincerely yours,

                              Raymond Weese
                              Principal

RW:gad

Congratulation

SITUATION: Norman Langley is a newspaper reporter. Recently, Dick Maloney, a longtime friend and colleague on the same paper, was the Eastern Division's Reporter of the Year. Dick works mostly out of the paper's new bureau in another city, so Langley writes to extend his congratulations.

LETTER ELEMENTS: In writing a letter of congratulations to his colleague, Langley does the following:

1.   He commends his friend on the honor, giving it its exact title (a courtesy gesture) and reflects on its meaning.
2.   He makes additional comments on the nature of the achievement.
3.   He closes with personal good wishes.

The Newark *Clarion*
Harcourt Building
Newark, ST 19711
109-340-5600

February 10, 19--

Mr. Richard Maloney
The Newark Clarion
Springton News Bureau
1413 Chestnut Street
Springton, ST 17101

Dear Dick:

A general announcement was made yesterday to the Clarion
staff of your selection as the Eastern Division's Reporter of
the Year. Congratulations! It is certainly a well-deserved
honor. It's also an honor that is well worth having, as you
and I and others here on the staff have frequently discussed.

If you had been in town, I would have extended these congratulations in person, of course. But since our schedules
seem to keep us at opposite ends of the state, I thought I'd
write and let you know how pleased I am for you.

I am very proud that you have received this honor, one of
the highest that can be bestowed in our field. I'm also proud
to be a colleague of yours. May you enjoy many years of continued success.

As always, please give my warmest wishes to Marcia and
the children.

Best wishes,

Norm

Consumer Relations Letter

—explaining a delay in service

SITUATION: Wright-Way Kitchen Supply finds itself in a predicament. Recently they began carrying a rarity—an all-metal mixer/blender at a price comparable to the same-size models made of plastic. The line sold out in a week, and the store is trying to get in more units. However, the factory that makes the mixer is unable to keep up with the demand, and there will be a shipping delay of at least three weeks. Meanwhile, customers continue to order the new product from Wright-Way. The products manager, Barney Cates, writes to each of them, explaining the situation.

LETTER ELEMENTS: In writing to the would-be customers, Cates develops a basic text that he can use for all of the letters. Each letter will, of course, be personalized with the name, address, and salutation of the recipient. In writing the basic text of the letter, Cates does the following:

1. He begins by acknowledging the new product's success, and goes on to explain that the line is presently sold out.
2. He keeps the second piece of bad news, the three-week delay in restocking, for the second paragraph—no need to hit the reader with two negative items in the first paragraph—and then puts the best face on it he can.
3. He gets to the question that the reader would ask if he and the products manager were face-to-face: What can be done in the meantime? He offers his solutions.
4. These solutions may or may not be agreeable to the reader, so the products manager does not push them. He closes by assuring the customer that he will be notified as soon as the new mixer units arrive at Wright-Way from the factory.

Wright-Way Kitchen Supply
1560 Wright Way, El Yuma, ST 89110
(717) 793-4118 / 795-8708

March 7, 19--

Mr. Hubert Johansson
Appleton Appliances
15 Appleton Way
Deep Springs, ST 89010

Dear Mr. Johansson:

We're pleased to hear that you are interested in the Speed-Mix Master Mixer 1500. This is truly a high-quality item at a reasonable price, and interest in this product has been very high. So high, in fact, that we sold out of this item in one week's time. As far as I know, that is a record for us.

As soon as we realized how quickly our stock of the Master Mixer was being depleted, we contacted the factory to order more. Unfortunately, this item is currently being manufactured at only one factory, and the factory's output cannot meet demand. I have been told that there will be a delay of at least three weeks before our order can be filled.

In the meantime we still do have available the smaller Speed-Mix model, the Master Mixer 1200. Like the 1500, it is made completely of metal and is an excellent value. Its disadvantage, of course, is that it lacks the blender attachment of the 1500. We also have in stock Brandwell's Model 30 all metal mixer/blender. That model does, however, sell at wholesale for $20.00 more than the Master Mixer 1500.

If either of these two options interests you, we'll be happy to fill your order. If, on the other hand, you prefer to wait for us to restock the Master Mixer, you may be assured that we will contact you as soon as our order comes from the factory.

Cordially,

Barney Cates

Barney Cates
Product Manager

BC/lar

Consumer Relations Letter

—to win back an inactive customer

SITUATION: Daniel McMillan is sales manager of the Hanson Company, an optical-supply wholesaler. He has recently noticed a fall-off in orders. The stores involved are located in several different areas, and the sales manager cannot attribute the drop in sales to any one factor. He writes to each inactive customer.

LETTER ELEMENTS: In writing to the inactive custmers, McMillan does the following:

1. He briefly reviews the customer's past history with the company, arriving at his reason for writing—the customer is now inactive.
2. He gets right down to reasons for the letter. He wants to know why the customer is no longer ordering from his company, and the only way to find out is to ask straightforward questions.
3. He mentions a postage-paid questionnaire enclosed with the letter. The preprinted form indicates to the customer that the company is serious about regaining his business.
4. He brings up sales items that may interest the customer. He is taking advantage of having the attention of the reader, and he treats the situation as a selling opportunity.

October 14, 19--

Mr. Ralph Chauncey
The Camera Shop
1397 Rosemont Avenue
La Crosse, ST 54601

Dear Mr. Chauncey:

Every year for the past seven years our company has been pleased
to fill at least one order from your Camera Shop. Recently, however, I had the opportunity to go over our sales list, and I've
made the somewhat disquieting discovery that we've not received
an order from you in 14 months.

Given the Camera Shop's past relationship with the Hanson Company,
this may indicate a problem at our end. Have you encountered a
delay or dissatisfaction with an order? I can't find any evidence
in our files that you've written to us with a complaint. If you've
experienced any problems in ordering merchandise from us, I'd very
much like to know what they are.

A business owner with a crowded schedule doesn't have time to sit
down and write us a letter. However, we'd still like to hear from
you. I'm sending along a brief, postage-paid questionnaire, and I
do hope you'll take a moment to check off the questions on it.
This is one way of making your feelings known to us.

I'm also sending along something else that may be of interest to
you. We're currently offering the entire Monatrex autofocus line
of cameras at one-third off our usual price. This is one of our
best-selling lines, and we think you'll spot some excellent buys
in the enclosed brochure. You'll find a handy form inside the
brochure.

Sincerely,

Daniel McMillan
Daniel McMillan
Sales Manager

lvt

Hanson Company
P.O. Box 1435, Front Street, Wyanchochee, ST 37651
Telephone (101) 543-6660 or (101) 543-6503

Credit Letter
—canceling credit

SITUATION: Seven years ago, Howard Harris, owner of Universal Electrical Service, opened an account with Kelley Electrical Supply Shop. For some time he paid his store's bills within 30 days. For the past several months, however, his payments have been very late, necessitating letters of reminder from Albert Terranova, the credit manager of Kelley Electrical. Universal Electrical is now several months behind in its payments, and Terranova has decided to cancel the account.

LETTER ELEMENTS: In writing to Mr. Harris to cancel his account, Terranova does the following:

1. Before getting to the problem, he commends Mr. Harris for prompt payment in the past. An immediate negative or aggressive approach may prevent the letter from being read any further, and Terranova wants to avoid that.
2. When he brings up the current problem, he does so as tactfully and politely as possible.
3. Avoiding the negative, he suggests a solution.
4. He offers special assistance.
5. He requests a prompt response, keeping his wording polite but firm.

Kelley Electrical Supply Shop
6802 Eastern Highway
Smithville, ST 56789
Telephone (507) 841-3841

November 5, 19--

Mr. Howard Harris
Universal Electrical Service
4628 Southern Boulevard
Smithville, ST 56789

Dear Mr. Harris:

Over the past seven years, we have valued your account
with us and considered it one of our best.

Recently with the turndown in business, we have
noticed that your practice of discounting your bills
every thirty days has ceased. Your last payment was
ninety days late.

It is imperative that we keep current on our accounts
receivable; therefore, regretfully, it is necessary
to ask you to make future purchases on a cash only
basis until your account is cleared.

Please accept the enclosed Special Courtesy Discount
card for future cash purchases. It will entitle you
to a three percent cash discount to help you through
this transition period.

May we hear from you soon, Mr. Harris.

Very sincerely,

Albert Terranova
Albert Terranova
Credit Manager

AT:jml

Enclosure

Credit Letter
  —extending credit

SITUATION: Martin Goodson is credit manager of Craft's, a luggage wholesaler. He has received an order and request for commercial credit from Carry-on, a retail luggage shop now expanding its merchandise lines. A review of Carry-on's credit references shows that the store has a good track record of paying its bills on time. Goodson writes to Charles Gordon, the owner of the shop, to let him know that credit has been approved, and to establish a friendly relationship.

LETTER ELEMENTS: In writing to Mr. Gordon to extend him commercial credit, Goodson does the following:

1. He begins by giving the store owner the good news. He welcomes him as a new customer, and lets him know that the store's order is being taken care of. This letter should be kept informal, and credit terms should not be part of it. They can be sent in the same letter as an enclosure (which may be preprinted).
2. He winds up with a restrained sales pitch, combining it with a personal touch and an assurance of future service.

Craft's

800 Thunderbird Road
Myers, ST 88061
Telephone: 707-488-9322

September 5, 19--

Mr. Charles Gordon
Carry-on
Silver City, ST 88061

Dear Mr. Gordon:

Welcome aboard! Craft's is pleased to have you as a credit
customer. We are sending out your order of 25 all-in-one
suitcases and 10 garment bags (totaling $1500) by truck, and
you should have it by the time you read this. Our credit
terms are explained in detail on the enclosed form.

We've also enclosed a brochure describing a new line of over-
night bags that we feel are an excellent buy. The bags have
proved to be best-selling items in markets similar to yours.
Congratulations on the expansion of your store, and if there
is any way we can be of service to you, please let us know.

Sincerely,

Martin Goodson

Martin Goodson
Credit Manager

MG/ph

Credit Letter

—requesting credit

SITUATION: Bret Atkins is the owner of The Pet Place, a large pet store, selling not only pets and pet supplies, but housing and fencing for large animals as well. A recent fencing innovation has been heavily advertised in specialty magazines. Atkins thinks it will sell well, even though it is a relatively expensive item. He writes to Gino Russo, the sales manager for the manufacturer, to request commercial credit terms.

LETTER ELEMENTS: In writing to Mr. Russo to request credit terms, the pet store owner does the following:

1. He opens by explaining how he came to hear of the new product. This information is helpful to the manufacturer.
2. He moves on to the heart of the letter—his order. His calculations are accurate, precise, and arranged in sequence so the manufacturer can see quickly how the store owner arrived at the total. He then requests credit terms.
3. He gives detailed, precise information on his business, and then supplies the names and addresses of credit references.
4. He also gives the name and address of a bank with which he does business. This may not be something the manufacturer will follow up on, but the store owner does give him the option. He closes by volunteering to give more information if the manufacturer wants it.

The Pet Place   South Carters Run Road   Fulton, ST 41823   Telephone 505-626-2626

June 15, 19--

Mr. Gino Russo, Sales Manager
William-Weeks Manufacturing, Inc.
4365 West LaSalle Street
Fairmont, ST 48790

Dear Mr. Russo:

This month's issue of <u>Pet World</u> features a full-page advertisement for your
company's Unseen Fencing. This "fenceless fencing" is something my customers
frequently inquire about, but up to now I've had to tell them there was no
such product. I'm very pleased at the reasonable cost, which is actually lower than the cost of conventional fencing.

According to <u>Pet World</u>'s ad, the Unseen Fencing kit wholesales for $400. I
would like to order 10 kits on sixty-day credit terms. I understand that
there is a $200.00 shipping charge for orders of 10 or more, so my order to-
tals $4,200. I would also like to establish sixty-day credit terms for the
future on purchases up to $5,000.

The Pet Place opened almost eight years ago, and it has proved to be a very
successful enterprise. The store is run in conjunction with a nearby board-
ing kennel owned by my parents. Consequently I have plenty of opportunities
to talk to pet owners and listen to their needs. The Pet Place is the only
store in this area to supply a wide variety of pet supplies, and I feel we
will continue to do well. Being able to provide innovative new products such
as your Unseen Fencing certainly helps.

I refer you to three businesses for information on our promptness in meeting
our financial obligations:

        Ace Feed, 1211 Amity Street, Fulton, ST 41823
        Biological Supplies, Inc., Winding Lane, Highland
        Park, ST 48203
        Carter Carriers, 37 Hunter Boulevard, Everett,
        ST 41245

We do business with Fulton National Bank, 49 Parker Street, Fulton, ST 41801.
I will be happy to give you more financial information if you'd like it.

                    Very truly yours,

                    Bret Atkins
                    Bret Atkins

ga

Credit Letter

—refusing credit

SITUATION: Thomas Polani is the office manager for Ardmore Office Products, a retail office supply store. Margaret Allen, the owner of Interior Enterprises, a newly formed interior-design firm, has placed a sizable order for office equipment and has asked for 120-day credit terms. Interior Enterprises has been a good customer for the past year; however, a review of their financial statement and of the information supplied by credit references indicates that Interior Enterprises is in some financial difficulty. Polani decides to refuse the credit request, but he wants very much to keep Interior Enterprises as a cash customer.

LETTER ELEMENTS: In writing to refuse credit, Polani does the following:

1.   He expresses appreciation for the order and for past patronage. He is letting Ms. Allen know that he sees their business relationship as an ongoing one and that he hopes it will continue in the future.
2.   He states that the application for credit has not been accepted. He avoids the word *refuse,* and he expresses regret that this decision had to be made. At this point, he is neutral in tone and does not criticize or offer advice, which can often seem condescending. Nor does he say anything specific about the financial situation of Interior Enterprises; he simply says that the information provided does not warrant the decision to grant credit.
3.   He holds out hope that the decision could be reversed if more information were provided. Most probably, such information is not available; however, he is making clear that he has not come to any negative conclusions about the company.
4.   He reminds Ms. Allen that the order can still be filled on a cash basis. He adopts a cheerful tone here to encourage her not to cancel the order.

ardmore office products

136 John T. Slocum Street
Colquitt, ST 18282
Telephone (104)999-8115

September 27, 19--

Ms. Margaret Allen
Interior Enterprises
Suite 101
1700 Blanford Road
Kings Crossing, ST 18540

Dear Ms. Allen:

Thank you very much for the order you placed with us last week. We appreciate your patronage, and we hope we can continue to serve you in the future.

We have carefully considered your application for 120-day credit terms. We are sorry to say that, on the basis of the financial information we have seen so far, we are not able to approve your request. However, if there is any added financial information that you could send us that would allow us to reconsider this decision, we would be happy to do so.

In the meantime, we will be happy to fill this order on a cash basis, with our customary 3 percent cash discount.

Sincerely,

Thomas Polani

Thomas Polani
Office Manager

TP/mbs

Follow-up Letter

SITUATION: Claire Odom is office manager for Holliston and Beem Associates, a management consulting firm. Six weeks ago, she sent a check and a purchase order to Jenkins Press for a one-year subscription to their newsletter *Monthly Management Records*. The purchase order included a note saying that she wished the subscription to begin immediately. So far, she has received her canceled check, but no issues have arrived. She writes to urge them to begin delivery as requested.

LETTER ELEMENTS: In writing this follow-up letter, Odom does the following:

1. She states the date, amount, product, and other details involved in the original order.
2. She summarizes the current situation as she understands it, and she expresses her concern about it.
3. She renews her request for immediate delivery.
4. She requests notification if immediate delivery cannot be provided.

Holliston and Beem Associates

Faunce Building, Fourth Floor
Market Street
Tacoma Heights, ST 92614
Telephone: 916-484-0411

June 24, 19--

Subscription Department
Jenkins Press
95 High Ridge Road
Park City, ST 67890

Ladies and Gentlemen:

On May 9, 19--, we sent you a check for $52.50 and
a purchase order for a one-year subscription to
Monthly Management Records, and we asked that the
subscription begin immediately. A copy of the purchase order is enclosed.

To date, we have not received any copies of the
magazine, although we have received our canceled
check. We are concerned that somehow our order may
have gone astray, and so we would like to repeat
our request that we begin receiving our copies of
your newsletter immediately. If there is some reason why this cannot be done, please let us know as
soon as possible.

Sincerely,

Claire T. Odom

Claire T. Odom
Office Manager

CTO:kt
enclosure

Inquiry

SITUATION: Thomas Domizio is marketing manager for Acme Equipment Company, an equipment company that does a large proportion of its business through its catalog. The company plans to add a line of tractors to the equipment it currently leases, and it has chosen Laprade's Harris Tractors for the purpose. Domizio writes to Harold Thomas, sales manager of Laprade Industries, for specifications that can be used in the upcoming catalog.

LETTER ELEMENTS: In writing to Mr. Thomas, Domizio does the following:

1. He immediately gets to the point, while complimenting the manufacturer on its product.
2. He details his request in an easy-to-read way. He avoids the unhelpful request, "Please send me all the information you have on this particular product." He lists precisely what he needs, and he sets it up in such a way that it stands out from the surrounding text. Both things facilitate a helpful reply.
3. He mentions that he needs the requested information quickly, and he explains why.
4. He closes politely.

Acme Equipment Company
42 Grove Street
Johnsonville, ST 56855
507-327-0605

September 17, 19--

Mr. Harold Thomas
Sales Manager
Laprade Industries
1525 State Street
Smithville, ST 56789

Dear Mr. Thomas

Presently we are planning to add yard and garden tractors to our line of leased equipment. It is my pleasure
to announce that we shall feature Harris Tractors.

Would you please send us a complete list of models and
specifications for Harris Tractors. It would be helpful to have the following data as soon as possible:

1. Horsepower/range of job function.
2. Commercial/homeowner equipment.
3. Contract samples/sale terms.

Since the publication date for our catalog is slated
for November, your early reply will be appreciated.

Sincerely yours

Thomas Domizio

Thomas Domizio
Marketing Manager

TD:jml

Introduction Letter

SITUATION: For eight years Anita Rothstein has worked as children's librarian at a library in a small town. Recently her husband has been transferred to a large city, and Anita intends to apply for a job at the city's main library. She has asked Diana Green, the head librarian at the small-town library, for a letter of introduction and recommendation to accompany her application. The head librarian responds.

LETTER ELEMENTS: In writing a combination letter of introduction and recommendation, the head librarian does the following:

1. She immediately makes the introduction.
2. She presents relevant professional information.
3. She gives her evaluation and a recommendation.
4. She offers more information upon request.

Carnegie Library of Munstead
510   10th Avenue
Munstead, ST 15120
(412)-461-0007

May 23, 19--

Mrs. Ruth Owens
Personnel Director
Atkins Memorial Library
47 Cooper Road
Montgomery, AL 36106

Dear Mrs. Owens:

    This is a letter of introduction and recommendation for Mrs. Anita N.
Rothstein, who has ably served as Children's Librarian here for eight years.
Mrs. Rothstein received her Bachelor of Arts degree in Comparative Literature just prior to coming to work here. She began studying for her Master's
in Library Science shortly after her arrival, and earned her degree two
years later.

    Mrs. Rothstein's main duties have been the reorganization of the chil-
dren's section, which was much in need of reorganization when she arrived
here, and the day-to-day running of this section, which has included the selection and ordering of new books and periodicals. In addition to her regular duties, she took on the added task of arranging special programming for
area children. She raised money for a wide variety of special speakers and
performers, and during her time here our children benefitted greatly from
her efforts. Because she so efficiently took over a multitude of duties
here, I don't feel that moving from a small establishment to a much larger
one will overwhelm her. She has been very quick to learn, to improvise when
necessary, and to accept responsibility.

    In short, I'm sorry to be losing Anita, but I do feel that our loss
will be your gain. If you'd like further comments regarding her, feel free
to give me a call.

                        Very truly yours,

                        Diana T. Green

                        Diana T. Green
                        Head Librarian

DTG:col

Invitation, Formal

SITUATION: The Friends of the Cheltenham Museum of Fine Arts invite members and honored guests to a Christmas ball with a formal printed invitation.

INVITATION ELEMENTS: The invitation should set out the pertinent information in a handsome, easy-to-read manner.

1. The invitation is printed in black on heavy cream paper. A small size, such as 4 by 5½ inches, is the usual choice for a good reason; large sizes, because of the heavy paper used, and because there is usually an insert (see item four below), may require extra postage. The envelope of the invitation is not mailable if it measures less than 3½ by 5 inches.
2. The information is separated by spaces. The lines are centered, not indented or placed flush left.
3. Typically the envelope of a formal invitation is handwritten, not typed.
4. The invitation is marked R.S.V.P. (the abbreviation for French *répondez s'il vous plaît*, "please reply"), and a name and telephone number are given. Alternatively, a formal invitation of this type may contain a card, printed in the same style as the invitation, that reads:

> I will _____ will not _____ attend the Christmas ball being given by the Cheltenham Museum Friends on Friday, December 15.
> Name _____

The card should be placed in a stamped envelope addressed in the same style as the envelope of the invitation.

The Friends of the Cheltenham Museum of Fine Arts

cordially invite you to their

Twenty-fifth Christmas Ball

on Friday, the fifteenth of December

Nineteen hundred and eighty-eight

at seven o'clock

at the Bradford Inn

Cheltenham, New Hampshire

R.S.V.P.

Roland Frasier

(603) 782-1864

Invitation, Informal

—to a business event

SITUATION: Wayne Thoren is sales manager for Global Hardware Associates, a sales promotion organization. They are hosting an exhibition of new industrial hardware products, and they are inviting leading retail and wholesale vendors to the show. The invitations will go out on business stationery and be individually signed by Thoren.

LETTER ELEMENTS: In writing this kind of invitation, Thoren does the following:

1.   He opens in a cordial and attention-getting way.
2.   He gives the date, time, and location of the event.
3.   He describes the event and offers a motivation for attending.
4.   He includes directions and other details.
5.   He closes by encouraging the reader to attend.

GLOBAL HARDWARE ASSOCIATES

87 Highland Drive
Chicago, IL 60147
Telephone 312-120-0444

June 26, 19—

Mr. William Mann
Baker Company
14 Bank Street
Bartlett, IL 60432

YOU'RE CORDIALLY INVITED:

to come to our Industrial Hardware Exhibits to be
held on July 10, 19—, at the Civic Center, 25 High
Boulevard, Chicago, Illinois, from 9 a.m. to 3 p.m.

The newest industrial hardware will be on display.
Representatives from leading hardware manufacturers
will be on hand to answer your questions.

Parking facilities will be available at the Civic
Center Garage. Travel directions and a map are
enclosed for your convenience.

Won't you join your business associates for an
interesting and rewarding day at the Civic Center's
Industrial Hardware Exhibits on July 10.

Wayne D. Thoren

Wayne D. Thoren, Sales Manager

jml

Enclosures (2)

Invitation, Informal

—to a social event

SITUATION: Sandra Wilhelm is president of Wilhelm and Cook, an industrial design and packaging firm. She has recently hired Jeffrey Nirenberg to be their new finance director. She has decided to give a dinner party so that Nirenberg and his wife can meet socially with the other executives of the company and their spouses, as well as with a few of the firm's most important clients. In all, ten couples are being invited. The wording for each couple's invitation may vary somewhat, but the basic text of the invitation remains the same. In this case, she is inviting Michael Rankin, the firm's design director, and his wife.

LETTER ELEMENTS: In issuing this invitation, Wilhelm does the following:

1.   She has the letter typed on her own personal stationery. The typing is appropriate because this is in some respects a business event. If it were to be a purely social event, a handwritten note would have been appropriate. Because she knows the recipients very well, she addresses them by their first names. There is no need for an inside address on this letter.
2.   She offers the invitation, giving the date, time, and a brief description of the event.
3.   She offers a few more details about the event, and she encourages Sheila and Michael to accept the invitation.
4.   She issues the invitation on a "regrets only" basis, and she gives her home phone number. For guests who don't work at Wilhelm and Cook, she may also include her work number.

Sandra B. Wilhelm
47 Bridgewater Road
Oxmoor, ST 21574

May 26, 19--

Dear Sheila and Michael,

Sam and I would like to invite you to a dinner party on June 28 at seven o'clock. The party is an informal one to help welcome Jeffrey Nirenberg, our new Finance Director, and his wife Christine to the area.

We are hoping all of the officers of the corporation and their husbands or wives will attend. In addition, we are inviting a few other friends of Wilhelm and Cook to join us. We know that Jeffrey and Christine would be delighted if you would accept.

Please let us know only if you can't come. Our home number is 987-8613. If we don't hear from you, we'll be expecting you.

Best regards,

Sandy

Job Letter
—offering a job

SITUATION: Brandon Kiley is director of administration for Communications Media Corporation, a holding company that owns several radio stations, newspapers, and a television station. Kiley has recently been interviewing candidates for the position of assistant director of administration. He has now chosen one of the candidates, and he has called to give her the news. However, he also sends out a letter that confirms the offer and sets out other necessary details.

LETTER ELEMENTS: In writing this confirming letter to Ms. Reeve, Kiley does the following:

1.   He restates the offer of the job, giving the exact title of the position.
2.   He reviews pertinent aspects of the terms of employment.
3.   He gives a starting date for the job.
4.   He reviews the documents she will have to bring with her so that the company can remain in compliance with federal regulations regarding citizenship and residency status of new employees. He reminds her that it is mandatory that she bring these documents.
5.   He requests a formal acceptance of the offer.

Communications Media Corporation/Hawthorne Building/Pierce and Fremont Streets/Houston, TX 77001

CMC

Telephone (713) 898-7642
898-2746

July 15, 19--

Ms. Donna A. Reeve
4527 Van Dam Boulevard
Fairfield, ST 12321

Dear Ms. Reeve:

This letter constitutes our formal offer to you of the position of Assistant Director of Administration at Communications Media Corporation. Your duties will consist of assisting the Director of Administration in all professional areas of corporate administration and in carrying out special projects that relate to corporate communications and staff development, as assigned by the Director of Administration.

This is a full-time position, paying a salary of $27,500 a year less the deductions required by law for federal and state taxes and Social Security. You will receive a salary review after six months and annually thereafter. Increases will depend on the company's general policy and on your contributions to our administrative activities. Fringe benefits and other details regarding employment are explained in the employee manual that is being sent to you separately.

We have agreed that you will begin work on August 1, 19--. On that day, please bring with you proof of your U.S. citizenship or resident-alien status. A driver's license with photo (or a state-issued identification card with photo) and a Social Security card will suffice. If one of these is not available, you may bring alternative documents as explained on the enclosed form I-9. Unfortunately, if you do not bring the appropriate documents, you will not be able to begin work.

If this offer is acceptable to you, please sign and date the carbon copy of this letter and return it to us for our files.

Sincerely,

Brandon W. Kiley
Brandon W. Kiley
Director of Administration

BWK/hva
enclosure

Job Letter

—turning down an applicant

SITUATION: Gloria Markham is sales manager for Batterston Furniture Company, a retail furniture store. She has finished interviewing a group of applicants for a sales position in the store. She has chosen a candidate, and the candidate has accepted. She now writes to the other applicants to tell them that they did not get the job. Markham will use the same basic text for each letter.

LETTER ELEMENTS: In writing her letter to the unsuccessful applicants, Markham does the following:

1. She briefly thanks the applicants for applying and quickly moves on to the bad news, telling them that they were not selected.
2. She expresses her appreciation to them. Markham is being extra polite here, because she wants to do nothing to alienate the candidates. After all, they might be potential customers.
3. She tells them that she is keeping their applications on file in case she has a suitable opening in the near future. This is unlikely to happen, but it might. In addition, this is another polite gesture that she can make.

Batterston Furniture Company
16 Flower Street
Malvern, ST 23406
(300)-604-3232

August 16, 19--

Mr. John F. Zimmerman
628 Humphrey Street
Oakdale, ST 23412

Dear Mr. Zimmerman:

Thank you for giving us the opportunity to consider your application for the sales position that we advertised recently. We are sorry to say that we have chosen another candidate to fill this position; however, we want you to know that we appreciate your interest in the Batterston Furniture Company.

Your application will be kept on file. If we have an opening that is suitable for you in the near future, we will be in touch with you again.

Sincerely,

Gloria R. Markham
Gloria R. Markham
Sales Manager

GRM:pgk

Order

SITUATION: Paul Thomas is the purchasing agent of Rodriguez, Inc., a large home-products store. He has just been informed that the store has run out of two types of popular hardware. It is imperative that the store's stock be replenished as soon as possible. He writes a letter ordering more stock from his supplier.

LETTER ELEMENTS: In ordering replacement stock for his store, the purchasing agent does the following:

1. He makes known his store's urgent need for the order. He gives the shipping address that will best facilitate delivery.
2. He lists clearly the quantity, description, and price of the ordered items. By using a tabular approach, instead of inserting the item descriptions into the body of his letter, he makes clear what his store needs.
3. He closes by explaining why prompt delivery of these two items is necessary and by emphasizing that a rush order is needed.

Rodriguez, Inc.
2255 West 189th Street
New York, NY 11250
Telephone: 212-598-1534

November 13, 19--

Mr. George Holmes, Manager
Baxter and Halloway, Inc.
Smithville, ST 56789

Dear Mr. Holmes:

Please accept this order for immediate shipment to
Rodriguez, Inc., Wood Products Division, 2255 West
189th Street, New York, NY 11250.

Quantity	Description	Unit Price	Total
1800	No. 202 T. Hinges, Brass Plate	$1.50 pr.	$1,350
600	No. 78 Corner Braces, Brass Plate	1.75 ea.	1,050
		Total	$2,400

An unexpected flurry of orders has depleted our stock.
Therefore, any assistance that you can give in expe-
diting our order and delivery will be greatly
appreciated.

Sincerely,

Paul Thomas

Paul Thomas
Purchasing Agent

PT:jml

Price Quotation

SITUATION: Barry Zubroski, sales representative for Waterville Type-setting, Inc., has received a request for a price quotation for typesetting a new book from Nancy Bains, managing editor of Hampden Press, a local publishing company. He responds with a letter that supplies all of the pricing information that Ms. Bains has requested.

LETTER ELEMENTS: In submitting his price quotation, Zubroski does the following:

1. He begins in a polite and respectful way.
2. He supplies the requested information in a complete and detailed manner.
3. He provides additional information regarding the terms of sale.
4. He closes with an offer to provide additional information if it is needed.

Waterville Typesetting, Inc.
2965 James Street, Waterville, ST 21270
(101) 444-3131 or (101) 444-3003

December 30, 19--

Ms. Nancy L. Bains
Managing Editor
Hampden Press
44 Lincoln Street
Canton, ST 21212

Dear Ms. Bains:

    Waterville Typesetting is pleased to submit the following quotation
for The New Homeowner's Encyclopedia:

COMPOSITION: Baskerville, 40 x 50 text area, 8 x 10 trim

Quantity	Description	Unit Price	Total
10 pages	Front Matter	$24.50	$ 245.00
354 pages	Text	28.95	10,248.30
118 pages	Space Allowance for Art	6.00	708.00
30 pages	Index	26.00	780.00
200 pieces	Line Art to Shoot and Strip	4.50	900.00
512 pages	Negatives	3.00	1,536.00
512 pages	Proofs of Negatives	.75	384.00
			$14,801.30

    These prices are FOB our plant in Waterville. The terms of sale are
net 30 days, with a progress billing at the end of the galley stage.

    Pricing is subject to review upon receipt of the fully edited manu-
script, specifications, and scheduling requirements. Estimate is valid for
90 days.

    Thank you for the opportunity to provide this quotation. If you have
any further questions, please do not hesitate to call me.

Sincerely,

Barry Zubroski

Barry Zubroski
Sales Representative

BZ/gic

Refusal of an Invitation

SITUATION: Patricia Meacam is a partner in the law firm of Jenkins and Danforth. Recently she and her firm have been in the news for their efforts in negotiating some very important real-estate development projects in downtown Stateville. She has just been invited to speak at the annual banquet of Stateville United, a volunteer service that supports many charitable activities in the city. Meacam writes to Emilia Sheridan, the banquet organizer, to say that she cannot attend their banquet.

LETTER ELEMENTS: In writing to decline the invitation, Meacam does the following:

1. She thanks Ms. Sheridan for the invitation, and she expresses her regrets that she cannot accept the invitation. She offers a reason why she cannot, but she keeps the explanation very general.
2. She compliments the organization. The compliment is sincere, but it also helps maintain good feelings with the organization.
3. She ends on a friendly and cheerful note.

Jenkins and Danforth
Attorneys-at-law
One Court Street, Suite H
Stateville, ST 34533
Telephone: 512-507-1440

November 12, 19--

Ms. Emilia Sheridan
Stateville United
3700 Main Street
Stateville, ST 34534

Dear Ms. Sheridan:

Thank you very much for your invitation to speak at your annual awards banquet. Unfortunately, my responsibilities at Jenkins and Danforth prevent me from accepting any outside speaking engagements at this time.

I have always been a great admirer of the work of your organization, and I am honored to have been asked to speak to your group. I wish you well with what I am sure will be a splendid evening.

Sincerely,

Patricia J. Meacam

Patricia J. Meacam

lol

Request
—for an appointment

SITUATION: Grace Diaz is a sales representative for Grayson Paper Company. She writes to set up a business appointment with Brian Watson, purchasing agent for the Pikeville School District. Diaz has done business with Mr. Watson in the past and is aware of at least one of his product needs that her company can now answer.

LETTER ELEMENTS: In writing to ask Mr. Watson for an appointment, Diaz does the following:

1. She opens by reminding her client in a low-key way that they have met before. She mentions one of her company's products that she feels will interest him.
2. She states her desire to meet with him, and she suggests a date and a time. She does this as a way of helping her own scheduling and also as a way of urging Mr. Watson to commit to a specific time for a meeting.
3. She says she will call later to confirm the appointment. This allows Mr. Watson the chance to suggest an alternate time or to decline the request entirely. It also allows Diaz the chance to speak to Mr. Watson before the actual appointment to get a better idea of his needs and to do some brief low-key preselling of her product.
4. She offers a number at which she can be reached. Whether or not the number is needed, it is a friendly gesture to offer it.
5. She closes in a mildly flattering way, saying that she is looking forward to the meeting.

GRAYSON PAPER COMPANY
12555 Berea Road
Fayette, ST 54778
Telephone: (123) 349-6200

March 3, 19--

Mr. Brian Watson, Purchasing Agent
Pikeville Township School District
Pikeville, ST 45101

Dear Mr. Watson:

Last year when I visited Pikeville, you found some essay paper in the Grayson line that you felt would suit several different needs within the district. At that time, you and I also discussed the problem you were having in finding multicolor file folders that would be large enough to accommodate your oversize record forms. Grayson was then in the midst of production planning for a new line of file folders, but manufacturing had not yet begun. Now I have samples of our new file folders, and I believe they will fill all your requirements.

I would like to call on you at your office later this month to show you samples of these folders and of some of our other new products that I think will be of interest to you. Perhaps sometime on the morning of Wednesday the 24th would be convenient for you. I will call you early in the week of March 15 to confirm this date or to set up an alternate time.

If you need to reach me before that time, please feel free to call me at Grayson headquarters in Fayette at (123) 349-6222.

I look forward to meeting with you and talking about the needs of the Pikeville School District.

Sincerely,

Grace Diaz

Grace Diaz
Sales Representative

GD/smb

Request

—for a price quotation

SITUATION: Nancy Bains is managing editor of Hampden Press, a small publishing company that produces a few new books each year. The company is about to begin work on another new title, and Bains wants to receive price quotations for the typesetting part of the project from several companies that she feels are qualified to do the job. One of the typesetting companies is Waterville Typesetting, and Barry Zubroski is their sales representative.

LETTER ELEMENTS: In writing to request a price quotation from Mr. Zubroski, Bains does the following:

1. She describes in detail the specifications of the product and services she is requesting.
2. She describes the particular way in which she wants the product delivered.
3. She provides additional information about other aspects of the project, including information about schedule requirements.
4. She gives a date by which time she expects to receive a quotation.
5. She offers to answer any questions that Zubroski may have.

HAMPDEN PRESS
44 Lincoln Street   Canton, ST 21212   Telephone: 101-555-6926

December 20, 19--

Mr. Barry Zubroski
Waterville Typesetting, Inc.
2965 James Street
Waterville, ST 21270

Dear Mr. Zubroski:

SUBJECT: The New Homeowner's Encyclopedia

We are writing to request a quotation for typesetting services for
the above new title.

The book will be 512 pages, composed of 10 pages of front matter,
472 pages of main text, and 30 pages of index. The text will include approximately 200 pieces of line art (equalling approximately 25% of the
text space), which we will ask you to shoot, reduce, and position in place.
The trim size will be 8" x 10". The text area will be 40 picas x 50 picas,
and the main text will be set in 10/11 Baskerville.

We will require one set of galleys, one set of page proofs, a set of
negatives, and a set of proofs of negatives.

The copy will be in the form of clean typed manuscript, which we expect to send in several batches, with the last of the copy arriving by
June 30, 19--. We would like to receive final negatives by December 30,
19--.

I hope to receive your quotation within two weeks. If you have any
questions, please do not hesitate to call.

Sincerely,

Nancy L. Bains

Nancy L. Bains
Managing Editor

NLB/rg

Request
—*for a speaker*

SITUATION: The program-committee chairman of the Altamont Conservation Club must find a speaker for the annual banquet. Several honored guests will be present at the banquet, and the club membership is anxious that the affair be a memorable one. Unfortunately funds are quite low this particular year. Elaine Goodrich, president of the club, writes to Susan Compton, the professional speaker mentioned by several club members as their first choice.

LETTER ELEMENTS: In asking Ms. Compton to speak at the club's annual banquet, Goodrich does the following:

1. She begins not by mentioning her club's event, but by complimenting the speaker. Only then does she bring up her group's banquet. She goes on to specify the date and location.
2. She continues with a description of the banquet and its setting and theme, using that to bring up the topic of the speech. She touches on the topic in a general way, leaving the specifics to the speaker. This is not only courteous to a professional speaker, but a compliment to Ms. Compton's judgment.
3. She does not offer a fee, but leaves it to the speaker to set one. Neither does she commit her club to something that may be too expensive for it. She waits to see the speaker's response before concluding the arrangements.
4. She closes with a courteous reminder that she is waiting to hear from the speaker.

Altamont Conservation Club/P.O. Box 60/Altamont, ST 72672

February 4, 19--

Ms. Susan Compton
29 Fairfax Lane
Jackson, ST 98499

Dear Ms. Compton:

You certainly do come highly recommended—every member of
our program committee has mentioned your name as a speaker for
the Altamont Conservation Club spring banquet. This year the
banquet will be held at the Marriott Hotel in downtown Jackson.
The date has been set for Thursday evening, May 30.

Our spring banquet is an annual event, and caps our year's
calendar of activities. Many of those activities are concerned
with environmental issues, both on the local and national level.
Because of our club's involvement with social issues, our past
speakers have tended to focus on that as a topic. I realize,
however, that is a broad area, and I leave the specific choice
of topic up to you. A length of thirty-five to forty minutes
for your talk, including time for a question-and-answer period,
would be ideal for us.

Could you let us know by the first of next month whether
or not you are available and what your fee will be. If you can
join us and if satisfactory financial arrangements can be made,
we will send along more information, including a map that shows
how to get to the Marriott.

I look forward to hearing from you!

Sincerely,

Elaine Goodrich

Elaine Goodrich

Sales Letter

SITUATION: Daniel Parsons is responsible for sales promotion at Parsons Office Management Services, a company that offers a monthly newsletter summarizing information on new office-supply equipment. Parsons wishes to increase the newsletter's circulation, and towards that end he has drawn up a list of the office-supply stores in his region that are not currently subscribing. He writes to each one individually to tell them about his company's product.

LETTER ELEMENTS: In writing a sales letter to the manager of Morris Office Supply, Parsons does the following:

1. He writes a formal business letter on good-quality company stationery, and he addresses the store manager *by name*. This approach lessens the possibility that his letter will be dismissed as junk mail.
2. He uses a unique opening that will catch the reader's attention immediately.
3. He lists the advantages of his product, and describes his company's services.
4. He provides the reader with a chance to look over the product and make a judgment. The implication here is that Parsons is fully confident of his product's appeal. He is not trying to trick the reader into paying for something that may be inferior or unsatisfactory.
5. He uses a close that will encourage the reader to take positive action right away.

PARSONS OFFICE MANAGEMENT SERVICES
15 Evergreen Street
Jonesville, ST 02680
Telephone (108) 935-0246

October 24, 19--

Mr. James Huntwell
Morris Office Supply
250 Maple Street
Smithville, ST 56789

WHAT'S NEW FOR THE OFFICE?

Today's office manager is challenged to constantly seek information
on this question. Parsons Office Management Services is a recognized
authority on the subject.

Each month a newsletter entitled <u>Office Products Update</u> summarizes
new entries in the office supply and equipment arena to aid the be-
leaguered office manager in making the right decisions <u>fast</u>. This
month's edition is enclosed. Please accept it with our compliments.

Gain an edge on your competitors by obtaining the latest office products information in summary form each month. It won't take long
until your customers will recognize Morris Office Supply as a leader
in What's New for the Office.

<u>Office Products Update</u> may be yours each month for the new subscriber
fee of only $6 for the entire year. If you will make use of the en-
closed special subscriber's card before the end of this month, you
will receive two extra issues for the year at no extra cost. May
we hear from you soon?

Daniel B. Parsons

DANIEL B. PARSONS — VICE-PRESIDENT

jml

Enclosures

Thank-you Letter
—for hospitality

SITUATION: George Kinsey, plant manager for Fairfield Textiles Company, recently attended an out-of-town convention and trade show. During the convention, he was entertained by Fairfield's sales representative in the area, Barbara Raycroft, and her husband. When he gets back in his office, Kinsey writes a thank-you note to express his appreciation for the hospitality shown him.

LETTER ELEMENTS: In writing his thank-you note, Kinsey does the following:

1.   Because all his contacts with Ms. Raycroft are business-related, he has the letter typed on company stationery. He is on a first-name basis with her, and so he addresses her by her first name. This is, however, a business-related letter, and so the colon after the salutation is appropriate.
2.   He thanks her for the hospitality he received, mentioning specifically each of the occasions on which he was entertained. Because Ms. Raycroft's husband Bill participated in the occasion, Kinsey refers to him as well in the letter.
3.   He adds some friendly phrases that convey his good feelings and sense of appreciation.

Fairfield Textiles Company
2900 Northrup Way
Fairfield, ST 64380
Telephone: 505-555-9318

December 1, 19--

Ms. Barbara Raycroft
Fairfield Textiles Company
2100 Broadway, Suite 901
Silver City, ST 78920

Dear Barbara:

    Thank you very much for all the kind hospitality that you and Bill showed to me during my stay in Silver City. I thoroughly enjoyed my tour of the city and the wonderful meal that you and Bill managed to put together on such short notice.

    I certainly hope to see you again at this year's sales meeting. And again, many thanks to you both for making my trip such a pleasant one.

               Sincerely,

               George Kinsey

Thank-you Letter

—for information or service

SITUATION: Christopher Soule is a free-lance writer who writes mostly on local-history topics. Recently he asked for and was granted an interview with Barbara Chase, a librarian in a neighboring town who has amassed a collection of historical papers relating to that town's history. He writes to thank her for the interview.

LETTER ELEMENTS: In writing his thank-you letter to Mrs. Chase, Soule does the following:

1. He thanks her for the interview, and he specifically states what it is she did for him.
2. He describes the benefit he derived from the interview.
3. He expresses his appreciation for the time she gave him for the interview, and he offers a pertinent compliment.

1292 Park Street
Stateville, ST 46788
September 27, 19--

Mrs. Barbara Chase
Middleville Public Library
Middleville, ST 46712

Dear Mrs. Chase:

    Thank you very much for giving me the chance to speak
with you and to see your impressive collection of papers
relating to the history of Middleville. You not only helped
me with my current project, but you have also made me aware
of a valuable resource which I hope to be able to draw upon
in the future. I certainly appreciate the time you spent
with me, and I applaud the work that you and your staff are
doing to preserve these valuable materials.

                           Sincerely,

Christopher Soule
Christopher Soule

Transmittal Letter

—for materials requiring no explanation

SITUATION: Jean Linamen is the public relations assistant for Fairmont Stainless Steel Corporation. James Wilhelm, a professor at a nearby university, has written to Fairmont Stainless, requesting copies of their annual report for use in his classroom. Linamen writes a letter to Professor Wilhelm, informing him that copies of the requested material are on the way.

LETTER ELEMENTS: In writing a letter of transmittal to Professor Wilhelm, Linamen does the following:

1. She opens by acknowledging his interest in Fairmont's annual report.
2. She gives precise details on the transmittal.
3. She offers further assistance, and she closes in a friendly fashion.

Fairmont Stainless Steel Corporation
1480 Hamilton Road
Fairmont, ST 67890   Tel: 519-643-7899

March 18, 19--

Professor James Wilhelm
DePaul Technical College
Smithville, ST 56789

Dear Professor Wilhelm:

It is good to know of your interest in the Annual Report of
the Fairmont Stainless Steel Corporation for use by the
students in your research seminar.

As you requested, a dozen copies of Fairmont's Annual Report
were mailed to you today. Since these reports were labeled
Priority Mail, you will have them well in advance of the
target date for their use.

Each year, if you will let us know the number of these reports that you will need, it will be our pleasure to send
them. We feel that the material will be our contribution
to the business and economic understanding of your students.

Sincerely yours,

Jean Linamen

Jean Linamen
Public Relations Assistant

FSS

Transmittal Letter
—for materials requiring some explanation

SITUATION: James Santiago is president of Santiago and Nussbaum, an architectural firm specializing in restoration of historical buildings. William Demetrius, a real-estate developer, has asked the firm to develop a proposal for the restoration of a building that his company is considering for purchase. Santiago's firm has completed the proposal, and Santiago includes a cover letter with the proposal.

LETTER ELEMENTS: In writing his cover letter, Santiago does the following:

1. He states clearly what it is that is being delivered.
2. He points out some important details pertaining to the proposal.
3. He adds a personal note, expressing his feelings about the proposal.
4. He closes with an offer of additional assistance if it is needed.

Santiago & Nussbaum

The Arcade · Hillsborough, ST 64529 · Telephone 411-820-3333

August 27, 19--

Mr. William Demetrius
Demetrius Brothers, Inc.
1200 High Street
Hillsborough, ST 64501

Dear Mr. Demetrius:

Here is our proposal for the renovation of the McKay Building at 1300 State Street. In developing this proposal we have kept in mind your stipulation that the result of this renovation should be a multi-use commercial space. We have also developed the proposal in such a way to ensure that it qualifies for favorable tax treatment as an historical restoration. The proposal assumes that Demetrius Brothers will be acquiring the property at 1308 State Street as well.

We think this is a very exciting project, and we look forward to hearing your reaction to our proposal. If you have any questions about any aspect of the proposal, please do not hesitate to call.

Sincerely,

James Santiago
President

JS:gic

Index